CONTENTS

Art in the
PRIMARY
SCHOOL

Page 1

THE VALUE OF
ART

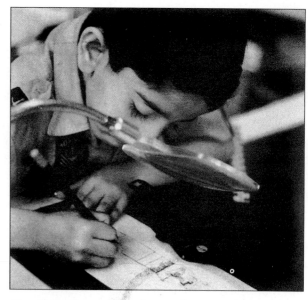

Below we set out some of the many strengths of art as a tool for learning in the primary curriculum. Above all, the concrete results of art activities provide a shared starting-point for discussion and a window into the thoughts and feelings of the child.

❏ Art is a unique 'visual language' through which children can organise and communicate their responses to experience.

❏ As with other 'languages' such as number, movement, sound, written and spoken language, there are some areas of experience which can only be recognised and communicated through visual language.

❏ Art combines the development of ideas and concepts with the exploration and education of feeling, educating the *'whole child'*.

'Learning to see' is an area where art has a special and unique role to play in each child's education through close observational study in a variety of media supported by discussion. The quality of later work from memory and imagination bears a close relationship with working from direct experience through art.

❏ Art values diversity and personal response. Rather than there being a 'right answer' there are as many answers as there are individuals. It is important to value and support the individual child's self-image as an artist.

❏ Through art children can develop skills, imagination, self-discipline, and the capacity to make decisions and solve problems. Creative work develops self-esteem and confidence.

❏ The visual language of art; the elements of line, tone, colour, pattern, texture, shape, form and space, is universal. There are no culturally-specific symbols to learn before expression and communication can begin.

❏ Art can provide an opportunity to learn about other cultures, an awareness of rich diversity and a celebration of and sensitivity towards cultural differences.

❏ Art has a major role in providing aesthetic education in the family of the Arts. The development of sensitivity to seeing and touching, the exploration of feeling and critical judgement, all contribute to developing aesthetic awareness.

❏ Through displays, festivals and productions, children can share and work co-operatively, gaining the sense of communal achievement which collaboration in the Arts can bring.

For all these reasons art must be seen as an entitlement and not as optional, purely recreational or therapeutic, a 'service' subject, or an area where children can teach themselves if provided with appropriate media.

HOW CHILDREN
Learn

Children learn through active experience, organising and expressing this experience through movement, sound, number, writing and speech and 'visual language'. The child comes to school with a range of experience, skills and understanding which must be assessed and built on in the early years of education. The integrated approach to primary education remains an ideal, despite the subject-based nature of the National Curriculum.

Art can initiate and support learning across the curriculum. However, the art National Curriculum supports our view that art must also be studied as a subject in its own right. Children should be involved in education through art, education in art, and education about art within their whole curriculum experience.

LEARNING THROUGH ART

Learning through art is widespread in primary schools. In the early years in some schools over 50% of the curriculum is taught through art activities. Topic work is supported by bookmaking, model making, illustration and display. Observation is sharpened and recorded through drawing for scientific investigation. Art materials are investigated and used constructively in historical, geographical, mathematical and technological contexts. (It must also be remembered that art itself draws on knowledge and understanding from across the curriculum). As so much of what we learn must be assimilated visually it makes sense to use art activities to stimulate, explore and record.

The processes of making also provide many rich contexts for language development. It would be worrying, however, if art education was limited to a supporting role.

LEARNING IN ART

The entitlement to learn art as a 'discrete' subject in its own right is recognised by its place as a foundation subject in the National Curriculum. Art has its own tools, equipment, processes, vocabulary and conventions.

The best way of learning in art is by making art!

Progression occurs as a result of experimentation and evaluation leading to the development of new ideas. Like any new language each child has to learn systematically from the basic elements to make more complex communications.

Support and interaction from a sensitive teacher speeds and enriches this process. Far from inhibiting creativity as some have claimed, interaction with a sensitive adult empowers the child to become more fluent and confident. Development in art should be supported alongside other areas and not allowed to wither once its vital role in promoting the development of writing has been achieved. Children need education in art activities - gaining control and developing the skills of 'Investigating and making' throughout their school career.

LEARNING ABOUT ART

There is now a widespread understanding that art education should be more than a practical expressive activity or a support for topic work. There is a wealth of art, craft and design, from the past and the present and from a variety of cultures, which children can learn to recognise, identify with and appreciate. In a sense this visual culture defines what art has been and gives us a context for inventing its future. It also gives us an insight into the diversity and richness of human ingenuity and expression.

The introduction of the art National Curriculum Attainment Target: 'Knowledge and Understanding' is aimed at ensuring that children learn about a wide variety of cultural traditions, and make connections with their own work. They also need to develop the ability to make their own judgements and to talk about their own and others' work developing 'visual literacy'.

VISUAL LANGUAGE

This view of art as *'visual language'* is an important one. Most primary teachers are experienced in language development and powerful analogies can be made between the development in written and spoken language and the development of visual literacy.

What, for instance, is the equivalent in art of the *'drafting'* process?

This question may help us in developing ideas for art activities which are not just *'one offs'* but provide opportunities for children to investigate, record, evaluate, discuss, change and refine their work. It may also help us with a policy for the use of sketch books in Key Stage 2.

Good writing comes from vivid experience. The same is true of art and we need to think about providing appropriate experiences and visual resources to stimulate and promote learning and expression. Visual language has a particular strength in expressing the results of visual enquiry - what things look like, how they are structured and how we feel about them. A written description may be far less efficient than a drawing or painting in this context.

Art has a basic visual vocabulary: **line, tone, colour, pattern, texture, shape, form and space, the visual elements of art**. Because of their importance we have devoted a whole section in these guidelines looking at each in depth (See 'The Visual Elements of Art').

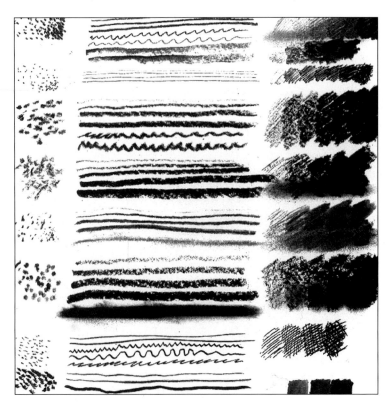

WRITING AN ART
Policy

Children will benefit if there is a consistent approach to the teaching and the organisation of art throughout the school. Simple 'agreements' can be recorded about the range of materials, labelling, organisation, resources and teaching strategies to be used, together with an overview of how art activities and experience will progress from year to year.

The first page of the Programme of Study for each Key Stage of the Art National Curriculum (sections 1 to 6) contains policy-like statements, defining the scope of the subject, which you can adapt for your own policy.

A good policy should be short!
However it may be combined with more detailed guidelines to support non-specialist or newly-appointed teachers. It should begin with a statement about why art is important in young children's education. If this is well expressed it will motivate teachers to provide quality art education. Our opening section *'The Value of Art'* provides ideas, but an important principle is that your policy should be *'owned'* by everyone and therefore should be produced through a process of discussion, drafting and consultation. One approach is to establish guiding principles, such as:

A balance should be sought between three important roles for Art Education:

❐ A means through which children can learn in all areas of the curriculum, **(integrated art)**. This is especially important in the early years and during Key Stages 1 and 2, art is an integral part of topic work.

❐ As an end in itself **(discrete art)**. Each practice (drawing, painting, collage, etc.) has its own unique areas of knowledge, skills, specialist language, tradition and value.

❐ To begin to develop **'Knowledge and Understanding'** of some of the world's artistic and cultural heritage making particular links with, and extending from the children's own cultural background and experience.

Children should be given access to:

- teacher-directed learning activities planned for continuity and progression

- self-directed or negotiated activities with the opportunity to work at their own pace, making choices about the content and direction of their work.

CURRICULUM TIME:

- The use of art media should feature as part of the daily experience of each class often in a supporting role. Each week a regular period of time must be found for specific teaching and learning in art. Establishing a regular weekly session for art activities is one of the best ways of ensuring that sufficient time is allocated.

- The National Curriculum Art Working Group's Final Report noted that on average, primary schools allocated approximately two hours per week to art for pupils in KS1 and one hour forty minutes in KS2. If art supporting other areas of the curriculum were to be taken into account, this proportion of time would be considerably more.

CORE ACTIVITIES

Some activities, such as observational drawing, colour mixing / matching, 3D construction using recycled materials and looking at and talking about art, are so important that they need to be seen as core activities which are returned to regularly in a variety of contexts. Others, such as *'Tie-Dye'*, may only need to be experienced once in each Key Stage. (Firstly, to learn the basic skills, technique and language and perhaps in Key Stage 2, to explore a cultural tradition and develop individual designs). The policy could, for example, detail how often children should have opportunities to work from direct observation, visit a gallery etc., and in which years *'Tie-Dye'* would feature.

HEADINGS

In many schools the art policy will share agreed headings with other subject areas as part of a whole school policy. This is becoming increasingly desirable as pressures for accountability mount, and documentation is required for OFSTED inspections.

Such a list might include

- Curriculum Content
- Planning
- Recording
- Equal Opportunities
- How to Involve Parents.
- Organisation
- Assessment
- Reporting
- SEN

A useful approach is to think in terms of a new teacher joining the school.

What information will she or he need in order to write and provide appropriate schemes of work ?

(Examples of all planning formats etc. can be provided in an appendix).

There is a growing expectation that the Curriculum Co-ordinator should help other staff to create appropriate schemes of work developing an overview to ensure continuity and progression. The Policy can provide a shared understanding and framework from which the more detailed termly or half-termly schemes of work can be derived, linked to class topics. It may be best to form a small committee to work on the Policy including a 'Curriculum Coordinator in training', and an NQT, or someone who is definitely not a specialist, to check that the group writes at a level which will be understood by all. An **'Audit'** of art activities already going on and the skills and experience of the staff will be a good place to start. These can be matched against the requirements of the art National Curriculum and the school's own aims.

Finally, once a policy is written and agreed in consultation with all staff, it needs to be accompanied by an action plan for implementation which should include resourcing, support, INSET, monitoring evaluation and review.

THE TEACHER'S ROLE

Teachers become adept at providing children with challenges to their existing understanding based on their previous experience to promote achievable goals.

Experiences need to be carefully planned to build coherently on the developing knowledge, skills, attitudes and understanding of the child in transition from home to school and from year to year in school.

Observation and interaction allows judgements to be made about the best way forward to support, stimulate and challenge. The processes of development in art are less widely understood than those of number and written and spoken language, and for this reason we have included a section on 'Drawing and Development'.

An understanding of these broad stages of visual development is valuable in all aspects of art education.

- Clear ground rules need to be established with children so that they can progressively take responsibility for their own organisation of equipment and materials and clearing up! This also means that the art area in the classroom needs to be arranged and labelled to encourage independence and choice.

- Art, craft and design flourish in a stimulating learning environment where there are visual resources to study: natural forms, artefacts and art, real and in reproduction. High quality accessible tools and materials should also be displayed to invite participation.

- Children need both teacher-led input and opportunities for self-directed paths of enquiry where the teacher's role is to provide the time, space and resources and support the child's own responses, decisions and ideas.

- A developing culture of discussing the children's own and other artists' work requires the gradual introduction of appropriate vocabulary. The teacher's skill lies in careful questioning to elicit the children's thoughts.

- Care needs to be taken not to judge children's work by inappropriate adult standards. This requires a respect for the nature of children's visual language at different stages of development and a determination not to try to achieve superficially more sophisticated work through copying, tracing, using templates or teacher-drawn outlines.

- Display can stimulate and celebrate achievement. Care should be taken not to communicate hidden messages by just displaying the work of more advanced or *'gifted'* children but to support every individual's efforts and achievement. Working alongside children can provide a model in which a shared sense of learning and discovery enhances the quality of interaction.

Display will stimulate and celebrate achievement.

Organisation of the
Art Area
WORK SPACE

There should be a specific art area with both work and display space and access to water. Ideally a table or tables should be set aside plus easels and drawing boards within the art area, specifically for art activities.

Equipment/materials should be accessible and clearly labelled. Thorough cleaning and tidying at the end of activities, especially after clay work, should be seen as an important skill to be developed from the nursery.

DISPLAY SPACE

Both wall and 3-dimensional display space should be found in the room. Examples of children's and other artists' work as well as collections of photographs, artefacts and natural objects should be present. The effect should be to provide stimuli for work of all kinds as well as showing that children's art work is valued.

STORAGE SPACE

Equipment and materials should be accessible and clearly labelled. Part of children's art education will be in recognising the importance of keeping equipment clean and in good working order; they need to be confident that they can find what they need easily.

RESOURCES

There are many kinds of resources for art:

- skills and experience of staff (and parents)
- resources from home
- collections of artefacts and natural forms
- books
- postcards
- slides
- reproductions
- art materials
- computer draw and paint programs
- albums showing good practice and successful displays
- the school buildings and grounds
- the local environment
- museums/galleries & places of interest
- artists in residence.

BASIC CLASSROOM EQUIPMENT

Each school will need to decide on a policy for provision in each classroom and needs will vary according to the age range of the children.

Here is one example:

RESOURCES FOR AT2 - ART, DESIGN & CRAFT

Drawing pencils - H, HB, 2B and 4B
Charcoal (medium)
Pastels, mixing palette with containers to store pastels
Black felt pens - thick, medium, fine.
Cartridge paper - A2 A3 A4
Brushwork/sugar paper - grey, white, black, assorted colours
File paper and newsprint
Coloured pencils
> black, blue, sky blue, dark brown, green, grass green, grey, orange, peach, pink, purple, crimson, vermilion, white, yellow

Paint - water colour tablet set
Powder, ready-mixed or block paints in the double primary system:
> vermilion red, crimson, brilliant yellow, lemon yellow, turquoise, brilliant blue, prussian blue, and white - black can replace prussian blue

Fine brushes (sable) No. 6
Stiff brushes (Hog) Nos. 6, 8, 10, & 12
Waterpots, aprons, palettes
Cold water paste,
Merlin / PVA glue and glue spreaders
Water-based block printing ink, rollers and ink trays
Collage materials (inc. threads and textiles), scissors, needles, craft dyes and wax pot.
Recycled materials for modelling
Clay, clay bin, modelling tools
Cleaning materials
> dustpan, brush, mop, sponges, hard bristled washing-up brush, washing-up liquid and Jif

Plasticised table cloth

In making up your own list, refer to the checklist in the next column. One list will be needed for classroom-based equipment and a second for shared centrally-held equipment.

CHECKLIST:

DRAWING
Pencil - H, HB, 2B, 3B etc. ☐
charcoal, chalk, pastel, wax ☐
Pens - pen & ink, felt tip, biro ☐
Brushes - with ink, paint etc ☐

PAINTING
Finger paints ☐
Powder colour, ready mix
or blocks ☐
Watercolour ☐

PRINTMAKING
Rubbings, wax-resist ☐
Mono-printing ☐
Unit-printing: cotton reels
lego bricks, potatoes etc. ☐
Relief Printing: paper, card
press-print ☐
found textured materials ☐

COLLAGE
Collage: paper, card, foil ☐
threads, fibres, fabrics ☐
plastic, wood, metal, stone ☐
Shells, pulses, feathers, grasses ☐

TEXTILES
Threads, fibres, fabrics ☐
dyed ☐
printed ☐
woven, knitted ☐
stitched, embroidered ☐
appliqued ☐

SCULPTURE
Malleable materials
clay, plasticine or dough ☐
papier maché / paper paste ☐
Resistant materials
carving - soap, plaster, etc. ☐
construction - card, wood, wire ☐
junk modelling materials ☐
kits - lego, meccano etc. ☐

RESPONSE TO ART & VISUAL EXPERIENCE.
Visual resources:
natural forms ☐
artefacts, books and reproductions ☐
displays and exhibitions ☐
visits to the local environment ☐
Craft & design, photography ☐
architecture. ☐
Own work and others' work ☐

The Art
National Curriculum

(To be read in conjunction with 'Art in the National Curriculum', January 1995, HMSO)

The art National Curriculum provides a framework which can be used flexibly for planning art activities. It is a minimum framework leaving schools free to decide on how to teach and balance the curriculum.

COMMON REQUIREMENTS

This first section has some important information about **access.** There is much greater flexibility for children with special educational needs (SEN) who may, where appropriate, work to Programmes of Study selected from earlier or later Key Stages, without the need for 'disapplication'. Allowances can also be made in applying End of Key Stage Descriptions.

PROGRAMMES OF STUDY

Each Key Stage Programme of Study is laid out on a double-page spread. The introductory paragraph and **Sections 1 - 6** provide an overview of the scope of the subject and the general principles which should guide the broad planning in each year and Key Stage.

Principles include that art should be interpreted as **'art, craft and design';** activities should bring together the two Attainment Targets, **Investigating and Making - AT1** and **Knowledge and Understanding - AT2,** wherever

possible; opportunities should include **individual, group and whole class work;** and children should be taught to develop their **visual perception** (learning to see) and **visual literacy** (learning to 'read', and communicate with, images and visual language).

Section 7 contains six 'strands'. These detail the opportunities children should be given to allow breadth and balance within units of work or a particular topic or project.

Sections 8 and 9 are the specific skills, knowledge and understanding to be taught, linked to the 'strands' and under the Attainment Target headings. These are detailed Programmes of Study and can provide objectives for individual lessons and references to ensure coverage and depth.

Rather than reproduce the Programmes of Study, below is a diagram which presents key aspects of the art National Curriculum in a format which can be used for broad planning, checking coverage and balance. The two outside columns list the 'Visual and Tactile Elements' and 'Techniques / Media - Practices', while the central column lists the important processes through which children learn in art. All can be found in the statutory Programme of Study for Key Stages 1 & 2, the references are included in brackets. A suggested proforma for more detailed planning using sections 7, 8 & 9 of the framework is overleaf.

Visual & Tactile ELEMENTS (8e)		Learning PROCESSES	Techniques & Media PRACTICES (8d)
(4a)	Pattern	(2a) Expressing Ideas & Feelings	Drawing
	Texture	2b) Recording (experience, observation and imagination)	Painting
(4b)	Colour		Printmaking
(4c)	Line	2c) Designing & Making	Collage
	Tone	Looking at art, craft & design (5a) locality (5b) past & present (5c) Western & non-Western Textiles	
(4d)	Shape		Sculpture
	Form	Talking about art, craft & design (8f, 9e) describing, explaining, expressing opinions	Textiles
	Space		IT (where appropriate)

Any art project will link one or more aspect from each column. For example, **Pattern** linked with **Recording** (from observation) and **Drawing**, describes a simple art activity and focus.

A more complex project could link **Pattern** and **Colour, Designing and Making** with **Printmaking** and **Textiles**. Most projects would also involve the learning processes of **Looking at**, and **Talking about art, craft and design**. In this example children could explore a collection of Indian textiles, influencing their own designs for a length of printed cloth.

Linking different aspects from each column will provide endless variations and possibilities.

(This framework is similar to one developed for the London and East Anglian Group for the GCSE Art & Design Syllabus. A detailed explanation of its application to the primary curriculum can be found in the 'Oxford Primary Art Teacher's Resource Book' by Norman Binch, Oxford University Press)

PLANNING & ASSESSMENT

In order to ensure a balanced art curriculum throughout the school it is necessary to agree a consistent planning and assessment policy. Schemes of work are now required with an overview linking individual units of work.

PLANNING

Planning for art will often take place within a topic or theme, though there is a growing use of a subject-based or discrete approach. Often, each subject will have its own planning linked by an overall 'topic web'.

Our 'Planning Proforma' overleaf is a good starting point and can be used for 'brain-storming' ideas and later for a more formal presentation of a unit of work. First an overview of the project can be identified by highlighting or outlining the Elements, Processes and Practices and identifying broad aims. Next, a sequence of activities can be planned using the six 'strands', printed for reference. As the project takes shape more detailed references can be made to the Programmes of Study. Finally, thought can be given to what will indicate that progress has been made, identifying opportunities for assessment.

Whatever format is chosen for schemes of work they should: build on previous work and achievement (progression); allow for different pace and style of learning with support and extension activities (differentiation); identify resources needed, particularly those which are outside normal classroom provision; and be referenced to individual Programmes of Study.

In each year pupils should have opportunities to work regularly with all six strands and cover all Programmes of Study. This will require a whole year forward-plan overview or an audit half-way through a year to enable planning to cover areas not yet addressed. For this we provide an **'Overview'** Proforma overleaf. This can be used for forward planning, auditing, or as a class record. Both proformas are offered not as prescriptions, but as examples. **They are copy-right free** and should be enlarged to A4 or A3.

In many schools whole-school or team planning is developing and it will be appropriate to plan across Key Stages in outline. Certain activities can be prioritised, such as observational drawing, opportunities to develop colour-mixing skills, 3D work, looking at art from a variety of cultures, and using sketch-books (KS2), until these are well established. The school art policy can identify priorities for development.

INSPIRATION

Teachers need inspiration for planning!

The best source is examples of good practice within the school which can be spread through display in public areas and formal and informal contact between staff. A collection of books and guidelines should be made available to provide models of good practice to adapt and inspire.

Practically-based staff meetings focusing on a particular technique, skill or approach are, in our experience, welcomed and enjoyed by the vast majority of staff once they become involved. Policy groups and team planning offer support and the additional energy stimulated by collaboration.

Once policy or schemes of work are in place, additional value can be gained through collaborative provision of resources such as collecting packs of images and information for AT2, or 'Topic Boxes' of objects and artefacts to support children's investigations. Quality of work is often directly related to the quality of resources and children cannot be expected to work effectively in a vacuum.

Below are five areas through which artwork can be stimulated.

(adapted from Rob Barnes 'Teaching Art To Young Children', Routledge).

This is a useful checklist for resourcing:

Something (direct experience)	**SEEN, FELT, HEARD, TOUCHED**
Something to stimulate the (music, stories...)	**MEMORY OR IMAGINATION**
High quality	**MATERIALS & EQUIPMENT**
Demonstration of a	**TECHNIQUE**
Related work by	**ARTISTS, CRAFTSPEOPLE & DESIGNERS**

ASSESSMENT, RECORDING AND REPORTING

Most important is everyday 'formative' assessment. This is the process based on informal observation and dialogue, through which the teacher is able to gauge progress and understanding and decide when to intervene or plan for further development.

Helping children to discuss and evaluate their own achievement and progress, individually and in groups, is particularly valuable. More formal assessment is periodic and will need to fit into patterns established for the whole curriculum. Criteria are needed to make judgements and in art the **End of Key**

Stage Descriptions describe the performance most children will achieve if they have been taught the appropriate Programmes of Study.

In planning, one or two focuses can be identified for assessment and recording in each project or topic.

REPORTING

Each year a report on progress must be made for each pupil for all National Curriculum subjects including art. At or near the end of each Key Stage an individual End of Key Stage assessment and report will need to match each child's achievement against the End of Key Stage Descriptions. At present many schools have insufficient space on their report forms to write more than one or two sentences and this will need to be addressed as experience in assessment develops.

Assessment in art will develop. The End of Key Stage Descriptions are linked broadly to level demands in other subjects, KS1 - Level 2, and KS2 - Level 4. To help teachers, some schools will develop 'above and below' descriptions, while others will develop eight level descriptions to match other core and foundation subjects. Opportunities to look at work and discuss its assessment in staff meetings or training days will bring the experience of moderation to art and help to build teachers' confidence.

SAMPLING

The best way of building up a record of evidence is to keep samples of children's work. Some schools are introducing individual central cross-curricular portfolios, though these may place limitations on the size (A4) and nature of work. A sample sheet could be used or the work simply annotated. Sketch-books with comments, could also be used as samples and include sketches of 3D or bulky work. A good principle is to involve children in the choice and preparation of their samples.

Better still is to keep individual folders of a selection of each child's work in each classroom. These can become a real source of ownership and pride, a focus for discussion and self-assessment, and can be passed on to the next teacher each year.

Folders of examples of successful work characteristic of each National Curriculum year could also be built up centrally by the Curriculum Coordinator. These would provide teachers with ideas, evidence of 'standards' and progression, and the likely range of stages of development and spread of ability.

ART	TOPIC/THEME: Teacher :	YEAR : Term: CLASS :	Elements	Processes	Practices

AIMS/DESCRIPTION:

	Elements	Processes	Practices
	Pattern	Expressing Ideas & Feelings	Drawing
	Texture		Painting
	Colour	Recording experience, observation & imagination	Printmaking
	Line		Collage
	Tone	Designing & Making	Sculpture
	Shape		Textiles
	Form	Looking at & Talking about art, craft & design	IT (where appropriate)
	Space		

PoS: 1 2abc 3 4abcd 5abc 6 7abcdef 8abcdef 9abcde

Record   Gather resources   Explore media   Review & modify   Develop understanding   Respond & evaluate

Sequence:	Week	Week	Week	Week	Week
Stimulus					
Activity Extension/ Support?					
Resources					
Assessment & evaluation					

ART OVERVIEW   CLASS   YEAR   TEACHER

Title of topic						
	Term One		Term Two		Term Three	
Recording from: Experience Observation Imagination						
Sketchbook (KS2) Gather resources Develop ideas						
Explore media: Drawing Painting Printing Collage Sculpture Textiles						
Visual elements: Pattern Texture Colour Line Tone Shape Form Space						
Review & Modify						
Understanding Art/Craft/Design Materials Techniques Context						
Respond to & **evaluate own &** others' work						

'Looking at Art'
Knowledge & Understanding

The Art National Curriculum requires that children are introduced to the work of artists, craftspeople and designers so they can respond to the ideas, methods or approaches used in different styles and traditions and apply this understanding to their own work.

This is a new responsibility for many primary teachers and requires a range of strategies and resources for successful implementation.

A selection of work from the locality, the past and the present and a variety of cultures should be made. The Programmes of Study do not identify particular artists, cultures or movements to be studied in Key Stages 1 and 2, but indicate that there should be a balance between Western and non-Western traditions. A wide view of art should be taken so that besides painting and sculpture, photography, printmaking, crafts (such as pottery and weaving), and design (such as clothing, buildings and graphic design) are considered.

In Key Stage 1 children should become used to looking at and talking about art and artefacts, recognising examples in the school and environment. They should be taught to recognise the visual elements and the differences and similarities between art from different times and places. Much work in this area will be from reproductions, so it will be important for children to gradually learn about the difference between real works and reproductions, as well as visiting galleries and museums when possible.

SHARED LOOKING

A useful approach to developing Knowledge and Understanding (AT2) is *shared looking*. This is where the teacher gathers the children on the carpet and displays a picture or reproduction on the easel. To be effective the size of the image really needs to be a minimum of A3.

By concentrating on one image and perhaps returning to it on a number of occasions, the children will develop a relationship with the image which will lead to understanding over time. Exploring the image in this way will need sensitive questioning from the teacher if the children are to discover different aspects of the work.

The following framework developed by Rod Taylor can help teachers prepare a series of key questions and be reassured that any image can be explored without prior knowledge.

Although this example focuses on painting, the framework can be adopted for a variety of artefacts (including the children's own work).

Content (subject matter)

✓ **What things can you see in the painting?**
(children can be asked to identify and name all the parts of people, objects, buildings etc).

✓ **Does it represent something real, imagined or tell a story?**

✓ **How did the artist paint the picture?**
(Was it from observation, memory or imagination?)

Form (the elements of art and their arrangement)

✓ **What colours has the artist used?**

✓ **Which colours has she used most?**

✓ **What other colours can you see?**
(These sort of questions can be repeated for lines, textures and patterns as appropriate)

✓ **What shapes has the artist used?**

✓ **How are they arranged?**
(This is the beginning of thinking about composition and design)

Process (the techniques, process, methods and time taken to make the work)

✓ What kind of paint has the artist used?

✓ Can you see any brush marks?

✓ What is it painted on?
(paper, canvas or wood).

✓ Was it painted quickly?
(inside or outside, from observation or sketches)

Mood (the mood, atmosphere and feelings evoked by the work)

✓ How does this picture make you feel?
(happy or sad, warm or cold, calm peaceful, uneasy, frightened, angry).

✓ What sort of mood has the artist created?

✓ How did she want us to feel?

Clearly, the level and intensity of questioning should be related to the age and experience of the pupils. Only the class teacher can really know what is appropriate to build and develop understanding. Repeated 'readings' of increasingly familiar images and artefacts can consolidate learning, as well as lead to new discoveries and awareness.

'Shared Looking' can be extended through writing, both prose and poetry, further investigation of the artists work, style, life and times, or practical exploration in the children's own artwork. Looking at art can have great significance for individual children. Many artists can recall early experiences which set them on a life-time's involvement in art, which Rod Taylor has called, the *'illuminating experience'.*

During Key Stage 2 the children should discuss and compare different kinds of art, using appropriate vocabulary. Children can study influential artists and develop some knowledge of the related historical back-ground. History is a good vehicle for extension, planning history topics to include looking at art, or the study of a particular artist or tradition.

The children should also be given the

opportunity to experiment with some of the methods and approaches used by the artist in their own work. Artists could be living and local, Leonardo da Vinci, designers or craftsworkers, or the anonymous creators of pottery, African masks or Bengali Kanthas (embroidered quilts).

CLASSROOM APPROACHES TO AT2

Below are some of the approaches used successfully in the classroom.

While children are involved in practical art work, make passing reference to and display, other artists' work who used similar subject matter or a relevant style, or the same media.

✓ Collect contrasting postcard reproductions linked by topic, theme, or to the children's own imaginative work.
Eg: water, weather, portraits, court painting, nativity scenes, flowers, masks, pattern, etc.

Children make a direct response to an artist's work, 'drawing from' the work rather than copying.

✓ Looking at small 'sections' of an image. Using a view-finder to focus on a small area, the children can explore colours, textures and brush marks.

This will encourage similar close observational study of other areas of the work.

For variation:

✓ A poster or reproduction is cut into rectangles. Each child can respond in a chosen media on a larger but similarly proportioned piece of paper. The children's work is re-combined to form a large version of the work for display as a basis for further discussion and comparison.

✓ Using a teacher's or other child's verbal description of an unseen printing / design/artefact as a starting point.

This is a good language development project which creates an intense visual interest in the original when finally revealed and compared! Reconstruction of the subject matter of a painting for work from observation; eg. a still life in the style of an influential artist , or dressing up and posing as a Degas dancer or a Rembrandt self-portrait.

✓ Studying an artist's working methods such as using 'egg tempera', watching and working with an artist in residence,

visiting an artist's workshop or studios, studying Leonardo da Vinci's or Turner's sketchbooks.

✓ Reconstruction in 3D of a 2D artwork.

This encourages reading of the 'space' in an image and can be used with a variety of styles and genres, eg. Egyptian painting, Indian miniatures, Japanese prints, Classical landscape, Cubism, Abstract art etc.

AT2 RESOURCES TRIANGLE

Artist Designer or Craftsperson 'in Residence'

Visit to Craft Workshop Design Studio, Artist's Studio etc.

Museum or Gallery visit

Working in the local environment

Theme/Topic-based resource collection, art, craft and design objects, real and reproduction

Classroom collections of reproductions, artefacts, books Use of illustrations in children's books

Above is a checklist for resources for AT2 - 'Knowledge and Understanding' of art, design and craft. Some resources at the bottom of the triangle are reasonably easy to provide, while those in the top half of the triangle require more organisation and perhaps special funding.

CHILDREN'S BOOKS

The illustrations in children's books provide an immediate source of images for AT2. Look out for the ones in which the artist or illustrator has used media similar to those available in the classroom so that direct connections can be made by the pupils.

Examples:

'The Very Hungry Caterpillar'
Eric Carle -
Free painting, cut and collaged.

'Tigress'
Helen Cowcher -
'Wet' painting techniques for backgrounds overlaid with more defined painting.

'Window'
Jeannie Baker -
A wordless book using a wide variety of collage techniques

Some make direct reference in their illustration style to cultural traditions:

'Lord of the Dance'
Veronique Tadjo -
West African art.

'My Grandpa and the Sea'
Katherine Orr -
Caribbean painting.

'Roughtail'
Gracie Green, Joe Tramacchi, Lucille Gill -
Aborigine art.

Working in the local environment can provide a wealth of art and design to be studied such as murals, public and ceremonial sculpture, garden and landscape design, the crafts of ornamental iron work, stone carving and ceramic tiles, architecture with Gothic churches, classical columns and pediments, Victorian and 1920's style to modern architecture. Children can make a 'crafts map' of the area round the school using photography and observational drawing.

LEARNING FROM OBJECTS

Handling objects can be a valuable starting point for learning in any area of the curriculum. Interest is stimulated and questions should be asked to motivate further exploration and recording. It is a growing practice to collect objects and artefacts for handling either in topic boxes or a mini school museum.

Objects for handling are not expensive or precious, rather they are everyday things found in nature, the home, or the world of work, now or in times gone by. They will include things from Britain and other countries.

As children handle objects and develop recording techniques they will understand the need to treat objects with care and respect. The English Heritage book *'Learning from Objects'* provides a helpful framework with questions such as,

✓ **What does it physically look, feel, sound, smell like?**

✓ **How was it made?**

✓ **What was it made for?**

✓ **Does it work?**

✓ **Is it decorated?**

✓ **Does it look good?**

✓ **What is it worth, and to whom?**

Observations can be recorded in a variety of forms, but clearly using art materials to record the visual aspects of an object will be an indispensable learning tool. Children will need experience of a variety of drawing materials so that they can select the most appropriate. They will need to be able to mix colours accurately and have the time to experiment and persevere.

ARTEFACTS FROM A VARIETY OF CULTURES

Examining and responding to artefacts can be a valuable first hand way of learning about other cultures.

Around this direct experience can be woven learning from other areas of the curriculum.

The Oxfam Development Education Unit , (Effa School, Barnwell Road, Brixton SW2 1PL) have published a useful checklist for teachers:

USING EVERYDAY OBJECTS FROM OTHER COUNTRIES IN THE CLASSROOM

Useful points to consider before you start:

Why and in what context are you teaching about this group?

Be aware of the backgrounds of the children in your class. Try to encourage positive images of all cultures and countries.

Be aware of attitudes / prejudices / stereotypes held by children in the class.

Be aware of what your own prejudices are and the need to involve yourself in the process of questioning, learning and discussion.

When teaching:

✓ Use the objects to encourage interest and respect for the identity of the people.

✓ Try to develop contacts with people from the relevant country and invite them into school to talk to pupils.

✓ Use the objects as a starting point for further work on the country.

✓ Encourage an on-going interest in the country. (e.g. a folder to which pupils can add information through the year.)

✓ Encourage a critical approach to media information and images of the country.

✓ Try to set the country in its historical context.

✓ Emphasise that a country is made up of very divergent groups and individuals and will not necessarily conform to any given generalisation.

✓ Do give women and men equal emphasis.

✗ Do **NOT** present the country as exotic or primitive.

✗ Do **NOT** use stereotypes unless to counter them.

✗ Do **NOT** encourage any sense of your pupils' cultural superiority.

✗ Do **NOT** be afraid to say that you don't know.

BILINGUAL / BICULTURAL CHILDREN

Bilingual children will have access to cultural traditions which are often markedly different in their values, skills and imagination to those of the dominant culture of Europe and the West. To work within Western conventions, particularly those which stress observational drawing and perspective may be similar to speaking in a foreign language. It is important that bilingual children see that their own cultural heritage is valued and can draw upon it in their work.

For example, in some cultures, a young child may be able to make fine embroidery work but have done little drawing. Clearly to judge newly arrived children by drawing skills may seriously underestimate their aesthetic understanding and ability. Many bilingual children born in Britain are still firmly embedded in their family and community culture and this 'bicultural' experience should be acknowledged.

Each child is unique and through observation and listening we can, as teachers, learn about individual patterns of belief and custom. We can, with sensitivity, draw upon the wide range of experience in a multi-cultural classroom to develop understanding and respect for a wide range of traditions and cultural contexts.

All children have an entitlement to learning both within the Western tradition and non-Western traditions. Bicultural children may need time to establish confidence and acceptance working within their own artistic language and skills before branching out to develop additional fluency within Western cultural conventions or finding ways of continuing traditions in new forms.

ART AND THE MUSLIM CHILD

There is a common misconception that there is no figuration in Islamic art and that children of the Muslim faith may only be able to work with pattern and calligraphy.

Figurative representation is forbidden in mosques, as is representation of Allah and the Prophet Mohammed. The creation of idols is condemned in the Koran and consequently Islamic art has not developed religious iconography as in the West.

The secular Islamic culture, however, abounds with figurative design. Many of the patrons of Islamic art were princes and caliphs who commissioned work in all media to beautify architecture and the objects of everyday life.

For Muslims, inscriptions take the place of icons. The arts of the book, calligraphy, illumination and binding, hold a special place as do their makers. Inscriptions are incorporated into all forms of art and design, religious and secular.

Pattern carries special meaning conveying a sense of order and possibility of infinite repetition as a characteristic of the divine. For this reason, it has been developed in great geometrical complexity in architecture, ceramics, textiles, and miniature painting.

The arabesque, rhythmic designs based on flowering vines, provides the other strongly characteristic element of Islamic pattern.

Images of flowers, the garden and water offer an earthly reflection of paradise and are to be found in surface decorations, carpets and painting.

Miniature painting is an art of the secular book. Figuration is used to illustrate the exploits, real and mythical, of the rulers and dynasties of the Islamic world. Accurate observation is combined with a stylised and decorative treatment. Images are full of narrative details and often need to be read sequentially. Borders are equally rich in their calligraphic, floral, geometric or figurative detail.

Muslim children can participate fully in the art curriculum providing the special requirements in relation to religious contexts are respected and treated with sensitivity. They can be involved in making all kinds of figurative art, except in the area of religious iconography. This does not mean that they cannot explore Western traditions of religious art alongside those of Islam. It does mean, however, that when responding in their own practical work they are able to use traditional Islamic forms such as calligraphy and pattern. Becoming familiar with some of the rich traditions of Islamic art, should be seen as an entitlement of all children.

Drawing

A key to developing confidence is to value each child's emerging drawing ability at their own level and not judge by inappropriate adult criteria and standards. See the section on 'Drawing and Development' for detailed information about children's stages of visual development.

THE EARLY YEARS

Children start drawing before they come to school and much of this early activity, before a child learns to make pictures that adults can recognise, can still be seen in the nursery and reception.

'Scribble' is of fundamental importance as children begin to discover the marks they can make with a variety of materials. Important stages are developing the ability to repeat marks, increased control, and the emergence of the circle and a variety of patterns.

Encourage children to talk about the marks they have made e.g. curved, straight, wiggly, and at times challenge them to make marks, lines and patterns to express these descriptions.

Children begin to 'compose' or 'design' from the earliest age and given the appropriate support and materials will discover a wide range of graphic possibilities.

As children mature they should still have opportunities to experiment with and explore the qualities of art materials, before moving on to use them for representation.

An opportunity to experiment can be built into the sequence of most projects and will often lead to media being used in fresh and inventive ways. Older children will enjoy taking an almost scientific approach, making a systematic exploration and recording results.

REPRESENTING EXPERIENCE AND 'NARRATIVE' DRAWING

As children develop the ability to make simple symbols for people, houses, trees, transport etc., they use these to represent their experience and tell stories, real or imagined. Progression can be seen in increasing complexity and detail, and inventive use of ways of depicting the three-dimensional world on paper. There should be opportunities for free, as well as teacher-directed work.

A chance to make a narrative drawing in response to topic work may be far more valuable than copying illustrations, as it gives an opportunity to use the imagination, to order and (re)present information and consolidate learning.

The art National Curriculum requires that children work from experience, observation, and imagination. Imagination requires a strong basis in real experience. It is impossible to imagine something totally new. When we use our imagination we are combining previously unlinked elements of experience in new ways.

Older children can explore the way artists make up imaginative pictures, studying their working methods and preparatory studies.

OBSERVATIONAL DRAWING

Children can be introduced to drawing from direct experience from their earliest time in school. It is important to focus on one or two simple aspects like shape and pattern, understanding that children will use their own visual language at whatever stage they are to represent their experience.

Observational drawing makes a valuable contribution to the science curriculum, allowing children to record what they observe - the growth of a plant, the colour of the sky or the effects of weather, or simply the arrangement of equipment used in an experiment.

The more discussion and if possible handling, if the drawing is of an object, the better. Children need help both in discussing the kind of lines and shapes they can use and the sequence in which they can make a drawing, where to start, what to put in next and so on.

Discussion can focus first on the broad aspects of what is being observed, e.g. flower, yellow, spring. Then you can delve into where this particular thing differs from groups of similar things, e.g. trumpet, six petals, long narrow leaves, 40 cm high, etc. Finally, you can search together for minute differences, e.g. petals: narrower, broader, smaller, greener yellow etc.

Another approach is to invite pupils to look at something for a short time, hide it and then ask questions about what they noticed about it. This game used regularly can help children to develop their visual perception and memory. A variation is to draw from memory and then give an extended opportunity for close observational drawing.

The non-specialist can be successful in encouraging drawing and visual awareness by asking the child to describe what he or she can see in terms of shapes, lines, textures, patterns, colour - the elements of art. Children can then be encouraged to really look and find their own equivalents using appropriate media. When finished, the work can be jointly evaluated by both teacher and pupil which may well lead on to further drawing, perhaps from a different viewpoint or in another medium.

RESOURCING YOUR CLASSROOM

A wide range of resources support drawing. Collections of things to draw chosen for their qualities, or related to a topic, as well as examples of drawings drawn from different times and cultures, are useful. Equipment and materials should be of the best quality and attractively stored and displayed to invite use. Clipboards for outside work, viewfinders and magnifying glasses can help children to focus and select areas for investigation. A range of papers of different sizes and qualities will encourage a diversity of scale and response.

Each medium has its own qualities and a selection which includes hard and linear (pencils, pens), soft and smudgy (pastel, charcoal and wax) and liquid (ink and paint) will provide a wide range of mark making qualities and possibilities. Combinations of media can be explored for even richer possibilities.

It is worth remembering that younger children draw by **accumulating details**. Accurate proportion is less important than the value attached to details or fitting them on to the page. For this reason, select drawing subjects with plenty of rich detail, and appreciate the often ingenious ways in which children organise this information on the paper.

Very young children respond best to familiar things and people, in their drawing. Later, children are stimulated by encountering new and unfamiliar objects and experience.

'I can't draw!' A CRISIS OF CONFIDENCE

As children mature and begin to compare their untroubled and spontaneous work with the sophisticated images to be found all around them, they can lose confidence and develop the familiar 'I can't draw' syndrome. This attitude can be picked up from the family, media or the teacher and is unfortunately often seen as acceptable.

The teacher needs to support each pupil, to develop their skills and to meet their new demands for realism. At the same time, it is important to provide a variety of creative activities which develop other aspects of craft and design to ensure success and continued aesthetic experience while skills are being acquired.

In a school where there is a policy ensuring that children work regularly from direct observation, skills develop gradually and progressively and there is less likelihood of such a crisis of confidence.

Children should have opportunities to develop their observational skills in a systematic way. Make it a policy that in each half-term there are at least several opportunities for observational drawing.

Pupils can be encouraged to learn from looking at an artist's work how particular problems have been solved. By studying a variety of cultures children should be helped to understand that there are many ways of expressing ideas and feelings through art and that the Western emphasis on photographic realism and perspective is just one of a family of equally valid conventions which they can work within.

LEARNING THROUGH DRAWING

Think of drawing as a tool for learning. Close observation of people, plants, animals, environments and made objects can be the starting point for learning across the curriculum.

Observational drawing helps children slow down their looking and therefore notice more. Noticing more leads to questions. Following these up into the scientific or mathematical implications of what has been observed, or the technological, cultural, historical, geographical or social context can provide stimulus for discussion, writing or further imaginative work.

The representational skills of art are often most effectively developed through close observational work. Children are challenged by what they see to invent new and more complex ways of representing their visual experience. These in turn can be used for work from memory or imagination where children use their existing visual repertoire to express their ideas.

SKETCHBOOKS

These can be seen as first draft working books, used for collecting observational drawings, paintings, notes, and details of artist's work. These will become a valuable personal resource for the development of their own work.

The use and functions of a sketchbook will need to be carefully negotiated with your class particularly when introducing them for the first time. On one hand you will want the children to feel ownership, but on the other hand you will not want sketchbooks used up quickly with superficial or inappropriate work. It will be useful to have a shared policy in the school, and an early introduction may help to promote richer self-directed work and progression in KS2.

Sketchbooks are particularly valuable for collecting information and recording on school journeys and visits. Besides observational work, notes can be made to record colours, materials seen and lists of descriptive words inspired by experience.

Ideas for imaginative and design work can be tried out, the best selected and developed further.

Sketchbooks should also be seen as a place for personal images and ideas, images from dreams, doodles, and special enthusiasms which may be developed into further self - directed work.

A wide variety of media should be encouraged, collage, water colour, felt tip, biro and coloured crayons. Dusty media (chalks, pastels, charcoal) which need fixing, should be avoided.

Written comments from the teacher acknowledging quality and achievement and suggesting further developments will increase motivation and sketchbooks can be an important source of evidence for end of year or Key Stage assessment in art.

Bulldog — NEAR River thames

Drawing and
Development

EARLY MARK-MAKING ('SCRIBBLE')

**There is great value in understanding the stages children pass through as they learn to draw.
It enables us to make judgements about how to help children progress and the most effective form of interaction and support.**

Children learn in different ways and at varying pace. At times children may seem to be making little progress, while at other times they may pass through a 'stage' in a matter of days, or even miss out a stage with no apparent ill effect. Above all this points to the need for sensitive observation.

Perhaps the most realistic view is that stages are cumulative. Each is an important building block in the development of visual literacy and aesthetic awareness. Children can operate in the 'stages' already developed, according to the demands of each task and can continue or slip to and fro between them.

Children's earliest marks are accidental results of movement often recorded in spilt food. This discovery opens up a whole range of experimental possibilities driven by the child's pleasure in movement and the visual 'magic' of the recorded marks as they appear. We as parents or teachers encourage this experience by providing drawing materials, paper and perhaps paint and malleable materials.

Children's earliest marks are made with one, or combinations, of three basic movements: pounding up and down, a push-pull action and a sweeping ark from side to side.
It is important to value and support this early learning. Although attention may be fleeting, important developmental steps are taken as s/he begins to be able to recognise and repeat marks and make deliberate choices about placement.

RESPONDING AND HELPING

Drawing, painting and modelling materials need to be organised for convenient use and children helped to become familiar with the routines of use and cleaning up.

As the work is about movement and the marks made, observations and questions should focus on the physical sensations of the materials, naming and discussing marks, dots, lines, patches, textures, colours and their arrangement.

Silent encouragement and attention is also important and although younger children are mainly involved while making and can soon forget their work, display is a valuable way of signalling the work's importance and encouraging later consideration.   Teachers should acknowledge the children's pleasure and involvement and comment on the expressive qualities of the work (lively, peaceful, delicate) but avoid interpreting them as representational.

EXPERIMENTING AND DESIGNING WITH DOTS, LINES, SHAPES, AND COLOURS

As children gain control and develop a vocabulary of lines, shapes and colours they need to explore the qualities and possibilities of each material used and ways of arranging and designing with them. It is valuable to

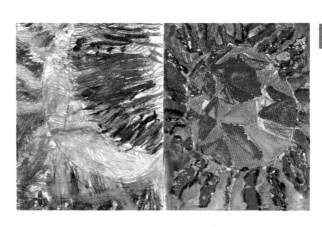

1 Free easel painting: lines, dots & patches, colour mixing and designing.

2 Experimenting with 'colour families', warm and cold colours, using the moon and sun as motives. Rich build up of mixed-media and aesthetic experiences.

3 Free pattern work using sponge brushes.

4 Group work exploring cold colours to encourage discussion and development of personal and social skills.

5 Collage of geometric shapes enhanced with a painted background using a limited colour range. Developing shape concepts, vocabulary, manipulative and design skills.

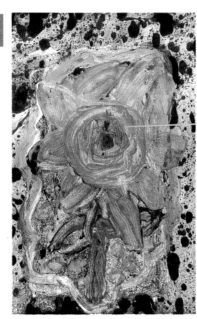

6. Water colour painting enhanced with a rich variety of collage materials.

7. Mixed media: marbling and finger painting.

8. Unit printing, painting and collage used to represent the city.

9 Free 'narrative painting', an expression of recent experience.

10 'Trafalgar Sq.' by Reception child. Observed and discussed with teacher on school trip, drawn from memory at school.

11 Imaginative painting of the Fire of London, confident & experienced use of paint to express the flames & smoke.

12 Children's work combined imaginatively & ambitiously in a 'walk-in' display on the Planets and space travel.

13 Imaginative illustration on the theme of 'friends'.

14 Portrait drawing in special frame.
Member of class posed in costume for observational drawing, following a trip to the National Portrait Gallery.

15 A well stocked and labelled Art Area.

16 Life sized carnival figures, collage and paper tie-dye. Part of a whole school carnival focus.

think of materials in terms of their characteristics:

hard and linear
pencil, pen

smudgy and crumbly
chalk, pastel, charcoal

waxy and oily
wax crayons, oil pastels

wet and runny
inks, dyes, paint

sticky and creamy
finger paints, glue

soft and malleable
clay, dough.

(adapted from Keith Gentle, in 'Children and Art Teaching', Routledge).

Children need structured opportunities to explore each in turn, moving on when the experience is thoroughly absorbed.
Some materials, such as paint and clay, offer a wide range of different states to be explored together with a variety of tools and equipment. At first, colour is used arbitrarily and colours mixed accidentally. Later conscious decisions will be made to use and mix specific colours. Paper in different sizes, shapes, surfaces and colours should be explored to encourage thought about scale, space, texture and colour combinations.

Children begin to explore the different design possibilities of dots, lines, patches in paint and three dimensional shapes in malleable materials. The circle begins to be used to represent enclosure, and parallel lines, dots and grids are explored in a rich diversity of ways.

Exploring variations and combinations provides a valuable focus both for the child's self-directed work and for teacher-led activities. Shapes form the basis for later representation, letter forms, handwriting and pattern design. Although children's work of this type may seem like adults' 'abstract art', to the child it is entirely concrete and a result of simply exploring visual elements and their possible arrangements driven by the excitement of aesthetic pleasure and discovery.

FIRST REPRESENTATIONS

Children begin to discover the possibilities of depicting things when they notice similarities between the marks and designs they make and real things, and begin to name them. Children draw 'what they know' rather than what they see: selecting and matching

experience from their existing repertoire of visual marks. A circle may stand for anything - with additional details added according to importance. Thus the 'big head' or 'tadpole' figure is one of the first images to appear recognised by adults. In the child's mind this 'schema' is quite sufficient to represent the whole person. In fact children at this stage actually prefer them to more realistic drawings if asked to choose! These schemas will gradually evolve in their complexity, detail and proportions. They are, in a sense, diagrams of ideas rather than attempts at realism.

RESPONDING AND HELPING

As with earlier stages, acceptance and understanding of the child's visual work is important. Silent attention as well as questioning can support. If a child wants to draw or paint a particular object, or the teacher wants children to focus on a particular subject, a discussion about its visual characteristics followed by questions about the kinds of marks, lines, and shapes which can be used to make the image, will help.

It will be important to help the children break down the task into manageable parts and simple sequences but not to be over-directive.

Looking at finished work is valuable both individually and in groups. Sensitive questions such as *'Would you like to tell me about your drawing'* can help, as can descriptions by the teacher of what s/he can see in terms of shapes, colours and arrangements . Subject matter can be followed up by asking about the original experience, which may shed further light on intentions and meaning.

THE 'AIR GAP'

At some point in this process of development the child's use of the paper space changes. At first the whole of the paper is used as a **free space for design**. Now the bottom of the paper becomes a base line and represents the ground, and a thin strip across the top of the paper, the sky. This so called **'air-gap'** is quite logical to a child of this age - the ground is beneath our feet and the sky above our heads and everything else goes on in between. This convention will disappear of its own accord when the child develops more complex ways of representing space.

Another type of drawing found is the 'x-ray' image where, for example, figures and events inside a building are shown through 'transparent' walls. Children will also represent movement with lines, such as the flight-paths of aeroplanes and super-heroes, or the movement of cars and people ('action representations'). If children are observed, they may be acting out experience in other ways, making appropriate noises and move-ments, mini-dramas in addition to drawing!

COMBINING SIDE AND 'BIRD'S EYE' VIEWS

Children develop the 'air gap' approach by introducing one or more base lines and combining side views and 'birds eye' views. The overall picture is still flat and scale is used to denote importance, so heads are often larger than bodies!

Parts of a picture are 'fitted in' to achieve a good design rather than accurate proportion. This is a powerful drawing system capable of great elaboration.

DISCOVERING 'ANGLED' LINES

Developmentally, the next step is the discovery that angled lines (the oblique) create an illusion of depth. This opens up a whole new range of possibilities, helping children to achieve sophisticated illusions of space and three-dimensional objects.

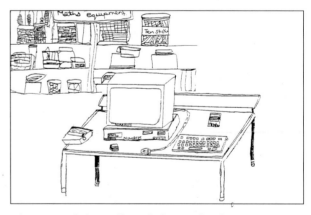

The use of these lines is inventive but unconnected across a drawing. This system has been used in many cultures, (Indian, Persian, Chinese, Japanese, Greek and Roman painting) as well as in modern Western art (Cubism) and should not be confused with perspective where the angled lines converge.

PERSPECTIVE

'Top juniors' can learn to draw in perspective from the experience of observational sketching combined with understanding gained from looking at and discussing art and photography. There is little value at this age in teaching the scientific or mathematical rules unless a child or class shows particular interest. By giving regular opportunities to draw from direct experience some will develop an intuitive grasp of perspective, while you will support others using alternative drawing systems. It is worth remembering that from a global viewpoint, perspective was only important in Europe between the 15th and 19th Centuries. It should be valued as just one of a range of powerful visual systems and not given undue pre-eminence.

PROGRESSION AND DEVELOPMENT

It can be seen that children are using drawing for a rich variety of purposes to represent their experience, drawing on the cumulative experience of early mark-making, the expressive qualities of the media, experiments with design, their developing 'schema' and a number of ways of representing space.

Collections of drawings of the human figure and of buildings, can be used as valuable indicators of children's' visual development. Collections made by class teachers from each class in a primary school could form the basis for discussion and comparison in INSET sessions, helping to develop a shared understanding of progression and development.

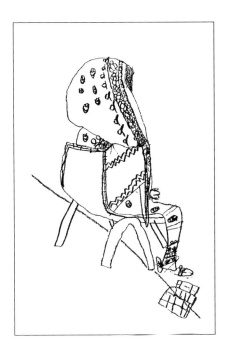

Painting

Gaining an appreciation and sensitivity towards colour is an essential element in each child's broad and balanced education. Helping children to *'learn to see'*, is a fundamental aim for art in education. This means that children develop a sharpened visual sense, the ability to perceive with greater insight, an attention to detail and an awareness of the innate characteristics and expressive qualities of the things around them.

There are many activities which contribute to this process but responding to direct experience and colour mixing from close observation, is recognised as an activity that, with regular practice, leads to this development. It is also highly valuable in exploring any visual resources brought into support topic or theme work. It leads to prolonged concentration and a depth of visual experience which aids memory, prompts questioning, discussion, language and conceptual development, and forms the basis for personal expression.

PRACTICAL CONSIDERATIONS

To encourage mixing all pupils should have their own pallet, brushes, water (two pots if possible!) and small rag or sponge to wipe or blot their brush. A central tray of powder colours or dispensed ready mixed paint can be shared if within easy reach, although children will benefit from having their own set. Block paints cannot be shared (as j25mixing takes place on top of the blocks). Pupils should have plenty of room and sit 'square' to the paper.

Some teachers use newspaper to protect tables. The value of this is questionable as the tables still need to be sponged. Plain coloured plasticised table clothes can protect tables from all types of practical work but care must be taken when working with craft knives.

Mixing paint with PVA glue and other additives such as sand, sawdust, etc. can extend the variety of experience. It is best to use recycled food containers for this kind of work as the PVA can stain and spoil water pots and pallets if allowed to dry. Mixing PVA glue used on top of block paints will seal the paint and is not recommended.

PAINT SYSTEMS

There are many different paints available for use in schools - powder colour, tempera blocks, ready mixed paint, finger paints and water colour. All provide educational experience and have advantages and disadvantages.

Very young children in nursery and reception should have access to the painting experience through finger paints and liquid paint, either ready mixed or mixed from powder. The paint should be thick enough not to run. A wide range of colours should be available and named. The foundations are being laid for understanding and knowledge about colour. Experimentation, building confidence and enjoyment, should be encouraged. Finger paint can be made with cold water paste and powder colour.

In the early years it becomes appropriate for children to begin to experiment with mixing and matching colour from observation, building on the earlier free mixing experience. At this stage a paint system is required which provides the full potential for mixing all colours in subtle shades. Without wishing to restrict the availability of a variety of types of paint for experimentation, best practice is often achieved when a teacher, or better still a whole school, adopts a standardised paint system and range of colours **(a 'limited palette')** as a basic set for the classroom.

This will almost certainly be a form of tempera - powder, blocks or ready mixed paint, using the **'double primary'** system of

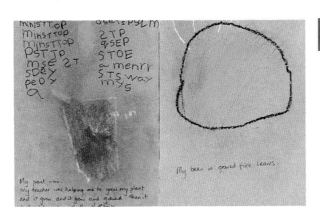

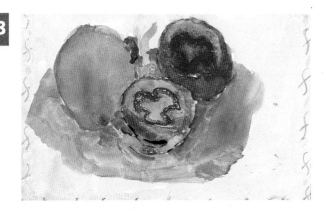

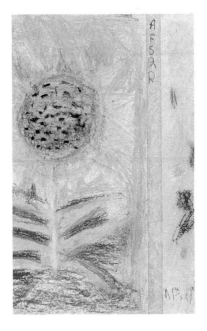

17 Observational drawing of a growing bean, recording for science in the Reception.

18 Sensitive water colour study of cut vegetables - top Juniors.

19 Direct observation of a sunflower in oil pastel.
Strip of paper provides an opportunity to try out colour mixing alongside the emerging drawing.

20 Painting combining direct observation, colour mixing skills and a rich textured surface.

21 Colour pastel studies of leaves, from a class book on 'Growth'. Close observation and colour matching.
22 Exploring pastel shades, responding to Monet's landscape painting and technique.
23 Working directly with natural materials outdoors to create ephemeral sculptures.
24 Children's animal drawings, observational plant and leaf paintings are combined in an impressive large scale collage.

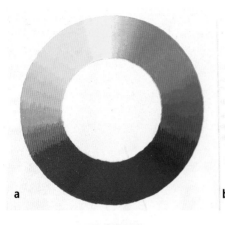
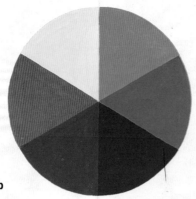
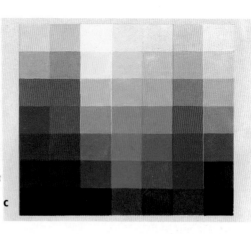

a

b

c

25

26 'Paper paste' models of decorative animal artefacts from India. The forms are simply crumpled newspaper 'bandaged' with strips of newspaper and wallpaper paste, painted white and decorated.

27 A classroom display to stimulate work on the colour 'Yellow'.

27

25a Colour theory: the visible spectrum bent round and joined at violet. Colours close to each other form harmonious 'colour families'.

25b The colour circle: Primary colours (red, yellow and blue) and Secondary colours (orange, green and violet). Colours opposite each other form 'complimentary contrasts'.

25c Primary and secondary colours mixed with white to form 'tints' and black to form 'shades'.

29 Group construction; a 'crab' sculpture!

28 **29**

28 An outdoor exhibition of a variety of sculpture using a range of construction techniques.

30 Look for examples of art, craft and design in school and the local environment. Older buildings are decorated with architectural crafts, ornamental iron, tiles, glass etc.

31 Make a map of the local area identifying interesting examples of art, design and craft. This would be a good assignment for older children and the map could be used by other teachers and classes as a resource for AT2, 'Knowledge and understanding'.

30 **31**

colours. This can be extended by the use of water colour boxes for small scale work and painting outside the classroom.

There is a consensus that primary age children should have access to quality art materials and that it is better to have a small quantity of good relatively inexpensive materials than a lots of cheap poor materials which may lead to lack of success and disappointment.

Theoretically, all colours should be able to be mixed from the primary colours plus white. Because pigments are not pure this does not work in practice. The 'double primary colour system' has been developed as the most limited set of colours which will truly provide the full range of colour mixing possibilities.

It is more important to standardise the range of colours available than the type of paint medium used.

The double primary colour system uses a warm and cold version of each of the primary colours, black and white. Powder and blocks require an appropriate eight-section palette to contain the paint. Powder and ready mixed paint require a mixing palette. Mixing is done on top of blocks, which are washed afterwards.

THE 'DOUBLE PRIMARY' COLOUR SYSTEM.

Choosing a range of colours:

Recipes can be developed for various colours. *'Pure'* primaries can be mixed from equal quantities of the warm and cold versions of the primary colour.

'Pure' secondaries are mixed from appropriate primaries:

orange - brilliant yellow and vermilion,
green - lemon yellow and turquoise,
violet - crimson and brilliant blue.

In mixing and matching from observation teachers and learners can share experimentation and research. A wide range of greens can be obtained by cross mixing all the blues and yellows extended into pastel tints with white and shades with black. A wide range of browns can be obtained mixing blues with vermilion and extended by adding brilliant yellow. 'Colour greys' and 'tertiary colours' are the technical terms used for the many subtle colours made from various proportions of all the primary colours.

Unfortunately the suppliers of paints provide what sells so it can sometimes be difficult to obtain the colours recommended here. Many 'special offers' include green and browns, which are not necessary and encourage children to go for superficial ready-made solutions.

Powder colour, tempera blocks and ready mixed paint are all tempera paint in different forms - pigment mixed with a binder. Tempera is meant to be used as an opaque paint (while water colour has a much finer pigment and is designed to be used in thin transparent washes on white paper).

Educational experts disagree and recommend their favourite paint which they back up with well-argued justification, but all three forms of tempera paint are capable of excellent results if used in an appropriate way.

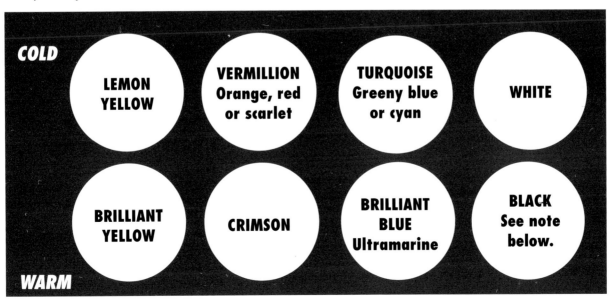

COLD			
LEMON YELLOW	**VERMILLION** Orange, red or scarlet	**TURQUOISE** Greeny blue or cyan	**WHITE**
BRILLIANT YELLOW	**CRIMSON**	**BRILLIANT BLUE** Ultramarine	**BLACK** See note below.
WARM			

Note: Some schools have decided not to automatically include black due to the tendency of some children to outline and mix darker shades using black alone. The turquoise can be replaced with Prussian blue which will produce a range of blacks when mixed with vermilion, alternatively black can be replaced with Prussian blue as a third blue.

POWDER COLOUR

Powder colour mixes easily to produce a thick consistency and the dry powder can be picked up with a wet brush to adjust mixing in progress. It is stored in trays with individual containers and used with a mixing palette (and like all painting systems plenty of clean water!). Trays require regular topping up and it is potentially messy when trays of powder are accidentally dropped.

TEMPERA BLOCKS

Blocks are stuck into eight-welled palettes with PVA glue. They are easy to stack and store and provided they are cleaned and drained after use, instantly accessible. They can be more difficult to mix to a thick consistency unless wetted before use, allowing time for the top surface of the block to soften up. Mixing is done in patches on top of the blocks themselves using a stiff brush and avoiding concentration in the centre of the block which will wear a hole in the centre. When a block is nearly finished the section of the palette can be filled with water and left to soak overnight. In the morning the remains will be soft and can be removed with a knife and stiff washing-up brush and replaced.

READY MIXED PAINTS

Ready mixed paints are set out in a palette in small quantities at the beginning of a painting session and need only a little water to mix to a painting consistency. They are best stored in a wine-rack and need to be shaken every so often as the liquid binder separates out from the pigment over time. The little plastic tops must be carefully replaced after use as blockages can result in messy accidents when bottles are squeezed!

THE BEST PAINT

Powder colour is perhaps the cheapest form of paint. It can be mixed to a variety of consistencies and also be used to cover large areas for mural and theatrical scale work. It requires preparation and can be quite messy which can be off-putting to some teachers. Some argue that the process of mixing from a dry powder is fundamental, while others maintain it distracts the learner from immediacy of response to colour!
Ready mixed paint overcomes this particular problem and can be used in many of the ways powder colour can. However thick and dryer forms of the paint cannot be mixed as the paint is already liquid. The dispensation of paint requires supervision and takes time. It is slightly more expensive and some argue

more wasteful as once paint is squeezed out it has be washed away at the end of a session.

Blocks are also slightly more expensive than powder but are more economical in use than ready mixed. They are perhaps the most accessible, economical in preparation time and trouble free in terms of classroom organisation, storage and use, encouraging independence. They are not suitable for large scale work and can provide disappointingly thin paint if children are not taught the appropriate mixing skills.

IMPLEMENTING A STANDARDISED PAINT SYSTEM

This can only be achieved if you can convince your colleagues of its value. It is also expensive so may have to be implemented in a phased programme. As it is more important to standardise colour than paint type make sure all future orders are only for the 'limited palette'. Make an audit of the colours you have which you can use. The first order you make can concentrate on the colours you don't have.
(Remember you will need to order twice as much yellow and white as other colours as they get used up more quickly!).

Blocks and powder colour will need the appropriate eight-section palettes so budget to buy enough for one room on each order if you haven't enough for a complete changeover. Most palettes are suitable for ready mixed paint.

Use National Curriculum implementation of Technology and Art as an argument for extra resources.

Remove all non- standard colours - these can be used for large scale theatrical work, model making, murals or in the Nursery/ Reception where a variety of mixed colours are appropriate.

PURCHASING THE 'DOUBLE PRIMARY COLOUR SYSTEM'

If you do not envisage whole group painting sessions, decide how big the group will normally be for painting and calculate accordingly. All the basic colours are available from Ocaldo. Special offers are available from suppliers on double primary sets in all types of paint. The Berol Colour Workshop is a high quality double primary system, which is economical when bought in 1 litre refill bottles.

Art and IT

The classroom computer should be seen as just another art medium. 'Electric' drawing and painting would be a good way to think about it! The National Curriculum requires that children should be given opportunities to develop and apply their information technology (IT) capability, where appropriate, in art, craft and design.

You will need to identify a draw and paint program which is suitable for the age range of your class. For example, Nimbus computers' 'Paint Pot' has two entry levels, one which only uses visual symbols and can be used from the nursery onwards. 'Paint Spa' is more suitable for older children with a wider range of 'tools', as is 'Drawmouse' which has some interesting pattern design facilities. All classroom computers should have appropriate programs.

It is important to be able to make prints, preferably in colour. You should become familiar with the program you are going to use and learn how to print. You can then offer guidance to children as they work, and cope with technical problems as they arise.

It is best to stick to one program and really get to know it before branching out. Encourage one or two children to use the computer every time you set a drawing or painting project exploring the similar ideas in 'electronic' line and colour. Younger children will explore mark-making freely, just as they do with graphic and liquid media. Use the computer extensively for observational drawing alongside traditional media, encouraging children to make comparisons. One difference is the lack of variation caused by pressure when using a 'mouse'.

The screen can be used for narrative drawing

and illustration; technical drawing using the straight lines, circles, squares, etc.; pattern making; and small design projects incorporating lettering, colour and image.

'Templates' can be created and saved as files, for example the 'net' of a sweet packet, or the outline of a postage stamp with the Queen's head for graphic design, garments for textile design, or a line drawing of a room for interior design. The children can design onto the templates, trying out different ideas and effects, saving only the best.

The following qualities of computer draw and paint programmes should be borne in mind when planning art/IT work.

❏ Highly responsive for experimenting, drafting, trying out, a rough sketch pad without the need to save.
❏ Colours can be changed rapidly, good for exploring the expressive and spatial effects of colour.
❏ Image has stepped 'pixel' structure (the dots on a television screen). This is a quality which should be accepted and worked with.
❏ Colour is inconsistent and often there are differences between screen image and print. A printed out colour chart could be provided to compare with colours on screen.
❏ Highly interactive medium with absorbing possibilities for individual work and potential for group work, joint decision making and discussion.
❏ Puts highly professional lettering and technical drawing within the reach of young children.
❏ For observational drawing it is often best to restrict use of tools using only 'free hand' lines, the 'spray gun' for shading and perhaps 'fill' for backgrounds and large areas of colour.
❏ The highest quality work will come through the use of 'zoom' to work pixel by pixel on adjustments to small areas of the image.

A more recent use of computers for art is the introduction of 'CD Rom'. This will eventually allow children to research encyclopedias of art, held on interactive compact disks, in the classroom. The National Gallery, London, has produced the most useful interactive CD Rom disk so far.

Printing

SURFACE EXPLORATION

A wide range of media and techniques can be used to explore and record surface textures and patterns. The same processes can be used to create and design surface decoration, starting from basic elements (lines, shapes, textures, colours), the study of natural patterns, or in response at art, craft, and design from a variety of cultures and times (AT2). Just a few are described below that we think are particularly useful in the primary school.

RUBBINGS

One of the easiest ways of recording surface texture and relief pattern is to use the technology of 'brass rubbing', dark wax crayon and thin but robust paper (shiny white printing paper is best).

A selection of textured surfaces can be provided in the classroom, as well as arranging excursions into the local environment to collect textures. The activity is complete in itself but can later be extended with coloured wax crayons and combined with paint washes (wax resist) or alternatively used as a collage material.

Other ways of recording texture are: silver foil rubbing, clay impressions, casting in plaster, photography, printing from found surfaces and of course, observation drawing and painting.

UNIT PRINTING

Children's early experience of creating surface patterns and texture can be enhanced through simple printing, finger, hand and foot prints, or 'unit printing' with a variety of materials such as crumpled paper, cut fruit and vegetables, wooden blocks, cotton reels, sponges, fabric or nets stretched over corks, etc.

Free printing can be followed up by challenges to create simple pattern structures - lines, spirals, concentric circles, symmetrical, border and 'all-over' patterns. Unit printing can progress to specially designed string and matchstick blocks. Potato 'blocks' can be carefully cut into a tessellating shape, such as a square or triangle, before the design is applied. These can then be used to explore more complex pattern repeats including 'rotation' and 'half drop'.

MONO PRINTING

Single prints can be taken from a finger painting done directly on a table top. Any impervious surface can be rolled up with water-based printing ink and drawn into with a variety of markmaking materials. Cutting special squares of Melamine board for this activity will give you a raised surface which allows easy control of the ink and gives clean sharp edges to the print.

RELIEF PRINTING

A raised 'relief' surface is created, rolled up with ink and printed. There are a variety of techniques each with its own possibilities and limitations to explore.

A wide variety of textured materials (string, card, fabrics, etc.) are made available to be cut or torn and collaged using PVA glue onto card (the glue itself can also be used to create textured effects). This method of creating a printing block can be used by younger children to explore texture, while older children can use the technique to make images. The pieces need to be carefully stuck down otherwise they will pick up on the roller when applying printing ink. It is best to keep the raised surface a reasonably even height for ease of inking and printing. Seal the finished block with a 1:1 solution of PVA and water and allow to dry.

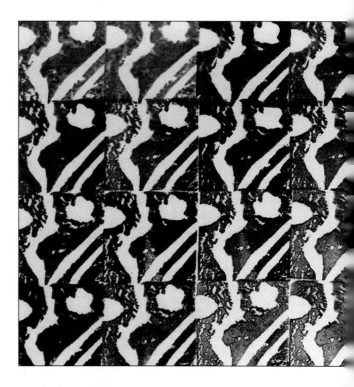

Colour is not always important when focusing on surface texture and pattern so use black ink or an earth colour. Use an inking tray, roller and water-based printing ink. Ensure an even distribution of ink on the 'block' starting with the edges, then inking in both directions, up and down and across the block. Place the paper onto the block and burnish the back of the paper with the soft part of the hand, a pad of cloth or the back of a spoon, rather than a roller.

Inking up and printing is a craft skill and it is best if you can practice yourself in advance in order to demonstrate to the children a technique which really works and can bring success!

Paper printing is a version of relief printing which just uses sugar / brushwork paper. The image is cut direct from one sheet of paper and carefully stuck down to a second sheet with PVA glue. This method is useful with older children because of the care needed in cutting and sticking. It can be used during direct observation as a form of drawing. The cut edge creates a fine sharp line set against a textured background when printed. (In this method, omit sealing with PVA solution).

PRESS-PRINT

Thin expanded polystyrene sheets can be purchased through supplies catalogues which are far superior to, and cheaper than polystyrene ceiling tiles which are not suitable! (Polyblocks - GLS, Easiprint - NES). The design or image is drawn into the surface with a ball pen or pencil, or objects are pressed into the surface to leave an impression. The surface is then inked up and printed.

This method of printing can provide a 'reduction' process similar to lino-printing without the resistance and danger of lino cutting blades. Smaller pieces can be cut to interesting tesselating shapes for pattern repeats.

Collage

Collage is a versatile medium which depends for quality on the bits and pieces available to work with. Rich collections of colours and qualities (hard, soft, smooth, rough, shiny, dull, stretchy, resistant, etc.) should be provided. Children can be involved in collecting and sorting colour family collections attractively labelled and stored in plastic sweet bottles.

The activity builds aesthetic experience, as children are involved in choosing shapes, colours and qualities of materials, placing them together and composing them on the paper. A feature of collage is that a number of arrangements can be tried before 'fixing' with glue.

The skills of discrimination, tearing, cutting, estimating, measuring, controlling and placing glue are all involved along with organising ideas and response to the focus of the activity.

Children can be progressively introduced to a variety of techniques that extend the ability to choose, such as self-made templates, the use of positive and negative shapes created by cutting, layering opaque and transparent materials, mixing media and extending use e.g. paper - tearing, plating, crumpling, curling, folding, distressing, scoring, pre-painting etc.

Children need the opportunity to explore independently, as well as with direction, to realise the full potential of the materials and their own creativity. Progression should be apparent in the increasing sophistication of response in projects which allow them to apply their accumulated skills and experience.

Textiles

Textiles are good media for surface decoration as well as being a unique area of knowledge and understanding in the art and technology curriculum.

It is beyond the scope of this booklet to explore the area in depth but the following framework can provide a starting point for planning.

The first column provides a breakdown of the field of textiles and the second an appropriate school-based activity to introduce skills, understanding and opportunities for creative art, craft and design.

TEXTILE PRACTICES	CLASSROOM PRACTICE
Fabric Construction ■ Spinning ■ Weaving ■ Felting ■ Knitting/Crochet	Hand Spinning Card Weaving
Dyeing ■ Fabric painting ■ Tie Dye ■ Batik (hot wax resist)	Fabric Painting Tie Dye(KS1) Batik (KS2)
Surface Decoration ■ Embroidery ■ Appliqué ■ Quilting	Binca / Canvas Appliqué as an extension of collage with embroidered detail
Printing ■ Block ■ Stencil/Silk Screen	String block unit printing Stencil printing
3D Work ■ Soft sculpture ■ Clothing ■ Accessories (eg.hats)	Mix-media headgear or costume project drama/celebration/ carnival etc.

A sewing machine in KS2 will open up a wider range of possibilities including machine embroidery. The traditional view of textiles as women's work, and as of lower status than fine art, needs to be challenged.

Sculpture

Children need to experience a wide variety of materials and modelling can be explored through clay, plasticine, dough and papier maché.

DOUGH

can be baked or left to harden and painted. One recipe (Saltdough) is to mix and knead equal quantities (300 g) of flour and salt with a tablespoon full of oil and a small amount of water. If put in an airtight bag or container, and particularly if stored in a refrigerator, it will last a long time. Foods dyes can be used to colour the dough, added during mixing.

PLASTICINE

is also a useful reusable modelling material. When new its coloured properties can be used expressively. However, unless it is carefully separated, all the colours become intermixed and have to be ignored. When cold it can be quite stiff and difficult to mould so it is best to warm it up before use. It is useful, particularly in the early years, for access to modelling, but has quite different properties to clay and like dough should not be seen as a substitute.

CLAYWORK

Modelling clay is perhaps the most ancient of art forms in human history. Figures, animals and simple decorated containers have been found in all ancient cultures where clay was available in the local environment.

Clay

Many testify to the unique feel and qualities of clay as a plastic malleable material. The clay that we use in the classroom is a cleaned version of the clay found in the ground. Clays gain their colours from minerals occurring naturally in them, for instance red or terracotta clay contains iron oxides. Clay changes properties according to the amount of water in it. It is best worked with when it is soft and malleable but not sticky. In this state it can be joined, retain marks and impressions and has a certain amount of structural strength, if not modelled too thinly.

As it dries it becomes `leather hard', more rigid and stronger, but less easy to bend and mould. In this state it can be carved. When dry it is rigid but easily broken. When fired (baked to a high temperature) in a kiln it changes chemical structure and becomes progressively harder, the higher temperature. In its 'sticky' state (slip) it can be used to join soft and leather-hard clay together.

Colouring Clay

Clay can also be coloured and given a variety of surface treatments after 'biscuit firing' (firing the dry clay to make it hard). You can also buy air hardening clay if you do not have a kiln ('Newclay'). It can be painted with ordinary classroom paints, blocks, powder, or ready-mixed. Wetting the fired clay first is advisable as the biscuit fired clay is like blotting paper. Painting onto fired or air dried clay should be done as sensitively as would be on paper. Models of natural forms, for instance, can be painted from direct observation. The painted object can then be varnished with matt, silk or glossy polyurethane varnish depending on the surface quality required. Fired clay can be coated with 'glaze', which is a creamy liquid containing a material like fine ground glass. This fuses onto the surface of the clay when fired for a second time in the 'glaze firing'.

Health and Safety

Clay is a safe clean material, Kaolin is used in medicines to settle the stomach! It is only dangerous as an irritant when breathed in as dry dust. Like any dust, if inhaled over a long period of time, it can lead to respiratory problems. For this reason, cleaning up is important and should be a 'wet regime' using sponges and mops rather than scraping and brushing.

Storing Clay

Plastic clay is delivered ready for use in strong airtight plastic bags sealed with a wire twist. Providing the bag has not been punctured it will keep in this state for months even years. You can feel its consistency by squeezing the clay through the bag.

Children can be given the clay directly from the bag which should be kept closed when not in use. Even leaving it open for half an hour can have an effect. Clay which has begun to dry out in this way can be reconstituted by spraying or splashing water down the sides of the inside of the bag around it and then resealing. The clay evenly absorbs the water over a day or two. This can be repeated until the right consistency is achieved. Bags which have been punctured should be sealed in another bag, used immediately, or transferred to the clay bin.

The Clay Bin

All primary classrooms should have a clay bin where clay can be stored in small lumps ready to use. The best clay bins are medium sized plastic dustbins with lids which can be sealed airtight. A 23 LITRE JOLLY BIN, available from your local hardware store, is ideal. It is 44cm/17.5 inches high and will often fit under the sink. It is large enough to hold more than enough clay for a class, but small enough to move without too much effort. The clay is stored in fist size lumps (relate this to the fist size of the children you are teaching rather than your own fist size) so that the damp air can circulate to the bottom of the bin. It goes without saying that the clay should be placed, rather than thrown into the bin to keep the lumps separate! The clay is covered

with a damp cloth, an old towel or double layer of Hessian. Then a piece of polythene, or opened out clay bag, is laid on top of the damp cloth and finally sealed in by the bin lid. Check from time to time that the cloth is still damp, if it is, then the clay will be in the right soft condition to use.

At the end of a working session all the unused clay should be reconstituted into fist size balls and put back in the bin for re-use. The cloth should be moistened, covered in the polythene and the lid replaced. The lid should always be put back on the bin when not in use, even during a session. Pupils should learn about this method as part of the process of working with clay so that they can help maintain the system. Unused dry clay can be reconstituted by soaking down in bins, drying to the non-sticky plastic state on wooden boards and then kneading (wedging) to get rid of air bubbles and gain a smooth consistency. For most primary teachers it will be more cost effective to throw away dried clay and replace with new clay, as this procedure takes time, effort, equipment and space.

Working with clay

All that is needed to get started is a bag of clay, sponges and perhaps some shaped lollipop sticks to use as clay tools. The children will need aprons or protective clothing of some sort.

Tools

Lollipop sticks can be shaped with a sharp knife or doweling with a pencil sharpener. Cocktail sticks and old blunt knives can be a useful addition to a tool collection. For rolling out clay to make 'slabs' or tiles, a rolling pin, batons and Hessian/linen backing cloth or paper are needed. Pupils need to be able work at a surface which can be easily sponged down. Formica tables are excellent. Some teachers like to cover tables with plasticised cloth for claywork. Clay worked directly on to a shiny surface will stick, therefore work should either be done in the hand, on a small wooden board, sugar paper or cloth.

It is best to work over an easily cleaned floor such as linoleum. Clay droppings can be swept up while still damp but not when dry. Dry clay, when trodden on, become dust which is easily transferred elsewhere as footprints, and into the air.

Many problems while working with clay are caused by children's access to water. Clay begins to dry from the moment it is removed from the bag or clay bin and this process speeds up as the clay becomes warm from the hands. The best practice is to supply a number of damp sponges which the children can use from time to time to keep their hands moist to transfer to the clay, keeping it at a working consistency. Some teachers even go so far as to put a board over the sink while work is in progress! It is a natural thing for a child to want to wet the clay, but once this has happened the whole thing becomes a slimy mess and there is no alternative but to start again.

If children have not worked with clay for some time, it is a good idea to give them a chance to explore clay as a material by giving them some quick exercises to encourage them to discover the full range of expressive and structural possibilities before moving on to project work.

SKILLS

At times, it is beneficial to teach skills as these allow children to be more creative. Below are just a selection of possible activities to allow children to explore the qualities and possibilities of clay. Many of these activities have been derived from clay workshops led by Maurice Barrett.

Holes

- ❑ modelling a spherical shape, gently push holes into it (one hand is needed to support the sphere)
- ❑ model-stretch-support-move, until a hollow 'golf ball' is created

Projections

- ❑ start with a spherical form, use straight fingers and gradually 'pull up' conical shapes (this is a very strong shape)
- ❑ smooth over cracks at all times, try to use all the fingers when pulling and keep the pressure even

Coils

- ❑ practice hand rolling coils, try to keep the pressure even to obtain an even coil
- ❑ practise making a coil pot with a circular or square base
- ❑ smooth the coils so that they are worked together on at least one side (inner or outer)

Thumb pots

- ❑ supporting a ball of clay in your cupped hand, gradually press out a hole with the thumb of your other hand
- ❑ smooth out the pot, until it is no thinner than 1/4" and is semi-spherical in shape
- ❑ flatten the rim by gently tapping on the table

Spheres

- ❑ make identical two thumb pots
- ❑ join the rims by roughening and cross-hatching (scoring) the surfaces
- ❑ paint on some slip (liquid clay) and gently push together, supporting with the hands and gradually smoothing
- ❑ make a small hole in the hollow sphere before drying to allow quicker drying (and prevent explosions if firing!)
- ❑ this basic shape can be used to model fruit and natural form, or the bodies of animals, portrait heads etc.

Rolling out clay

- ❑ a piece of Hessian or linen is needed to prevent the clay from sticking to the table, use two batons which should be the same thickness you require the clay
- ❑ shape the clay roughly to the size and shape you want the final slab and place between the batons
- ❑ roll the clay out using a rolling pin, lift the clay up from time to time, to allow

the clay to expand

- ❑ slabs can be used to make tiles, model furniture, houses, or used as surfaces to impress or build with texture

Formers

- ❑ use existing shapes, such as cardboard tubes and blocks of wood, as 'formers' to support the clay while it dries
- ❑ wrap newspaper around the former first (to stop the clay sticking)-roll out slabs of clay and wrap around former, joined together using the cross-hatching and slip method
- ❑ when 'leather hard' extract shape and newspaper before the clay shrinks and becomes dry and brittle

People

- ❑ start with a ball of clay and pull out projections for the arms, legs and head
- ❑ try to use all fingers in modelling, keeping the pressure even
- ❑ 'clothes' can be made using thin hand-made slabs of clay wrapped and smoothed onto the figure
- ❑ hair can be made by pushing clay through a sieve and joining to the head with slip
- ❑ the smaller you are able to make figures, the more skill you have!

Carving

- ❑ when the clay is 'leather hard', it may be carved
- ❑ projections and additions can be joined using the cross-hatching and slip method.

PAPER PASTE CONSTRUCTION AND 'JUNK MODELLING'

Papier maché (mashed paper) can be made by soaking torn newspaper in water and mashing to form a stiff pulp. Cold water paste is added and the resulting material can be modelled into any sort of shape. Avoid pastes with fungicide as they are toxic. PVA glue can also be added for extra strength. This is actually quite a difficult process as modern papers are difficult to break down.

A more versatile and suitable method is **'Paper Paste Construction'**. Torn strips of newspaper are painted with paste and laminated over some sort of 'former' such as crumpled newspaper, recycled packaging, card, wire, balloons, wood, or a combination of these. Alternatively strips of newspaper can be laid into or over moulds, using a thin layer of 'cling film' as a releasing agent.

These moulds could be existing containers and objects, or specially made from clay or plasticine, for instance in mask making. When dry, models can be painted. They can be further strengthened by varnishing with matt, silk or glossy polyurethane varnish depending on the surface quality required.

'Paper Paste' therefore ranges from plastic modelling to mixed media construction and it has much potential as a cheap, yet versatile three-dimensional medium. It incorporates and extends the tradition of 'Junk Modelling' using recycled materials, which links technology and art and is fundamental to developing children's three-dimensional experience and understanding.

Display

It would be unwise to make hard and fast rules about what contributes to good display. It helps, however, to form some general guiding principles.

- ☞ At the centre of 'display' should be an emphasis on valuing and giving meaning to children's work. Children's self-image develops through others' response to their work so it should be available to as wide an audience as possible. Not every piece of work by each child can be displayed but over time all children should have some work selected.

- ☞ Children should have opportunities to learn the skills of display themselves, mounting their work and contributing to decision-making through class discussion.

- ☞ Good display fulfils two main overlapping functions, to serve educational purposes and to create a visually interesting and aesthetically pleasing environment. Everyone works and learns better in an attractive and stimulating environment.

- ☞ Display is of crucial importance because so much information is received visually. Art is an important area, but there is also a wide variety of visual education across the curriculum, including the use of photographs, illustrations, maps, diagrams, graphs, written language and mathematical symbols.

- ☞ Display can act as stimulus and starting point for questioning and further investigation as well as celebrating children's work.

- ☞ There is a need for classroom and whole-school policy to ensure a balance of curriculum areas, equal access and opportunity. This should ensure representation from all age groups in public areas and sensitivity to providing positive images for all sections of our multi-cultural community. Displays made in the classroom can be moved into public areas to stimulate further learning, sharing ideas and good practice.

- ☞ Skills and understanding developed in the process of making high quality work are perhaps more important than the finished product. All stages, including first attempts should be seen as worthy of display so that with appropriate captions children and adults can see the processes, struggle and achievement involved.

- ☞ Display is an important aspect of the 'hidden curriculum'. If a special kind of work is produced just for display it de-values children's everyday work. It is, however, the responsibility of each teacher to present the children's real work in ways which will enhance and bestow value. A consistent approach to a high quality learning environment will help to foster a caring attitude towards the wider environment in life outside the school.

PRACTICAL CONSIDERATIONS

Displays are made up of varying proportions of:

Display materials & equipment:

- ❑ display boards
- ❑ surfaces
- ❑ backing papers
- ❑ borders
- ❑ fabrics / drapes
- ❑ rotatrim
- ❑ glue
- ❑ staple-gun etc.
- ❑ boxes and shelves for three dimensional display,

Input

- ❑ source material
- ❑ pictures
- ❑ reference material
- ❑ objects
- ❑ other visual material
- ❑ artefacts
- ❑ natural forms
- ❑ books etc.

Output

- ❑ Children's work - in progress / finished, for celebration, discussion and evaluation.

Captions

- ❑ Captions to explain
- ❑ headlines
- ❑ key questions to invite involvement.

Form

The nature of a display can change over time, starting in the classroom as a stimulus with source and reference material, gradually incorporating work in progress and finally

...ecoming a full documentation of the learning process for exhibition in a public area.

Displays are better if they are interactive, with questions to answer, objects to handle, books to look at and read.

Children will not necessarily look at a display. They must be engaged in various ways by drawing attention to various aspects, asking appropriate questions and inviting their involvement e.g. through observational drawing or a questionnaire.

Display can take a number of forms. For an exhibition of work, backing and mounts should be neutral and layout simple to throw the emphasis onto the work. For a thematic display all elements - lettering, colour, backing, borders, can contribute to an all-over effect relating to the theme. A group conceived and produced picture can involve children contributing in various ways with the teacher 'orchestrating' the separate parts into a unified whole. Care should be taken not to undermine the children's confidence in their own drawing skills with teacher-drawn outlines.

Scale and height

This should be considered from the children's, not the teacher's level, particularly in the nursery where ground-level display is important. 3D objects and books should be below eye-level with the smaller things at the front. Written work and small illustrations should be at eye level; 4-8 ft is useful for artwork and visual material with larger lettering; above 6 ft should be reserved for large scale work, things that can be read across the classroom and long term display (use a ladder, don't overstretch, call assistance!).

Layout

There are two ways of planning layout. One is to lay out all the pieces on the floor, arrange and rearrange until a satisfactory composition is achieved. Secondly a display can grow organically from a central area over time. In both cases you need to be guided by invisible grid lines, lining up edges to achieve a coherent design. Most two dimensional work will be in squares and rectangles, avoid mounting at angles, cutting off corners or 'amoeba' cutting, otherwise you look at the shape and not the content! Three-dimensional work can be arranged and rearranged until it looks right, like a still-life. Display can be symmetrical or asymmetrical. If asymmetrical, a balance between elements should be achieved overall.

Mounting

Work may be single or double-mounted or single-mounted with a drawn line. The side and top edges should be of equal width with the bottom edge slightly larger to achieve an aesthetic balance. The larger the picture, the larger the space needed around it, either on the mount or in the design of the layout. Three dimensional work can be enhanced through placing on draped fabric or white painted boxes or blocks of wood used as 'plinths'.

Adhesive

PVA glue spread thinly is the best mounting adhesive. Spread thickly it will make paper 'buckle' as paper expands when it gets wet. Pritt stick is only strong enough for small-scale work. Copydex will turn brown and stain through paper after a few weeks, ruining the work.

Changing displays

Remember tissue paper's colour quickly bleaches out on exposure to light and can only be used for short-term display. Sugar/brushwork paper bleaches out over a period of weeks, while more expensive coloured card and poster paper are 'colour fast'. Old displays become invisible with familiarity, therefore display must be seen as a continuing process and changed at least termly.

Lettering

Younger children can have difficulty reading captions or headlines made up of capital letters. Lettering must be clearly written and of an appropriate size and type-style for easy reading. Hand lettering needs practice, pencil guidelines are helpful and can be rubbed out later. Commercial templates in wood or plastic are excellent for larger headlines and the paper can be painted beforehand to create special effects. Computers can be used to produce large lettering and some photocopiers allow enlargements to be made from A4 to A3.

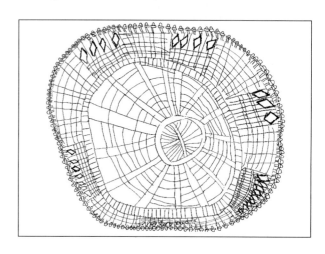

THE VISUAL
Elements of Art

Art has a basic visual vocabulary:

- ☐ line
- ☐ colour
- ☐ texture
- ☐ form
- ☐ tone
- ☐ pattern
- ☐ shape
- ☐ space.

These form the visual and tactile elements of art. These have their own direct expressive power and can also be combined in pictorial images and three-dimensional work to describe objects and events in the real and imagined world. Comparison between the 'elements' also reveals their difference.

Whether making two- or three-dimensional work, children will always be using one or more of the 'elements' of art.

We see the world in colour and tone (light and shade) which reveals the texture of surfaces and the shape and form of things. We also understand texture and form through touch, and the space around us through moving in our environment. Certain repeated shapes or arrangements we recognise as patterns.

To represent these in two dimensions we have drawing materials, paints and collage materials, with which we can arrange, compose or design. We can also work directly with line, form and texture in three dimensions, using wire, clay and other materials, adding colour and tone if needed.

References to the elements of art can be found in the art National Curriculum Programmes of Study (4a-d, 8e, 9b). It is important to ensure that children get a balance of experience and activity with each element, sometimes separately, sometimes in combination, in each year.

In the following sections a number of artists and cultural traditions are suggested as being particularly relevant and can be followed up initially by looking in art encyclopedias.

They are of course, non-statutory!

LINE

A single mark on a page will produce a point or a dot. A slight movement will make a dash. A longer movement creates a line which is a basic component of all early drawing.

Starting Out

At first, children should be allowed to play freely to explore, experience and develop a range of marks and lines, absorbing the qualities and expressive potential of each medium, gradually achieving control.

Progression

Children can be guided or challenged to:

- ☞ explore line in its own right: straight, curved, wiggly, zig zag

define shapes: (literally an 'outline'): circles, squares, triangles, 'egg' shapes, natural and made

☛ create direction and movement: horizontal, vertical, diagonal, meandering, branching, exploding, spiralling

☛ create patterns: by repetition, overlapping, direction and rhythm

☛ create texture through scribbling and cross-hatching.

Children will use line naturally in their narrative drawing for all kinds of imagery, people, houses, trees, the sun, animals, transport, etc. Lines will be used both for outline, detail and to show paths of movement.

Line is a fundamental language for observational drawing and can be used to explore:

☛ familiar things: toys, clothing, shoes, pets.

☛ human things: finger prints, hair styles, portraits

☛ natural things: feathers, shells, leaves, grasses, flowers, seeds, fruit

☛ made things: clock workings, electrical circuits, bicycles, ironwork, buildings, bridges.

☛ artefacts: baskets, weave, fabric patterns, pottery

Looking at Art - AT2

Children's understanding of line can be extended and stimulated by looking at and responding to other artists' work.

Here are just a few examples:

❑ Australian Aborigine bark drawings - animal images and patterns created with line.
❑ Vincent Van Gogh's pen and ink drawings
❑ Islamic art - calligraphy and linear patterns
❑ Henri Matisse - deceptively simple line drawing
❑ Bengali Kanthas - linear pattern and images created with running stitch
❑ Bridget Riley - early black and white work exploring linear optical illusion
❑ African wire sculpture

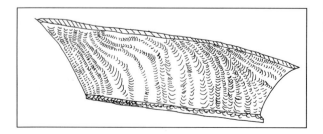

Vocabulary : Line

Angular	Broad	Broken	Circular
Contour	Curved	Dark	Diagonal
Flowing	Grid	Hard	Horizontal
Light	Linear	Long	Outline
Rhythmic	Short	Smooth	Soft
Spiralling	Straight	Sweeping	Thick
Thin	Vertical	Wiggly	Zig Zag

TONE

Tone in art refers to the range of values from dark to light usually represented in a black, through grey to white scale.

Tone can be used as an expressive element in its own right or to depict light and shade.

Starting Out

Children can be introduced to the basic concepts of light and dark, black, white and grey in their early mark making and mixing activity. Gradually they will gain control and learn how to make a range of tones in drawing media, collage and paint.

Progression

Limiting children at times to the use of black and white media can be very useful as it focuses on the expressive qualities of tone, texture and light and shade.

Charcoal, chalks, pastels, ink and paint are the best tonal media. Soft pencils can be very effectively used if children learn the skills of shading. Demonstrations of techniques and opportunities to practice 'scales' can lead to richer tonal expression in both narrative and observational work.

Older children can benefit from analysing the tonal values of a coloured object, or responding to the highlights and shadows of an observed scene, in tonal media.

Using the light from a window, a spot light or table lamp to create stronger contrasts of light and shade can help children focus on tonal values and the moods created by dramatic lighting.

Looking at Art - AT2

❑ The tonal drawings of Georges Seurat, the Pointillist Painter, are excellent examples of 'drawings without lines', made in conté (a kind of black pastel) on rough textured paper.
❑ Renaissance artists were very interested

in making things look 'real,' using tone in their drawings. A good example is the 'Virgin with St Anne' Cartoon, by Leonardo Da Vinci in the National Gallery.

- ❑ African masks and sculpture make use of strong expressive shapes which catch the light and create strong shadows. They are best drawn in tonal media.
- ❑ Black and White photography is the great tonal medium of the twentieth century, from fine art photography found in the gallery, to the daily newspaper.
- ❑ Picasso's 'Guernica' uses only line and tone to express terrifying images of war. Many of Picasso's and Braque's early Cubist paintings use only a tonal range of whites, blacks and browns.
- ❑ Many artists have used tone and light to create special moods or atmosphere. Look at Caravaggio and Rembrandt.

Vocabulary : Tone

Black	Contrast	Dark
Grey	High key	Highlight
Light	Low key	Monotone
Shade	Shadow	

TEXTURE

Texture refers to the surface quality of things. Things within reach can be experienced through touch as well as sight. Texture can be recreated in clay, or suggested through illusion in drawing and painting. Real bits of the world can be incorporated into art through collage, direct impressions through clay, wax rubbings, printing and casting, or recorded in photography.

Starting Out

Children need to begin exploring texture through direct experience with their environment. A good way to start would be to make a collection of objects and materials of various textures for classroom display. The children could handle, sort and discuss, helping them to develop their vocabulary.

They could then be introduced to the various ways of exploring texture through different art media.

Progression

Objects can be explored unseen to intensify the tactile experience, hidden in a bag, 'feeley box' or using blindfolds. The provision of collage boxes with differently surfaced papers and card, and other materials such as seeds, feathers and fabrics, will encourage a rich response and growing 'bank' of experience.

At times subjects can be chosen for drawing which avoid pattern and colour to focus more strongly on textural response. Surface textures and qualities are particularly important in sculpture and crafts where things are made to be handled.

LOOKING AT ART - AT2

- ❑ Crafts: Baskets, woven and knitted textiles, clay objects, carved wood, etc.
- ❑ Sculpture: Elizabeth Frink, Barbara Hepworth, Henry Moore, African sculpture, Benin bronzes.
- ❑ Painting: the techniques of realism, illusions of textures, of metal, glass, fur, textiles, fruit etc. can be studied in Dutch still-lives, Chardin and Titian
- ❑ Collage: - Cubist collages of Braque, Picasso and Kurt Schwitters.
- ❑ Black and White Photography: Bill Brandt, Ansel Adams.

Vocabulary : Texture

Coarse	Dry	Feathery
Furry	Glossy	Hard
Matt	Rough	Scratchy
Shiny	Silky	Slimy
Smooth	Soft	Waxy
Wet		

PATTERN

Pattern refers to the repetitions of lines, shapes and colours to be found in the natural and made world. In nature patterns are the result of growth structures, natural forces or the needs of living things to attract or disguise. In the made world they may be accidental, functional or decorative, or a combination.

Starting Out

Early experiences should offer opportunities to recognise and create simple pattern structures. Simple unit printing with found objects - cotton reels, corks, small bits of sponge; hand, foot and finger printing; sorting and arranging activities all contribute to early pattern experience.

Progression

Drawing and painting from a wide variety of patterned papers, textiles and artefacts, perhaps using a viewfinder to focus on a manageable area, can extend appreciation of a variety of cultural forms of surface decoration.

Opportunities to design patterns for a variety of needs, in real contexts, eg wrapping paper, wallpapers, furnishing fabrics, book covers, can consolidate basic understandings and link to Maths and Design Technology.

More complex pattern systems can be explored with string, potato, stencil or relief printing, or on a computer paint programme.

LOOKING AT ART - AT2

- ❏ Islamic patterns in architecture, calligraphy, carpets and book illustrations.
- ❏ Indian miniature painting
- ❏ Costume and Textile Arts from a variety of cultures: Japanese Kimono tradition, Indian, African, Guatemalan.
- ❏ Architectural crafts; wrought ironwork, ceramic tiles, mosaic
- ❏ William Morris

Vocabulary : Pattern

Arabesque	Border	Counter change
Decorative	Geometric	Grid
Half-drop	Irregular	Natural
Regular	Repeat	Rhythm
Rotation	Symmetrical	Tessellation

COLOUR

Colour can be a great source of enjoyment as well as providing a powerful language to express responses to the world. Primary colours (red, yellow and blue) are pure colours which cannot be mixed from other pigments. Secondary colours (orange, green and violet) can each be mixed from two primary colours completing the six-part colour circle. The addition of white or black allows us to mix 'tints' or 'shades'.

Colours which are close to each other on the colour circle 'harmonise' and give us a 'colour family'(eg cool blues and greens). Colours opposite each other contrast and are called 'complementary' colours (e.g. red and green, blue and orange, yellow and violet). They are perhaps called complementary because artists and designers have found that a small amount of a complementary colour brings its opposite to life.

Starting out

Young children need to experience colour in a wide range of media to become sensitive to its expressive qualities and be able to recognise and name each colour in its many hues in the environment. Colour displays, or collections in 'colour boxes', and collecting and sorting games can support this process alongside mixing games and activities in wet and dry media.

Many children will not have used paint until they start school. Colour differentiation develops through early 'free painting' with fingers and with brushes at the easel. Much of the time the primary colours, plus white, should be available and other colours can be added to extend experience. At other times just two colours will encourage further experimentation. Opportunities should be provided to explore warm and cold colours, colour related to mood, weather and seasons.

Progression

In Key Stage 1 the art National Curriculum requires that children should learn to mix from primary colours(4b). Introducing the 'double primary system' (described in the Painting section) will ensure that the range of colour available will enable children to mix any colour they can see, avoiding the disappointment and difficulties associated with a more limited pallet. Collect colour charts from paint shops for a wide range of names of colours to extend vocabulary.

In Key Stage 2 pupils should continue to experiment and apply their understanding of colour mixing principles both expressively and from direct observation.

LOOKING AT ART - AT2

- ❑ Paul Klee: expressive colour in simple structures
- ❑ Cave painting: natural pigments
- ❑ Guatemalan embroidery: bright colours, complementary contrast
- ❑ Mondrian: primary colours in geometric structures
- ❑ -'Les Fauves': Fauvism, exaggerated expressionist colour
- ❑ Impressionists: the effects of light, weather and atmosphere on colour
- ❑ Seurat: Pointillism, optical mixing of dots of pure colour
- ❑ Matisse: flat decorative colour

Vocabulary : Colour

Binder	Bright	Clashing
Cold	Contrast	Dark
Deep	Dull	Earth
Hue	Intense	Light
Pale	Pastel	Pallet
Pigment	Primary	Prism
Rainbow	Secondary	Shades
Shape	Tints	Warm
Complementary		

SHAPE

Shape and form are often used interchangeably. However, in art shape is more correctly used to refer to the two dimensional outline, while form refers to three dimensional shape.

Starting Out

Shape recognition is fundamental to drawing. The first steps are taken as the teacher encourages each child to see and name simple shapes in objects, the environment and their own emerging free art work. Learning to draw geometric shapes is a gradual process.

First the circle followed by the rectangle, then the triangle and finally the diamond. Shape can be explored through collage, first from ready made shapes, later carefully cut, either composing directly or responding to things seen.

Printing allows shape exploration and repetition starting with found units, corks, cotton reels, etc. and later exploring natural shapes through leaf printing and cut fruit and vegetables. Tessellating shapes can be explored with carefully cut potato blocks or stencils. Throughout there is a close relationship with mathematical learning.

Progression

Helping each child to analyse the shapes he or she can see in something observed is very supportive to all forms of observational work. Artists' work can also be analysed to identify the underlying shapes and their arrangement. Spaces in between, 'negative shapes', can be as important as the shapes themselves.

LOOKING AT ART - AT2

- ❑ Matisse cut outs: such as the 'Snail' in the Tate Gallery.
- ❑ Buddhist Mandalas: complex geometrical images for meditation
- ❑ Paul Klee: compositions with geometric shapes
- ❑ Architecture: identifying shapes in the local built environment
- ❑ Symbolic Shapes: Road signs, flags, logos, religious symbols.

Vocabulary : Shape

Asymmetrical	Complex	Geometric
Large	Made	Natural
Negative	Simple	Small
Symmetrical	Solid	Tessellating

MudChute Farm

FORM

Form in art can refer to all the characteristics of an object or artefact. More specifically it refers to three dimensional shape. In three dimensional art, form can be created directly, in clay or construction materials, in two dimensional art it can be represented through illusion.

Getting Started

Children experience the three dimensional world and objects and structures within it through active experience in movement and play. Provision of malleable materials, clay, plasticine and dough (together with water, sand and building blocks) provides not only a tactile experience and material investigation but also a media for representation, the three dimensional equivalent of drawing and painting.

Simple construction materials such as cardboard boxes and tubes (recycled 'junk') and joining devices - clips, pegs, rubber bands,

Sellotape and glue give an opportunity to make a lasting artefact rather than something ephemeral (as with construction kits).

Progression

Both clay and paper paste construction (using strips of newspaper and wallpaper paste) provide simple technologies which can, as skills develop, provide increasingly sophisticated outcomes.

LOOKING AT ART - AT2

- ❑ African sculpture - simplified and powerful expressive form
- ❑ Henry Moore - sculpture inspired by natural form
- ❑ Michaelangelo - classical form in painting and sculpture
- ❑ Andy Goldsworthy, David Nash - ephemeral and natural form
- ❑ Brancusi - pure sculptural form

Vocabulary : Form

Carving	Cone	Construction
Cylinder	Cube	Erosion
Mass	Malleable	Modelling
Natural	Organic	Rigid
Sculpture	Sphere	Streamlined
Structure	Volume	Weight

Note: Most of the vocabulary for shape and texture can also be applied to form.

SPACE

Objects exist in three dimensional space. Some art makes use of only two dimensional space such as flat decorative design. Much painting and drawing makes use of systems to represent space, some by suggestion and convention, others by illusion. Many cultures have seen realism as unnecessary or unimportant in art.

The West's quest for realism has seen the invention of perspective in 15th Century Italy, photography in 19th Century France and Britain, followed by colour photography, film, television and holography in the 20th Century.

The invention of photography freed modern art from the role of providing realistic images. The legacy is strong, however, and many people still think that 'proper art' should be an accurate representation in perspective and that other forms are of a lesser importance. This view needs to be challenged as it distorts and narrows what we see and value as art.

Starting out

Young children intuitively design and compose two dimensionally with lines, dots and shapes taking into consideration the empty space on the paper as well as the image. For this reason the original dimensions of the paper used should be respected when mounting and displaying work, so as not to give the hidden message that only the image is important and not the space round it. Space can be enclosed, filled and structured. It is explored by young children in sand and water play, through movement, in the climbing frame and through a wide variety of construction toys as well as through art media.

Progression

Much of children's two dimensional work represents space in one way or another and making connections with appropriate artists' work will enhance understanding.

Space enclosing or bridging structures can be explored using art straws or on a larger scale newspaper 'spills' (rolled tubes of newspaper). Fabric and carpet tubes which can be picked up free in rag trade areas provide the potential to make 'walk-in' large scale structures.

The casting process is a way of making a lasting three-dimensional record of an enclosed space. Pressing clay, pouring plaster or laminating strips of newspaper with wallpaper paste, are all possible in the primary classroom.

LOOKING AT ART - AT2

- ❐ Surface decoration and textile traditions from a variety of cultures using decorative two dimensional space.
- ❐ Mark Rothko, Joseph Albers: colour space
- ❐ The Eiffel Tower, steel bridges; spatial structures
- ❐ Egyptian Painting: combined front and side views in 'shallow space'. Wall paintings, papyrus and 'low relief' sculpture
- ❐ Indian and Persian miniature painting, Japanese prints (Hiroshige, Hokusai): the use of diagonal lines (the oblique) to create spatial effects
- ❐ The Italian Renaissance painters: the invention of perspective to create illusions of 'real' space
- ❐ Claude Lorraine: atmosphere or 'Aerial Perspective', the use of gradations of tone to create perspective
- ❐ Cubism (Braque, Picasso, Juan Gris): The combination of a variety of points of view in a single image.
- ❐ parks, gardens, squares, stadiums, streets, architecture and the built environment: functional and aesthetic spaces, 'spirit of place'.

Vocabulary : Space

Airy	Atmospheric	Broad
Busy	Claustrophobic	Enclosed
High	Large	Narrow
Open	Quiet	Small
Wide		

Resources

MUSEUMS AND GALLERIES

Many Museums and Galleries have an Education Department. If your school is not already on the mailing list, it is worth phoning or writing to the Education Officer. You can request information packs and details of current exhibitions, educational services and teachers' evenings. Some galleries will also organise staff INSET free or for a small fee.

RESOURCES FOR AT2

Packs of reproductions are expensive. In our experience the best are:

'The Primary Art Pack'
Robert Clement & Shirly Page, Oliver & Boyd

'Oxford Primary Art'
Norman Binch, Oxford University Press

'Approaches to Art'
Peppin, Smith &Turner, Ginn

Resources for non - Western art are often difficult to find. In the following two publications a wide range of non - Western art, craft and design is documented, making an excellent starting point for planning:

'World of Crafts'
Smith & Mahoney, Merilion Arts Library

'World Crafts'
Jacqueline Herald, Oxfam

In the case of World Crafts many of the artefacts featured in the book can be obtained through Oxfam Shops or Mail-Order.

Some of the best books currently available are:

'A Year in the Art of a Primary School'
Clement, R. & Tarr, E. (1992), NSEAD

'Learning from Objects'
Durbin, G. (1989), English Heritage

'Children and Art Teaching'
Gentle, K. (1984, 1988), Routledge

'Children and Computers'
Matthieson K. (1994), Hodder and Stoughton

'Teaching Art at Key Stage 1'
Meager N (1993), NSEAD

'Art in Practice'
Morgan, M. (1994), Hodder and Stoughton

'Experience and Art, Teaching Children to Paint'
Smith, N (1983), Teachers College Press

'The Arts in the Primary School'
Taylor, R & Andrews, G. (1986), Falmer

East Anglia Guide 1996

Welcome to East Anglia

The East Anglia Guide provides you with hundreds of ideas for a great day out. Whether you are on a short break or holiday, visiting friends or family, or a resident of the region, the Guide gives you all the information you need to explore this beautiful region.

Contents

Prices appear in the order of Adults/Children/Senior Citizens. When prices are not available at the time of going to press, the 1995 (95) prices are given. If no prices are given, admission is free.

See Touring Maps on pages 122 to 128 for locations of places to visit.

(NT) = National Trust (EH) = English Heritage

Published by the East Anglia Tourist Board, Toppesfield Hall, Hadleigh, Suffolk IP7 5DN

Tel: (01473) 822922   Fax: (01473) 823063

Internet: http://www.e-anglia-tourist-board.org.uk/eatb/

Look out for the Welcome Host sign.

A COMMITMENT TO COURTESY AND SERVICE

WELCOME HOST

Quality and friendliness are the key themes of the Welcome Host programme, a nationally recognised customer care initiative which aims to promote the highest standards of service and a warm welcome for all visitors.

A sign of quality at over 23,000 places to stay in England...

Knowing what to expect is vital when choosing a place to stay in England. But how can you be sure that what you read about in the brochures will be reflected in reality? With a little help from the ENGLISH TOURIST BOARD, you can take a short-cut through the maze of brochures and guides to find the place that will be right for you.

Most are graded for quality – including general decor, furnishings, fittings and level of hospitality. Graded establishments are awarded APPROVED, COMMENDED, HIGHLY COMMENDED or DE LUXE. And each establishment is checked every year to ensure standards are being maintained.

...and a sign that shows the facilities offered.

As well as grading for quality our inspectors also check the facilities offered. Crowns, Keys and Moons indicate the range you can expect in three different types of serviced and self-catering accommodation. The Q scheme relates to caravan, chalet and camping parks.

CROWN CLASSIFICATION
If you're looking for a hotel, guesthouse, inn, B&B or farmhouse, look for the CROWN. The classification LISTED or One to Five Crowns tells you the range of facilities/services you can expect. The more Crowns, the wider the range.

KEY CLASSIFICATION
If you're looking for a self-catering holiday home, look for the KEY. The classification One to Five Keys tells you the range of facilities and equipment you can expect. The more Keys, the wider the range.

MOON CLASSIFICATION
If you're looking for somewhere convenient to stop overnight on a motorway or major road route, look out for the 'Lodge' Moon. The classification One to Three Moons tells you the range of facilities you can expect. The more Moons, the wider the range.

THE Q SCHEME
If you're looking for a holiday caravan, chalet or camping park, look for the Q Scheme. The Q symbol indicates the quality, the more Ticks in the Q (from One to Five) the higher the quality standard.

More detailed information on all our grading and classification schemes is available at any Tourist Information Centre or your Regional Tourist Board. Please check to see if your choice of accommodation has been inspected, graded and classified by the English Tourist Board before reaching a decision on booking. Only establishments that have been inspected are able to display the official Crown, Moon, Key and Q symbols and the four quality grades: Approved, Commended, Highly Commended and De Luxe.

CAMBRIDGE

When in Cambridge make the most of your visit.

Join a Walking Tour, accompanied by a Blue Badge Guide.

Tours leave the Tourist Information Centre daily throughout the year.

For further information or details regarding the special arrangements necessary for groups, please contact:

The Tourist Information Centre, Wheeler Street, Cambridge CB2 3QB Tel: (01223) 322640/463290 Fax: (01223) 463385

Norwich Cathedral and Diocese, Anniversary Celebrations 1996

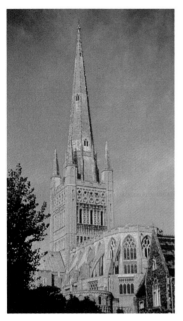

In 1996 Norwich will be celebrating 900 years of the foundation of its great Cathedral, the first stone was laid on the greenfield site by Herbert de Losinga in 1096. It will also be a whole year of celebration for the Diocese, which covers 1804 square miles of rural Norfolk as well as Lowestoft in North Suffolk, since it was also 900 years ago that Herbert de Losinga moved his See from Thetford to Norwich, and founded a religious community of Benedictine monks.

Today the Cathedral's role is mother church of the Diocese, drawing people to its great services and festival events, its concerts and recitals as well as those who come to marvel at its magnificence and treasures.

The surrounding tree-lined Close is filled with medieval and Georgian houses, and is the largest and most charming collection of Cathedral houses surviving in Europe. From the Close visitors can wander down to the River Wensum which winds through the centre of medieval Norwich and now is filled with colourful pleasurecraft.

On 25 May 1996 a commemorative piece of stone, given by the citizens of Caen (home of the stone used in the construction of the Cathedral), will be shipped to Norwich to launch the Celebration Year. It will be carried from Great Yarmouth on the last black-sail trader, the wherry 'Albion', escorted by other wherries. Amid much celebration, the stone will be ceremoniously hauled on a tumbrel up the Close to the Cathedral door. The procession will be accompanied by music and dance, together with hundreds of school children. 900 balloons will be released and church bells will be rung throughout the city and county. The inscribed stone will be used in a Cathedral project.

There are many events planned throughout 1996 including music, dance, theatre, cinema, arts, concerts, hot air balloons, garden parties, flower festivals, fetes and exhibitions. The highlight of the whole year will take place within the Cloisters - which are the largest of any English Cathedral. 'Fire from Heaven' will be a live outdoor drama spectacular that unfolds the rich tapestry of events in Norwich Cathedral's long history.

In early September there will be a large open-air concert, performed by the renowned Wren Orchestra of London, with a grand firework finale, all against the magnificent backdrop of the Cathedral, and at the end of this month the Archbishop of Canterbury will visit.

And, of course, as well as the fun element, there is the contemplative. A time to reflect, to join the quiet times, as well as the great services that will be taking place.

Time to be part of living history and an unforgettable year.

Programme of Events 1996

May

25th French Connection: Public Launch of Celebrations
Commemorative stone from Caen, France. Ceremonial arrival by river at Pull's Ferry, on the wherry Albion.

June

1st Pasadena Roof Orchestra
Internationally renowned orchestra performing live in outdoor concert.

13th Medieval Festival Living history fair involving schools in Diocese. Over 3000 children in costume in Pageant of Medieval Market in Cathedral and Close.

20-21st Noye's Fludde by Benjamin Britten
Performances by Norfolk secondary schools and professionals in Cathedral.

July

1-5th Schools Celebration Week
Exhibitions and displays in the Cathedral by school children. Music events and drama. Teddy bears' picnic. Display in Cathedral of Schools' 900 Poems Competitions.

6th 900 Years of Music
Choral and orchestral concert, in Cathedral, of music through the ages - a piece for each century. Finale, première of new work commissioned for Cathedral and Diocese 900, written and conducted by Malcolm Archer.

11-14th Flower Festival in Cathedral
'Flowers in Celebration': approx. 150 arrangements thoughout Cathedral.

13th Lord Mayor's Procession
Annual procession of colourful floats through streets of city centre.

August

6-11th 'Fire from Heaven'
Live outdoor drama spectacular with son et lumière that unfolds the rich tapestry of events in Norwich Cathedral's long history. Magnificent music and choral singing from cast of 100, plus extravagant sound and lighting effects. Cathedral Cloisters.

September

7th September Symphony Musical Extravaganze with Fireworks
Large open-air concert with fireworks within The Close, against the spectacular backdrop of the Cathedral. Concert performed by the renowned Wren Orchestra from London, plus pre-concert early evening entertainment: jazz, hog roast, etc.

The above are just some of the events which are planned for the special anniversary year. For further details on the programme of events contact:

The Tourist Information Centre, The Guildhall, Gaol Hill, Norwich NR2 1NF Fax: (01603) 765389, or
Events Co-ordinator, Cathedral & Diocese Anniversary, 12 The Close, Norwich NR2 4DH Fax: (01603) 766032

The Best Days Out Are Yesterdays

England's superb historical heritage is especially rich in East Anglia. Here you'll find splendid houses, elegant gardens, peaceful parks, lakes and country walks.

Often with restaurant meals, light refreshments, gift shops and many special events.

Blickling Hall
NORFOLK

Felbrigg Hall
NORFOLK

Oxburgh Hall
NORFOLK

Sheringham Park
NORFOLK

Ickworth
SUFFOLK

Lavenham Guildhall
SUFFOLK

Anglesey Abbey
CAMBRIDGESHIRE

Wimpole Hall & Home Farm
CAMBRIDGESHIRE

Free Visitors Guide to East Anglia

Telephone 01263 733471 Mon - Fri 9-5 for your copy
or write to: The National Trust,
Blickling,
Norwich
NR11 6NF

The National Trust

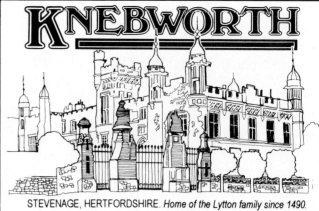

Historic Houses

Bedfordshire

☙ **Elstow Moot Hall,** Elstow Green, Church End, Elstow: Medieval Market Hall containing exhibits of 17th century life, including beautiful period furniture on show. Publications and antique maps for sale. *1 Apr-31 Oct, Tue-Thu, Sat and Bank Hol Mon, 1400-1700; Sun, 1400-1730; last admission 45 mins before closing. 60p/30p. Tel: (01234) 266889.*

Mentmore Towers, Mentmoor, Leighton Buzzard: An example of the Victorian 'Jacobean' revival at its best. Built in 1855 for Baron Meyer Amschel de Rothschild, this grand romantic house is a reminder of the enormous wealth and power of the Rothschilds in the 19th century. The architect was Sir Joseph Paxton, designer of the Crystal Palace. Mentmore Towers is now the headquarters of the Maharishi Foundation. *All year, Sun, 1430 guided tours. £3.00/£1.50/£2.00. Tel: (01296) 662183.*

☙ **Woburn Abbey,** Woburn: One of the finest houses in England, Woburn Abbey has been the home of the Dukes of Bedford for over 300 years. Set in a 3,000 acre deer park, it was built in the mid 12C and extensively altered by Henry Holland, the Prince Regent's architect, in the mid 18C. Contains an important and extensive art collection, including paintings by Canaletto, Rembrandt, Holbein, Velazquez and many others. *Mar-Oct, Mon-Sat 1100-1600, Sun, Bank Hol, 1100-1700; closed Nov, Dec; Open 1 Jan; Weekends only until Mar. £6.80/£2.50/£5.80. Tel: (01525) 290666.* ♿

☙ **Wrest Park House and Gardens,** Wrest Park, Silsoe: 150 years of English gardens, laid out in the early 18C. Includes a painted pavilion, Chinese bridge, lake, classical temple and Louis XV style French Mansion. *1 Apr-29 Sep, Sat, Sun, Bank Hol Mon, 1000-1800. £2.30/£1.20/£1.70 (95). Tel: (01525) 860152.* ♿

☙ **Luton Hoo** - The Wernher Collection, Luton: Historic house built in 1767. Collection incs. paintings, tapestries, porcelain, bronzes, ivories. Display of Fabergé and mementoes of the last Russian Imperial Family in and around the recently restored Russian Orthodox consecrated Chapel. *1 Apr-13 Oct, Fri, Sat, Sun, garden & restaurant 1200, house 1330, Bank Hol Mon 1030. £5.50/£2.50/£5.00. Tel: (01582) 22955.* ♿

Cambridgeshire

☙ **Anglesey Abbey,** (NT) Lode: The house, dating from 1600, is built on the site of an Augustinian Abbey, and contains the famous Fairhaven collection of paintings and furniture. It is surrounded by an outstanding 100 acre garden and arboretum with a wonderful display of hyacinths in spring and magnificent herbaceous borders and a dahlia garden in summer. A watermill in the grounds is in full working order and the machinery is demonstrated on the first Saturday of each month. *House, 23 Mar-13 Oct, Wed-Sun, Bank Hol Mon, 1300-1700; Garden, 23 Mar-7 Jul, Wed-Sun, Bank Hol Mon, 1100-1730; 8 Jul-8 Sep, daily, 1100-1730; 11 Sep-3 Nov, Wed-Sun, 1100-1730; Mill, 23 Mar-3 Nov, Wed-Sun, Bank Hol Mon, 1300-1700; last admission 1630, closed 5 Apr. £5.50/£2.75/£5.50. Tel: (01223) 811200.* ♿

Burghley House, Stamford: The largest and grandest house of the first Elizabethan age. House was built in 1585. Features paintings, tapestries, silver fireplaces, porcelain, furniture. *1 Apr-6 Oct, daily, 1100-1700; Closed 7 Sep, 25 Dec, 1 Jan. £5.10/£2.50/£4.80. Tel: (01780) 52451.*

⊚ **Elton Hall,** Elton: Historic House and Gardens open to the public. Fine collection of paintings by Gainsborough, Reynolds, Alma Tadema, Constable, Millais, etc. Furniture, books. Henry VIII's prayer book. Restored rose garden. Knot and sunken garden and arboretum. No guided tours on Bank Holidays. *8 Apr, May, Aug, Bank Hol Sun & Mon, 1400-1700; Jul, Wed, Sun, 1400-1700; Aug, Wed, Thu, Sun, 1400-1700. £4.00/£2.00. Tel: (01832) 280468.*

Hinchingbrooke House, Brampton Road, Huntingdon: Large country house - origins in 12th century Nunnery, home of the Cromwell family and Earls of Sandwich. *12 May-25 Aug, Sun, 1400-1700. £2.00/£1.00/£1.00. Tel: (01480) 451121.* &

⊚ **Island Hall,** Godmanchester: An important mid 18C mansion of great charm owned and being restored by an award winning interior designer. Tranquil riverside setting with ornamental island forming part of the grounds. *30 Jun, Jul, Sun only, 1430-1700 (last admission 1630). £3.00/£2.00/£3.00. Tel: (0171) 491 3724.*

Kimbolton Castle, Kimbolton: Tudor house remodelled by Vanbrugh. Pelligrini mural paintings, Adam gatehouse, fine parklands. Now occupied by an independent school. *7, 8 Apr, 26, 27 May, 14, 21, 28 July, 4, 11, 18, 25, 26 Aug, 1400-1800. £1.00/50p/50p. Tel: (01480) 860505.*

⊚ **Peckover House,** (NT) North Brink, Wisbech: Merchant's house on North Brink of River Nene, c. 1722. Fine plaster and wood rococo interior, notable and rare Victorian garden with unusual trees. *1 Apr-30 Oct, House & Garden, Wed, Sun, Bank Hol Mon; Garden only, Sat, Mon, Tue; times for both 1400-1730; Possible Sat House opening for 1996, please ring Property Manager for details. £2.50/£1.25. Tel: (01945) 583463.*

Wimpole Hall, Cambridgeshire

⊚ **Wimpole Hall and Home Farm,** (NT) Arrington: 18th century house in landscaped park. Folly and Chinese bridge. Plunge bath and yellow drawing room in house, work of John Soane. Home Farm - rare breeds centre. Museum, children's corner, adventure playground. *23 Mar-3 Nov, Tue-Thu, Sat, Sun, Hall, 1300-1700; Farm 1030-1700; 3 Nov-Mar 1997, Sat, Sun, Hall, 1300-1700, Farm 1030-1700. Closed 23-27 Dec, 1 Jan 1996. £5.00/ £2.25. Tel: (01223) 207257.* &

Essex

⊚ **Audley End House and Park,** (NT) Saffron Walden: Palatial Jacobean house remodelled in 18th-19th century. Magnificent Great Hall, 17th century plaster ceilings. Rooms/furniture by Robert Adam. Park by 'Capability' Brown. *1 Apr-30 Sep, Wed-Sun, Bank Hol Mon, Grounds 1000-1700, House 1200-1700, last admission 1700. Please telephone for admission prices and Christmas opening times. Tel: (01799) 522842.* &

Gosfield Hall, Gosfield: Tudor house built around courtyard with later alterations. Old well and pump house. 100 foot Elizabethan galley with oak panelling. *1 May-30 Sep, Wed, Thu, 1400-1700. Guided tours of House £2.50/£1.00/£2.50. Tel: (01787) 472914.*

⊚ **Hylands House, Park and Gardens,** Hylands Park, Writtle: Hylands House beautifully located in over 400 acres of Hylands park, in Writtle near Chelmsford. The first phase of internal restoration completed in May 1995 is open to view. Four areas are restored including entrance hall and old drawing room, also available is the history exhibition and views into other unrestored areas on ground floor. The parkland and gardens are well worth a visit too. *Please phone for details of opening arrangements. House £2.00/£1.00/£2.00. Park & Gardens free. Tel: (01245) 490490.*

⊚ **Ingatestone Hall,** Ingatestone: Tudor house and gardens, the home of the Petre family since 1540. Family portrait collection, furniture and other heirlooms on display. *13 Apr-29 Sep, Sat, Sun, Bank Hol Mon, 1300-1800; 17 Jul-30 Aug, Wed-Fri, 1300-1800. £3.50/£2.00/£3.00. Tel: (01277) 353010.*

⊚ **Layer Marney Tower,** Layer Marney, Colchester: Tallest Tudor Gatehouse in the country built by Henry 1st Lord Marney, Lord Privy Seal to Henry VIII. Flamboyant Italianate style with fine terracotta work. Formal gardens and deer in surrounding fields. Rare Breed Farm Park allowing chance to meet the animals. *1 Apr-30 Sep, Sun-Fri, 1400-1800; Sun during Jul & Aug, 1200-1800; Bank Hol Sun & Mon, 1100-1800. £3.25/£1.75/£2.50. Tel: (01206) 330784.*

Moot Hall, High Street, Maldon: Originally built in the 15th century, C1440, for the D'Arcy family by Sir Robert D'Arcy (1358-1448), a Royal Official in the County of Essex and M.P. for Maldon in 1422. This historic building has been the centre of local government in the town of Maldon since 1576 when it was purchased for a sum of £55.00. It is said that the tower was intended to form part of a much larger house. In 1539 it was described as Master D'Arcy's chief mansion. *All year, Mon-Sat, 1000-1530. £1.00/50p. Tel: (01621) 857373.*

⊚ **Paycockes,** (NT) West Street, Coggeshall: Half-timbered merchant's house built c. 1500. Richly carved interior. Small display of Coggeshall Lace. *5 Apr-31 Oct, Tue, Thu, Sun and Bank Holiday Mondays, 1400-1730 (last entry 1700). £1.40/65p. Tel: (01376) 561305.*

Hertfordshire

⊚ **Hatfield House,** Hatfield Park, Hatfield: Twenty-one miles north of London, easy to reach by road and rail. There are two exhibitions, the National Collection of Model Soldiers and a William IV kitchen built in 1833. *5 Mar-13 Oct; House, Tue-Sat, Guided tours only, 1200-1600; Sun, no guided tours, 1330-1700; Bank Holiday Mon (excl. 5 Apr), no guided tours, 1100-1700; Park; 1030-2000, daily, except 5 Apr; Gardens 1100-1800, daily, except 5 Apr. £5.20/£3.30/£4.40. Tel: (01707) 262823.* &

Historic Houses

Knebworth House, Gardens and Park, Knebworth: Home of the Lytton family since 1490, refashioned in the 19C by Bulwer-Lytton. There is a fine collection of manuscripts, portraits and furniture. Jacobean Banquet Hall with Minstrels Gallery. British Raj Exhibition. Formal gardens with Jekyll Herb Garden, large adventure playground with 'Fort Knebworth'. Set in 250 acre country park which is the setting for many special events throughout the summer. Gift shop, licensed cafeteria in restored 400 year old Tithe Barn. *29 Mar-15 Apr, 25 May-3 Sep, Tue-Sun, Bank Hol Mon; 20 Apr-19 May, 7-29 Sep, Sat, Sun, Bank Hol. House 1200-1700; Park/Fort Knebworth 1100-1730. Please telephone for admission prices. Tel: (01438) 812661.*

Knebworth House, Hertfordshire

The Priory, High Street, Ware: The Priory was founded in 1338 as a Franciscan friary. 200 years later under Henry VIII it was dissolved and became a private house. It remained a home until 1st World War when it was used as a convalescent home for wounded soldiers. By this time the owner was Mrs Anne Elizabeth Croft and in 1920 she leased the Priory to Ware Urban District Council. The lease was for 999 years at an annual rent of 3 shillings (15p). It is now home to Ware Town Council. Set on the banks of the River Lea in several acres of gardens and lawns, it is a Scheduled Ancient Monument and Grade I Listed building. *All year, daily, 0900-1700. Telephone for details of Bank Hol opening; closed 25-26 Dec. Tel: (01920) 460316.* &

Rye House Gatehouse, Rye House Quay, Rye Road, Hoddesdon: The Gatehouse is the only surviving part of a memorial house built for Sir Andrew Ogard and is one of the finest examples of early English brickwork in the country. Famous for the conspiracy to assassinate Charles II in 1683 and in Victorian times the estate became a pleasure park attracting people from London by train. *5 Apr-31 Sep, Sat, 1300-1700, Sun, Bank Hols & school summer hols, 1100-1700. 95p/50p/50p. Tel: (01992) 713838.*

Shaw's Corner, (NT) Ayot St Lawrence: Home of George Bernard Shaw from 1906 until his death in 1950. Literary and personal relics in five rooms maintained as in his lifetime. *30 Mar-31 Oct, Wed-Sun and Bank Holiday Mon, 1400-1800 (last admission 1730); Closed 5 Apr, on event days house and gardens closed at 1600. £3.00. Tel: (01438) 820307.*

Norfolk

Blickling Hall, (NT) Blickling: Jacobean red brick mansion. Garden, orangery, parkland and lake. Fine tapestries and furniture. Picnic area, shop and restaurant. Plant centre. *23 Mar-3 Nov, Sun, Tue, Wed, Fri, Sat, Bank Hol Mon, Garden 1000-1700, Hall 1300-1700; Closed 5 Apr; Parkland open all year. £5.50/£2.40. Tel: (01263) 733084.* &

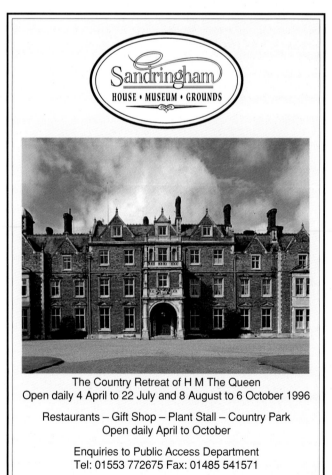

Dragon Hall, 115-123 King Street, Norwich: A magnificent medieval merchants hall, described as, 'The secular equivalent of East Anglia's great medieval churches'. With a wealth of beautiful features including an outstanding crown-post roof, intricately carved and painted dragon and screens passage, the hall is a monument to medieval craftsmanship. Built for the sale and display of cloth, a staple of the local economy for five centuries, Dragon Hall is also a unique legacy of 15th century mercantile trade. *1 Apr-31 Oct, Mon-Sat, 1000-1600; 1 Nov-31 Mar, Mon-Fri, 1000-1600; closed 22 Dec-2 Jan. £1.00/25p/50p. Tel: (01603) 663922.* &

Felbrigg Hall, (NT) Felbrigg: 17C country house with original 18C furniture and pictures. Walled garden, orangery, parkland and lake. Walks, picnic area, shop. *23 Mar-3 Nov, Mon, Wed, Thu, Sat, Sun, 1300 - last visit 1630, Bank Hols, 1100-1700. £5.00/£2.50. Tel: (01263) 837444.* &

Holkham Hall, Wells-next-the-Sea: Classic 18C Palladian style mansion, home of the Earls of Leicester and a living treasure house of artistic and architectural history. One of Britain's most majestic stately homes, situated in a 3,000 acre deer park on the beautiful north Norfolk coast, it is part of a great agricultural estate. Attractions include: Bygones Museum, a collection of over 4,000 items from cars, crafts and kitchens to steam. The History of Farming exhib, with audio visual aids and dioramas. Garden Centre, in a beautiful 18C walled garden. Pottery, Gift Shop, Art Gallery, Tea Rooms and Lake. *26 May-30 Sep, Sun-Thu, 1330-1700; Easter, May, Spring & Summer Bank Hols, Sun & Mon 1130-1700. Last adm. 1640. Hall or Bygones: £3.00/£1.50. Combined ticket £5.00/£2.50. Tel: (01328) 710733.*

Houghton Hall, Houghton, King's Lynn: Built for Sir Robert Walpole, first Prime Minister of England, in early 18C. Much of the original furnishings by William Kent in the State Rooms. Collection of approx. 20,000 model soldier and other militaria. Heavy horses and ponies. Picnic area, cafeteria, gift shop, children's playground. Newly restored walled garden open for the first time in 1996. *7 Apr- 29 Sep, Sun, Thu, Bank Hol Mons, Easter Sun & Mon, 1400-1730, last adm. 1700. £5.50/£3.00. Tel: (01485) 528569.* &

Oxburgh Hall, (NT) Oxborough, King's Lynn: 15C moated red brick fortified manor house. Magnificent 80ft gatehouse. Mary Queen of Scots needlework. Catholic priests' hole. Garden. Woodland walks. Catholic chapel. *30 Mar-3 Nov, Sat-Wed; Hall 1300-1700; Garden, 1200-1730; Bank Holiday Mons; 1100-1700. House & Garden £4.00/£2.00 (95); Garden only £2.00/£1.00 (95). Tel: (01366) 328258.* &

Sandringham, Sandringham: Country retreat of H.M. The Queen. Set in 60 acres of beautiful grounds and lakes, Sandringham is complemented by a museum of Royal vehicles and memorabilia. House and grounds are surrounded by 600 acres of country park with visitor centre and shop. *House, 4 Apr-22 Jul, 8 Aug-6 Oct, 1100-1645; Grounds & Museum, 4 Apr-27 Jul, 7 Aug-6 Oct, Grounds, 1030-1700; Museum, 1100-1700. £4.00/£2.00/£3.00. Tel: (01553) 772675.* &

Suffolk

Bridge Cottage, (NT) Flatford, East Bergholt: 16th century building, tea garden and shop. Constable Exhib. *Mid Mar, Apr, May, Oct, Wed-Sun, 1100-1730; 1 June-30 Sep, daily, 1000-1730; Open Bank Holidays; Closed on Good Friday, Christmas, New Year. Tel: (01206) 298260.* &

Christchurch Mansion, Christchurch Park, Ipswich: Fine Tudor Mansion built between 1548 and 1550, later additions. Good collection of furniture, panelling and ceramics, clocks and paintings from 16-19C. Suffolk Artists' gallery, lively temporary exhibition programme in Wolsey Art Gallery. *All year, Tue-Sat, 1000-1700, Sun, 1430-1630; closes at dusk in winter; Open 7-8 Apr, 27-31 Dec; Closed 24-26 Dec, 5 Apr. £2.50/£1.00/£1.00. Tel: (01473) 253246.* &

Euston Hall, Euston Estate Office, Thetford: Euston Hall was built in the 1660s by the father-in-law of the first Duke of Grafton, Lord Arlington. His fine collection of portraits of Charles II, his family and court, still hangs in the house and includes works by Van Dyck, Lely and Stubbs. The Pleasure Grounds were designed by John Evelyn and the Park and Temple by William Kent. The 17th century church of St Genevieve close to the house has a beautiful panelled interior and contains monuments to members of the FitzRoy family. *6 June-26 Sep, Thurs 1430-1700. 30 June and 1 Sep, 1430-1700. £2.50/50p/£2.00. Tel: (01842) 766366.*

Guildhall, Market Place, Hadleigh: Medieval timber framed complex Grade 1 Listed (with Victorian addition) 14-15th century. Timbered Guildroom and old Town Hall with fine crown post roof, Georgian assembly room, Victorian ballroom. *27 May-Mid Sep, Sun, Thu, 1400-1700. £1.50/free/£1.00. Tel: (01473) 823884.*

Haughley Park, Haughley: Jacobean manor house with lovely gardens and woods set in parkland. *May-Sep, Tue, 1500-1730; Closed Easter, Christmas. £2.00/£1.00. Tel: (01359) 240205.* &

Ickworth House, Park and Gardens, (NT) Ickworth: Ickworth is one of England's most extraordinary houses, a Rotunda begun in 1795, the inspiration of the Earl of Bristol also Bishop of Derry, housing a major collection of pictures, including works by Titian, Gainsborough and Velasquez, fine furniture and Georgian Silver. The house is set in a 'Capability' Brown Park and surrounded by an Italian Garden. Range of waymarked woodland walks, deer enclosure with hide, adventure playground and picnic area. *Closed 5 Apr. House open 23 Mar-3 Nov, Tue, Wed, Fri, Sat, Sun, Bank Hol Mon, 1300-1700; Park, all year, daily, 0700-1900; Gardens, 23 Mar-3 Nov, daily, 1000-1700; 4 Nov-end Mar '97, daily, 1000-1600. £4.75/£2.00. Tel: (01284) 735270.* &

Kentwell Hall, Long Melford: Mellow red brick Tudor Manor surrounded by moat. Family home interestingly restored. Tudor costume display. XVIth century, and earlier. House equipped XVth century style, Mosaic Tudor Rose Maze. Unique Re-Creations of everyday domestic Tudor Life over Bank Holidays, other selected weekends and during 16 Jun-14 Jul when Kentwell Hall re-creates a given year in the Tudor period with up to 250 people in costume taking part each day. *Open Easter-end Oct on certain days including daily mid Jul-mid Sep. Special events on all Bank Holidays; Great Annual Re-Creations 16 Jun-14 Jul. Telephone for programme and prices. Tel: (01787) 310207.*

⊛ **Lavenham Guildhall of Corpus Christi,** (NT) Market Place, Lavenham: See Museums section.

⊛ **Little Hall,** Market Place, Lavenham: 15C hall house. A warm, friendly, furnished house with a beautiful garden in the heart of historic Lavenham, Restored by the Gayer-Anderson twins in the 1930's, Little Hall, a Grade II Listed building with a magnificent Crown Post roof, reveals five centuries of change. Its history mirrors the rise and fall of Lavenham's cloth trade, the years of industrial depression, the influx of evacuees during WWII and the start of the preservation of Suffolk's historic buildings. Links also with Ancient Egypt & Persia. *5 Apr-31 Oct, Wed, Thu, Sat, Sun, Bank Holiday Mon, 1430-1730. £1.00/50p. Tel: (01787) 247179.*

⊛ **Melford Hall,** (NT) Long Melford: Turreted brick Tudor Mansion with 18th century and Regency interiors. Bought by Sir Harry Parker of the famous naval family in 1786. Chinese porcelain; ivories captured from a Manilla galleon. Fine Dutch and naval pictures. Memorabilia of Beatrix Potter, a member of the family who often visited the hall. *Apr, Sat, Sun and Bank Hol Mon, 1400-1730; 1 May-30 Sep, Wed, Thu, Sat, Sun and Bank Hol Mon, 1400-1730; Oct, Sat, Sun, 1400-1730. £4.00/£2.00. Tel: (01787) 880286.* ⅋

⊛ **Otley Hall,** Hall Lane, Otley: Outstanding beautiful 15C moated medieval hall. Rich in architecture and family history, set in ten acres of garden, incl. canal, mount, nuttery, herbacious and rose garden. *7, 8 Apr, 26, 27 May, 25, 26 Aug, 1400-1800. £4.00/£2.50. Tel: (01473) 890264.* ⅋

⊛ **The Priory,** Water Street, Lavenham: Through the ages the home of Benedictine monks, medieval wool merchants and an Elizabethan rector. Timber-framed. Herb garden, with culinary, medical and dyers' herbs. Kitchen garden, orchard and pond. Superb medieval building in the heart of Lavenham, yet backing onto rolling countryside. *5-8 Apr, 4-6 May, 25-27 May, 20 Jul-8 Sep, daily, 1030-1730. £2.50/£1.00/£2.50. Tel: (01787) 247003.*

⊛ **Somerleyton Hall and Gardens,** Somerleyton Hall, Somerleyton: The home of Lord and Lady Somerleyton. Rebuilt in Anglo-Italian style in 1846. Magnificent state rooms, furnishings and paintings. Fine gardens, maze, garden trail and miniature railway. Shop and refreshment room for light luncheons and teas. *7 Apr-29 Sep, Apr, May, Jun, Sep, Thu, Sun, Bank Hol, 1230-1730; Jul, Aug, Tue, Wed, Thu, Sun, Bank Hol, 1230-1730. Closed Christmas. £3.75/£1.75/£3.25 (95). Tel: (01502) 730224.* ⅋

⊛ **Wingfield College,** Wingfield: Founded in 1362 on the 13C site of the Manor House by Sir John de Wingfield. Magnificent medieval great hall. Mixed period interiors with 18C neo-classical facade. Walled gardens and topiary. Homemade teas, celebrated arts and music season based at Wingfield College. Regular exhibitions Adjacent church with tombs of college founder and benefactor the Dukes of Suffolk. *6 Apr-29 Sep, Sat, Sun, Bank Hol Mon, 1400-1800. £2.50/£1.00/£2.30. Tel: (01379) 384888.*

Otley Hall, Suffolk

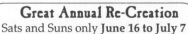

Gardens & Vineyards

Bedfordshire

⦿ **Stockwood Craft Museum and Gardens,** Stockwood Park, Farley Hill, Luton: Museum set in period gardens and Hamilton Finlay sculpture garden. Craft demos at weekends. The Mossman Collection of horse drawn vehicles is housed in a separate museum within the complex. This collection traces the history of transport from Roman times to the 1940's. *Mar-Oct, Tue-Sat, 1000-1700, Sun, Bank Hol Mon, 1000-1800; 1 Nov-31 Mar, Sat, Sun, 1000-1600; Closed 25, 26 Dec, 1 Jan. Tel: (01582) 38714.* &

⦿ **The Swiss Garden,** Biggleswade Rd, Old Warden: A unique, ornamental 18th century example of an English garden affording splendid shrubs, mature trees, intertwining islands and ponds, tiny bridges and buildings. *Jan, Feb, Oct, Sun and New Year's Day, 1100-1600; 1 Mar-30 Sep, Sat, Sun, Bank Hol Mon, 1000-1800; Mon, Wed-Fri, 1330-1800; last admission 45 mins before closure. £2.00/75p/£1.00. Tel: (01234) 228671.* &

⦿ **Wrest Park House and Gardens,** Wrest Park, Silsoe: 150 years of English Gardens, laid out in the early 18C. Includes a Painted Pavilion, Chinese Bridge, lake, classical temple and Louis XV style French Mansion. *1 Apr-29 Sep, Sat, Sun, Bank Hol Mon, 1000-1800. £2.30/£1.20/£1.70 (95). Tel: (01525) 860152.* &

The Swiss Garden, Old Warden, Beds

Cambridgeshire

⦿ **Anglesey Abbey,** (NT) Lode: See entry under Historic Houses.

⦿ **Chilford Hundred Vineyard,** Chilford Hall, Balsham Road, Linton: Winery housed in interesting old buildings. Collection of sculptures on view, vineyard, cafe, shop. *5 Apr-30 Sep, daily, 1100-1730; Tours on the hour 1100-1600. £3.85/free/£3.85. Tel: (01223) 892641.* &

Crossing House, 78 Meldreth Road, Shepreth: Crossing keepers cottage. Small plantsmans garden. Very wide variety of plants. *All year, daily, Dawn-Dusk. Tel: (01763) 261071.*

Docwra's Manor Garden, 2 Meldreth Road, Shepreth: Walled gardens round 18C red brick house and wrought iron gates. Barns, 20th century folly and unusual plants. Plants for sale. *All year, Mon, Wed, Fri, 1000-1600; Apr-Oct, first Sun of month, 1400-1600; Bank Holiday Mon, 1000-1700. £2.00/free/£2.00. Tel: (01763) 261473.* &

⦿ **Elton Hall,** Elton: Historic House and Gardens open to the public. See entry under Historic Houses.

Herb Garden, Nigel House, High Street, Wilburton: Herb garden laid out in collections culinary, aromatic, medical, biblical, Shakespearian, dye bed, astrological etc. *1 May-31 Sep, telephone for opening times. Tel: (01353) 740824.* &

⦿ **Peckover House,** (NT) North Brink, Wisbech: See entry under Historic Houses.

University of Cambridge Botanic Garden, Cory Lodge, Bateman Street, Cambridge: Arboretum, rockgarden, scented garden, winter garden, glass-houses. *Nov-Jan, daily, 1000-1600; Feb-Apr & Oct, daily, 1000-1700; May-Sep, daily, 1000-1800; closed 25, 26 Dec. £2.00/£1.50/£1.50. Tel: (01223) 336265.* &

Essex

⦿ **BBC Essex Garden,** Ongar Road, Abridge: Garden; Decorative with shrub beds, seedsowing, flower border, vegetable plot, two greenhouses, summer house and dahlia area. Weekends are worked in summer by Jack Kinns (vegetable and dahlias) with Sheila Love working remainder. Organic garden and junior trial plot. Tea shop and adjoining retail nursery. Meet Ken Crowther gardening presenter. *All year, daily, 0930-1730; closed 25-29 Dec. Tel: (01708) 688581.* &

Bridge End Gardens, Bridge End, Saffron Walden: A Victorian garden of great interest, featuring garden ornaments, rose garden, Dutch garden and pavilions. Hedge maze - only open by appointment through TIC. Some fine trees. *All year, daily, any time. Tel: (01799) 510445.* &

Felsted Vineyard, The Vineyards, Crix Green, Felsted: Wine and cyder making, vineyard work. Wine and vines may be bought and other local produce. *5 Apr-31 Sep, Tue-Sat, Bank Hol Mon, 1000-1800, Sun, 1200-1700; 1 Oct-Easter '97, Sat, 1000-1600, Sun, 1200-1700. Tel: (01245) 361504.*

The Gardens of Easton Lodge, Warwick House, Easton Lodge, Great Dunmow: Gardens created since 1971 on foundations of kitchen and stable block at Easton Lodge (home of 'Darling Daisy' countess of Warwick) features include cobbled and herringbone courtyard with fountain (Harold Peto), fishpond, mosaic walk, dovecote, pergolas. There are a further 20+ acres of Harold Peto's gardens designed in 1903 and abandoned in 1950. Features include balustraded pool in sunken garden, tree house and Japanese garden. Restoration has commenced with an exhibition of history in the dovecote. *Feb, Sat, Sun, 1200-1600; Easter-27 Oct, Sat & Sun, Bank Hol Mon, 1400-1800 or dusk. £2.00/free/£2.00. Tel: (01371) 876979.* &

⊕ **Hylands House, Park and Gardens,** Hylands Park, Writtle: See entry under Historic Houses.

⊕ **Ingatestone Hall,** Ingatestone: See entry under Historic Houses.

Mark Hall Gardens, off First Avenue, Muskham Road, Harlow: Three walled gardens, one landscaped as unusual fruit garden. Formal garden including herbs & parterre. Large garden demonstrating a number of styles. *Open all year, Mon-Fri, 1000-1700; Apr-Sep, Sun, 1100-1900; Oct-Mar, Sun, 1100-1600; Closed on public holidays. £2.50/£2.00/£2.00. Tel: (01279) 439680.* &

New Hall Vineyards, Chelmsford Road, Purleigh: Guided tours, May-Sep. Vineyards and cellars where wine can be tasted. Vineyard trail through vines. Press house, slide shows, fermentation, bottling and wine tasting. *All year, Mon-Fri, 1000-1700, Sat, Sun, 1000-1330. Tel: (01621) 828343.* &

⊕ **R H S Garden - Hyde Hall,** Rettendon, Chelmsford: All year round garden of 8 acres set in a hill with fine views. Woodland garden, spring bulbs, extensive rose garden ornamental ponds with lillies and fish, flowering shrubs and trees, herbaceous borders, glasshouses and national collections of malus and viburnum. *24 Mar-27 Oct, Wed-Sun, Bank Holidays, 1100-1800, gates close 1700, 1 hour earlier Sep-Oct. £2.70/70p/£2.70. Tel: (01245) 400256.* &

Saling Hall Garden, Great Saling: 17th century house not open. 12 acre garden with old walls, fish pond, water garden, and well-known landscaper arboretum including many rare trees. *1 May-31 July, Wed, 1400-1700; 30 Jun, 1400-1700. £2.00/free/£2.00. Tel: (01371) 850243.* &

Hatfield House, Hertfordshire

Hertfordshire

⊕ **The Gardens of the Rose,** The Royal National Rose Society, Chiswell Green, St Albans: The Royal National Rose Society's Garden, 20 acres of showground and trial grounds for new varieties of rose. 30,000 roses of all types with 1,700 different varieties. *8 Jun-13 Oct, Mon-Sat, 0900-1700, Sun and Aug Bank Holidays, 1000-1800. £4.00/free/£3.50. Tel. (01727) 850461.* &

⊕ **Hatfield House,** Hatfield: See entry under Historic Houses.

⊕ **Knebworth House, Gardens and Park,** Knebworth: See entry under Historic Houses.

Norfolk

Alby Gardens, Cromer Road, Erpingham: Beautiful relaxing plantsmans garden of 4 acres. Island beds, ponds, wild area. An interesting collection of unusual bulbs, plants and shrubs. *1 Apr-30 Sep,Tue-Sun and Easter Sat 6 Apr, 1000-1700. £1.00/free/£1.00. Tel: (01263) 761226.* &

R H S Garden, Hyde Hall, Essex

⊕ **Blickling Hall,** Blickling: See entry under Historic Houses.

⊕ **Bressingham Steam Museum and Gardens,** Bressingham: A working steam museum in a nationally known garden setting. Narrow gauge railway rides, Victorian steam roundabout. Fire Museum, Locomotive Sheds, Stationary Engine Display, Royal Coach, Traction Engines, Gardens, 2 acre Plant Centre and display area. Services vary according to steaming programme. *Opening times to be confirmed but likely to be open Apr-Sep, daily, 1000-1700; reduced operation during Oct. Please phone Steam Information line in advance to confirm times - (01379) 687382. Closed Nov-Mar to general visitors, access is available during this time for groups if pre-booked. £3.90/£2.85/£3.15 (95).* &

⊕ **Congham Hall Herb Garden,** Lynn Road, Grimston: Over 250 herbs in formal beds with wild flowers and potager garden. Over 150 herbs for sale in pots. *1 Apr-30 Sep, Sun-Fri, 1400-1600. Tel: (01485) 600250.*

Elmham Vineyard and Winery, Elmham House Cottage, North Elmham: Vineyard, winery tours, slide show. Wine tasting, wines for sale. *All year, tours daily, 1000, 1200, 1400, 1600. £2.50/free. Tel: (01362) 668167.* &

⊕ **Fairhaven Garden Trust,** School Road, South Walsham: These delightful woodland and water gardens with private Inner Broad have something of interest for everyone who loves natural beauty. At all seasons there is sense of peace and tranquility, and the combination of cultivated and wild flowers makes this garden quite unique. In Spring there are masses of Primroses and Bluebells, and Azaleas and Rhododendrons in several areas. Candelabra Primulas and some unusual plants grow near the waterways, which are spanned by small bridges. In summer the wild flowers come into their own. Also, a separate bird sanctuary for bird watchers. *5 Apr-1 Oct, Tues-Sun, Bank Hol Mon, 1100-1730, Sat, 1400-1730. £3.00/£1.00/£2.00. Tel: (01603) 270449.* &

Gardens & Vineyards

Norfolk Lavender Ltd

◉ **Felbrigg Hall, Felbrigg:** See entry under Historic Houses.

◉ **Fritton Lake Countryworld,** Fritton, Gt Yarmouth: 250 acres of woodland and water which features boating, fishing, 9 hole golf, putting, childrens adventure playground, wildfowl collection, mature gardens, cafe with home baking, gift shop. Main attractions are the large undercover falconry centre with flying displays twice daily (not Friday) whatever the weather. The stables with Shires and Suffolks are open daily with cart rides. *1 Apr-29 Sep, daily, 1000-1730, last admission 1615. £3.50/£2.50/ £3.20 (95). Tel: (01493) 488288/488208.*

Harling Vineyards, Eastfield House, Church Road, East Harling: Guided tour of part of 7-acre vineyards. Indoor or outdoor tasting of up to 8 wines. Wine and gift shop, toilets, picnic area, large car park. Gardens of Victorian mansion beside C15th Church. Grounds extend to river. *All year, daily, 1030-1800; tours and tastings, 5 Apr-mid October, closed 25 Dec. £2.50/free/£2.50. Tel: (01953) 717341.*

◉ **Hoveton Hall Gardens,** Hoveton Hall, Wroxham: Approx 10 acres gardens featuring principally daffodils, azaleas, rhododendrons and hydrangeas in a woodland setting. Large walled herbaceous garden. Victorian kitchen garden. Woodland and lakeside walks.*7 Apr-15 Sep, Sun, Wed, Fri, Bank Hol Mon, 1100-1730. £2.50/£1.00. Tel: (01603) 782798.* ᚬ

◉ **Mannington Gardens and Countryside,** Mannington Hall, Norwich: Gardens with lake, moat and woodland. Outstanding rose collection. Heritage rose exhibition. Saxon church and Victorian follies. Country walks and trails. Coffee, lunches home-made teas and snacks. Manor house by prior arangement for specialist groups. *Walks all year, daily, 0900-1700 (or dusk); Gardens, 7 Apr-27 Oct, Sun, 1200-1700; Jun-Aug, Wed-Fri, 1100-1700; £3.00/free/£2.50. Tel: (01263) 584175.*

Natural Surroundings, Bayfiled Estate, Bayfield, Holt: A wild flower centre set in 8 acres of the Glaven Valley. Demonstration gardens, nature trail, bird hide, information room and a well stocked shop and sales area, ideal for the wildlife and organic gardener. Learn how to create your own wildlife garden area or just enjoy the hundreds of wild flowers. *1 Jan-31 Mar, Thu-Sun, 1000-1600; 1 Apr-30 Sep, Tue-Sun, 1000-1730; 1 Oct 20 Dec, Thu-Sun, 1000-1600. £1.50/50p/£1.00. Tel: (01263) 711091.*

◉ **Norfolk Lavender Ltd,** Caley Mill, Heacham: Caley Mill is the home of the National Collection of Lavenders. See many varieties of lavender and a large miscellany of herbs. Hear about the harvest and the ancient process of lavender distillation. The Countryside Gift Shop stocks the full range of Norfolk Lavender products, together with a wide choice of other gifts to suit all pockets. The Herb Shop has many varieties of lavender and herb plants, plus unusual gifts for gardeners. The Cottage Tea Room specialises in cream teas, home made cakes and light lunches. *All year, daily, 1000-1700; closed 23 Dec '96-13 Jan '97. Tel: (01485) 570384.* ᚬ

Raveningham Gardens, Raveningham: Extensive gardens surrounding an elegant Georgian house provide the setting for many rare, variegated and unusual plants and shrubs. Large nurseries, sculptures, parkland and church. *Mid Mar-Mid Sep, Wed, 1300-1600; Sun, Bank Hol Mon, 1400-1700. £2.00/£0.00/£2.00. Tel: (01508) 548222.* ᚬ

The Fairhaven Garden Trust, South Walsham, Norfolk

The Tropical Butterfly Gardens, Long Street Nursery, Great Ellingham: The central attraction is the tropical butterfly gardens, with 2,400 sq feet of landscaped gardens, heated to a year round temperature of 75⁰F. The gardens contain hundreds of tropical trees and flowers, and several hundred exotic tropical butterflies and birds flying freely around the visitors. Other attractions include a garden centre stocked with over 2000 different plant varieties, a gift shop and the Bamboo Coffee Shop, serving lunches, teas and light meals all day. *25 Mar-2 Nov, Mon-Sat, 0900-1800, Sun, 1000-1800. CLosed 25, 26 Dec. £2.45/£1.45/£2.15. Tel: (01953) 453175.* ᕫ

Willow Farm Flowers Dried Flower Centre, Cangate, Neatished: Growers and suppliers of quality dried flowers and arrangements. Dried flower arranging workshop open all year, for advice and help. Walk around show field in summer. *All year, Tue-Sat, 1000-1600, Sun, 1100-1600, also Mon, Jul, Aug, 1000-1600 and all Bank Hol Mon; closed 23 Dec-mid Jan. Tel:(01603) 783588.*

Suffolk

Akenfield, 1 Park Lane, Charsfield: 0.5 acre council house garden full of flowers and vegetables. Homemade wine on view. As seen on BBC Gardeners World. New fish pool. *5 Apr-30 Sep, daily, 1030-1900. £1.00/free/75p. Tel: (01473) 737402.*

Blakenham Woodland Garden, Little Blakenham, Ipswich: 5 acre woodland garden with many rare trees and shrubs. Especially lovely in the spring with blue-bells, camellias, magnolias and cornus followed by roses in the early summer. Free parking. No dogs please. *1 Mar-30 Jun, Sun-Fri, 1300-1700; 5-8 Apr, 1300-1700. £1.00/£1.00/£1.00. Tel: (01473) 831214.*

Boyton Vineyard, Hill Farm, Boyton End, Stoke by Clare: Vineyard with vines growing. Gardens of listed period farmhouse. Tours of vineyard followed by talk and wine tasting. *1 Apr-31 Oct, daily, 1030-1800. Tel: (01440) 61893.*

Bruisyard Vineyard and Herb Centre, Church Road, Bruisyard: 10 acre vineyard, picturesque winery, herb and water gardens wooded picnic area and childrens' play area. English wine, herbs, crafts, souvenirs, etc for sale. Producers of the award winning Bruisyard St Peter English wine and herbs. Picturesque and tranquil establishment with restaurant in beautiful countryside, well worth a visit. *16 Jan-24 Dec, daily, 1030-1500. £3.00/£1.50/£2.50. Tel: (01728) 638281.* ᕫ

East Bergholt Place Garden, East Bergholt Place, East Bergholt: East Bergholt Place Garden covers 15 acres and was laid out at the turn of the century by Charles Eley, the great grandfather of the present owner. A fine collection of trees and shrubs, many of which are rarely seen in East Anglia and originate from the great plant hunters such as George Forest. The garden is particularly beautiful in spring when the many mature rhododendrons, magnolias and camellias are in full flower. Also, Topiary hedges, ornamental ponds and a camellia walk. Large range of plants can be bought from within the walled garden. *1 Mar-30 Sep, Tues-Sun, Bank Hol Mon, 1000-1700. £1.50/free/£1.00. Tel: (01206) 298385.*

Akenfield, Charsfield, Suffolk

Giffords Hall, Hartest: 33 acre small country living. Vines, winery, rare breed sheep, pigs, free range chickens, rose garden, wild flower meadows, organic vegetable garden, cut flowers incl. sweet peas and small apiary. *5 Apr-31 Oct, daily, 1000-1800. £2.75/free/£2.25. Tel: (01284) 830464.*

Helmingham Hall Gardens, Estate Office, Helmingham: Moated and walled garden with many rare roses and possibly best kitchen garden in Britain. Highland cattle and safari rides in park to view Red/Fallow deer. *28 Apr-8 Sep, Sun, 1400-1800. £3.00/£1.50/£2.60. Tel: (01473) 890363.* ᕫ

Ickworth House, Park and Gardens, Ickworth: See entry under Historic Houses.

James White Cider & Apple Juice Co, White's Fruit Farm, Helmingham Road, Ashbocking: Cidermaking and apple juice production and bottling on view. Downie Produce Farm Shop selling Apple Juice and Ciders produced on site. Free tastings. Downie Produce also sells fruit and vegetables and Pick Your Own soft fruit. *All year, daily, 1000-1700. Closed 25, 26 Dec. Tel: (01473) 890202.* ᕫ

Helmingham Hall Gardens, Suffolk

Letheringham Watermill Gardens, Letheringham Mill, Woodbridge: Watermill (with newly restored wheel) in nearly 5 acres of gardens, river walk and watermeadows. Home made teas. Plants for sale. Well stocked aviary of exotic pheasants. Gallery and aviary. *3 Mar-27 May, 7 Jul-5 Sep, Sun, Bank Hol Mon, 1400-1730; 7, 8 Apr 1400-1800. £1.50/free/£1.00. Tel: (01728) 746349.* ᕫ

Otley Hall, Hall Lane, Otley: See entry under Historic Houses.

Paradise Centre, Twinstead Road, Lamarsh: Feature enclosed paddock where visitors can hold and photograph pets such as Pygmy goats. Gardens on slope with lovely view over Stour Valley. *2 Apr-1 Nov, Sat, Sun, Bank Hol Mon, 1000-1700. £1.50/£1.00/£1.00. Tel: (01787) 269449.*

The Priory, Water Street, Lavenham: Through the ages the home of Benedictine monks, medieval wool merchants, an Elizabethan rector. Timber-framed. Herb garden, with culinary, medical and dyers herbs. Kitchen garden, orchard and pond, superb medieval building in the heart of Lavenham, yet backing onto rolling countryside. *5-8 Apr, 4-6 May, 25-27 May, 20 Jul-8 Sep, daily, 1030-1730. £2.50/£1.00/£2.50. Tel: (01787) 247003.*

Shawsgate Vineyard, Badingham Road, Framlingham: 17 acre vineyard with modern winery making award winning English wines. Guided tours, vineyard walk, wine tastings, picnic area, children's play area. Shop open all year for wine sales. *31 Mar-30 Nov, daily, 1030-1700. £2.75/free/£2.25. Tel: (01728) 724060.*

Somerleyton Hall and Gardens, Somerleyton Hall, Somerleyton: See entry under Historic Houses.

Wissett Vineyards, Valley Farm, Wissett: A10 acre (4 hectare) vineyard set in tranquil suffolk countryside with 16th century farmhouse and barns surrounded by exquisite gardens, a wine shop, picnic area and nature walks *All year, daily, 1000-1800. Tel: (01986) 785216.*

Wyken Hall Gardens and Wyken Vineyards, Stanton, Bury St Edmunds: Seven acres of vines and four acres of garden. An Elizabethan Manor House and 16th century barn. Spectacular woodland walk through ancient woodland. Well known cafe for which you should book, countrystore selling wine, quilts, garden tools, baskets, local pottery and other countryware. *7 Feb-24 Dec, Thu, Fri, Sun, Bank Hol Mon, 1000-1800. £2.00/free/50p. Tel: (01359) 250240.*

Nurseries & Garden Centres

Bressingham Plant Centre

Bressingham, nr Diss, Norfolk
(3 miles west of Diss on A1066).

Unique 2 acre Plant Centre adjacent to Bressingham's world famous Display Gardens. A 'Mecca' for plant lovers with a superb range of over 5,000 varieties. Included in the 2,000 varieties of perennials are many of the 200 plants introduced by nursery founder Alan Bloom VMH during 70 years of gardening. Inspiring plant displays and plantings, plus our Pavilion Tea Room for light refreshments. Above all, you'll find the choice, quality, service and value which have made Bressingham a byword for excellence since 1946.

Open daily including Sun, 1000-1730,
except Christmas Day and Boxing Day.
Tel: Bressingham (01379) 687464/688133.

Norfolk Lavender Ltd.

Caley Mill, Heacham, Norfolk
(on A149)

Caley Mill is the home of the National Collection of Lavenders. See many varieties of lavender and a large miscellany of herbs. Hear about the harvest, and the ancient process of lavender distillation. The Countryside Gift Shop stocks the full range of Norfolk Lavender's famous products, together with a wide choice of other gifts to suit all pockets. The Conservatory Shop has many varieties of lavender and herb plants, selections of cottage garden fragrant plants and unusual gifts for gardeners. The Cottage Tea Room specialises in cream teas, home made cakes and light lunches. Admission to car park and grounds free.

Open daily 1000-1700 (closed for Christmas holiday).
Tea Room opening – Please see Afternoon Teas
Section.
Tel: (01485) 570384

Wootten's of Wenhaston

Wootten's Plants, Blackheath, Wenhaston,
Suffolk IP19 9HD.
1.5 miles off the A12 south of Blythburgh.

A beautifully laid out nursery with superbly grown herbaceous plants, many of them rare. An extraordinary range of plants thumping with health. Masses of salvias, a huge collection of Barnhaven primulas, at least 10 different sorts of foxgloves and more than 40 irises. More than 80 kinds of old fashioned scented leaved pelargoniums. "To get there, I spent seven hours in the car driving through a monumental Cloud burst. It was worth it" Anna Pavord, The Independent.

Open daily 0930-1700.
Tel: (01502) 478258.

Taverham Garden Centre

Fir Covert Road, Taverham, Norwich
(Situated 7 miles from Norwich on the A1067
Norwich/Fakenham road).

Taverham Garden Centre is set in 15 acres of beautiful countryside in the pretty Wensum Valley to the west of the city of Norwich. The Garden Centre offers a riot of colour all year round, with acres of greenhouses packed with beautiful flowers and pot plants, all grown to the highest standards in the on-site propagating unit. For gardeners, there is an unrivalled choice of plants, shrubs and trees and an extensive range of bulbs and seeds, as well as attractive garden furniture and ornaments, terra-cotta pots and planters, paving slabs, pools and conservatories. Plus dried and silk flowers, books petfood, coffee bar, craft complex. Disabled facilities, coach parties welcome. Parking for 1000 cars.

Open Mon-Sat, 0900-1730. Sun, 1000-1730.
Tel: (01603) 860522

Notcutts Garden Centres

Ipswich Road, Woodbridge, Suffolk
Also at Station Road, Ardleigh, Essex
Daniels Road (Ring Road), Norwich
Oundle Road, Orton Waterville, Peterborough

Notcutts Garden Centres are wonderlands for gardeners. Over 2000 varieties of hardy plants always in stock, all guaranteed of course. You don't need to be a specialist because there's plenty of help and informed advice always on hand. So why not spend some time wandering at leisure. There's so much to see - display borders, pools, furniture, stoneware, books, gift ideas and pot plants, plus lots of tips on how to improve your garden. Whatever your interests, there will be plenty for you at Notcutts.

Woodbridge Tel: (01394) 383600.
Ardleigh Tel: (01206) 230271.
Norwich Tel: (01603) 453155.
Peterborough Tel: (01733) 234600.

Laurel Farm Herbs

Main A12 at Kelsale between Saxmundham and
Yoxford.

Grow your own souvenir of East Anglia at Laurel Farm Herbs where you'll find a wide selection of top quality potted herb plants. They are attractive, fragrant, tasty, easy to grow and the ideal way to remember your holiday in East Anglia - every time you take a cutting. Meet local herb specialist Chris Seagon who will be glad to take you round the 160 herb varieties in his gardens.

Open every day (except Tue) from 1000-1700
so come along and say hello.
Tel (01728) 668223.

Norfolk Herbs

Blackberry Farm, Dillington,
Nr Gressenhall, Dereham
*(approx 1 mile north of Dereham on the B1110, turn
left on bend at end of golf course and we are approx.
1.5 miles on right).*

Norfolk's specialist Herb Farm, situated on a
new, larger site in a beautiful wooded valley
renowned for its wildlife. Visitors may browse
through a vast array of aromatic, culinary and
medicinal herb plants and learn all about
growing and using herbs.

*Open Apr-Jul, daily, Aug, Tue-Sun, 0900-1800;
Sep-Mar, Wed-Sat, 0900-1700.
Tel: (01362) 860812.*

Bruisyard Vineyard and Herb Centre

Church Road, Bruisyard,
Saxmundham,
Suffolk IP17 2EF

One of the largest ornamental herb gardens in
East Anglia. We have a wide variety of culinary,
medicinal and pot-pourri herbs for sale as well
as a good range of vines. We also offer vineyard
and winery tours, a secluded picnic area,
children's play area, restaurant, a shop selling
herb seeds, wines, herbal teas, local produce
and crafts. Admission to the car park and
gardens is free.

*Open daily from 15 Jan-24 Dec, 1030-1700.
Tel: Badingham (01728) 638281.*

The African Violet Centre

Terrington St Clement,
King's Lynn, Norfolk
Beside the A17, 5 miles from King's Lynn.

Wide variety of gold medal winning African
Violets on show. Cultural advice given. Good
selection of African Violets and other seasonal
plants for sale. Attractive nursery shop and
tearoom for light refreshments. Ample parking,
coach parties welcomed. Talk and demonstration
to parties, by appointment.

*Open daily 1000-1700. Closed Christmas/New Year.
Tel: (01553) 828374.*

Fisk's Clematis Nursery

Westleton, nr Saxmundham, Suffolk IP17 3AJ
*(midway between Aldeburgh and Southwold
on the B1125)*

Call and see many varieties of clematis in
flower, on walls, pergola and in greenhouses, or
send 75p for our colour catalogue.

*Open Mon-Fri,0900-1700 Sat and Sun in summer
1000-1300, 1400-1700.
Tel: Westleton (01728) 648263.*

Frinton Road Nurseries Ltd

Kirby Cross, Frinton-on-Sea, Essex.

On your way to the peaceful resort of Frinton-
on-Sea call and inspect our wide range of top
quality plants, shrubs and trees. Many of these
are grown in our own nurseries, which you are
invited to wander around at leisure. Our attractive shop and pot plant house stocks a wide
range of sundries, tools and furniture and offers
service from friendly and helpful staff. 'The
Applegarth' coffee shop is also open.

*Open Mon-Sat, 0830-1730.
Tel: (01255) 674838.*

Thorncroft Clematis

*On the B1135 exactly halfway between Wymondham
and East Dereham, Norfolk.*

A small family run nursery specialising in
growing clematis, they have a large sales area
displaying around 200 varieties, as well as a
display garden showing different ways to grow
them. There is always someone available to give
advice on selecting and planting.

*Open from 1 Mar-31 Oct from 1000-1630 daily
except Wed when it is closed all day.
Tel: (01953) 850407.*

Bedfordshire

◎ **Bromham Mill,** Stagsden Road (Bridge End), Bromham: Watermill and art gallery alongside River Great Ouse. Milling demos and guided tours to suit any age. Crafts outlet with changing art gallery exhibits. *1 Mar-31 Oct, Wed-Fri, 1030-1630; Sat, Sun and Bank Hol Mon, 1130-1800; last admission 45 mins before closure. 70p/35p/35p. Tel: (01234) 824330.* &

◎ **Stevington Windmill,** Stevington:Fully restored 18thC postmill. Entry via keys from the Royal George Public House in Silver Street for a small returnable deposit. *All year, daily, 1000-1900. Tel: (01234) 228671.*

Cambridgeshire

Bourn Windmill, Caxton Rd, Bourn: Pre-Civil War post mill which may be the oldest of its type in England. Restored in 1980s for which a Civic Trust Commendation and a Europa Nostra Diploma were received. *7 Apr, 12, 26 May, 23 Jun, 28 July, 25 Aug, 29 Sep, 1400-1700. £1.00/25p/£1.00.*

Downfield Windmill, Fordham Road, Soham: Working windmill, dating back to 1726. Flour for sale to visitors and local shops. *All year, Sun, Bank Hol Mon, 1100-1700; closed 25 Dec-2 Jan. 70p/35p. Tel: (01353) 720333.*

Hinxton Watermill, Mill Lane, Hinxton: 17th century watermill restored to working order. Working machinery that grinds flour. *12 May, 9 Jun, 7 Jul, 4 Aug, 8 Sep, 1430-1730. £1.00/25p/£1.00.*

◎ **Houghton Mill,** (NT) Houghton: Large timber built water mill on island in River Ouse. Much of the 19c mill machinery intact, and some restored to working order. *31 Mar-23 Jun, Sat, Sun, Bank Hol Mon, 1400-1730; 24 Jun-6 Sep, Sat-Wed, Bank Hol Mon, 1400-1730; 7 Sep-31 Oct, Sat, Sun, 1400-1730. Sat, Mon-Wed, £1.80/90p; Milling days, Sun, Bank Hol Mon, £2.20/£1.00. Tel: (01480) 301494.*

◎ **Sacrewell Farm and Country Centre,** Sacrewell, Thornhaugh: Childrens play area with maze, trampolines etc. 500 acre farm, with working watermill, farmhouse gardens, shrubberies farm, nature and general interest trails, 18C buildings, displays of farm, rural and domestic bygones. *All year, daily, 0930-1800 summer, 0930-dusk winter; closed 25 Dec. £3.00/£1.00/£2.00. Tel: (01780) 782222.* &

◎ **Wicken Fen Nature Reserve,** (NT) Lode Lane, Wicken: Last remaining undrained portion of great Fen levels of East Anglia. Rich in plant, bird and invertebrate life. Working windpump. Fen cottage restored as it might have been in the 1930's. ¾ board walk gives easy access to heart of the Fen. *All year, daily, except 25 Dec. £2.50/£1.25/£2.50. Tel: (01353) 720274.*

The Windmill, Swaffham Prior, Cambridge: Tarred brick and clunch four storied tower mill built c1855 and worked commercially until 1946. Restored by present owner and producing traditional stoneground wholemeal flour with french burr stones powered by four double-shuttered patent sails. *By appointment only. Tel: (01638) 741009.*

Essex

◎ **Aythorpe Roding Post Mill,** Aythorpe Roding: The largest remaining post mill in Essex, occupying an ancient mill site, in use before 1615. Present mill built about 1779 worked until 1936. Restored to working order by Essex County Council, ground corn in 1982. There is evidence that the mill was comprehensively modernised late in the nineteenth century. *Last Sun of each month Apr-Sep and 2nd Sun of May (National Mills Day), 1400-1700. £1.50/£1.00/£1.50.*

Bocking Windmill, 272 Church Street, Bocking: Listed ancient monument, post mill. Outside viewing all year. Inside viewing: *11 open afternoons, 7 Apr-30 Sep, 1400-1700 but phone for exact dates. Tel: (01376) 552458.*

◎ **Bourne Mill,** (NT) Bourne Road, Colchester: 16thC fishing lodge converted into a mill. Machinery in working order. *All Bank Hol Sun, Mon, Jul, Aug, Sun, Tue, 1400-1730; £1.30/65p/£1.30. Tel: (01206) 572422.*

John Webb's Windmill, Thaxted: Four floors of mill can be explored. Main machinery is intact and on view. Rural museum on two lower floors. Two pairs of sails are now clothed enabling them to turn when wind is favourable and if a volunteer is available. *1 May-30 Sep, Sat, Sun, 1400-1800. 50p/25p. Tel: (01371) 8303285.*

◎ **Mountnessing Windmill,** Roman Road, Mountnessing: Early 19th century post mill restored to working order. *12 May - National Mills Day then 3rd Sun of each month May-Oct, 1400-1700.*

Rayleigh Windmill & Museum, rear of Mill Hall, Bellingham Lane, Rayleigh: Windmill with sails. No mechanism on ground floor. Museum of local artifacts. *UPPER FLOORS NOT OPEN. 6 Apr-28 Sep, Sat, 1030-1300. 20p/10p/10p.*

Stansted Mountfitchet Windmill, Millfields, Stansted: Best preserved tower mill in Essex, built 1787. Most of original machinery remains including rare boulter and curveed ladder to fit cap. *Apr-Oct, first Sun in month, every Sun in Aug, 11400-180050p/25p50p. Tel: (01279) 813160.*

◎ **Stock Tower Mill,** Mill Lane, Stock: Nineteenth century tower mill on an older site which contained 3 windmills in that century. The mill has recently been restored to a high standard and is an excellent example of nineteenth century tower mill construction and millwrighting. Mill was comprehensively 'modernised' late in 19C. *14 Apr, 12 May, 9 Jun, 14 Jul, 11 Aug, 8 Sep, 13 Oct, 1400-1700. Tel: (01621)828162 / (01245) 437663.*

◎ **Thorrington Tide Mill,** Brightlingsea Road, Thorrington: Early 19thC mill, built on an ancient site, fully restord by Essex County Council. The water wheel & associated machinery are in full working order. *For opening times please telephone (01245) 437663 or (01621) 828162.*

Hertfordshire

◎ **Kingsbury Watermill,** St Michael's Street, St Albans: 16C watermill with working machinery, collection of farm implements, art gallery and gift shop. Also Waffle House tearoom/restaurant. *All year, Tue-Sat, 1100-1800, Sun, Bank Hol Mon 1200-1800. Closed 25 Dec-2 Jan. £1.20/60p/80p. Tel: (01727) 853502.*

Norfolk

◎ **Berney Arms and Mill,** (EH) Gt Yarmouth: Highest remaining Norfolk marsh mill in working order, 7 floors. Built late 19th century by millwrights Stolworthy. Situated on Halvergate Marsh. Access by boat (river trips from Gt Yarmouth) or train, difficult walk across marshes. Site exhib. *1 Apr-30 Sep, daily, 0900-1700. £1.00/50p/80p. Tel: (01493) 700605.*

Billingford Windmill, Billingford: Restored cornmill - all internal machinery intact, in addition to wind driven machinery. *Key available all year from Horseshoes Public House, daily during opening hours, 1100-1500, 1900-2100. 70p/30p. Tel: (01379) 740414.* &

◎ **Bircham Mill,** Great Bircham: Norfolk cornmill with working machinery. Small working bakery museum. Tea rooms, ponies, cycle hire *31 Mar-30 Sep, 1000-1800. Bakery closed Sat. £2.20/£1.20/£2.00. Tel: (01485) 578393.* &

◎ **Boardman's Mill,** How Hill Trust, Ludham: Windpump is a unique open framed trestle windpump with turbine. No exhibits. *On view: All year, daily, 24 hours.*

◎ **Clayrack Windpump,** How Hill, Ludham. Remains of Ranworth Hollow Post, taken to How Hill and rebuilt. *On view: All year, daily, 24 hrs.*

Cley Mill, Cley next the Sea: Tower mill used as a flour mill until 1918, converted to guest house in 1983. Built early 1800's. Outstanding example of preserved mill with sails. *27 May-30 Sep, daily, 1400-1700. £1.50/75p/75p. Tel: (01263) 740209.*

Horsey Windmill, Norfolk

Mills

🌀 **Dereham Windmill,** Cherry Lane, Norwich Road, Dereham: Brick tower mill built in 1836. Restored 1984-87. Now complete with a cap, fantail and sails. Some machinery intact. Permanent exhibition on windmills. Opening times available from Breckland District Council. *Tel: (01362) 695333 during normal working hours.*

🌀 **Gunton Park Sawmill,** Gunton Park, Hanworth: Grade II water powered. Timber framed and weatherboarded. Saw frame inside fully restored. Thatch roof, unique in Britain. *For opening times/prices Tel: (01603) 222705.*

Stanton Post Mill, Suffolk

🌀 **Horsey Windmill,** (NT) Nr B1159, Horsey: This windmill is four storeys high and the gallery affords splendid views across the marshes. *30 Mar-3 Nov, daily, 1100-1700. Closed 5 Apr. £1.00/50p/£1.00.*

Letheringsett Watermill, Riverside Road, Letheringsett: Working mill (1802) restored to working order. Mills approx 2 tons of flour per week. Doomsday site. On working days fully demonstrated displays of mill working with staff on hand to help and explain workings of mill. Tues-Sat 0900-1300/1400-1700. *Demos Tues, Wed, Thu, Fri, 1400-1630. Bank Hols 1400-1700. Closed at Christmas. £1.50/£1.00. Tel: (01263) 713153.*

Little Cressingham Mill, Fairstead Lane, Little Cressingham: Combined wind and water mill in process of restoration. Pumphouse with water powered cylinder pump built by Joseph Bramah. Hydraulic rams. Picnic area. *12 May, 9 Jun, 14 Jul, 11 Aug, 8 Sep, 13 Oct, Sun 1400-1700. 70p/30p.*

Saint Olaves Windpump, St Olaves: Tiny timber trestle windpump in working order. Parking, with permission, Bell Inn, or lay-by over bridge. *All year, daily; key held by Mr Miller at Bridge Stores, St Olaves.*

Sculthorpe Mill, Lynn Road, Sculthorpe: Grade II Listed watermill, set within six acres of watermeadow. Plans to set up a nature trail (working with Wensum Valley Conservation Trust). Unbridged ford. Riverside walk. *All year, daily, Mon-Sat, 1100-2300, Sun 1200-2230; please phone for Christmas opening arrangements. Tel: (01328) 856161.* ♿

Starston Windpump, Starston: Restored windpump. *All year, daily. Tel: (01379) 852393.*

Stracey Arms Drainage Mill, Stracey Arms, Acle: Exhibition of photos and history of drainage mills in Broadland. Restored drainage mill. Access by 2 ladders to cap showing brakewheel and gears. Also shop selling souvenirs and snacks. *1 Apr-30 Sep, daily, 0900-2000.* ♿

Thurne Dyke Windpump, Thurne: Fully restored windpump. Exhibition of windpumps in Broadland. Tower very distinctive-painted white. *May-Jul, Sun, Bank Hol Mon; Aug, Sat, Sun, Bank Hol Mon; Sep, Oct, Sun; all times 1400-1700. Tel: (01692) 670764.*

Suffolk

🌀 **Alton Watermill** - Museum of East Anglian Life, Stowmarket: Dating from 1780 this water-powered cornmill has been meticulously dismantled and re-erected on the Museum site, and can be seen milling flour several times throughout the season. *Open to visitors every Museum working day.*

🌀 **Buttrums Mill,** Burkitt Road, Woodbridge: Six storey brick tower dating from 1836. Fully restored with 4 shuttered sails and working fantail for turning cap and sails to face the wind. Last worked in 1928, it retains intact milling machinery including 4 pairs of millstones. Ground floor contains a display of the history and workings of the mill. *4 May-29 Sep, Sat, Sun, Bank Hol Mon, 1400-1800. 50p/20p/50p. Tel: (01394) 382045/(01473) 265162.*

🌀 **Eastbridge Windpump** - Museum of East Anglian Life, Stowmarket: Windpump from 1850, one of four draining the Minsmere Level, re-erected on riverside site. Wooden eight sided body, boat shaped cap and four sails.

Herringfleet Marsh Mill, Herringfleet: Octagonal smock drainage mill clad in tarred weatherboards with a boat-shaped cap. 4 common sails, spread with cloth when the mill works. Cap turns to face the wind by means of a winch. External scoopwheel. Dating from the 1830's, it is now the last of the old wooden pumping mills in Broadland. In working order. *National Mills Day, 12 May, 1300-1700; also special days advertised locally, on these days the mill is set to work (wind permitting). Tel: (01473) 265162.*

Holton Saint Peter Post Mill, Holton St Peter: Restored post mill dating from the mid 18th Century on a two storey roundhouse. Still turned to face the wind by a fantail. Replicas of last working sails were fitted in 1992 Most of the machinery has been removed except for the brakewheel. *27 May, 26 Aug, 1000-1800. Tel: (01986) 872367/(01473) 265162.*

🌀 **Museum of East Anglian Life,** Stowmarket: See entry under Museums.

Pakenham Water Mill, (EH) Mill Road, Grimestone End, Pakenham: Fine 18C working Water Mill on Domesday site, complete with oil engine and other subsidiary machinery. Mill restored by Suffolk Preservation Society. Situated in quiet country lane with wonderful unspoilt countryside with a beautiful short river walk and a mill pool to enjoy a picnic or barbeque or just rest or paint. *5 Apr-31 Oct, Wed, Sat, Sun, Bank Holiday Mon, 1400-1730. £1.35/75p/£1.00. Tel: (01787) 247179.* ♿

🌀 **Saxtead Green Post Mill,** The Mill House, Saxtead Green: Elegent white windmill dating from 1776. Fine example of traditional Suffolk post mill. Climb stairs to 'buck' to see machinery all in working order. *1 Apr-30 Sep, Mon-Sat, 1000-1800; £1.30/70p/£1.00. Tel: (01728) 685789.*

Stanton Post Mill, Mill Farm, Upthorpe Road, Stanton: Post Mill dating from 1751 which is intact and in full working order. 4 'Patent' sails drive the two pairs of French stones, stoneground flour being produced. The Mill is winded by a fantail and there is a brick roundhouse below the 'buck'. There are displays of local mills, also Post Mills in general. *Open at any reasonable time but if travelling long distances please phone beforehand. Guaranteed times: 7, 8 Apr, 5, 6, 26, 27 May, 14 Jul-29 Sep, Sun, Bank Holiday Mon, 1000-1900. £1.50/20p/£1.50. Tel: (01359) 250622.*

Thelnetham Windmill, Mill Road, Thelnetham: Early 19thC four floor towermill with conical cap, powered by four large 'Patent' sails which drive two parts of French millstones. The mill is working whenever possible (wind permitting) on open days. Visitors may purchase stoneground flour and other grain products. *Jul-Sep, Sun, Bank Hol Mon, 1100-1900. Telephone for further information. £1.00/20p/£1.00. Tel: (01359) 250622.*

Thorpeness Windmill, Thorpeness: Working windmill housing displays on Suffolk coast and Thorpeness village as well as mill information. *4 May-8 Sep, Sat, Sun, Bank Hol Mon, 1100-1700; Jul, Aug, Mon-Fri, 1400-1700. Tel: (01473) 265177.*

Woodbridge Tide Mill, Tide Mill Quay, Woodbridge: Possibly the best known building in Suffolk. Standing on the picturesque Woodbridge quayside. This mill is very popular with visitors in the summer months. This mill was built in 1793, and used until 1957. After full restoration it was opened to the public in 1973. The machinery works at varying times and for varying periods, depending on tides. *5-8 Apr, 1 May-30 Sep, daily, 1100-1700; Oct, Sat, Sun, 1100-1700. 90p/40p/90p. Tel: (01473) 626618.* ♿

Machinery & Transport

Bedfordshire

◉ **Leighton Buzzard Railway,** Page's Park Station, Billington Road, Leighton Buzzard: A preserved narrow gauge railway operating rare steam and diesel engines on passenger trains through uniquely varied scenery around the historic market town of Leighton Buzzard. A large locomotive collection includes eleven steam engines and many preserved diesels. Wagons are restored and demonstrated in authentic industrial train displays and a variety of special events are held. This volunteer run railway is a true working museum. *24 March-13 Oct, Sun, Bank Hol Mon, 1100-1630; 29 May-28 Aug, Wed, 1100-1510, 1-31 Aug, Thu, Sat, 1100-1510. 1-22 Dec, Sat, Sun, 1030-1530. Train ride £4/£1/ £3. Tel: (01525) 373888.* &

Baby Peugeot, Shuttleworth Collection

◉ **The Mossman Collection,** Stockwood Country Park, Farley Hill, Luton: Over 70 historic vehicles depicting the history of horse-drawn transport from Roman times to the Second World War. There is a splendid, possibly unique, example of a Royal Mail Coach, state coaches and examples of omnibuses. *1 Apr-31 Oct, Tue-Sat, 1000-1700, Sun, Bank Holiday Mon, 1000-1800; 1 Nov-31 Mar, Sat, Sun, 1000-1600; Closed 25, 26 Dec, 1 Jan. Tel: (01582) 38714.* &

◉ **Shuttleworth Collection,** Old Warden Aerodrome, Biggleswade: Unique historic collection of aircraft from 1909 Bleriot to 1942 Spitfire in flying condition and cars dating from 1898. Panhard in running order. Flying displays and many other events held throughout the year including

several Aeromodeller and Motor Rally events. *2 Jan-31 Mar, 1 Nov-22 Dec, 1000-1500 (last admission), 1 Apr-31 Oct, 1000-1600 (last admission), closing time 1 hour later than last admission. Closed 23 Dec-1 Jan. £5.00/£2.50/£2.50. Tel: (01767) 627288.* &

Cambridgeshire

◉ **Imperial War Museum,** Duxford Airfield, Duxford: Duxford Airfield, a former Battle of Britain fighter station, is home to the largest collection of military and civil aircraft in Britain. Special exhibitions, ride simulator, adventure playground, shops, restaurant and picnic area are all available. Pleasure flying during summer weekends. Education groups welcome. Special events during summer. *1 Jan-15 Mar, 27 Oct-31 Dec, daily, 1000-1600; 16 Mar-26 Oct, 1000-1800; closed 24-26 Dec. £6.00/£3.00/£4.00. Tel: (01223) 835000.* &

Shuttleworth Collection, Bedfordshire

◉ **Nene Valley Railway,** Wansford Station, Stibbington: Regular steam trains operate over the line to Peterborough a return trip of 15 miles. Many steam locomotives are kept on this line including both British and Continental types. The railway has featured in television series including 'Hannay', 'London's Burning', 'Christobel' etc and for breathtaking stunts in the James Bond film 'Octopussy'. *Site open 1 Jan-31 Dec. Closed 25, 26 Dec. £2.00/£1.00/£1.00. For full timetable Tel: (01780) 782921.* &

Prickwillow Engine Museum, Main Street, Prickwillow: Mirrlees Bickerton and Day diesel engine. Five cylinder, blast injection, 250 bhp, working unit. Vicker-Petter 2 cylinder 2 stroke diesel, and others. A complete attraction on how water 'works' in Fen drainage. *1 Apr-30 Oct, daily, 1000-1700; 31 Oct-31 Mar, Sat, Sun, 1100-1600; closed 22 Dec-5 Jan. £2.00/£1.00/£1.00. Special days £3.00/£1.50/£1.50. Tel: (01353) 624337.* &

◉ **Railworld,** Oundle Road, Peterborough: Train exhibitions, mainly modern rail travel and worldwide, some historic items and locomotives. Exhibition titles are: Rail and the Environment, sponsored by British Rail and Eastern Electricity, with an impressive model railway; Global Rail Travel, in association with Long Haul Leisurail, a Thomas Cook company; Rail Industry Showcase, outline of an international industry; Local Rail History, to celebrate Peterborough's 150 railway years (1845-1995). *All year, daily, 1100-1600. £2.00/£1.00/ £1.50. Tel: (01733) 344240.* &

Museum of Technology, The Old Pumping Station, Cheddars Lane, Cambridge: Preserved Victorian pumping station containing gas and steam engines, working printshop and other items from the industrial past. *1 Jan- 31 Mar, 1 Nov-31 Dec, 1st Sun in every month, 1400-1700; 1 Apr-31 Oct, Sun, 1400-1700; 7,8 Apr, 1100-1700. £1.50/75p/ 75p. Special Steam days £3.00/ £1.50/£1.50. Tel: (01223) 68650.*

Imperial War Museum, Duxford, Cambs

Essex

Audley End Miniature Railway, Audley End: Steam and diesel locomotives in 10.5 gauge running through attractive woodland for 1.5 miles. Crosses the River Cam twice. *23 Mar-20 Oct, Sat, Sun, Bank Holiday Mon, from 1400; 14, 15, 21, 22 Dec, Santa Specials from 1100. £2.00/£1.00/£2.00. Tel: (01799) 541354.*

East Anglian Railway Museum, Chappel Station, Essex

Castle Point Transport Museum Society, 105 Point Road, Canvey Island: 1935 Museum housing collection of buses, coaches and commercial vehicles in restored condition. Some examples are unique. Some now being restored and commercial vehicles. *1 Apr-31 Oct, 2nd and last weekend, 1000-1700. Tel: (01268) 684272.*

⊚ **Colne Valley Railway,** Yeldham Road, Castle Hedingham: Pretty award winning station and pleasant ride in most attractive part of Colne Valley. Incorporating the largest and most interesting collection of operational heritage railway rolling stock, steam and diesel locomotives in the country. Large riverside and woodland picnic nature area, signal box and station to explore, shops, restaurant-buffet cars. *Rides every Sun and Bank Holiday from 17 March-October and Tue, Wed and Thu throughout school summer holidays, and many special events. Santa Special prior to Christmas, closed 25 Dec-31 Jan. Steam days £4.00/£2.00/£3.00. Non Steam days £2.00/£1.00/£2.00. For free timetable Tel: (01787) 461174. &*

⊚ **East Anglian Railway Museum,** Chappel Station, Colchester: The most comprehensive collection of period railway architecture and engineering in East Anglia. Based upon a busy Victorian country junction station. Preserved locomotives, passenger and freight rolling stock, working signal boxes, heritage centre. Fine transport bookshop, giftshop, buffet. Steam train rides on approx 30 days/year, miniature railway, free parking. *1 Mar-31 Oct, daily, 1000-1700; 1 Nov-28 Feb, daily, 1000-1600. Steam days £4.00/£2.00/£2.00. Non Steam days £2.25/£1.25/£1.25. Tel: (01206) 242524. &*

Mangapps Railway Museum, Burnham-on-Crouch: Large collection of railway relics, restored station, locomotives, coaches and wagons. Working railway line (half a mile). Also farm bygones and animals. *All year, Sat, Sun, 1300-1730; Steam days held on Bank Hols and first Sun of every month, 1130-1730; Open daily throughout school holidays, 1300-1730. Prices vary depending on service, tele-phone for details. Tel: (01621) 784898. &*

Bressingham Steam Museum

Mark Hall Cycle Museum, off First Avenue, Muskham Road, Harlow: A unique collection of over 60 cycles and accessories illustrating the history of the bicycle 1880-1980's. Housed in converted stable block. *All year, Mon-Fri, 1000-1700; Apr-Sep, Sun, 1100-1900; Oct-Mar, Sun, 1100-1600; Closed on public holidays, 24 Dec-2 Jan.£2.50/£2.00/£2.00. Tel: (01279) 439680. &*

National Motorboat Museum, Pitsea Hall Country Park, Pitsea: Museum devoted to the history and evolution of the motorboat Racing hydroplanes, power boats and leisure boats. Racing trophies etc. *All year, Thu-Mon, 1000-1700; during school holidays daily, 1000-1700; closed 24-31 Dec. Tel: (01268) 550088. &*

North Weald Airfield Museum, Ad Astra House, Hurricane Way, Epping: Ground floor fine old house at former main gate of North Weald Airfield. Historic record of the airfield from 1916 to 1964. A comprehensive and accurate collection of archives, photographs, detailed records of all activities, models, uniforms and equipment relating to Royal Flying Corps and Royal Air Force, all in immaculate condition and surroundings. *All year, Sat, Sun, 1200-1600. All other times by arrangement with Secretary. £1.00/50p/50p. Tel: (01992) 572705.*

⊚ **The Working Silk Museum,** New Mills, South Street, Braintree: Show of textiles and mill shop. Looms and ancient textile machines restored and working. Working looms Mon-Fri, Sat pm on the hour with weaving demonstrations. Evening tours with demonstrations by appointment. *All year, Mon-Fri, 1000-1230, 1330-1700; Sat, 1330-1700; closed 5, 8 Apr. £2.85/£1.60/£1.60. Tel: (01376) 553393. &*

Working Silk Museum, Braintree, Essex

Hertfordshire

St. Albans Organ Museum, 320 Camp Road, St Albans: A permanent playing exhibition of mechanical musical instruments. Organs by DeCap, Bursens and Mortier; Mills Violano-Virtuoso; reproducing pianos by Steinway and Weber; musical boxes; Wurlitzer and Rutt theatre pipe organs. *All year, Sun, 1400-1630; Sat evening theatre organ concerts, 18 Feb, 25 Mar, 22 Apr, 27 May, 24 Jun, 5, 26 Aug, 16 Sep, 14 Oct, 11 Nov, 8, 9, 31 Dec. £2.00/60p/£1.50. Tel: (01727) 851557. &*

Norfolk

Barton House Railway, Hartwell Road, The Avenue, Wroxham: 3.5" gauge miniature steam passenger railway. 7.25" gauge battery-electric railway. Full size M & GN accessories including signals and signal box. *21 Apr-20 Oct, third Sunday of each month, 1430-1730. 30p/10p/30p. Tel: (01603) 782470.*

Machinery & Transport

Bressingham Steam Museum and Gardens, Bressingham: A working steam museum in a nationally known garden setting. Narrow gauge railway rides, Victorian steam roundabout. Fire Museum, locomotive sheds, stationary engine display, Royal Coach, traction engines, gardens, 2 acre plant centre and display area. Services vary according to steaming programme. *Admission only £3.90/£2.85/£3.15 (95). Steam information line for full programme and prices. Tel: (01379) 687386.* &

Victorian Gallopers, Bressingham Steam Museum

Bure Valley Railway, Aylsham Station, Norwich Road, Aylsham: This new narrow-gauge steam railway runs on 9 miles of the old Great Eastern trackbed through some of Norfolk's most beautiful Broadland countryside. Trains can be joined at either end of the route and the stations are conveniently placed in each town. Parking available in both places. Connections are possible with both the National Trust's Blickling Hall and The Broads. *5 Apr-30 Sep, please phone for details of rail times. £6.50/£3.50/£5.50. Tel: (01263) 733858.* &

Duxford
Europe's Top
Aviation Museum

See Europe's largest collection of historic aircraft at this preserved Battle of Britain airfield.

Walk through dramatic battlefield scenes of tanks and artillery in the Land Warfare Exhibition Hall.

Enjoy Duxford's world famous airshows staged regularly during the summer months.

For a day to remember - make Duxford a must this summer.

DUXFORD
IMPERIAL WAR MUSEUM

Open daily from 10am.
Just south of Cambridge at Junction 10 of the M11.
For a free brochure send SAE to Dept. EAG,
Duxford Airfield, Cambridge CB2 4QR. Tel 01223 835000

Charles Burrell Museum, Minstergate, Thetford: The Museum draws together an impressive collection of exhibits to tell the story of Charles Burrell & Son, a name once famous throughout the world. The large exhibits are housed on the ground floor, together with a series of re-created workshops with original tools and machinery. Up in the gallery a series of photographs, letters and documents tell the story of the company and of the Burrell Family. *30 Mar-27 Oct, Sat, Sun, 1000-1700. Prices on application. Tel: (01842) 751166.* &

City of Norwich Aviation Museum, Old Norwich Road, Horsham St Faith: Exhibition building with displays of aviation memorabilia, photographs, models, maps and pictures. RAF Horsham St Faith display, 8th USAAF display, 2nd Air Division display, 458th Bomb Group display, collection of aircraft including Vulcan Bomber from Falklands Task Force. Souvenir shop. *1 Apr-31 Oct, Sun, Bank Holiday Mon, 1000-1700; 7 May-29 Aug, Tue, Thu, 1930-Dusk, Wed, 1400-1700; 1 Nov-31 Mar 1000-1530. £1.50/75p/75p. Tel: (01603) 861348.* &

Cockley Cley Iceni Village & Museums: See entry under Museums.

County School Station, North Elmham: Restored country railway station. Exhibitions about the railway, the county school and the Wensum Valley. Small length of track with working diesel train and brake-van. Small tea room providing light refreshments. Picnic area and way-marked circular walks (4.5 and 6 miles) with free leaflet. *Walks open all year, daily; Station/Museum please telephone for opening times. Tel: (01362) 668181 or (01362) 695333.*

Fenland & West Norfolk Aviation Museum, Bambers Garden Centre, Old Lynn Road, West Walton: The Vampire T11 aircraft is one of the finest examples in the country and has just undergone a complete respray and airframe check. Members of the public are welcome to sit in the cockpit and

Bressingham Steam Museum

study the aircraft at close quarters. Recently acquired 2 TS EE Lightning T5's. *1 Mar-30 Sep, Sat, Sun, Bank Hol Mon, 0930-1700. £1.00/50p/50p. Tel: (01945) 585946.* &

Forncett Industrial Steam Museum, Low Road, Forncett St Mary: Unique collection of large industrial steam engines including one that used to open Tower Bridge. Seven of the largest can be seen working on steam days. Museum won a 1989 Steam Heritage Award. *5 May, 2 Jun, 7 Jul, 4 Aug, 1 Sep, 6 Oct, 3 Nov, 1 Dec, 1000-1730; please ring for details of special events. £3.00/free/£2.50. Tel: (01508) 488277.* &

Lydia Eva Steam Drifter/Mincarlo Side Fishing Trawler, South Quay, Great Yarmouth and Yacht Basin, Lowestoft Harbour: Lydia Eva is the last survivor of over 3,000 drifters which came every autumn to Yarmouth and Lowestoft to fish for herring. Displays the hardships of life aboard and ashore in an industry which dominated the two towns for a century. Lydia Eva was built in 1930 in King's Lynn and her engines and boiler were fitted in Great Yarmouth. She was one of the last steam drifters to be built and was destined to be the last survivor. The owner, Harry Eastick, sold his fleet in 1938 and Lydia Eva became a Royal Air Force salvage vessel, servicing the bombing ranges. *5 Apr-mid Oct, 1000-1600, days and times dependent on manning availability, check with Gt Yarmouth or Lowetoft Tourist Information Centres for details, including location of ship.*

Muckleburgh Collection, Weybourne Old Military Camp, Weybourne: The original NAAFI complex of this former military camp now houses the largest private military collection in the country incl. tanks, armoured cars, lorries, bombs, artillery and missiles used by Allied armies during WWII and since. It incorporates the Suffolk & Norfolk Yeomanry Museum of uniforms, weapons, photographs and documents. Items of artillery used in the Falkland Islands, and uniforms, weapons and other equipment recovered from Coalition and Iraqi armies in the Gulf War. Some post war aircraft on display and a maritime and RNLI exhibition. *18-25 Feb, 10 Mar-3 Nov, daily, 1000-1700. £3.50/£2.00/£2.80. Tel: (01263) 588210.* &

Machinery & Transport

Norfolk Motor Cycle Museum, Railway Yard, North Walsham: Wide collection of motor cycles dating from 1920 to 1960. *2 Jan-31 Mar, Mon-Sat, 1 Apr-31 Oct, daily, 1 Nov-31 Mar, Mon-Sat, all 1000-1630; closed 24, 25 Dec, 1 Jan. £2.00/£1.00/£1.50. Tel: (01692) 406266.* &

⊙ **North Norfolk Railway,** Sheringham Station, Station Approach, Sheringham: The North Norfolk Railway operates steam trains along the 5.5 mile line from the seaside resort of Sheringham to the market town of Holt. The journey affords beautiful views of the sea, pine forest and heathland. At Sheringham there is a museum of railway memorabilia, static exhibits, a station buffet and souvenir shop. Weybourne station gives access to Kelling Heath Nature Trail and is a typical rural station. Here is our engine shed where historical loco's and rolling stock are maintained and restored. *A regular steam or vintage diesel hauled service. 3 Mar-27 Oct; telephone for full timetable and prices. Tel: (01263) 822045.* &

Reepham Station Museum of Shops & Adventure Cycle Hire, Station Road, Reepham: Independent museum with principal exhibits illustrating Britain's shopping past, with special displays on the Victorian Reepham railway station which houses the museum Also, off-road cycle hire on the 21 mile Marriott's Way on the trackbed of the Historic M&GN and GE Railway route. Other facilities include free play on giant outdoor games, unusual gifts and refreshments. On and off-road cycle hire, local walks and bridleways. *Phone for opening times & prices. Tel: (01603) 871187.*

Seething Airfield Control Tower, Station 146, Seething Airfield, Seething: Seething a B24 Liberator base during World War II. Renovated U.S.A.A.F. control tower has model a/c room, diorama of Seething base, 448th Honour roll, display of WWII memorabilia, exhibition of 'The 448th Bomb Group Collection'. This includes diaries, photographs and personal stories from Americans based at Seething 1943-1945. *5 May-6 Oct, first Sun in every month, 1000-1700. Tel: (01508) 494850.* &

Sheringham Station, North Norfolk Railway

The Thursford Collection, Norfolk

Strumpshaw Hall Steam Museum, Old Hall, Low Road, Strumpshaw: Collection of steam vehicles including working beam engines showman's road engine, portable and stationary Steam Engines, Steam Wagon and

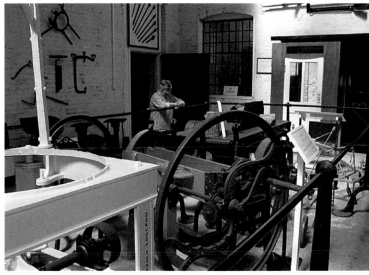
Long Shop Museum, Leiston, Suffolk

fairground organ. Railway running every day, *5, 7, 8 Apr, 14 Jul-2 Oct, Sun-Fri, 1100-1600; £2.00/£1.00/£1.50. Tel: (01603) 712339.* &

⊙ **Thursford Collection,** Thursford Green, Thursford: Musical evenings every Tue from mid Jul to end Sep. Live musical show every opening - nine mechanical organs and Wurlitzer show starring Robert Wolfe. *1 Apr-31 May, daily 1300-1700; 1 Jun-31 Aug, daily, 1130-1700; 1 Sep-27 Oct, daily, 1300-1700. £4.40/£4.00. Tel: (01328) 878477.* &

Wells Walsingham Railway, Stiffkey Road, Wells-next-the-Sea: Four miles of railway. The longest 10¼ inch railway in the world. New locomotive, Norfolk Hero now in service, largest of its kind ever built. *7 Apr-30 Sep, daily. Last week of October for schools half term holiday. Closed Christmas/New Year. £4.00/£3.00, Tel: (01328) 856506.* &

Wolferton Station Museum, Wolferton: The former Royal retiring rooms built for King Edward V11 and Queen Alexandra in 1898. Items and furniture from Royal trains. Queen Victoria's travelling bed. Rrailway relics and curios. Victorian/ Edwardian fashions, jewellery, furniture and ephemera. Personal royal letters. A representation of a royal train carriage housed in an 1880's GER coach and much more. *1 Apr-30 Sep, Mon-Fri, 1030-1730, Sun 1300-1700; closed 25 Dec, 1 Jan. £1.95/ 90p/£1.50. Tel: (01485) 540674.* &

Suffolk

Boat World, Sea Lake Road, Oulton Broad: Working exhibition of boat building craft skills. Visitors can view a variety of interesting craft under construction. *May-Sep, Mon-Thu, 1000-1500, Fri, 1000-1400. £1.50. Tel: (01502) 569663.* &

⊙ **East Anglia Transport Museum,** Chapel Road, Carlton Colville: A museum which is under constant development, where the emphasis is on movement. There are working trams, trolley buses and narrow gauge railway, other vehicles include buses, cars and commercial vehicles and steam rollers, all included in a re-constructed 1930's street scene. Visitors may travel on Trams, trolleybus and narrow gauge railway. A period street is being developed complete with authentic street furniture. *7, 8 Apr, May-Sep, Sun, 1100-1700; Jun, also Sat, 1400-1600; Jul-Sep, Mon-Sat, 1400-1600, Sun 1100-1700. £3.00/£2.00/£2.00. Tel: (01502) 518459.* &

Ipswich Transport Museum, Old Trolleybus Depot, Cobham Road, Ipswich: A collection of over 90 historic commercial vehicles, housed in a former Ipswich Corporation Trolleybus Depot. The vehicles date from 1850-1983 and all have been built or used in the area. *7 Apr-27 Oct, Sun, Bank Hol Mon, 1100-1630. £2.00/£1.00/£1.50. Tel: (01473) 715666.* &

Machinery & Transport

Long Shop Museum, Main Street, Leiston: One of the largest Industrial museums in East Anglia, the Long Shop Museum once belonged to Richard Garrett Engineering Company, best known for its traction engines and agricultural machinery. Built in 1852 the Long Shop, Grade II Listed building, was one of the earliest production line assembly halls in the

Lowestoft & East Suffolk Maritime Museum

world. It was known locally as the cathedral amongst its workforce. By 1980 Garretts had gone and the cathedral lay derelict. A trust was formed and the Long Shop and many Garrett products were rescued and have been restored and displayed. Winner of the 1995 Suffolk Coastal Museum of The Year Award. *1 Apr-27 Oct, Mon-Sat, 1000-1700, Sun, 1100-1700. £2.00/75p/£1.00. Tel: (01728) 832189.* &

Lowestoft and East Suffolk Maritime Museum, Sparrows Nest Park, Whapload Road, Lowestoft: Models of fishing and Commercial ships old and new, shipwrights tools and fishing gear. Lifeboat display and gallery. Drifter's cabin with models of fishermen. *5, 7, 8 Apr, 1 May-30 Sep, daily, 1000-1700. 50p/25p/25p. Tel: (01502) 561963.* &

Lydia Eva Steam Drifter/Mincarlo Side Fishing Trawler, Lowestoft and Great Great Yarmouth: See entry in Norfolk.

Mid Suffolk Light Railway Society Museum, Brockford Station, Brockford: The setting up of a working museum dedicated to the Mid Suffolk Light Railway. Restoration of station and trackwork on part of original route of railway. Preservation of artefacts and memorabilia

relating to the Railway stimulation of historical and educational interest. *7 Apr-29 Sept, Sun, BH Mon, 1100-1700; Aug, Wed, 1400-1700. £1.00/50p/£1.00.*

◉ **Museum of East Anglian Life,** Stowmarket: Unique Burrell Steam Ploughing Engines can be seen working on special days (see museum brochure). 'Empress of Britain' a general purpose agricultural steam engine by Charles Burrell is also housed here. Walsh and Glarke are represented by a pair of paraffin run ploughing engines and one can also see a Whitmore and Binyon Single Cylinder Horizontal Steam Engine from a flour mill at wickham Market. *Telephone for opening times and admission prices. Tel: (01449) 612229.* &

Norfolk and Suffolk Aviation Museum, The Street, Flixton: 24 aircraft on display. Unique collection housed indoors, from the early pioneers of flight up to the present day. Also the Royal Observer Corps Museum, the 446th Bomb Group Museum and 446th Bomb Group Memorial. USAAF 8th Air Force. Donations encouraged. *5, 7, 8 Apr, 15 Apr-27 Oct, Sun, Bank Hol Mon, 1000-1700; School summer holiday period, Tue-Thu, 1000-1700.* &

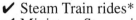
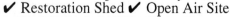
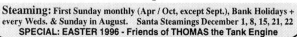

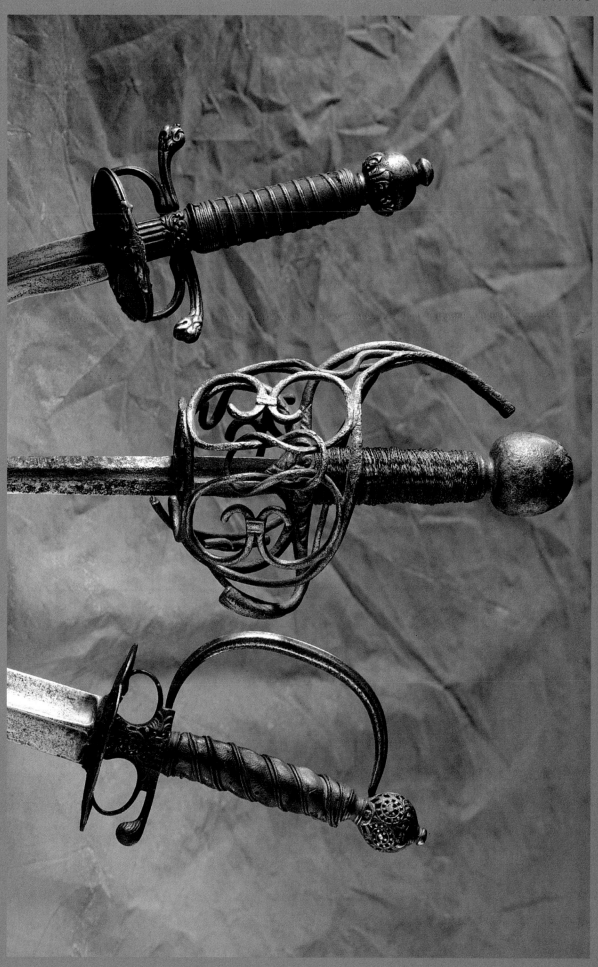

Museums

Bedfordshire

BEDFORD

⊚ **Bedford Museum,** Castle Lane, Bedford: Bedford Museum is housed in a former brewery in a setting close to the River Great Ouse. The displays show aspects of community life in Bedford, re-created interiors of farmhouse and cottage, local rocks and fossils, birds and mammals from town and countryside, archaeology through the ages including important local archaeological finds and lacemaking. There is a full programme of temporary exhibitions, children's activities and special events. *All year, Tue-Sat, 1100-1700; Sun, Bank Hol Mon, 1400-1700; Closed 5 Apr, 25 Dec, telephone for details of remainder of Christmas. Tel: (01234) 353323.* ⅃

Bunyan Museum & Bunyan Meeting Free Church, Mill Street, Bedford: Personal effects of John Bunyan (1628-1688) and copies of 60 of Bunyan's works including 'The Pilgrim's Progress' in 169 languages, together with items relating to over 300 years of Church history. The Church contains bronze doors and stained glass windows depicting scenes from the 'Pilgrim's Progress'. *1 Apr-31 Oct, Tue-Sat, 1400-1600; Jul-Sep, Tue-Sat, 1030-1230, 1400-1600. 50p/30p/30p. Tel: (01234) 358075.* ⅃

⊚ **Cecil Higgins Art Gallery and Museum,** Castle Close, Bedford: Award winning re-created Victorian Mansion, original home of Cecil Higgins. Rooms displayed to give 'lived-in' atmosphere including bedroom with furniture designed by William Burges (1827-1881). Adjoining gallery with outstanding collections of ceramics, glass and watercolours and prints. *All year, Tue-Sat, 1100-1700, Sun, Bank Hol Mon, 1400-1700; Closed 5 Apr. Tel: (01234) 211222.* ⅃

ELSTOW **Moot Hall,** Elstow Green, Church End: See entry under Historic Houses.

Elstow Moot Hall, Bedfordshire

LUTON

⊚ **Luton Museum and Art Gallery,** Wardown Park, Luton: Striking Victorian Mansion housing interesting and diverse collections, including lace, costume, re-created Victorian displays, toys, natural history and archaeology. The house is set in beautiful parkland and offers free parking and admission, a lovely gift shop and a small tea room. *All Year, Mon-Sat, Bank Hol Mon, 1000-1700; Sun, 1300-1700; closed 25, 26 Dec, 1 Jan. Tel: (01582) 746739.* ⅃

⊚ **Stockwood Craft Museum and Gardens,** Stockwood Park, Farley Hill, Luton: Museum set in period gardens and Hamilton Finlay sculpture garden. Craft demonstrations at weekends. The Mossman collection of horse drawn vehicles is housed in a separate museum within the complex. This collection traces the history of transport from Roman times to the 1940's. *Mar-Oct, Tue-Sat, 1000-1700, Sun, B.H. Mon, 1000-1800; 1 Nov-31 Mar, Sat, Sun, 1000-1600; Closed 25, 26 Dec, 1 Jan. Tel: (01582) 38714.* ⅃

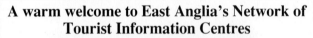

Cambridgeshire

BURWELL Museum Trust, Mill Close, Burwell: Rural village museum housed in re-erected 18C timber framed barn. Smithy and wheelwrights shop. Waggon sheds with display of waggons, carts, tractors etc and video room and further period displays in new buildings. *7 Apr-29 Sep, Sun, Thu, Bank Hol Mon, 1400-1700.* &

CAMBRIDGE

Cambridge and County Folk Museum, 2-3 Castle Street, Cambridge: Building was 16thC farmhouse. From 17thC to 1934 was an Inn. Houses wide variety of objects relating to everyday life of people in City and Country. Museum also has temporary exhibition programme and activity days. *1 Apr-30 Sep, Mon-Sat, 1030-1700, Sun, 1400-1700; 1 Oct- 31 Mar, Tue-Sat, 1030-1750, Sun, 1400-1700; closed 5 Apr, 23-29 Dec. £1.00/50p/50p. Tel: (01223) 355159.* &

Cambridge Univ Collection of Air Photographs, The Mond Building, Free School Lane, Cambridge: This is a private reference collection, but enquiries by general public are welcome. *2 Jan-22 Dec, Mon-Thu, 0900-1700; Fri 0900-1600, (closed for lunch 1300-1400); closed 5-8 Apr. Tel: (01223) 334578.* &

Museum of Classical Archaeology, Sidgwick Avenue, Cambridge: Plaster casts of Greek and Roman sculptures. *All year, Mon-Fri, 0900-1700; closed 5-8 Apr, 24 Dec-1 Jan. Tel: (01223) 335153.* &

Fitzwilliam Museum, Trumpington Street, Cambridge: The museum contains fascinating Egyptian, Greek, Roman and other antiquities, an internationally renowned collection of European paintings, an outstanding and varied display of ceramics, some fine furniture, clocks, watches, bronzes, medals, armour and fans. The original magnificent buildings dating from the mid-19th century and the additions built this century provide a splendid setting, resulting in one of the best museums of its type outside the major cities. *All year, Tue-Sat, 1000-1700, Sun, 1415-1700. Also open Spring & Summer Bank Holidays. Tel: (01223) 332900.* &

Kettle's Yard, Castle Street, Cambridge: Major collection of 20th century paintings and sculpture exhibited in a house of unique character. Temporary exhibitions gallery with changing contemporary art exhibitions, talks and discussions. *All year, Gallery, Tue-Sat, 1230-1730; Sun and Bank Hol, 1400-1730; House, Tue-Sun, Bank Hol, 1400-1600; Closed 25 Dec. Tel: (01223) 352124.* &

Sedgwick Museum, Dept of Earth Sciences, Downing Street, Cambridge: Large collection of vertebrate and invertebrate fossils from all over the world. Some mounted skeletons of dinosaur, reptiles and mammals. Also collection of rocks and building stones. Mineral Gallery. *All year, Mon-Fri, 0900-1300, 1400-1700; Sat, 1000-1300; closed 5-8 Apr, 23 Dec- 2 Jan. Tel: (01223) 333456.*

University Museum of Archaeology & Anthropology, Downing Street, Cambridge: The museum is primarily a University institution devoted to teaching and research, but its public display galleries have recently been totally refurbished and contain much to interest the non-specialist visitors. The Archaeology Gallery surveys world prehistory from the origins of mankind to the rise of literate civilisation, and also contains an important collection of local antiquities. The Anthropology Gallery surveys culture and art from all continents, and special exhibitions are also held from time to time. *All year, Mon-Fri, 1400-1600; Sat, 1000-1230; closed 4-10 Apr, 24 Dec-1 Jan. Tel: (01223) 337733.*

Whipple Museum of the History of Science, Free School Lane, Cambridge: Extensive collection of scientific instruments. *All year, Mon-Fri, 1400-1600. Tel: (01223) 334540.*

ELY

Ely Museum, 28C High Street, Ely: Displays investigate the history of Ely and the surrounding area from the prehistoric period onwards. Particular exhibits include an archeology and Medieval history gallery, Fenland life (incl. audio-visual films), crafts. The Cambridgeshire Regiment, and the cycle of James Moore used on the day of the world's first bicycle race. *All year, daily, 1030-1700. £1.00/50p/50p. Tel: (01353) 666655.*

★ **Oliver Cromwell's House,** 29 St Marys Street, Ely: The family home of Oliver Cromwell recently extended to give the visitor a deeper insight into 17th Century life. In addition to the Parlour Kitchen and Tithe Office, the first floor opened in 1995 and contain a large Civil War Exhibition as well as Cromwell's Study and Haunted Room. There are two films to watch, one on Oliver Cromwell and another on the Drainage of the Fens. The front of house contains Ely's Tourist Information Centre and a comprehensive Gift Shop. *1 Apr-30 Sep, daily, 1000-1800; 1 Oct-31 Mar, Mon-Sat, 1000-1715; Closed 25, 26 Dec, 1 Jan. £1.80/£1.30/£1.30. Tel: (01353) 662062.*

Stained Glass Museum, The Cathedral, Ely: Examples of stained glass from 13C to present day in specially lighted display boxes. Models of a modern workshop which explain the manufacture of a stained glass window. There are approximately 80 panels on display. Audio tour available. *All year, Mon-Fri, 1030-1600, Sat, Bank Holidays, 1030-1630, Sun, 1200-1500 (summertime 1200-1800); Closed 5 Apr, 24, 25 Dec. £1.80/75p/£1.00. Tel: (01353) 667735/6.*

HUNTINGDON

Cromwell Museum, Grammar School Walk, Huntingdon: The foremost collection of Cromwelliana in the UK attractively displayed in the former school room of the Lord Protector. Many paintings and personal items from the descendants of Cromwell can be seen in this presentation of one of England's most significant historical figures, 'warts and all'. *2 Jan-31 Mar, Tue-Fri, 1300-1600, Sat, Sun, 1100-1600, 1 Apr-31 Oct, Tue-Fri, 1100-1700, Sat, Sun, 1100-1600; 1 Nov-31 Dec, Sat, 1000-1600, Sun, 1400-1600; where applicable closed between 1300-1400 for lunch. Tel: (01480) 425830.*

William Burges Decanter, 1865, Fitzwilliam Museum, Cambridge

MARCH March & District Museum, High Street, March: General collection of artefacts relating to social history. Agricultural tools, many local photos and 19C record material. Restored blacksmiths forge and Fen Cottage. *All year, Wed, 1000-1200, Sat, 1000-1200, 1400-1600; Closed 23 Dec-2 Jan. Tel: (01354) 55300.*

★ **PETERBOROUGH Museum & Art Gallery,** Priestgate, Peterborough: Local history. Geology, archaeology, natural history, folk life, industry, world famous collection of Napoleonic POW work, costume period shop and many temporary exhibitions. *All year, Tue-Sat, 1000-1700 (except June when closed for building work); closed 5 Apr, 23-30 Dec. Tel: (01733) 343329.* &

RAMSEY Rural Museum, The Wood Yard, Cemetary Road, Ramsey: Rebuilt farm buildings housing a collection of old farm implements of the fens and Victorian life in the home. Now including a chemists shop and a cobblers shop. *31 Mar-31 Sep, Sun, Thu, 1400-1700. £1.00/50p/50p. Tel: (01487) 815715.* &

ST IVES Norris Museum, The Broadway: The Norris Museum is the Museum of Huntingdonshire, with exhibits from every part of the County and every period of history. Oldest items on show are fossils and reconstructed models of animals that lived here in the time of the dinosaurs; more recent specimens include remains of the Woolly Mammoth, and archaeological remains from the Stone Age onwards. There are special displays on the Civil War, on French prisoner-of-war work from the prison camp at Norman Cross, and the local sport of ice-skating on the flooded Fens. The Museum is set in a picturesque riverside garden. *1 Oct-30 Apr, Mon-Fri, 1000-1300, 1400-1600, Sat, 1000-1200; 1 May-30 Sep, Mon-Fri, 1000-1300, 1400-1700, Sat, 1000-1200, 1400-1700, Sun 1400-1700; Closed 5, 8 Apr, Bank Hol. Tel: (01480) 465101.* &

Museums

ST NEOTS **St Neots Museum,** The Old Court, New Street, St Neots: The building, a former police station and Magistrates' Court contains rare examples of Victorian cells, in near-original condition. The Museum collection illustrates the history of the area through archaeological and local history exhibitions including a range of crafts, costume and much photographic and other pictorial material. *2 Apr-21 Dec, Tue-Sat, 1000-1600. £1.25/75p/£1.00. Tel: (01480) 388788.*

THORNEY **Heritage Centre,** Station Road, Thorney: Models, development from monastic days, Walloon, Fleming influence after Vermudens drainage. 19C model housing by Duke of Bedford, recent village life. *1 Apr-31 Oct, Sat, Sun 1400-1700; 1 Jul-30 Sep, Wed, Sat, Sun, 1400-1700. Tel: (01733) 270780.* ♿

WATERBEACH **Farmland Museum** PROVISIONALLY OPENING EARLY SUMMER 96, Denny Abbey, Ely Road, Waterbeach: New Museum. Farmyard setting, 1 acre site, next to Denny Abbey (English Heritage). Brings history of Cambridgeshire farming to life. Displays on rural life, the Fens. Housed within a Grade 2 Listed stone barn, cow sheds and modern grain store. This site has been an agricultural estate from medieval times to today, where the modern farm sits alongside the Museum. *Opening early summer 1996, details to be decided. Tel: (01223) 860988.*

WHITTLESEY **Whittlesey Museum,** Town Hall, Market Street, Whittlesey: Archaeology, agriculture, hand tools, brickmaking, collection of local photographs. Sir Harry Smith exhibition, railways, costume display, temp. exhibitions. Non-working forge. *All year, Fri, 1430-1630, Sat, 1000-1200, Sun, 1430-1630; Closed 25 Dec. 50p/20p/50p. Tel: (01733) 203608.*

WISBECH **Wisbech & Fenland Museum,** Museum Square, Wisbech: Museum founded in 1835. Premises purpose built in 1846/7. Collections cover: Applied Art, for example ceramics and Townshend collection, local geology, zoology, archaeology, topography and history. Personalia of Richard Young, Chauncey Townshend and the Peckover family. Ethnography - mainly African. Two historic libraries, open by appointment, as well as local archives, inlcuding Parish Records and maps. We also have a temporary Exhibition Gallery. New gallery on Thomas Clarkson, slavery and the slave trade. *2 Apr-28 Sept, Tue-Sat, 1000-1700; 1 Oct-29 Mar 1997, Tue-Sat, 1000-1600. Tel: (01945) 583817.*

Essex

BILLERICAY

⊚ **Barleylands Farm Museum,** Barleylands Road, Billericay: Over 2,000 exhibits, working craft shops, narrow gauge steam railway, farm animals, farm trail, farm shop and Pick-Your-Own Unit. Large free car and coach park, toilets, picnic area, shop and tea rooms. Guided tours of our museum and busy modern working farm for schools and groups at any time by prior arrangement. *All year, Wed-Sun, 1000-1700; Closed Mon, Tue except Bank Holiday. £2.00/£1.00/£1.00. Tel: (01268) 282090.* ♿

Cater Museum, 74 High Street, Billericay: Victorian sitting room and bedroom. Folk museum of Bygones. *All year, Mon-Sat, 1400-1700; Closed Easter, Christmas. Tel: (01277) 622023.*

⊚ BRADWELL **Bradwell Power Station,** Bradwell-on-Sea: Exhibits in Centre on energy production, the environment and nuclear power. Visits to reactors and generating station. The new visitor centre contains interactive videos, an audio visual room, classroom, cafeteria etc. *1 Apr-31 Oct, daily, 1000-1600; 1 Nov-31 Mar, Sun-Fri, 1000-1600. Tel: (01621) 873395.* ♿

⊚ BRAINTREE **District Museum,** Manor Street, Braintree: 'Threads of Time' tells the story of Braintree District and its important place in our island's history. By creativity and skill the people of the area developed ideas which shaped 20thC life. Gallery exhibits interpret the diverse local industrial heritage; the production of fabrics for State occasions during the past 200 years and innovation in metal window design and man-made textiles in which our District led the world. *All year, Tue-Sat, Bank Holidays, 1000-1700, Sun 1400-1700. Closed Sun, Jan-Mar. £2.00/£1.00/£1.00. Tel: (01376) 325266.* ♿

BRIGHTLINGSEA **Brightlingsea Museum,** 1 Duke Street, Brightlingsea: Maritime and Social History Museum of Brightlingsea (limb of the Cinque Port of Sandwich) showing a collection relating to the towns Cinque Port connections. Also its history of fishing, yachting, stowboating and oystering - the one-time rail link with Colchester. *1 Apr-30 Sept, Mon-Thu, 1400-1700, Sun 1000-1600. 50p/25p/25p.*

BURNHAM ON CROUCH **Burnham on Crouch & District Museum,** Tucker Brown Boathouse, Coronation Road, Burnham-on-Crouch: Museum specialising in local history, maritime and agricultural features of Dengie Hundred. *Easter-Mid Dec, Wed, Sat, 1100-1600; Sun, Bank Hol, each day of Burnham Week (Last week in August) 1400-1630. 50p/20p.*

CANVEY ISLAND **Dutch Cottage Museum,** Canvey Road, Canvey Island: Early 17 century cottage of one of Vermuydens Dutch workmen (responsible for drainage schemes in East Anglia). *27 May, 1030-1300, 1430-1700; 29 May-29 Sep, Wed, Sun, 1430-1700. Tel: (01268) 794005.*

⊛ CHELMSFORD **Chelmsford and Essex Museum,** Oaklands Park, Moulsham Street, Chelmsford: Permanent collections of fossils and rocks, archaeology, costume, decorative arts (Castle Hedingham Ware, English tinglaze pottery) glass, natural history, taxidermy, live observation beehive, also Essex Regiment Museum. New permanent display - 'The Story of Chelmsford', from the Ice Age to Present day. Temporary exhibition programme. *All year, Mon-Sat, 1000-1700, Sun, 1400-1700; closed 5 Apr, 25, 26 Dec. Tel: (01245) 353066.*

COLCHESTER

⊛ **Colchester Castle,** Colchester: Spectacular new displays of Colchester's early history including the destruction of Colchester at the hands of Boudica and the Iceni. Roman Colchester galleries feature many hands on exhibits of appeal to children and adults alike. Look out for the imaginative holiday events programme. New displays about Medieval and Norman Colchester plus imaginative interpretation of Castle prisons. *All year, Mon-Sat, 1000-1700; Mar-Nov, Sun, 1400-1700. £2.80/£1.80/£1.80. Tel: (01206) 282931.* &

⊛ **Hollytrees Museum,** High Street, Colchester: Collection of toys, costume and decorating arts from eighteenth to twentieth century displayed in an elegant Georgian Town House built in 1718. *All year, Tue-Sat, 1000-1700; closed for lunch 1200-1300. Tel: (01206) 282931.*

The Minories Gallery, 74 High Street, Colchester: This beautiful Georgian building, with its peaceful garden complete with Gothic folly, now houses a major art gallery. Exhibitions focus on the art of today and range from video installations to painting and sculpture, from international figures to artists who live and work in the area. Firstile aims to make today's art accessible and arranges workshops, talks and events both in the gallery itself and around Colchester. We can also provide information about visual art, craft & media activity at other venues in the area. The garden is an ideal spot to relax after sightseeing. *All year, Tue-Sat, 1000-1700; closed 25, 26 Dec. Tel: (01206) 577067.* &

⊛ **Natural History Museum,** All Saints Church, High Street, Colchester: A 13 century church housing natural history of Colchester and Essex dioramas. Recently re-displayed to a high standard with 'hands on' activities for children. *All year, Tue-Sat, 1000-1700; closed 1300-1400. Tel: (01206) 282932.* &

⊛ **Social History Museum,** Holy Trinity Church, Trinity Street, Colchester: Town and country life in the Colchester area over the last 200 years displayed in the medieval former Church of Holy Trinity with its Saxon tower. *Apr-Oct, Tue-Sat, 1000-1200, 1300-1700. Tel: (01206) 282931.* &

⊛ **Tymperleys Clock Museum,** Trinity Street, Colchester: A fine collection of Colchester made clocks displayed in Tymperleys, a restored late fifteenth century timber framed house which Bernard Mason restored and presented to the town. *Apr-Oct, Tue-Sat, 1000-1700. closed 1300-1400. Tel: (01206) 282931.*

DEDHAM **Toy Museum,** Dedham Centre, High Street, Dedham: Collection of dolls, teddies, toys, games, play house and pictures displayed in section of beautifully converted church. Touch and Try corner. Museum shop. Small but fascinating museum. *All year, Tue-Thu, Sat, Sun, Bank Hol, 1030-1645, flexible lunch time closing between 1200-1400; closed 25, 26, 27 Dec. 50p/30p/30p. Tel: (01206) 322666.*

EAST TILBURY **Coalhouse Fort,** Princess Margaret Road: Best example of a Victorian Casemate fortress in the South East, built as a front line defence for the Thames. Public access to fort incl. guided tours of magazines and roof. Displays in the fort: a World War II display team, Thameside Aviation Museum, military vehicles, etc. The Fort is in a riverside park with Thames foreshore walk. *Feb-Nov, last Sun in month, Bank Hol, 1200-1600 (GMT), 1300-1700 (BST). £1.50/50p/£1.50. Tel: (01375) 859673.*

FINCHINGFIELD **Finchingfield Guildhall,** Church Hill, Finchingfield: 15th Century Guildhall (a) Museum of local items including Roman remains (Sunday p.m. only). (b) Exhibition Hall (the old school room). Art Exhibitions from time to time. *7 Apr-30 Sep, Sun and Bank Holidays, 1430-1700. Tel: (01371) 810456.*

GRAYS **Grays Thurrock Museum,** Thameside Complex, Orsett Rd, Grays: An interesting display of artefacts, maps and models showing Thurrock's history from prehistoric to modern times. *All year, Mon-Sat, 0900-2000; (phone for closing arrangements on Wed & Sat). Tel: (01375) 382555.* &

GREAT BARDFIELD

Bardfield Cage, Bridge Street, Great Bardfield: Great Bardfield Cage is a 19thC village lock-up. *6 Apr-29 Sep, Sat, Sun, Bank Hol Mon, 1400-1730.*

Cottage Museum, Dunmow Road, Great Bardfield: 16th Century Charity Cottage: A collection of mainly 19th and 20th Century domestic and agriculture artefacts - some Rural Crafts mainly straw plaiting and Corndollies. *6 Apr-29 Sep, Sat, Sun, Bank Hol Mon, 1400-1730.*

HARLOW

Harlow Museum, Passmores House, Third Avenue, Harlow: 5 Galleries covering archaeology and history of area geology and natural history. Temporary exhibition gallery. *All year, Tue-Sat, 1000-1700; closed Bank Hols. Tel: (01279) 454959.* &

Harlow Study and Visitors Centre, Netteswellbury Farm, Harlow: Visitors Centre is a medieval tithe barn, containing an exhibition telling Harlow's New Town story. Study Centre is 13C church. *All year, Mon-Fri, 0930-1630; closed Easter, Christmas. Tel: (01279) 446745.*

HARWICH

Harwich Lifeboat Museum, Timberfields, off Wellington Road, Harwich: Lifeboat Museum contains 34ft Oakley class lifeboat with facilities to go on board, also full illustrated history of lifeboat service in Harwich. *May, Sep, Sun, 1000-1300, 1400-1700; 1 Jun-31 Aug, daily, 1000-1300, 1400-1700. 50p/free/50p.*

Harwich Maritime Museum, Low Lighthouse, The Green, Harwich: Special displays related to Royal Navy and commercial shipping. Fine views over unending shipping movements in harbour. *7 Apr-31 May, Sun, 1000-1300, 1400-1700; 1 Jun-31 Aug, daily, 1000-1300, 1400-1700; Sep, Sun, 1000-1300, 1400-1700. 50p/free/50p. Tel: (01255) 503429.*

KELVEDON

Feering & Kelvedon Local History Museum, Maldon Road, Kelvedon: *1 Mar-31 Oct, Mon, 1400-1700, Sat, 0930-1230, 1 Nov-28 Feb, Sat, 1000-1230. Closed Bank Holidays. Tel: (01376) 570307.*

Museums

Kelvedon Hatch Nuclear Bunker, Kelvedon Hall Lane, Kelvedon Hatch, Brentwood: A large 3 storey ex-government regional H.Q. buried some 100ft below ground. Complete with canteen, BBC studio, dormitories, plant room, plotting floor, communications and scientists' rooms and entrance tunnel. This bunker was active until as recently as 1992. *All year, daily, 1000-1700; closed 25 Dec. £5.00/£3.00. Tel: (01277) 364883.*

LEIGH-ON-SEA **Leigh Heritage Centre,** 13A High Street: Photographic exhibition - historical, interpretive displays, Granny's kitchen. Number of local artefacts. *Daily, 1100-1500 (subject to volunteers being available); Closed 25 Dec. Tel: (01702) 470834.* &

LINFORD **Walton Hall Farm Museum,** Walton Hall Road, Linford: Main collection housed in 17th Century english barn and other farm buildings. Collection includes farming bygones, tools, wagons, implements, harnesses, military, rare breed animals, shire horse, donkey, sheep, goats, fowl, pigeons, peacock, parrot, domestic bygones, motoring bygones. Representations of Victorian and Edwardian childs' nursery with dolls, toys, collection of prams. Representations of old time dairy, milk delivery pram, churns, milk delivery, bottles. Bird garden and picnic lawn. *30 Mar-22 Dec, Thu-Sun, 1000-1700. Open all school holidays & Bank Holiday. £2.00/£1.00/£1.00. Tel: (01375) 671874.* &

MALDON

Maldon & District Agricultural and Domestic Museum, 47 Church Street, Goldhanger: Museum has extensive collection of items of every kind, products of Maldon Ironworks and printing machines from 1910. Bygones include mangles, 1860 washing machines, irons, old cookers and stoves, shoe making machine, typewriters and printing machines, wirelesses and clocks, a 1945 room setting. A range of road signs from Maldon Ironworks and petrol pumps. A collection of photographs, display of birds eggs, stuffed birds and animals. Farming implements include tractors, hayrake, seed drills, scythes, flails and mowers; cattle cake breakers, butter *churns, etc. 1 Apr-30 Nov, Sun, 1000-1800, Wed, 1400 1800. £1.00/ 75p/75p. Tel: (01621) 788647.*

Maldon District Museum, The Promenade Lodge, 47 Mill Road, Maldon: Small museum devoted to Maldon town and with many articles of general and domestic nature displayed in a charming, small Listed building. *Please telephone for opening times and admission prices. Tel: (01621) 852749 or 772103.*

MANNINGTREE **Manningtree & District Local History Museum,** Manningtree Library, High Street, Manningtree: Local History Museum with displays of old photographs, artifacts, books and local maps and plans. Some permanent displays with two major exhibitions of local interest each year (wartime, schools etc). The Museum provides a resource for local historical study by children and adults as well as an archive for research and a repository for the continuing acquisition of historical material. The public library is housed in what was the Corn Exchange of 1865. *All year, Fri, 1000-1200, 1400-1600; Sat, 1000-1200; closed Easter, 25 Dec, 1 Jan. Tel: (01206) 392747.* &

◎ MISTLEY **Essex Secret Bunker,** Crown Building, Shrublands Road, Mistley: The former Essex County Nuclear War HQ bunker. Just as it was as it came off the Official Secrets List. Communications rooms. Operations rooms, offices and dormitory. Radio room and the central command centre with all its original equipment and war telephones. Two cinemas show authentic cold war film never before seen and there is a main AV show theatre and presentation. A gift shop and cafe complete your visit to the unique world of official secrets all hidden inside this vast concrete bunker. *5 Apr-30 Sep, daily, 1000-1630 (last admission). £4.00/£2.00/£3.00. Tel: (01206) 392271.*

SAFFRON WALDEN

Fry Public Art Gallery, Bridge End Gardens, Castle Street, Saffron Walden: The gallery displays the artistic heritage of N W Essex featuring Edward Bawden, Eric Ravilious, Michael Rothenstein, John Aldridge, Michael Ayrton and others continuing to the present day, who have made a significant contribution to British art. Two or three changing exhibitions additionally. *7 Apr-27 Oct, Sat, Sun, Bank Holidays, 1445-1730. Easter Sun & Mon afternoons. Tel: (01799) 513779.* &

◎ **Saffron Walden Museum,** Museum Street, Saffron Walden: 150 year old museum of local history, decorative arts, ethnography, Great Hall gallery of archaelogy and early history. Ancient Egyptian room/tomb. New geology displays. Natural history collections. Norman castle ruins in grounds. *Mar-Oct, Mon-Sat, 1000-1700, Sun, Bank Holidays, 1430-1700; Nov-Feb, Mon-Sat, 1100-1600, Sun, Bank Holidays, 1430-1630; closed 24, 25 Dec; £1.00/50p. Tel: (01799) 510333.* &

SOUTHEND-ON-SEA

◎ **Central Museum & Planetarium,** Victoria Avenue, Southend-on-Sea: Edwardian building housing displays of archaeology, natural history, social and local history. Also houses only planet arium in South East of England outside London. *Museum all year, Mon, 1300-1700; Tue-Sat, 1000-1700; Planetarium open, Wed-Sat, 1000, 1100, 1200, 1400, 1500, 1600; closed 5, 8 Apr, 24 Dec-3 Jan; Museum free; Planetarium £2.00/£1.50/£1.50. Tel: (01702) 330214.*

◉ **Prittlewell Priory,** Priory Park, Victoria Avenue, Southend-on-Sea: Remains of 12th century priory with later additions. Displays of natural history, medieval religious life and radios, gramophones and TV's. Set in Priory Park about 200 yards from the entrance. *All year, Tue-Sat, 1000-1300, 1400-1700. Phone for details of Easter, Christmas and New Year opening. 50p/50p/50p. Tel: (01702) 342878.* ♿

◉ **Southchurch Hall Museum,** Southchurch Hall Gardens, Southchurch Hall Close, Southend-on-Sea: Moated timber-framed 13th and 14thC manor house set in attractive gardens. *All year, Tue-Sat, 1000-1300, 1400-1700; closed, 5-8 Apr; 24 Dec-3 Jan. Tel: (01702) 467671.* ♿

Southend Pier Museum, Southend Pier, Marine Parade, Southend-on-Sea: Being 1.33 miles long, Southend pier is the longest in the world. Originally built of English oak, it was first opened in 1830 as a commercial pier but quickly proved to be so popular as a pleasure pier, the old structure was replaced by the present iron pier in 1889. Its unique feature, apart from its length, has always been its various forms of transport, from hand carts to horsedrawn tram to electric trams and trains and now diesel trains. The piers history is vast and fascinating and the museum depicts this in its entirety using train and pictorial exhibits. *11 May-27 Oct, Fri-Mon, 1100-1730; 1 Jul-31 Aug, Fri-Mon, 1100-1830. 50p/free/50p. Tel: (01702) 611214.* ♿

◉ STANSTED **House on the Hill Toy Museum,** Stansted Mountfitchet: Exciting, animated Toy Museum covering 7,000 sqft featuring a huge collection of toys from Victorian times to the 1970's, offering a nostalgic trip back to childhood. Many animated displays. *17 Mar-10 Nov, daily, 1000-1600; Weekends and School Holidays throughout the Winter. Closed 24-26 Dec. £3.00/£2.00/£2.50. Tel: (01279) 813237.*

THAXTED **Thaxted Guildhall,** Town Street, Thaxted: 15thC building, permanent display of old photographs and relics mainly relating to history of Thaxted. Exhibs on some weekends. Small museum. *Easter-Sep, Sun, 1400-1800; Bank Hol weekends, 1100-1800. 25p/10p. Tel: (01371) 831339.*

WALTHAM ABBEY **Epping Forest District Museum,** 39-41 Sun Street, Waltham Abbey: A lively community museum covering the social history of the Epping Forest district. Permanent and temporary exhibition galleries include exhibition of Victorian life, and varied programme ranging from contemporary art to historical spectaculars. Workshops for children and adults, special events, shop. *All year, Fri-Mon, 1400-1700, Tue, 1200-1700; closed 24, 25 Dec, 1 Jan. Tel: (01992) 716882.*

WALTON-ON-THE-NAZE **Walton Maritime Museum,** East Terrace: 100 year old former lifeboat house, carefully restored. Exhibitions of local interest change annually eg. maritime, urban, seaside, development etc. *23 Jul-31 Aug, daily, 1400-1700. £1.00/free/50p.* ♿

◉ WESTCLIFF-ON-SEA **Beecroft Art Gallery,** Station Road: A local topographical collection of watercolours, oils, prints etc. plus occasional displays of works from the permanent collection of 16th-20thC contemporary art. Varied programme of temporary exhibitions, both local and regional. *Tue-Sat, 0930-1700; Closed Sun-Tue of a Bank Holiday, Easter, Christmas and New Year. Tel: (01702) 347418.* ♿

WEST MERSEA **Mersea Island Museum,** High Street, West Mersea: Local history, natural history, display of methods and tools used in marine, and wildlife. fishing equipment, social history, fossils and mineral display. Special exhibitions. *1 May-29 Sept, Wed-Sun, 1400-1700. 50p/25p/25p. Tel: (01206) 385191.* ♿

Hertfordshire

BISHOPS STORTFORD

Rhodes Memorial Museum and Commonwealth Centre, South Road, Bishop's Stortford: Birthplace of Cecil John Rhodes, founder of Rhodesia. Two Victorian villas made to look as one. 15 rooms with photographs, portraits and memorabilia of Rhodes' life and times. Refurbished in 1992. *All year, Tue-Sat, 1000-1600, closed all bank holidays. £1.00/free/50p. Tel: (01279) 651746.*

HATFIELD **Mill Green Museum and Mill,** Mill Green, Hatfield: 18thC Watermill, restored to working order, museum in Miller's House, local and social history, archaeology, craft tools and Victorian kitchen. *All year, Tue-Fri, 1000-1700, Sat, Sun, Bank Hols, 1400-1700. Closed 25, 26 Dec. Tel: (01707) 271362.* ♿

◉ HERTFORD **Hertford Museum,** 18 Bull Plain, Hertford: 17th century building with main exhibits on the archaeology, natural history and local history of Hertfordshire. Collection of Hertfordshire Regiment. Changing exhibitions. Jacobean garden plus activity room for pre-booked schools/groups. *All year, Tue-Sat, 1000-1700; closed Bank Hols. Tel: (01992) 582686.* ♿

ROYSTON **Royston and District Museum,** Lower King Street, Royston: Small local history museum housed in former Congregational church, with regularly changing exhibitions, 20thC ceramics and glass, Royston embroidery project. *All year, Wed, Thu, Sat, 1000-1700; last visitors at 1645; 3 Mar-27 Oct, Sun and Bank Hol Mon, 1400-1700; Tel: (01763) 242587.*

ST ALBANS

Museum of St Albans, Hatfield Road, St Albans: Discover the long history of St Albans town at the gate of a Medieval Abbey, coaching centre, market town, manufacturing centre and commuter city. Story told through lively new displays opened in 1990 and the Salaman Gallery of Trade & Craft Tools and regular special exhibition. *All year, Mon-Sat, 1000-1700, Sun, 1400-1700. Please trephone for Christmas opening times. Tel: (01727) 819340.* ♿

◉ **Verulamium Museum,** St Michaels, St Albans: Verulamium Museum is the museum of everyday life in Roman Britain. The award-winning displays include re-created Roman interiors, access to computer databases, 'hands-on' areas, excavation videos and accessible collections of glass, pottery, jewellery, coins as well as magnificent mosaics, wall paintings and reconstructions of the City of Verulamium. *All year, Mon-Sat, 1000-1700 (last admission), Sun, 1400-1700 (last admission); Closed 25, 26 Dec. £2.50/£1.75/£1.75. Tel: (01727) 819339.* ♿

WARE **Ware Museum,** The Priory Lodge, 89 High Street, Ware: An independent museum, featuring the 'Story of Ware' and temporary displays on the town's history. Exhibits include Mesolithic and Roman finds, including Roman jewellery and a 'slave shackle', and tools associated with Ware's importance as a malting centre from the 18th-20th centuries. Many publications are on sale associated with Ware and Hertfordshire. *1 Apr-30 Sep, Sat, 1100-1700, Sun, 1400-1600; 1 Oct-31 Mar, Sat, 1100-1600, Sun, 1400-1600. Tel: (01920) 487848.* ♿

Norfolk

ALBY

Alby Bottle Museum, Alby Craft Centre, Cromer Road, Erpingham: The Bottle Museum is part of a large craft complex complete with gallery, working craftsmen and gardens. Coaches welcome by prior arrangement if possible. *1 Mar-31 Dec, Tue-Sun, Bank Hol Mon, 1000-1700. 30p/10p. Tel: (01263) 761327.*

Alby Lace Museum and Study Centre/Stitches & Lace, Alby Craft Centre, Cromer Road, Alby Hill: Wide variety of lace exhibits up to 300 years old, easily studied with magnifying glasses provided. Lacemaker's cottage shows conditions under which lace would have been made in late Victorian times. Memorabilia and some modern lace on display. Bobbin lace demonstrated and sold, wide variety of equipment, books etc. for sale. DMC main agent for all embroidery supplies. *New Year-mid Mar, Sun only, mid Mar-Christmas, Tue-Fri, Sun, 1000-1700 . Tel: (01263) 768002.* ♿

BURSTON **Burston Strike School,** Burston: Scene of the longest strike in British History - 25 years. Building erected to house scholars of strike school. Interpretative exhibit of artefacts, documents and photographs. *All year, daily, 0700-dusk. Tel: (01379) 741565.* ♿

COCKLEY CLEY **Iceni Village and Museums,** Cockley Cley: Nestling in a valley on a Breckland country estate lies the picturesque Iceni village and museums complex. Comprising a reconstruction of an Iceni tribal village, a medieval cottage/forge with museum. A Saxon church c630AD and carriage, vintage engine and farm museums. Nature trail by a stream and a lake completes this most attractive and unique venue. *31 Mar-31 Oct, daily, 1000-1730. £2.80/£1.30/£1.80. Tel: (01760) 724588.* ♿

Museums

CROMER

Cromer Lifeboat Museum and Lifeboat, The Pier and Gangway, Cromer: In the museum is found the Oakley class lifeboat H F Bailey which served at Cromer from 1935 to 1947 in which Henry Bloggs served as Coxwain. This boat and crew saved 818 lives. The history of Cromer lifeboats is displayed in pictures, models, photographs. Henry Bloggs' medals are also on display. The present lifeboat 'Ruby and Arthur Read II' is a new Tyne Class lifeboat and can be viewed at the Lifeboat house on the pier at the same times as the museum. *5 Apr-31 Oct, daily, 1000-1600. Tel: (01263) 512503.* &

◎ **Cromer Museum,** East Cottages, Tucker Street, Cromer: Late Victorian fisherman's cottage, displays on local history (fishing, bathing resort) geology, natural history archaeology. *All year, Mon-Sat, 1000-1700, (closed for lunch, Mon, 1300-1400), Sun 1400-1700; closed 5 Apr, 23-26 Dec, 1 Jan. £1.00/50p/60p. Tel: (01263) 513543.*

DEREHAM

Bishop Bonners Cottage Museum, St Withburga Lane, East Dereham: Built 1502. Framed building. Walls of brick, flint, wattle and daub. Thatched roof, coloured pargetting. Collection of artefacts and bygones from local trades and industries. Local personalities include William Cowper, George Barrow and William Hyde Wollaston. *1 May-1 Oct, Tue-Sat, 1430-1700.*

Hobbies Museum of Fretwork & Craft Centre, 34-36 Swaffham Road, Dereham: Museum of fretwork machines dating back to 1900, magazines and hobbies weeklies from 1895 and samples of old fretwork designs. *9 Apr-31 Aug, Mon-Fri, 1000-1200, 1400-1600. Tel: (01362) 692985.* &

DISS **Diss Museum,** Market Place, Diss: Ever changing displays in our tiny museum reflect the history of Diss and its local area. See Victorian photos, work tools and clothing in the historic Shambles building. *All year, Wed, Thu, 1400-1600, Fri, Sat, 1030-1630; Closed 5 Apr, Bank Hol and 25 Dec-1 Jan. Tel: (01379) 650618.*

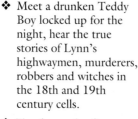

◎ DOWNHAM MARKET **Bridge Farm** - A Country Christmas, River Ouse Bank: Bridge Farm is a working arable farm with over a mile of frontage to the River Ouse. It is on the site of a medieval hermitage and there is the Hermitage Pilgrims Hall. The Chapel of the Nativity is unique. The main feature is a journey back to Dickens' Christmas with Victorian street scenes. The visit concludes in the Barbara Cartland room with a 'hot tot' of Norfolk Punch.

ERPINGHAM **Hawk & Owl Trust National Centre for Owl Conservation,** Wolterton Park, Norwich: An exciting walk-through display explaining in words and photographs the ecology and life style of the barn owl, and showing other British owls and birds of prey. There is also a Raptor Ramble (approximately 2 miles) within the private grounds of Wolterton Park on which examples of conservation can be seen. *7 Apr-30 Oct, Wed, Fri, Sun, Bank Holiday Mon, 1200-1700. Tel: (01263) 761718.* &

FAKENHAM **Museum of Gas and Local History,** Hempton Road, Fakenham: Complete small town gasworks with local history section; displays of working gas meters and ancillary exhibits. *8-11 Apr, 6-9 May, 27 May-19 Sep, Tue, Thu, and Bank Hol Mon, 1030-1530 (last admission 1500). £1.50/25p/£1.00. Tel: (01328) 863150.* &

GREAT YARMOUTH

◎ **Elizabethan House Museum,** 4 South Quay, Great Yarmouth: Merchant's house with late Georgian front and 16C panelled rooms. Exhibits showing 19C domestic life; Victorian toys; Lowestoft porcelain and glass. *1-14 Apr, daily except Sat and Good Fri, 1000-1700, Sun 1400-1700; 17 May-30 Sep, daily except Sat, 1000-1700. £1.00/50p/60p. Tel: (01493) 855746.*

◎ **Maritime Museum,** Marine Parade, Great Yarmouth: Maritime history of Norfolk, with herring fishery and Norfolk wherry, large collection of ship models. World War II and Home Front exhibition. *1-14 Apr, Mon-Fri except 5 Apr, 1000-1700, Sun, 1400-1700; 27 May-30 Sep, daily except Sat, 1000-1700. £1.00/50p/60p. Tel: (01493) 842267.*

◎ **North West Tower,** North Quay, Gt Yarmouth: Medieval Tower which was originally part of the towns walls of Great Yarmouth. Exhibition about trading wherries, traditional craft used on the Broads. Broads information Centre. *Please telephone for opening times. Tel: (01493) 332095.*

◎ **Old Merchant's House,** (EH) Row 111, South Quay, Great Yarmouth: Typical 17C town houses. One with splendid plaster ceilings contains of local architectural and domestic fittings salvages from other 'Row' houses. *1 Apr-1 Oct, daily but telephone to confirm days and times. £1.30/70p/£1.00. Tel: (01493) 857900.*

◎ **Tolhouse Museum,** Tolhouse Street, Great Yarmouth: One of the oldest municipal buildings in England. Once the towns courthouse and gaol, prison cells can still be seen. Displays illustrating the long history of the town. *1-14 Apr, daily except Sat and Good Fri, 1000-1700, Sun, 1400-1700; 27 May-29 Sep, daily except Sat, 1000-1700. 50p/30p/40p. Tel: (01493) 858900.*

◎ GRESSENHALL **Norfolk Rural Life Museum,** Beech House, Gressenhall: Former workhouse illustrating history of Norfolk over last 200 years. Union Farm is a working 1920s farm with traditional breeds of livestock. Crafts and exhibits, special events and activities, exhibitions. *1 Apr-31 Oct, Mon-Sat, 1000-1700, Sun, 1200-1730. £3.50/£1.50/£2.50. Tel: (01362) 860563.* &

HARLESTON **Harleston Museum,** King Georges Hall, Broad Street, Harleston: Exhibition of items of historical interest relating to Harleston and district. *1 May-30 Sep, Wed, 1000-1200, 1400-1600; Sat, 1000-1200.*

KING'S LYNN

◎ **Guildhall of St George,** 27 King Street, King's Lynn: Regional Arts Centre. Medieval Guildhall now houses theatre. Regular programme of daytime and evening events for people of all ages; film, concerts, galleries and annual Arts Festival. *All year, Mon-Fri, 1000-1600; Sat, 1000-1230, 1400-1530; 10 Jun-13 Jul, 1000-1230; closed all Bank Hol Mon, 5 Apr, 25, 26, Dec, 1 Jan. Guildhall is not usually open when performances are on. Refer to King's Lynn Arts centre brochure for details or contact box office on (01553) 773578. Galleries closed Sun and Mon. 50p/25p/50p. Tel: (01553) 774725.*

◎ **Lynn Museum,** Market Street, King's Lynn: Mid-Victorian church, includes natural history, archaeology, local history; also temporary exhibitions. *All year, Mon-Sat, 1000-1700. Closed all Bank Holiday Mondays and Public Holidays. 60p/30p/40p. Tel: (01553) 775001.* &

◎ **Tales of the Old Gaol House,** The Old Gaol House, Saturday Market Place, King's Lynn: 'The Tales of the Old Gaol House', King's Lynn, charts the history of Crime and Punishment over the last 3 centuries. Once through the Gaol House the tour takes you into the Undercroft of the Trinity Guildhall to view the King John Cup, Four Maces, Royal Charters and Mayoral Insignia. *5 Apr-31 Oct, daily, 1000-1700; 1 Nov-Good Fri '97, Fri-Tue, 1000-1700. Closed 25,26 Dec. £2.00/£1.50/£1.50. Tel: (01553) 763044.* &

◎ **Town House Museum of Lynn Life,** 46 Queen Street, King's Lynn: Discover the merchants, tradesmen and families who for nine hundred years have made Lynn such a prosperous place. The past comes to life in historic room displays, including costume, toys, a working Victorian kitchen and a 1950's living room. *1 May-30 Sep, daily except Mon, 1000-1700, Sun 1400-1700; 1 Oct-30 Apr, Tues-Sat, 1000-1600. £1.00/50p/60p. Tel: (01553) 773450.* &

◎ **True's Yard Heritage Centre,** 3-5 North Street, King's Lynn: Two fully restored fisherman's cottages with research facilities for tracing ancestry in Kings Lynn, museum, gift shop and tea room. *All year, daily, 0930-1630; closed 25 Dec. £1.90/£1.00/£1.50. Tel: (01553) 770479.* &

LITTLE DUNHAM **Dunham Museum,** Little Dunham: Exhibition building showing collection of old working tools and machinery. Dairy, Leathersmith, Shoemakers. Bygones. *All year, Sun, 1000-1700. 50p/free/free. Tel: (01760) 723073.* &

◎ LITTLE WALSINGHAM **Shirehall Museum,** Common Place, Little Walsingham: A Georgian country courthouse, local museum and tourist information centre. *4 Apr-30 Sep, Mon-Sat, 1000-1700 (closed Mon 1300-1400), Sun 1400-1700; 1-31 Oct, Sat, Sun only. 60p/30p/40p. Tel: (01328) 820510.*

LUDHAM **Toad Hole Cottage Museum,** How Hill, Ludham: 18C building; 5 small rooms plus Broads information area. Cottage museum giving impression of home and working life of a family on the marshes, about 100 years ago. *5 Apr-31 May, daily, 1100-1700, 1 June-30 Sep, 1000-1800, Oct, daily, 1100-1700. Tel: (01692) 678763.*

NORWICH

◎ **Bridewell Museum of Norwich Trades & Industries,** Bridewell Alley, Norwich: Display illustrating local industry during the past 200 years. *All year, Tue-Sat, 1000-1700, 1 May-30 Sep, 22 Dec, Sun, 1400-1700; Closed 5 Apr, 23-26 Dec. £1.40/70p/£1.20. Tel: (01603) 667228.*

◎ **Castle Museum,** Castle Hill, Norwich: Large Collection of art (including an important collection by Norwich School artists). Large collection of British Ceramic Teapots. Archaeology, natural history, temporary exhibitions. Early 12thC Castle Keep. Tour battlements and dungeons. *All year, Mon-Sat, 1000-1700, Sun, 1400-1700; closed 5 Apr, 23-26 Dec, 1 Jan. £2.20/£1.00/£1.50(95). Tel: (01603) 223624.* &

Inspire Hands-On Science Centre, St Michael's Church, Coslany Street, Norwich: Inspire is a hands-on science centre housed in a Medieval Church. Suitable for all ages it allows everyone to explore and discover the wonders of science for themselves. Features regular new hands-on exhibitions and special events. *All year, Tue-Sun 1000-1700; closed 24 Dec-2 Jan. £2.50/£2.00/£2.00. Tel: (01603) 612612.*

The Norwich Gallery, Norwich School of Art and Design, St Georges Street, Norwich: The Norwich Gallery exhibits the work of living artists who come to Norwich to install their exhibitions. There is a comprehensive programme of talks, seminars and events for the public. The emphasis is on providing exhibitions of new work for the public with ten exhibitions a year featuring artists of an International reputation. The longer EAST International open exhibition runs through the Summer. *Telephone for opening times. Tel: (01603) 610561.* &

◎ **Royal Norfolk Regimental Museum,** Shirehall, Market Avenue, Norwich: Displays devoted to the history of the County Regiment from 1685. Includes the daily life of a soldier. Audio-visual displays and

graphics complement the collection. Linked to Castle Museum by prisoners' tunnel and a reconstructed 1st World War communication trench. *All year, Mon-Sat, 1000-1700, Sun, 1400-1700; closed 5 Apr, 24-27 Dec, 1 Jan. £2.20/£1.00/£1.50. Tel: (01603) 223649.*

◎ **Sainsbury Centre for Visual Arts,** University of East Anglia, Norwich: The Robert and Lisa Sainsbury Collection is wide-ranging, remarkable and of international importance. With the recent addition of Sir Norman Foster & Partners superb Crescent Wing 700 paintings, sculptures and ceramics are on permanent display with Picasso, Moore, Bacon and Giacometti shown alongside art from Africa, the Pacific and the Americas. The Centre also houses the Anderson Collection of Art Nouveau. Three special exhibitions a year. The Centre has a restaurant, buffet and coffee bar and is accessible to disabled visitors. *All year, Tue-Sun, 1200-1700; closed 23 Dec-2 Jan 1997. £1.00/50p/50p. Tel: (01603) 456060.* &

◎ **Saint Peter Hungate Church Museum,** Princes Street, Norwich: 15C church with fine hammerbeam roof and Norwich painted glass. Displays on art and craft in service of Christianity. Illuminated books, brasses, musical instruments. *All year, Tue-Sat, 1000-1700, Sun 1400-1700; Closed 5 Apr, 23-26 Dec. Tel: (01603) 667231.* &

◎ **Strangers' Hall Museum of Domestic Life,** Charing Cross, Norwich: Late medieval town house with furnished rooms illustrating tastes and fashions 16th-19th century. Fine costume and textile collection. *All year, Tue-Sat, Bank Holiday Mon, 1000-1700; May-Sep, Sun, 1400-1700; Closed 5 Apr. £1.40/70p/£1.20. Tel: (01603) 667229.*

SHERINGHAM **Sheringham Museum,** Station Road, Sheringham: Local history museum. All things to do with the social history and life of the town. *1 Apr-End Dec, Tue-Sat, 1000-1600, Sun, Bank Holidays, 1400-1630. Sat, Sun only in Nov. Tel: (01263) 822895.*

SWAFFHAM **Swaffham Museum,** Town Hall, London Street, Swaffham: 18th century building, formerly brewers' main house. Local history museum with significant temporary exhibitions. Displays on local heroes: Howard Carter and the discovery of Tutankhamen's Tomb, W E Johns, author of Biggles; Admiral Sir Kynvet Wilson VC. *1 Apr-31 Oct, Tue-Sat, 1100-1300, 1400-1600. 50p/free. Tel: (01760) 721230.*

THETFORD

◎ **Ancient House Museum,** White Hart Street, Thetford: A museum of Thetford and Breckland life in a remarkable early Tudor House. Displays on local history, flint, archaeology and natural history. Herb garden in courtyard with Tudor plants. The building is noted for its fine carved oak ceilings. Museum is also the local Tourist Information Point with displays and leaflets. Occasional temporary exhibitions and special events. *All year, Mon-Sat, 1000-1700, (closed Mon 1300-1400); additionally 26 May-29 Sep, Sun, 1400-1700; closed 5 Apr, 24-26 December. 60p/30p/40p. Tel: (01842) 752599.*

Museums

Charles Burrell Museum, Minstergate, Thetford: The Museum draws together an impressive collection of exhibits to tell the story of Charles Burrell & Son, a name once famous throughout the world. The large exhibits are housed on the ground floor, together with a series of re-created workshops with original tools and machinery. Up in the gallery a series of photographs, letters and documents tell the story of the company and of the Burrell Family. *30 Mar-27 Oct, Sat, Sun, 1000-1700. Telephone for admission prices. Tel: (01842) 751166.* &

WELLS-NEXT-THE-SEA ◎ **Bygones Collection.** See Holkham Hall entry under Historic Houses.

WYMONDHAM **Heritage Museum,** Bridewell, Norwich Road, Wymondham: The museum established in 1984 and has exhibits of local origin. Displays are generally changed annually or biannually. *Telephone for times and prices as museum moving location. Tel: (01953) 604650.*

Suffolk

ALDEBURGH **Moot Hall and Museum,** Aldeburgh: 16th century Town Hall which is a listed ancient building with museum containing items of local interest. Photographs and artefacts depicting life in Aldeburgh with emphasis on fishing industry and the part played by the lifeboat and its crews. *1 Apr-31 May, Sat, Sun, 1430-1700; Jun, Sep, Oct, daily, 1430-1700; Jul, Aug, daily, 1030-1230, 1430-1700. 45p/free/45p. Tel: (01728) 452871.*

BECCLES **Beccles & District Museum,** Former Sir John Leman School Building, Ballygate, Beccles: Varied items - printing, Waveney, agricultural costumes, cultural and domestic varied items. *7 Apr-31 Oct, daily, 1430-1700; closed Mon except Bank Holidays. Tel: (01502) 712941.*

BUNGAY **Bungay Museum,** Waveney District Council Office, Broad Street, Bungay: Two small rooms upstairs. *All year, Mon-Fri, 0900-1300, 1400-1600. 50p/free/30p. Tel: (01986) 892176.*

BURY ST EDMUNDS

Abbey Visitor Centre, Samons Tower, Abbey Precinct, Bury St Edmunds: The Abbey Visitor Centre is housed in Samsons Tower, part of the west front of the now ruined Abbey of St Edmund. The Centre has displays reflecting major aspects of the Abbey's long history including objects found on the site. The interpretation is completed with the use of displays, a model of the Abbey and an audio tour. *Apr, Oct, daily, 1000-1700; May, Sep, daily, 1000-1800; 1 Jun-31 Aug, daily, 1000-2000; 1 Nov-31 Mar, Wed-Sat, 1000-1600; Sun, 1200-1600. 80p/60p/60p. Tel: (01284) 763100.*

Bury St Edmunds Art Gallery, Cornhill, Bury St Edmunds: Market Cross. Robert Adam's only public building in the East of England, a magnificent cruciform gallery space, now using the upper floor for changing exhibitions of painting and applied arts. Small area devoted to sale of art books, prints postcards, wood, ceramics, glass and jewellery. *All year, Tue-Fri, 1030-1700; Sat 1030-1630; Closed 25 Dec-8 Jan. 50p/30p/30p. Tel: (01284) 762081.* &

◎ **Manor House,** Honey Hill, Bury St Edmunds: Collection of clocks and watches, fine and decorative arts, of national importance in magnificent 16th and 18thC buildings. *All year, daily, 1000-1700, Sun 1400-1700; closed 5 Apr, 25, 26 Dec. £2.50/£1.50/£1.50. Tel: (01284) 757072.* &

◎ **Moyse's Hall Museum,** Cornhill, Bury St Edmunds: Norman domestic building containing local history, archaeology of West Suffolk. Relics of Maria Marten Red Barn Murder. Temporary exhibitions. *All year, daily, 1000-1700, Sun 1400-1700; Closed 5 Apr, 25, 26 Dec. £1.25/75p/75p. Tel: (01284) 757488.* &

CAVENDISH **Sue Ryder Foundation Museum,** Sue Ryder Foundation Headquarters, Cavendish: Displays showing the reason for establishing the Sue Ryder Foundation and its work, past, present and future. *All year, daily 1000-1730, closed 25 Dec. 80p/40p/40p. Tel: (01787) 280252.* &

COTTON **Mechanical Music Museum Trust,** Blacksmith Road, Cotton: A large selection of mechanical musical items the small music boxes, polyphones and organettes, larger street pianos and player organs and the large fair organs, dance band and cafe organs plus a number of unusual items and the Wurlitzer theatre pipe organ, housed in a purpose built building with the interior roof adorned with hundreds of old records and horned gramophones. *2 Jun-29 Sep, Sun, 1430-1750; 6 Oct, 1000-1700. £3.00/£1.00/£3.00. Tel: (01449) 613876.* &

DUNWICH
Dunwich Museum, St James's Street, Dunwich: History of Dunwich from Roman times chronicling its disappearance into the sea. Local wildlife. *Mar, Sat, Sun, 1400-1630; Apr-Sep, daily, 1130-1630; Oct, daily, 1200-1600. Tel: (01728) 648796.* &

FRAMLINGHAM
Lanman Museum, Framlingham Castle, Framlingham: Rural exhibits relating to everyday life in Framlingham and surrounding area, including paintings and photographs. *6 Apr-30 Oct, Tue-Sat, 1030- 1300, 1400-1630, Sun, Mon, 1400-1630. 40p/20p/20p.*

HALESWORTH **Halesworth & District Museum,** The Almshouses, Steeple End, Halesworth: Two rooms in 17th century almshouses plus former fire engine shed adjacent to library and under art gallery. Local geology and archaeology including fossils, prehistoric flint and medieval finds from recent excavations. Farming, rural life and local history exhibitions. *1 May-30 Sep; Wed, 1030-1230, 1400-1630; Sat, 1030-1230; Sun and Bank Hol, 1400-1630. Tel: (01986) 873030.*

HAVERHILL **Haverhill and District Local History Centre,** Town Hall, High Street, Haverhill: A collection of over 2000 items relating to Haverhill & District. Also a vast collection of photographs. *All year, Tue, 1900-2100; Wed, 1400-1600; Thu, Fri, 1400-1600, 1900-2100; Sat, 1030-1530. Tel: (01440) 714962.*

IPSWICH

◎ **Christchurch Mansion,** Christchurch Park, Ipswich: Fine Tudor Mansion built between 1548 and 1550, later additions. Good collection of furniture, panelling and ceramics, clocks and paintings from 16-19thC. Suffolk Artists' gallery, lively temporary exhibition programme in Wolsey Art Gallery. *All year, daily except Mon, 1000-1700, Sun, 1430-1630; closes at dusk in winter. Open 6-8 Apr, 27-31 Dec; closed 5 Apr, 24-26 Dec. £2.50/£1.00/£1.00. Tel: (01473) 253246.* &

◎ **Ipswich Museum and Gallery,** High Street, Ipswich: Roman Suffolk galleries, Peoples of the world. Suffolk geology, Ogilvie Bird Gallery, Victorian Natural History Gallery, Suffolk Wildlife Gallery. *All year, Tue-Sat, 1000-1700. £1.00/50p/50p. Tel: (01473) 213761.* &

Moyse's Hall Museum, Bury St Edmunds, Suffolk

⊚ **Tolly Cobbold Brewery & The Brewery Tap,** Cliff Road, Ipswich: Taste the malt and smell the hops on a fully guided tour of this magnificent Victorian Brewery. Follow the brewing process and see the many brewing artefacts, some dating back to 1723 when Thomas Cobbold founded the Brewery. Key exhibits include a steam engine, the cooperage, malt and hop displays and the oldest brewing vessel in the world. Afterwards relax in the Brewery Tap pub and enjoy a complimentary glass of beer. Featured on the BBC programme 'Troubleshooter with Sir John Harvey-Jones'. *Jan-5 Apr, Oct-Dec, Fri, 1200; 6 Apr-30 Sep, daily, 1200. £3.75. Tel: (01473) 231723.*

⊚ LAVENHAM **Guildhall of Corpus Christi,** (NT) Market Place, Lavenham: Impressive timber framed building dating from 1520s. originally hall of Guild of Corpus Christi, now local museum with information on medieval wool trade. *23 Mar-3 Nov, daily, 1100-1700; closed 5 Apr, 25 Dec. £2.60/70p/70p. Tel: (01787) 247646.*

LOWESTOFT **Lowestoft Museum,** Broad House, Nicholas Everitt Park, Lowestoft: Local history, Lowestoft china, fossils, flint implements, medieval artefacts from local sites. Domestic history. *1-14 Apr, 20 May-6 Oct, Mon-Sat, 1030-1300, 1400-1700, Sun 1400-1700; 20 Apr-19 May, Sat, Sun, 1400-1700; 12-27 Oct, Sat, Sun, 1400-1600; Autumn half term week, Mon-Sat, 1030-1300, 1400-1600, Sun, 1400-1600. Tel: (01502) 511457.* ᕒ

MILDENHALL **Mildenhall and District Museum,** 6 King Street, Mildenhall: Local voluntary Museum housed in early 19C. Cottages with modern extensions. Exhibitions on RAF Mildenhall, Fenland and Breckland. Includes local archaelogy and local history. *1 Mar-24 Dec, Wed, Thu, Sat, Sun, 1430-1630; Fri, 1100-1600. Tel: (01638) 716970.* ᕒ

⊚ NEWMARKET **National Horseracing Museum,** 99 High Street, Newmarket: 5 permanent galleries of fine paintings, bronzes, memorabilia and trophies relating to the development of horse racing. Temporary exhibitions to supplement the permanent exhibition. Two galleries of works the property of the British Sporting Art Trust. Equine tours by arrangement to studs, racing yards and training facilities. *2 Apr-8 Dec, Tue-Sat, 1000-1700; Sun, 1200-1600; Bank Hol Mon and Mon in Jul and Aug 1000-1700. £3.30/£1.00/£2.00. Tel: (01638) 667333.* ᕒ

ORFORD

Dunwich Underwater Exploration Exhibition, The Orford Craft Shop, Orford: The Exhibition has been extended to include 'Suffolk Underwater Studies' (on a temporary basis, until suitable accom is found). Exhibits showing progress in the underwater exploration of the former city and underwater studies off the Suffolk Coast. *All year, daily, 1030-1700; closed 25, 26 Dec. 50p/50p/50p. Tel: (01394) 450678.*

Orford Museum, Rear of Crown & Castle Hotel, Orford: Exhibits, photos, articles showing the history of Orford and District. Special exhibits for 1996 will include a display of Borough Regalia over one weekend to be decided. *1 Apr-30 Sep, daily, 1400-1600. 50p/free/50p.*

SHOTLEY **HMS Ganges Association Museum,** Unit 4 & 5, Shotley Marina, Shotley Gate: The Museum is an old building of the original HMS Ganges 'Stone Frigate' which closed in 1976. It was a training establishment for boys of the age 15-16 years and was closed when the school leaving age rose to 16. There are still boys who trained there serving in the modern navy. *1 Apr-31 Sep, Sat, Sun, 1100-1700.* ᕒ

⊚ SIZEWELL **Sizewell Visitors Centre,** Sizewell B Power Station, Sizewell: Visitor centre giving details about all aspects of electricity generation. *All year, daily, 1000-1600; closed Bank Hol, 25, 26 Dec, 1 Jan. Tel: (01728) 642139.* ᕒ

SOUTHWOLD **Lifeboat Museum,** Gun Hill, Southwold: RNLI models, photographs of lifeboat, relics from old boats. *27 May-30 Sep, daily 1430-1630; open Easter Week subject to weather. Tel: (01502) 722422.*

Southwold Museum, Bartholomew Green, Southwold: Local history, archaeology and natural history. Exhibits relating to Southwold railway, and Battle of Sole Bay. Domestic bygones. *5 Apr-30 Sep, daily, 1430-1630. Tel: (01502) 723725.* ᕒ

Southwold Sailors Reading Room, East Cliff, Southwold: Building of character where retired seamen have a social club and reading room. Maritime exhibits and local history. *All year, daily, 0900-1730, later in summer.*

⊚ STOWMARKET **Museum of East Anglian Life,** Stowmarket: 70 acres of superb Suffolk countryside in the centre of Stowmarket housing collections of historic buildings, domestic life, agriculture, industrial history and crafts. The famous Suffolk breeds of animal can be seen around the site - horses, pigs, sheep and cattle. A nature walk alongside the river provides a view over traditional water meadows. Bring a picnic or eat in the Museum refreshment room and calculate that your visit will last 4½ hours. *31 March-27 Oct excluding Mon (except Bank Holidays) in April, May & Oct. Telephone for admission prices. Tel: (01449) 612229.* ᕒ

⊚ SUDBURY **Gainsborough's House,** 46 Gainsborough Street, Sudbury: Gainsborough's House is a well established arts centre in the birthplace of Thomas Gainsborough RA (1727-88). The Georgian fronted town house, with an attractive walled garden, displays more of the artist's work than any other Gallery. The collection is shown together with 18C furniture and memorabilia in chronological sequence following the artist's career. Commitment to contemporary art is reflected in a varied programme of exhibitions throughout the year. Fine art, photography, craft, printmaking and highlighting in particular work of East Anglian artists. *1 Apr-30 Oct, daily except Mon, 1000-1700, Sun, Bank Hol Mon, 1400-1700; 1 Nov-31 Mar, daily except Mon, 1000-1600, Sun, Bank Hol Mon, 1400-1600; closed 5 Apr, 24 Dec-1 Jan. £2.50/£1.25/£2.00. Tel: (01787) 372958.* ᕒ

WOODBRIDGE

Suffolk Horse Museum, The Market Hill, Woodbridge: An indoor exhibition about the Suffolk Punch Breed of Heavy Horse. This illustrates the history of the breed through paintings, photographs and exhibits, and shows how the breed was used. It includes shoeing, harness, the life of the horseman and depicts how Suffolks are bred and used today. *5 Apr-30 Sep, daily, 1400-1700. £1.50/80p/80p. Tel: (01394) 380643.*

Woodbridge Museum, 5 Market Hill, Woodbridge: Sutton Hoo, Burrow Hill and other exhibits which change each year. *6 Apr-30 Oct, Thu-Sat, Bank Hol Mon, 1000-1600, Sun, 1430-1630; 1 May-30 Sep, daily except Wed, 1000-1600. Sun, 1430-1630. 50p/20p/50p. Tel: (01394) 380502.*

WOOLPIT **Bygones Museum,** The Institute, Woolpit: 17thC timber framed building with one permanent display of brickmaking and other displays changing yearly depicting life of a Suffolk village. *6 Apr-29 Sep, Sat, Sun, Bank Hol Mon, 1430-1700; Closed 25 Dec, 1 Jan. Tel: (01359) 240822.*

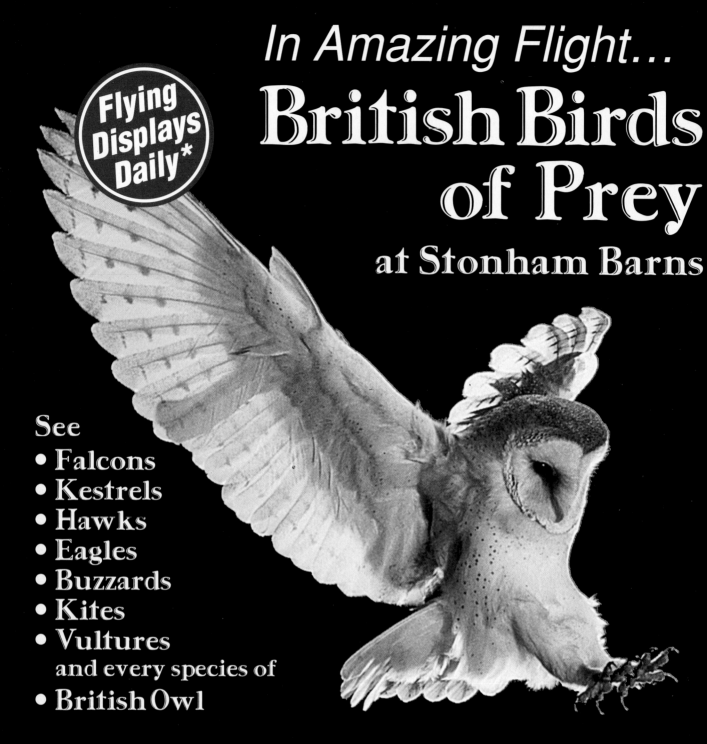

In Amazing Flight...

British Birds of Prey

at Stonham Barns

Flying Displays Daily*

See
- Falcons
- Kestrels
- Hawks
- Eagles
- Buzzards
- Kites
- Vultures

and every species of
- British Owl

A GREAT NEW FAMILY ATTRACTION INCLUDING*

★ Up to Five Different Flying Shows Daily ★ Indoor & Outdoor Flying Arenas ★ Large Aviaries featuring Rare & Popular Birds of Prey from Britain and Around the World ★ The Owl Barn & Every Species of British Owl ★ Information Centre ★ Children's Activity Programmes ★ Play & Picnic Areas ★ Lecture Areas ★ Bird Handling & Management Courses ★ Large Car & Coach Park ★ Café ★ Gift Shop & Bookshop ★ Easy Access for the Disabled.

Stonham Barns
STONHAM ASPAL, A1120 SUFFOLK
(just off the main road between Ipswich & Norwich)

Photo: Kim Taylor @ Bruce Coleman.

*Outdoor Flying Displays subject to weather conditions.

Animal Collections

Bedfordshire

⊛ **Mead Open Farm & Rare Breeds,** Stanbridge Road, Billington, Leighton Buzzard: A working farm with a wide range of traditional farm animals and rare breeds. Pets corner, childrens play area and tea room. Animals housed in farm buildings and paddocks. *1 Mar-31 Oct, daily exc. Mon (exc. Bank Hol), 1000-1700. £2.50/£1.50/£2.00. Tel: (01525) 852954.* &

⊛ **Toddington Manor**, Toddington: Beautiful gardens and woods with lakes (given 'star' in Good Gardens Guide 1994) covering an area of 20 acres. Rare breeds of livestock, vintage tractors. Very peaceful and natural surroundings. Well kept but not very commercial. Excellent for children and for all the family. Cricket matches on pitch in front of house at weekends. Good contact with animals - they roam freely amongst visitors. A truly relaxing day reminiscent of a gentler life. *10 Apr-29 Sep, Wed-Sun, 1100-1800; closed Mon and Tue including Bank Hols. £3.50/£1.50/£2.50. Tel: (01525) 873924.* &

Whipsnade Wild Animal Park, Zoological Society of London, Dunstable: Whipsnade is a conservation centre for rare and endangered species as well a home to chimps, bears, zebras penguins and tigers. Animals are housed in spacious paddocks providing a near natural environment. Daily events include Birds of the World, Sealions Demonstrations and Elephant Encounters. Children's Farm, Runwild Playcentre, BP Bear Maze and Great Whipsnade Railway. Special events throughout the season such as Hunt the Easter Egg and August Teddy's Party. *All year, daily, 1000-1600; closed 25 Dec. £7.60/£5.50/£6.30 (95). Tel: (01582) 872171.* &

⊛ **Woburn Safari Park,** Woburn Park, Woburn: Drive-through safari park and Wild World leisure area boating lake, pets corner, and parrot, sea lion and elephant show. Adventure Ark adventure playground, wild watch computer centre. All inc. except Great Woburn Railway. New walk-through aviary, feed the birds nectar at Rainbow Landing. *2 Mar-27 Oct, daily, 0900-1700; Winter weekends 1100-1500, weather permitting; phone for Christmas opening times. £.90/£5.40/£.5/40 (95). Tel: (01525) 290407.* &

Woodside Farm & Wildfowl Park, Mancroft Road, Slip End: 6 acre park with farm shop, poultry centre, arts and crafts centre, wildfowl collection, rare breeds centre, farm animals, children's play area and coffee shop. Waterfowl area, large indoor rabbit warren. *All year, daily excl. Sun, 0800-1730, Closed 25 and 26 Dec, 1 Jan. £1.70/£1.30£1.30. Tel: (01582) 841044.* &

Cambridgeshire

Grays Honey Farm, Cross Drove, Warboys: Bee and honey exhibition showing rural and modern beekeeping around the world. Beekeeping video. Bees can be seen at work in the different observation hives. A Black Forest model railway layout shows how bees talk to each other. Make your own beeswax candles - no heat required. Picnic area includes Guinea piggery and Aviary. *31 Mar-24 Dec, daily except Sun, 1030-1800. £1.00/50p£1.00. Tel: (01354) 693798.*

⊛ **Hamerton Wildlife Centre,** Hamerton: Lemurs, marmosets, meerkats, wallabies, unique bird collection with rare and exotic species from around the world. Also gibbons, sloths, wildcats. Adventure playground. Gift shop/coffee shop and covered picnic area. *All year, daily, 1030-1600 winter; 1030-1800, summer. Closed 25 Dec. Please telephone for prices. Tel: (01832) 293362.* &

⊛ **Home Farm,** (NT) Wimpole Hall, Arrington: 19th century thatched farm building with farm museum, video loft, rare breeds of cattle, sheep and pigs. Suffolk Punch horse wagon rides. *23 Mar-2 Nov, daily except Mon, Fri (excluding Bank Hol), 1030-1700; 3 Nov-Mar 97, Sat, Sun, 1030-1700. £3.90/£2.20/£3.90. Tel: (01223) 207257.*

Linton Zoo, Hadstock Road, Linton: A wonderful combination of beautiful gardens and wildlife from all over the world. Lots to see including big cats, lynx, binturongs, tapir, zebra, parrots, owls, cranes, giant tortoises, snakes, tarantula spiders and many others - set in 16 acres. *All year, daily, 1000-1800 or dusk; Last admission 45 mins pre-closing; closed 25 Dec. £4.00/£3.00/£3.75 (95). Tel: (01223) 891308.* &

Peakirk Waterfowl Gardens Trust, Peakirk: Flock of Chilean flamingos and some 122 species of duck, geese and swans in 20 acres of water gardens. Refreshment room and shop. Nature walk and elevated picnic area, childrens play area, disabled access throughout. *All year, daily, 0930-1730; closed 24, 25 Dec. £2.50/£1.50/£1.50. Tel: (01733) 252271.* &

The Raptor Foundation, 490 Hern Road, Ramsey St Marys: The Raptor Foundation provides life care to injured birds of prey and wild disabled birds. Has a collection of hand reared owls used for fund raising for the hospital. Photographers and artists alike can capture these wonderful birds on film or canvas in pleasant surroundings and enjoy the hospitality of our tea room and gift shop. *All year, daily, 1000-1830 summer, 1000-1730 winter; Closed 22 Dec-2 Jan. Tel: (01733) 844266.*

Sacrewell Farm & Country Centre, Sacrewell, Thornhaugh: Children's play area with maze, trampolines etc. 500 acre farm, with working watermill, farmhouse gardens, shrubberies farm, nature and general interest trails, 18thC buildings, displays of farm, rural and domestic bygones. *All year, daily, 0930-1800 summer, 0930-dusk winter; closed 25 Dec. £3.00/£1.00/£2.00. Tel: (01780) 782222.*

Stags Holt Farm Park, Stags Holt, March: Victorian farm buildings set in ancient parkland. Visitors can see Suffolk Punches and farming bygones. Tea room. Traditional farm animals, picnic area; play area and caravan park. *5 Apr-30 Sep, daily except Mon (excluding Bank Holiday Mon), 1030-1700. £2.30/£1.20/£1.75. Tel: (01354) 52406.*

Willers Mill Wild Animal Sanctuary, Station Road, Shepreth: The Willersmill Wildlife Sanctuary was started in 1979 by Terry Willers to care for wild animals that were either road, gun and gassing casualties, unwanted pets or saved from the meat markets. In 1984 the sanctuary's fish farm opened to the public. To fund the work of running the Sanctuary, by 1988 Willersmill had grown into a fully fledged wildlife park with about 69000 visitors a year. Wolves, monkeys, owls, otters, pinemartens, very large carp and koi feed from your hands. *1 Apr-31 Oct, daily, 1000-1800; 1 Nov-31 Mar, daily, 1000-1700; closed 25 Dec. £3.50/£1.75/£2.75; Sun, Bank Hol £3.95/£2.00/£3.25. Tel: (01763) 262226.*

Wood Green Animal Shelters, King's Bush Farm, London Road, Godmanchester: Set within 50 acres, the shelter takes in 13,000 animals which are unwanted or injured each year, housing them in spacious runs until new homes can be found. Some, particularly farm and exotic animals eg. Llamas, Vietnamese Pot-Bellied Pigs, become permanent residents and they welcome visitors. Restaurant, Coffee Shop & picnic facilities. Pet Care Centre, Gift shop & Thrift Shop. Nature Trail to explore. Indoor Arena with special events including Riding & Driving for the Disabled. Access & facilities for the disabled. Ample Parking. Parties by appt. *All year, daily; Site, 0830-1700; Homing runs, 0900-1500. Tel: (01480) 830014.*

Essex

Ada Cole Memorial Stables, Broadlands, Broadley Common, Harlow: Stable yard and fields. Rescues horses, ponies, donkeys and mules. Sometimes young foals. Stable yard, gift shop. *All year, daily, 1400-1700; closed 25 Dec. Tel: (01992) 892133.*

Basildon Zoo, London Road, Vange: Birds of prey, patting pens, baby animals, cafe and gift shop. Big cats, otters, bats, sand pit, swings etc. Pet shop, birthday parties. *Winter 1000-dusk, Summer 1000-1800, last admission 1630. Closed 25, 26 Dec. £2.75/£1.50/£1.25. Tel: (01268) 553985.*

Capybara with babies, Willers Mill Wild Animal Sanctuary, Cambs

Colchester Zoo, Stanway, Maldon Road, Colchester: One of England's finest Zoological collections. 170 species set in 40 acres of natural parkland. Daily presentations include meet the elephants, snake handling, sealion, seal, parrot, penguin and falconry displays. Childrens pet area, two adventure play areas, road train. Restaurant, take away snack and ice cream kiosks, gift shops. New enclosures include Penguin Shores, Wilds of Asia for Orangutans, Serengeti Plains for African Lions. Winner of Best Essex Visitor attraction 4 years running. *All year, daily, 0930-until 1 hour before dusk. Closed 25 Dec. £6.50/£4.50/£5.00 (95). Tel: (01206) 330253.*

Dedham Rare Breed Farm, Mill Lane, Dedham: Dedham rare breeds farm is situated on 16 acres of land in the Dedham Vale. The animals are displayed in open paddocks and in buildings. Children's play area and paddock where they can touch the animals. Wide walk ways separate the field and pond, all of which are safely fenced. There is a large car park and picnic area, all set near the river Stour and only a short way from Flatford Mill. All children are given a bag of food to feed the animals. *2 Apr-27 Oct, daily 1000-1730. £3.00/£1.75/£2.50. Tel: (01206) 323111.*

Woburn Safari Park, Bedfordshire

Hayes Hill Farm, Stubbins Hall Lane, Crooked Mile, Waltham Abbey: Traditional farmyard - farm animals in pens and paddocks. Working commercial dairy and arable farm. Viewing at milking. Guided tours bookable in advance. *All year, daily, 1000-1630, Sat, Sun, 1000-1800 (dusk). £2.20/£1.60/£1.60. Tel: (0199289) 2291.*

Hobbs Cross Farm, Theydon Garnon: Modern working farm with 180 breeding sows, beef cattle, sheep, hens and chicks. Farm trail, adventure playground, straw jump, picnic area, blacksmith's forge. Licensed restaurant and farm shop. *All year, Mon-Fri, 0830-1700; Sat, Sun, 0830-1800, closed 25 Dec-3 Jan. £2.50/£2.00/£2.00. Tel: (01992) 814862.*

Jakapeni Rare Breeds Farm, Lillyville Farm, Burlington Gardens, Hullbridge: Working organic smallholding specialising in rare breed farm animals and poultry. Pets corner, picnic area, country walk, refreshments. 30 acres of rolling countryside. The farm has been specifically designed for customer access and offers the opportunity to touch and stroke the animals. There are staff on hand to talk about and advise on all aspects of animal welfare. The farm also caters for caravans, birthday parties and is available to groups to hire for country pursuits such as dog training, falconry, archery etc. *7 Apr-27 Oct, Sun, Bank Holiday Mon. £1.50/ 75p/75p. Tel: (01702) 232394.*

Layer Marney Tower, Layer Marney: See entry under Historic Houses.

Marsh Farm Country Park, Marsh Farm Road, South Woodham Ferrers: Farm Centre with beef cattle, sheep, pig unit, free range chickens, milking demos, adventure play area, nature reserve, walks picnic area and pets corner. Gift shop and tea rooms. *17 Feb-1 Nov, daily, 1000-1630, Sat, Sun, Bank Hol, 1000-1730; 2 Nov-15 Dec, Sat, Sun, 1000-1730; last adm. 30 minutes before closing. £2.25/£1.50/£1.50. Tel: (01245) 321552.*

Mistley Place Park Environmental and Animal Rescue, New Road, Mistley: 25 acres of woodlands, pastures and lakeside walks. Horses, sheep, goats, pigs, peacocks, turkeys, geese, ornamental fowl, rabbits and guinea pigs roam freely (where practical and safe) around the site. Nature trail and maze. Tearoom and shop. Majority of over 1000 animals and birds rescued from ill treatment, neglect or slaughter. *All year, daily, 1000-1730 (or Dusk). £2.00/£1.00/£1.00. Tel: (01206) 396483.*

Animal Collections

Mole Hall Wildlife Park, Widdington: Otters, chimps, guanaco, lemurs, wallabies, deer. owls, waterfowl etc. Butterfly pavilion. Attractive gardens. Picnic, play areas and pets corner. Park is in gardens and fields adjoining the fully moated Manor. House of Mole Hall has records dating back to 1287. *All year, daily, 1030-1800 summertime, 1030-dusk wintertime; closed 25 Dec. £4.00/£2.60/£3.20. Tel: (01799) 540400.*

Old MacDonalds Educational Farm Park, Weald Road, South Weald: Old MacDonalds Educational Farm Park has been created to offer a greater understanding of our British farm livestock, wildlife and countryside. The new buildings follow the traditional Essex barn style, set in 17 acres of pasture and woodland. Hard paths around the site ensure dry feet and access for wheelchairs. Many opportunities to get close to the birds and animals. Interpretation displayed on paddocks and pens to heighten the visitors awareness to the animals, picnic sites, playground, baby changing room, disabled toilets, first aid post are just a few of our facilities. *All year, daily, 1000-1800 in the Summer, 1000-Dusk in the Winter; Closed 25, 26 Dec. £2.50/£1.50/£2.00. Tel: (01277) 375177.*

SeaQuarium, Clacton Pier, 1 North Sea, Clacton-on-Sea: SeaQuarium enables visitors to come face to face with the world beneath the waves, 15 themed displays showing marine life from around the coast of the UK. Included is a chance to step back in time through the time tunnel illustrating Clacton of the past to the origins of the world. *1 Mar-19 Jul, daily, 1000-1700 (except 5-8 Apr, daily, 1000-1800); 20 Jul-1 Sep, daily, 0930-2200; 2 Sep-31 Oct, daily, 1000-1700; please telephone for opening arrangements during winter. £2.50/£1.50/£2.00. Tel: (01255) 422626.*

Southend Sea Life Centre, Eastern Esplanade, Southend-on-Sea: A Native Marine Aquarium takes you on a journey beneath the waves. The very latest in marine technology brings the secrets of the mysterious underwater world closer than ever before. An amazing underwater tunnel allows an all round view of some of the most sensational creatures ever seen in British waters, culminating in a thrilling interactive Shark Encounter. Discover hundreds of fascinating species displayed in natural surroundings. Follow the exciting Quiz Trail, explore the Touch Pool. *All year, daily, from 1000; closed 25 December. Please telephone for prices. Tel: (01702) 601834.*

Hertfordshire

Bowmans Open Farm, Coursers Road, London Colney: Bowmans is a working open farm of 1,100 acres. 360 cows, 250 pigs, sheep, shire horse, 500 chickens, 200 turkeys and rabbits, guinea pigs, ducks in the pets corner. There is a farm walk, nature trail. Facilities for picnics and barbeques plus two adventure playgrounds for the children. The farm shop sell freshly gathered produce and cards. The olde worlde style restaurant sells delicious snacks and refreshments. *Daily, 0900-1730. Closed 25, 26 Dec. £3.00/£2.00/£2.00. Tel: (01727) 822106.*

Paradise Wildlife Park, White Stubbs Lane, Broxbourne: Britain's most interactive wildlife park with many animal activities daily. An ideal place to learn about a range of animals including tigers, lions, monkeys, zebras, camels and many domestic animals. Also, many other attractions including woodland railway, crazy golf, children's rides (50p/ride) plus three themed adventure playgrounds, woodland walk, picnic areas, environmental education centre, cafeteria and restaurant. *All year, daily, 10001800 (last admission 1700). £4.50/£3.50/£4.00. Tel: (01992) 468001.*

Gray Wolf, Willers Mill Wild Animal Sanctuary, Cambridgeshire

India, Siberia, Essex?

Once You're in It's All in

Just one of 170 species at Colchester Zoo, this Siberian Tiger was born in England and resides in Essex. This picture was taken in Tiger Valley, one of Colchester Zoo's superb glass panelled enclosures, but you could be forgiven for thinking it was taken in the wild. Our aim is to create environments as close to nature as possible. Taking our animals' needs into consideration as well as yours. With 15 unique displays and a 'once you're in it's all in' policy we think you'll find that you can't have more fun than a day out at Colchester Zoo and that **You Can't get Closer to Nature.**

COLCHESTER ZOO MALDON ROAD STANWAY COLCHESTER ESSEX 01206 330253

Save £1 OFF TOTAL admission in a group of up to six people
Not valid in conjunction with any other offer, on bank holidays or in August VALID TO 30.11.96

COLCHESTER Zoo ...A CONSERVATION CENTRE

A new breed of Zoo

Lincolnshire

🦋 **Butterfly and Falconry Park**, Long Sutton: One of Britain's largest walk through butterfly houses. Hundreds of exotic butterflies. Insectarium. Gift shop, gardens, adventure playground, pets corner and picnic areas. In the attractive surroundings of the Park the Falconer gives two displays every day with eagles, owls and falcons. *1 Apr-31 Aug, daily, 1000-1800; 1 Sep-27 Oct, daily, 1000-1700. £3.80/£2.50/£3.50. Tel: (01406) 363833.* ♿

Norfolk

🦋 **Banham Zoo**, The Grove, Banham: See the wonders of the world's wildlife at Banham Zoo. Set in 25 acres of beautiful landscaped countryside, Banham provides a secure haven for animals and birds, some of which have reached near extinction in the wild. Daily animal feeding times and keeper talks are not only fun but educational too! Find out more about the Penguins, Seals and Squirrel Monkeys. Animals to be seen include Cheetahs, Snow Leopards, Grevy's Zebra, and an extensive collection of primates. Jungle clearing adventure playground, road train and all weather Activity and Information Centre. *All year; daily from 1000; closed 25, 26 Dec. Please telephone for prices. Tel: (01953) 887771.* ♿

Cranes Watering Farm & Shop, Rushall Road, Starston: This is a working farm, not a farm park, therefore it is very much a 'take us as you find us' sort of place. Some days there is a lot happening, other times a tour of the buildings/machinery may be all there is to offer. Wellies advisable. Pigs and cows always on site. Milking daily at 1600. Farmshop. Picnic lawn. Toilet. Space for a few caravans. Written guides and children's quiz, free. Small charge for groups which must pre-book, groups will be given a guided tour. *1 Feb-24 Dec, Tues, Wed, Fri, Sat 0900-1700. Please telephone for Easter and Christmas opening times. Tel: (01379) 852387.*

International League for the Protection of Horses, Anne Coluin House, Snetterton: Equine rest and rehabilitation centre. *All year, Sun, Wed, 1430-1600. Tel: (01953) 498682.*

Jungle Butterflies, Marine Parade, Central Seafront, Great Yarmouth: 5000 square yards of tropical gardens under glass with free flying butterflies, tarantula, scorpions, iguana and terrapins. Gift and souvenir shop. *1 Apr-31 Oct, daily, from 1000. £3.00/£1.50/£2.50. Tel: (01493) 842202.*

Norfolk Rare Breeds Centre, Decoy Farm house, Ormesby St Michael, Gt Yarmouth: Rare breeds of domestic farm animals, cattle, sheep, pigs, goats, poultry, donkeys, heavy horses and rabbits. Incubator and brooder on display. Info. area, shop and farm museum. *1 Apr-31 Oct, daily except Sat, 1100-1700; all year, Sun, 1100-1700. £2.50/£1.50/£2.00. Tel: (01493) 732990.* ♿

🦋 **Norfolk Shire Horse Centre**, West Runton Stables, West Runton: Shire horses demonstrated working twice daily. Native ponies, bygone collection of horse drawn machinery etc. Childrens farm. *31 Mar-27 Oct, daily except Sat (excluding Bank Holiday weekends) 1000-1700; £4.00/£2.25/£3.00. Tel: (01263) 837339.* ♿

Norfolk Shire Horse Centre

Norfolk Wildlife Centre and Country Park, Great Witchingham: Large collection of British and European wildlife exhibited in spacious natural enclosures in 40 acres of parkland. Unique team of trained reindeer pull their wheeled sledge or cart round the park most afternoons giving free rides to children. Commando and adventure play areas. Clear-water carp pool. Mystery rides on the woodland steam railway. Model farm with rare domestic breeds, where many of the animals are tame enough to be stroked. Attractive tea room, gift shop, picnic areas, peacock lawn and free car park. This is not a zoo. *1 Apr-31 Oct, daily, 1000-1800. Please telephone for prices. Tel: (01603) 872274.* ♿

Otter Trust, Earsham: World's largest collection of otters exhibited under near natural conditions. Trust specialises in breeding European Otters in captivity for re-introduction into the wild and its collection of British Otters is unique. Set in beautiful surroundings on banks of the river Waveney, riverside walks, picnic areas, copses with Muntjac Deer and Chinese Water deer, three lakes with large collection of European wildfowl, attractive Visitor Centre, incl. tea room and gift shop. *1 Apr-31 Oct, daily, 1030-1800. £4.00/£2.50/£3.50 (95). Tel: (01986) 893470.*

Overa House Farm Equine Rest and Rehabilitation Centre, Larling: Stable yard and paddocks. Horses, ponies and donkeys can be seen. Exhibition room and lecture theatre. Video of the work on the International League for the Protection of Horses. *6 Apr-29 Sept, Wed, Thu, Sat, Sun, Bank Hol, 1100-1600; Winter, Wed, Sun, 1430-1600; closed 25, 26 Dec. Tel: (01953) 717309.*

Woburn Safari Park, Bedfordshire

🦋 **Park Farm & Norfolk Farmyard Crafts Centre**, Snettisham: Discover Park Farm, whatever the weather, 45 min safari tours into red deer park, archaeological and discovery trails, sheep centre, gigantic adventure play area, indoor animal barn, lambs, calves, piglets, chickens, pets area. Information room, '5000 Years of Farming at Park Farm' film. 329 acres of farming fun, wildlife, horse riding centre. Craft centre in beautifully restored farm building with workshops, art gallery, orchard tea room and gift shop. *All year, daily, 1000-1700. entrance or safari £3.50/£2.50/£3.00; entrance and safari £6.00/£4.00/£5.00. Tel: (01485) 542425.* ♿

🦋 **Pensthorpe Waterfowl Park**, Pensthorpe: A world of wild and endangered waterbirds in 200 acre nature reserve. Courtyard Gallery and audio-visual centre, featuring wildlife, photographic, painting and craft exhibitions. Conservation gift shop. Licensed restaurant. Heated wildlife observation gallery, Children's adventure playground. Free car and coach parking. One of the largest waterfowl collections in the world. Many endangered species. Woodland, meadow, lakeside and riverside nature trails. Disabled access. Water gardens. Party bookings welcome. *Jan-Mar, Sat, Sun, 1100-1600; Apr-Dec, daily 1100-1700 (1100-1600 winter months). Tel: (01328) 851465.* ♿

Redwings Horse Sanctuary, Hill Top Farm, Hall Lane, Frettenham: Visitors are able to meet the rescued horses and ponies. Stalls, craft shops, bric-a-brac and refreshments. *5-8 Apr, daily, 1300-1700; 14 Apr-30 Jun, Sun, Bank Hol Mon, 1300-1700; 1 Jul-26 Aug, Mon, 1300-1700; 1 Sep-8 Dec, Sun, 1300-1700. £2.00/£1.00/£1.00. Tel: (01603) 737432.* ♿

🦋 **Sea Life Centre**, Southern Promenade, Hunstanton: A breathtaking display of British marine life. Stroll around over 20 settings as you view more than 2,000 fish from 200 different species. The environments have been specifically designed to recreate their natural habitats. 50,000 gallons of water surround you in the ocean tunnel with creatures of the deep inches away. Observe both resident seals and pups in the process of being rehabilitated for their release back to the wild, in the seal pools. *All year, daily, from 1000, closed 25 Dec. Please phone for prices. Tel: (01485) 533576.* ♿

🦋 **Sea Life Centre**, Marine Parade, Great Yarmouth: Walk underwater tropical reef shark tank; sand tank with Ray fish and British sharks, plus 25 themed displays depicting British marine life and local settings. Amazing display of tropical reef fish. *All year, daily, from 1000, closed 25 Dec. Please telephone for prices. Tel: (01493) 330631.* ♿

Animal Collections

◎ **Thrigby Hall Wildlife Gardens,** Thrigby Hall, Filby: Wide selection of Asian mammals, birds and reptiles, including tigers, crocodiles, storks, etc. 250 year old landscaped garden. Play area. Superb Willow Pattern Gardens. Dramatic New Swamp House for large crocodiles and other tropical swamp dwellers. *5 Apr-31 Oct, daily, 1000-1800, 1 Nov-Apr 97, 1000-1600. £4.50/£3.00/£4.00. Tel: (01493) 369 477.* &

◎ **The Tropical Butterfly Gardens,** Long Street Nursery, Gt Ellingham: The central attraction is the tropical butterfly gardens, with 2,400 sq feet of landscaped gardens, heated to a year round temperature of 75ºF. The gardens contain hundreds of tropical trees and flowers, and several hundred exotic tropical butterflies and birds flying freely around the visitors. Other attractions: a garden centre stocked with over 2000 different plant varieties, a gift shop and the Bamboo Coffee Shop, serving lunches, teas and light meals all day. *25 March-2 Nov, daily, 0900-1800, Sun, 1000-1800. Closed 25, 26 Dec. £2.45/£1.45/£2.15. Tel: (01953) 453175.* &

◎ **Junior Farm at Wroxham Barns,** Tunstead Road, Hoveton: Junior Farm where visitors can help feed and groom our friendly animals and collect freshly laid eggs. Part of a craft centre with 13 workshops, Gallery Craft and Gift Shop, Tea Rooms and Williamson's traditional family fair. *Daily 1000-1700, closed 25, 26 Dec. Farm entry £1.90. Tel: (01603) 783762.*

Suffolk

Baylham House Rare Breeds Farm, Baylham House Farm, Baylham, Ipswich: Small farm, located on a scheduled Roman site, maintaining breeding groups of rare farm animals; cattle, pigs, sheep and poultry. Walks through paddocks and along riverside. Children's paddock with friendly animals. Calves, piglets, lambs and chicks in season. Picnic area. Visitor's centre providing information on rare breeds and the Roman site, together with refreshments, gifts and cards. Special activity events as appropriate, e.g. shearing, foot trimming, lambing and calving. *2 Apr-29 Sep, daily, 1100-1700; closed Mon except Bank Hol. £2.75/£1.50/£2.00. Tel: (01473) 830264.*

British Birds of Prey & Conservation Centre at Stonham Barns, Pettaugh Road, Stonham Aspal: The Centre offers a variety of attractions including flying displays of Owls and Raptors daily, indoor facilities during bad weather, a comprehensive information centre, aviaries featuring most species of British Owls and Raptors, conservation and activity projects for children, a gift shop, kiddies play area and a cafe on site. *All year, daily, Jan-May, 1030-1700; May-Sep, 1030-1730; Oct-Dec, 1030-1700; Closed 25 Dec. £2.95/£2.00/£2.00. Tel: (01449) 711425.*

Cow Wise, Meadow Farm, West Stow: A modern working dairy farm with Friesian and Jersey cows, calves, goats, lambs, and free range hens. Visitors can see cows milked from a specially constructed gallery. Touch table, freshwater life, sense boxes. *Mar, Sun; 7, 8 Apr, 5, 6, 26, 27 May, 25, 26, 27, 28 All Aug; 1400-1700. £2.00/£1.50. Tel: (01284) 728862.* &

'Remus', Museum of East Anglian Life, Stowmarket

◎ **Museum of East Anglian Life,** Stowmarket: Suffolk breeds of animals can be seen on the 70 acre site in the centre of Stowmarket. 'Remus' the Suffolk Punch Horse together with 'Blackie' his Shetland pony companion enjoy stables here. 'Remus' can often be seen working on the site. Suffolk Red Poll cattle enjoy lush pastures near the river and Suffolk sheep thrive amid the tranquil setting. See entry under Museums for opening times and admission prices. *Tel: (01449) 612229.*

◎ **Easton Farm Park**, Easton, Wickham Market: Victorian farm setting for many species of farm animals incl. rare breeds. Modern milking unit, Victorian dairy, Suffolk horses. Farm trail. Food and farming exhib. Pets paddock. *24 Mar-30 Sep, daily. £3.85/£2.20/£3.15. Tel: (01728) 746475.* &

◎ **Kentwell Hall,** Long Melford: Mellow red brick house surrounded by moat. Rare breed domestic farm animals in tranquil setting around timber framed farm buildings. See entry under Historic Houses for opening times and prices. *Tel: (01787) 310207.*

◎ **Rede Hall Farm Park,** Rede Hall Farm, Rede: Working farm based on agricultural life of the 1930-50's including working Suffolk horses, use of agricultural implements and wagons. Management of cattle and sheep of the era. Working farrier shop. Cafeteria and gift shop. Children's pets corner and play area. Nature trail, cart ride Bygones and working displays of seasonal farm activities. *1 Apr-30 Sep, daily, 1000-1730; 22-24 Dec 1996, evening Christmas Celebration. £3.00/£1.50/£1.75. Tel: (01284) 850695.* &

◎ **Suffolk Wildlife Park,** Kessingland: Enjoy a walking safari among rare and endangered African wildlife and animals from around the world. You can see Zebra, Cheetahs, Chimpanzees, Arabian Oryx, Ankole Cattle, Sitatunga, Bontebok and many exotic birds. See how the African Lions and Ring Tailed Lemurs are fed and cared for, plus the chance to talk to the keepers. Take the Safari Road Train or follow one of the three explorer trails around the park; Livingstone, Stanley and Baker; each one varies in length. Indoor amusement centre; Explorers cafeteria with patio seating; baby changing/nursing facilities. *Daily, 1000. Closed 25, 26 Dec. Please telephone for prices. Tel: (01502) 740291.* &

Valley Farm Camargue Horses, Valley Farm Riding and Driving Centre, Wickham Market: Britain's only herd of breeding Camargue horses from the South of France as featured on Television. Also the well televised white animal collection, including Gobi the Arabian Dromedary and Baa Baa the driving sheep of the BBC's 'That's Life'. *All year, daily except Wed, 1000-1600; closed 25, 26 Dec, 1 Jan. Tel: (01728) 746916.*

Experience a day out that will stay with you for the rest of your life.

No memory will remain with you for quite so long as a visit to one of East Anglia's English Heritage sites of historical interest. Whether you're holidaying at home, or visiting from abroad, there's something for everyone to experience.

While 'Palace' is usually only associated with royalty, **Audley End** in Essex was a 17th century palace in all but name. Built by Thomas Howard, Earl of Suffolk, later owners had rooms designed by Robert Adam and landscaping by Capability Brown. On the east front of the house, the early Victorian garden has been recently restored by English Heritage.

Essex also boasts England's largest example of 17th century military engineering.

Tilbury Fort houses an exhibition demonstrating how it protected London from attack by the sea.

Once as common a site in Norfolk as they still are in Holland, windmills are a rarity now. The **Berney Arms Windmill** has seven floors and is visible for miles around. One of the largest remaining marsh mills in Norfolk, it was in use until 1951.

Still rising to its full height is the elaborately decorated west front of the 12th century church of **Castle Acre Priory**. Other remains include the prior's lodgings and his chapel. The walled herb garden is definitely not to be missed.

Another fine example of 12th century architecture can be found at **Castle Rising Castle**. The keep with many walls still intact in set in defensive earthworks.

One of the only English Heritage sites to be found underground is **Grime's Graves**, a unique Neolithic flint mine. You can descend into a shaft by ladder to see where flint for knives and axes was excavated.

One of the lesser known, yet fascinating attractions of the busy seaside resort of Great Yarmouth, is The **Old Merchant's House**, one of two 17th century row houses, with a display of local architectural detail.

Far from being the fairytale castle that it appears, **Framlingham Castle** in Suffolk has been a fortress, an Elizabethan prison, a work house and a school. Still remarkably intact, this 12th century castle's curtain walls link 13 towers, you can walk the entire circuit and enjoy superb views of Framlingham and nearby lake.

The first view of **Orford Castle** will be its immense keep, stretching 90 feet skywards. But inside this 12th century royal castle you'll find fascinating rooms to explore.

At first glance, it doesn't look real. But **Saxtead Green Post Mill** is still very much in working order. And you can have the run of the mill; study the machinery and climb the stairs to the top.

If you'd like further information about English Heritage's 400 sites and the 1996 Visitor's Guide, call English Heritage Customer Services on 0171 973 3434, or write to English Heritage Customer Services Dept, PO Box 9019, London W1A 0JA.

Orford Castle

Castle Rising Castle

Berney Arms Windmill

Audley End

Castle Acre Priory

Framlingham Castle

ENGLISH HERITAGE
A Legendary Day Out

Ancient Monuments

Bedfordshire

⚜ **Bushmead Priory,** (EH) Colmworth: Small Augustinian priory founded c1195. Magnificent 13thC timber roof of crown-post construction. Medieval wall paintings and stained glass. *Jul-Aug weekends only, 1000-1800; closed between 1300-1400. £1.30/70p/£1.00. Tel: (01234) 376614.*

⚜ **De Grey Mausoleum,** (EH) Flitton: Large mortuary chapel of the Greys of Wrest Park, containing some fine sculptured tombs and funeral monuments. All year, Sat, Sun, key may be obtained from keykeeper at *3 Highfield Road, access through Flitton church. Tel: (01536) 402840.*

⚜ **Houghton House,** (EH) Ampthill: Ruins of 17th century country house built on the 'heights' near Ampthill. Believed to be 'The House Beautiful' in Bunyan's 'Pilgrim's Progress'. Includes work attributed to Inigo Jones. *Any reasonable time . Tel: (01536) 402840.* ♿

Cambridgeshire

Cambridge American Cemetery, Coton: Visitors reception building for information, graves area and Memorial Chapel. Operated and maintained by The American Battle Monuments Commission. *16 Apr-30 Sep, daily, 0800-1800; 1 Oct-15 Apr, daily, 0800-1700. Tel: (01954) 210350.*

⚜ **Denny Abbey,** (EH) Ely Road, Chittering: Remains of 12thC church and 14thC dining hall of religious house. Run as hospital by Knights Templar. Became Franciscan Convent in 1342. *1 Apr-30 Sep, Sat, Sun, 1000-1800; closed 1300-1400. £1.50/80p/£1.10. Tel: (01223) 860489.* ♿

⚜ **Duxford Chapel,** (EH) Whittlesford: 14th century chapel once part of the hospital of St John. Keys available from Audley End House. *Tel: (01799) 522842.*

⚜ **Ely Cathedral,** Chapter House, The College, Ely: One of England's finest Cathedrals. The Octagon is the crowning glory. Guided tours and tours of Octagon and West Towers available in summer. Brass Rubbing and Stained Glass Museum. *Summer: daily, 0700-1900, Sun, 0730-1700. Winter: Daily, 0730-1800, Sun, 0730-1700; No facilities Good Friday & Christmas Day. £3.00/£2.20/£2.20. Tel: (01353) 667735.* ♿

⚜ **Flag Fen Bronze Age Excavations,** Fourth Drove, Fengate: Semi floating visitor centre, with Museum of the Bronze Age, gift shop and cafe. Facilitates entry into Bronze age landscape, roundhouses, primitive animals and one of the most important excavations ongoing in Europe today. Has to be seen! Preservation Hall housing 3000 year old remains in situ, surrounded by a 60m mural of the Bronze Age Landscape. *All year, daily except 25, 26 Dec, 1100-1600. £2.80/£1.95/£2.55. Tel: (01733) 313414.* ♿

⚜ **Isleham Priory Church,** (EH) Isleham: Norman church with much 'herringbone' masonry. *Any reasonable time.*

Kings College Chapel, Kings College, Cambridge: The exhibition in Northern side chapels shows why and how the chapel was built in pictures, works of art and models. *All year, Mid Mar-Mid Oct, daily, 0930-1630, Sun, 1000-1700; Mid Oct-Mid Mar, daily, 0930-1530; Tourists are advised to check with the local TIC or College before visiting the Chapel. £2.00/£1.00/£2.00. Tel: College (01223) 331100; TIC (01223) 322640.* ♿

⚜ **Longthorpe Tower,** (EH) Thorpe Road, Longthorpe: 14th century tower of a manor house. The wall paintings form the most complete set of domestic paintings of the period, in England. Exhibitions are held from time to time by local artists. *Jul, Aug, weekends only, 1000-1800. £1.00/50p/80p. Tel: (01733) 268482.*

Peterborough Cathedral

⚜ **Peterborough Cathedral,** 14 Minster Precincts, Peterborough: Magnificent Norman Cathedral with early English West Front and perpendicular retrochoir. 13thC painted nave ceiling. Tomb of Catherine of Aragon, former burial place of Mary Queen of Scots. Saxon sculpture. *All year, daily, 0830-1815 (2000 in summer); closed to tourists 5 Apr 1200-1500, 7 Apr 0830-1200, 25 Dec. Tel: (01733) 343342.* ♿

⚜ **Ramsey Abbey Gatehouse,** (NT) Abbey School, Ramsey: Ruins of 15thC gatehouse. *1 Apr-31 Oct, daily, 1000-1700. Tel: (01263) 733471.*

Saint Ives Bridge Chapel, Bridge Street, St Ives: St Ives Bridge and Chapel was built in the 1420's. It is a superb example of a very rare kind of building, with the midstream chapel rising directly from the waters of the Great Ouse, and views all round of the river and the historic St Ives Quay. The hatches through which bridge tolls were passed into the chapel can still be seen, as can the rebuilt arches on the south side of the bridge, a relic of the Civil War when the bridge was broken and replaced with a drawbridge, to defend the line of the river against attack by the Royalists. *All year, daily, 1000-1700; 1 May-30 Sep, Sun, 1400-1700; closed 5, 8 Apr and Bank Holidays. Tel: (01480) 465101.* ♿

Saint Wendreda's Church, Church Street, March: The church is noted for it's exceptional double hammer-beam timber roof which contains 120 carved angels. *All year, daily, 0930-1600. Key accessible at nearby shop, which is signed on church notice board.* ♿

Thorney Abbey Church, Thorney, Peterborough: Norman nave (c1100). Fine church organ originally built in 1787-1790. *All year, daily, 1000-dusk. Tel: (01733) 270388.*

Colchester Castle, Essex

Essex

⚜ **Chelmsford Cathedral,** Cathedral Office, Guy Harlings, Chelmsford: Medieval church, reordered in 1984 blending old and new. Modern sculpture, tapestry etc. All year, daily, 0800-1800. Tel: (01245) 263660. ♿

⚜ **Colchester Castle,** Colchester: See entry under Museums section.

⚜ **Cressing Temple,** Witham Road, Braintree: Site of Knights Templar settlement from 1137. Two magnificent timber-framed barns survive from that period. The Barley Barn circa 1200 and the Wheat Barn circa 1250. The site has connections with many of the great moments of England's past, sacked during the Peasants Revolt (1381) and threatened again during the Civil War. Tudor Court Hall, Granary and stables on show. Interpretive exhibition and beautiful Tudor style walled garden. *7 Apr-30 Sep, Mon-Fri, 0930-1630, Sun, 1000-1730; 7 Apr, 1000-1700; 8 Apr, 1400-1630. £3.00/£1.50/£1.50. Tel: (01376) 584903.* ♿

⚜ **Grange Barn,** (NT) Coggeshall: Restored 12th century barn. Earliest surviving timber framed barn in Europe. Small collection of early 20th century farm carts and wagons. *31 Mar-13 Oct, Sun, Tue, Thu, Bank Holiday Mon, 1300-1700 £1.50/75p/£1.50. Tel: (01376) 562226.*

⚜ **Hadleigh Castle,** (EH) Hadleigh: Familiar from Constable's picture, the castle stands on a bluff overlooking the Leigh Marshes. Single large tower 50 feet high. 13thC and 14thC remains. At any reasonable time. *Tel: (01702) 555632.*

Harwich Redoubt, Main Road, Harwich: Anti Napoleonic circular fort commanding harbour. *1 Jan-31 May, Sun, 1000-1300, 1400-1700, 1 Jun-31 Aug, daily 1000-1300, 1400-1700, 1 Sep-31 Dec, Sun, 1000-1300, 1400-1700; closed Easter, Christmas, New Year. £1.00/free/£1.00. Tel: (01255) 503429.*

Ancient Monuments

☼ **Hedingham Castle**, Castle Hedingham: Splendid Norman keep built in 1140 by the famous de Veres, Earls of Oxford. Approached by lovely Tudor bridge. Visited Kings Henry VII and VIII and Queen Elizabeth I, and besieged by King John. Magnificent Banqueting Hall with Minstrels' Gallery and finest Norman arch in England. Beautiful grounds, peaceful woodland and lakeside walks. Beside medieval village with fine Norman Church. *5 Apr, Bank Holiday Mondays, 1000-1700; For all other opening times please telephone.* £2.75/£1.75/£2.50. Tel: (01787) 460261.

Leez Priory, Hartford End: Scheduled Ancient Monument comprising 13thC Priory ruin and 16thC red brick Tudor Mansion and tower. 15 acres parkland, lakes, walled gardens and extensive Tudor tunnels. Oak panelled Great Hall and other public rooms available for private parties. *Open Bank Holidays and Wed evenings but see local press and telephone first to ensure opening.* £3.50/£2.00/£2.00. Tel: (01245) 362555. ⓑ

☼ **Mistley Towers**, (EH) Mistley: Two towers designed by Robert Adam in 1776 as part of the Parish Church. A rare example of Robert Adam's ecclesiastical work. *Any reasonable time. Key available on application to area Manager.* Tel: (01536) 402840.

☼ **Mountfitchet Castle,** Stansted Mountfitchet: Re-constructed Norman Motte and Bailey. Castle and village of Domesday period. Grand hall, church, prison, siege tower and weapons, domestic animals roam site. *17 Mar-10 Nov, daily, 1000-1700; Closed Christmas/New Year.* £3.85/£2.85/£3.50. Tel: (01279) 813237. ⓑ

Parish Church Of St Mary The Virgin And All Saints, Stambridge Road, Great Stambridge: St Mary The Virgin And All Saints is of outstanding historical, architectural and national importance. Of pre-Conquest origin, this Saxon building was founded by St Cedd and his followers in AD653. Beautifully restored Victorian interior with fine 19/20thC glass. Of particular interest is the outstanding Henry Holiday window depicting Faith and Charity, one of only 8 examples of his work in the country. Important stained glass window commemorating John Winthrop, 1st Governor of Massachusetts and founder of Boston who led great Puritan migration in 1630. *31 Mar-31 Oct, daily, 0900-1700, Sun 0900-1030, 1200- 1700; 1 Nov-30 Mar, daily, 0900-1600, Sun 0900-1030, 1200-1700.* Tel: (01702) 258272. ⓑ

☼ **Saint Botolphs Priory,** (EH) Colchester: Remains of 12thC priory near town centre. Nave with impressive arcaded west end, of the first Augustinian priory in England. *At any reasonable time.* Tel: (01728) 621330.

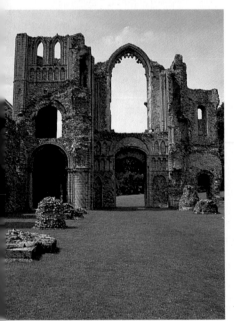

Castle Acre Priory, Norfolk

☼ **Tilbury Fort,** (EH) No 2 Office Block, The Fort, Tilbury: One of Henry VIII's coastal forts. Remodelled and extended in the 17thC in continental style. The best and largest example of 17th century military engineering in England, showing development of fortifications over the following 200 years. Exhibitions, the powder magazine and bunker-like 'casemates' show how the fort protected London from seaborne attack. *1 Apr-30 Sep, daily, 1000-1800, 10 Oct-31 Mar, Wed-Sun, 1000-1600; closed 1300-1400 for lunch throughout season; closed 24-26 Dec, 1 Jan.* £2.00/£1.00/£1.50. Tel: (01375) 858489. ⓑ

Waltham Abbey Church, Highbridge Street, Waltham Abbey: Norman church. Reputed site of King Harold's tomb. Lady Chapel with crypt. Crypt houses exhibition of history of Waltham Abbey, and shop. *All year, daily, 1000-1600 (GMT), 1000-1800 (BST); Wed 1100-1600; Sun 1200-1600.* Tel: (01992) 767897. ⓑ

Hertfordshire

☼ **Berkhamsted Castle,** (EH) Berkhamsted: extensive remains of 11th century motte and bailey castle. The work of Robert of Mortain, half brother of William of Normandy who learnt he was King here. *All year, daily, 1000-1600.* Tel: (01536) 402840.

☼ **Castle Mound,** The Castle Gardens, Bishop's Stortford: The remaining mound of a castle built by William I set in a pleasant spot in the gardens minutes from town centre. Key to gate available from Bishop's Stortford District Council. *All year, Mon-Fri, 0900-1600.* Tel: (01279) 655261.

☼ **Cathedral and Abbey Church of St Alban,** The Chapter House, St Albans: Norman Abbey church on the site of Martyrdom of St Alban, Britain's first Christian martyr in the third century AD. A Benedictine monastery was founded here by King Offa of Mercia in 793 AD. The present church was built in 1077 with Roman brick from nearby Verulamium. The 14th century shrine of St Albans has been recently restored and is a centre of ecumenical worship. A thriving parish church which since 1877 has been cathedral of the diocese of St Albans serving the people of Hertfordshire and Bedfordshire. Acclaimed multi-image audiovisual presentation 'The Martyr's Cathedral'. *29 Oct '95-30 Mar '96, daily, 0900-1745; 31 Mar-26 Oct, daily, 0900-1845.* Tel: (01727) 860780. ⓑ

Clock Tower, Market Cross, St Albans: Curfew Tower built in approximately 1405. Small exhibitions, aspects of local history, 1866 clock mechanism and belfry can be viewed. Fine views from roof. *5 Apr-15 Sep, Sat, Sun, Bank Hols, 1030-1700. Closed Christmas/New Year.* 25p/10p/25p. Tel: (01727) 860984.

☼ **Hertford Castle,** Hertford Tourist Information Centre, The Castle, Hertford: Norman motte, curtain walls constructed in the reign of Henry II. Gatehouse (known as 'The Castle') rebuilt between 1463 and 1465 in the reign of Edward IV. Attractive grounds with river running through (formerly part of the moat system). *Free band concerts and visits to the gatehouse on 1st Sun in months May-Sep, 1430-1700. Disabled access to gardens and ground floor.* Tel: (01992) 552885. ⓑ

Roman Theatre of Verulamium, Gorhambury, St Albans: The only completely exposed Roman theatre in Britain. Remains of town house and underground shrine. *Any reasonable time.*

Royston Cave, Melbourn Street, Royston: Man-made cave with medieval carvings made by Knights Templar dated around end of 13thC. Possibly a secret meeting place for initiation etc. *5 Apr-30 Sep, Sat, Sun, Bank Holiday Mon, 1430-1700; closed 25 Dec, 1 Jan.* £1.00/free/£1.00.

Scott's Grotto, Scott's Road, Ware: Grotto built in 1760 extending 67 feet into hill, making up 6 chambers. Features a covering of shells, ore and pebbles. The Grotto is unlit so torches are required. *1 Apr-30 Sep, 1400-1630.* Tel: (01920) 464131.

Norfolk

☼ **Baconsthorpe Castle,** (EH) Baconsthorpe: Guide books and postcards on sale at Baconsthorpe Post Office. 15th century semi-fortified house. The remains include the inner and outer gatehouse and curtain wall. *All year, daily, 1000-1600.*

Binham Priory, (EH) Binham: Remains of early 12th century Benedictine Priory. *At any reasonable time.*

Burgh Castle Church Farm, (EH) Burgh Castle, Great Yarmouth: One of the few monuments in private ownership. Can only be approached on foot. Info. and tearoom available only Easter to October. Remains of Roman fort, overlooking the River Waveney. *At any reasonable time.*

Caister Roman Town, (EH) Great Yarmouth: Remains of Roman commercial port. Footings of walls. *At any reasonable time.*

Castle Acre Castle, (EH) Castle Acre: Remains of a Norman manor house which became a castle. *At any reasonable time.*

Castle Acre Priory, (EH) Stocks Green, Castle Acre: Impressive ruins of Cluniac priory by William de Warenne, c1090. Church and decorated West front, 16th century gatehouse and priors lodging. *Please telephone for opening times and prices. Tel: (01760) 755394.*

Castle Rising Castle, (EH) Castle Rising: Fine mid 12th century keep with notable history. Set in the centre of a massive earthwork. Remains include bridge and gatehouse. *Please telephone for opening times and prices. Tel: (01553) 631330.*

Creake Abbey, (EH) Burnham Market: Remains of an Abbey church dating from 13th century, including presbytery and north transept with chapels. *Any reasonable time.*

Shrine of our Lady, Walsingham Abbey, Norfolk

Grimes Graves, (EH) Lynford: The wearing of a safety helmet is compulsory in accordance with safety regulations. Site exhibition. Remarkable Neolithic flint mines 4000 years old. First excavated in 1870s. Over 300 pits and shafts. One pit open to the public. 30ft deep - 7 radiating galleries. *Phone for opening times and prices.*

Nelson's Monument, South Beach Parade, Gt Yarmouth: Monument erected in honour of Nelson in 1819: 144 feet high, 217 steps to top. Views from top. *7 Jul-25 Aug, Sun, 1400-1700. 50p/30p/40p (95). Tel: (01493) 855746.*

New Buckenham Castle, New Buckenham: A Norman Mott and Bailey Castle and chapel with remains of later additions or other periods. A solid thick keep surrounded by an earthwork bailey some 40 ft high. *All year, daily, 0800-1730, Sun by arrangement; Key from garage opposite. £1.00/free/50p. Tel: (01953) 860374.*

North Elmham Chapel, High Street, North Elmham: The remains of a Norman chapel later converted into a house and enclosed by earthworks. It was built on the site of a Saxon Cathedral. *At any reasonable time.*

Norwich Cathedral, 62 The Close, Norwich: Norman Cathedral (1096). 14thC roof bosses depicting bible scenes from Adam & Eve to the Day of Judgement. Saxon Bishop's throne and the largest monastic cloisters in England. Cathedral Close. Shop and buffet. *Sep-May, daily, 0730-1800; May-Sep, daily, 0730-1900. Tel: (01603) 764385.* ♿

Saint Benets Abbey, (Parish of Horning), Ludham: Ruins of monastery founded 1020 AD by King Canute. Gatehouse with interesting carvings. 18th century windmill tower. Perimeter wall round 34 acres. Fishpond. *Permanently open.*

Saint Peter Mancroft Church, Haymarket, Norwich: Norman foundation (1075) New (present) church consecrated in 1455. Perpendicular font (1463). Flemish Tapestry (1573). East Window & Thomas Browne memorial. *All year, Mon-Fri, 0930-1630, Sat, 1000-1230; Closed on Public Holidays. Tel: (01603) 610443.* ♿

Shrine of our Lady of Walsingham, Holt Road, Walsingham: Pilgrimage church containing Holy House standing in extensive grounds. All year, morning till dusk. *Tel: (01328) 820266 .*

Slipper Chapel - Catholic National Shrine, Houghton St Giles, Walsingham: Roman Catholic National Shrine of Our Lady. Small 14thC Chapel connected with ancient shrine in Walsingham (latter now destroyed). New shrine complex including tea room, repository and Chapel of Reconciliation. *All year, daily, dawn to dusk. Tel: (01328) 820495.* ♿

Thetford Priory, Thetford: Custodian on duty selling literature at weekends from 5 Apr-30 Sept. During the week obtained at the 'Ancient House Museum', White Hart Street, Thetford. Founded by Norman warrior Roger Bigod. Henry VIIIs natural son Duke of Richmond formerly buried here. *At any reasonable time. Tel: (01842) 756127.*

Thetford Warren Lodge, (EH) Thetford: Ruins of a small two-storey hunting lodge. Can only be viewed from the outside. *Any reasonable time.*

Weeting Castle, (EH) Weeting: Remains of moated castle. *At any reasonable time.*

Suffolk

Bungay Castle, Bungay: The remains of this large Norman castle, built by the Bigods in 1165 and further developed in 1294, contains many interesting features. The massive gatehouse towers remain as do the bridge pit and curtain walls. A mine tunnel driven into the keep walls is exposed as is the adjacent forebuilding with its latrine chamber (garderobe). The inner bailey, a pleasant grassed area, commands fine views across the Waveney Valley. *All year, daily, 0900-1800; closed Christmas day, key must be collected from choice of nearby locations. Tel: (01986) 893148. RW*

Bury St Edmunds Abbey, (EH) Bury St Edmunds: Remains of Abbey in beautifully kept gardens. The two great gateways are the best preserved buildings. *At any reasonable time.*

Eye Castle, Castle Street, Eye: Norman motte and bailey with medieval walls and Victorian folly. The castle has always had close associations with Royalty since the Norman Conquest in 1066 and was probably used as a defensive site for many centuries before that. Now, rather than dominating the surrounding area with military might, the castle offers a tranquil setting for restoring them. *30 March-31 Oct, Daily, 0900-1900 (dusk if earlier); List of key holders on gate if site is closed.* ♿

Framlingham Castle, (EH) Framlingham: 12th century curtain walls with 13 towers and Tudor brick chimneys. Built by Bigod family, Earls of Norfolk. Wall walk. 17th century almshouses. Home of Mary Tudor in 1553. *1 Apr-30 Sep, daily, 1000-1800; 1 Oct-31 Mar, daily, 1000-1600; closed 24-26 Dec, 1 Jan. £2.00/£1.00/£1.50. Tel: (01728) 724189.*

Leiston Abbey, (EH) Leiston: Remains of 14thC Abbey including transepts of church and range of cloisters. *Any reasonable time.*

Orford Castle, (EH) Orford: Magnificent 90 foot high keep with views across River Alde to Orford Ness. Built by Henry II for coastal defence in 12thC local topographical display. Sculpture of Orford Merman on display. *31 Mar-30 Sep, daily, 1000-1800; 1 Oct-30 Mar, daily, 1000-1600; closed 25, 26 Dec, 1 Jan. £2.00/£1.00/£1.50. Tel: (01394) 450472.*

Walsingham Abbey, Norfolk

Ancient Monuments

Saint Edmundsbury Cathedral, The Cathedral Office, Angel Hill, Bury St Edmunds: 16C Nave (was St James church, made Cathedral in 1914). East End added post-war, completed late 1960. North Side built 1990. *Services: Sun 1000 Sung Eucharist, 1130, Choral Mattins or Communion; Choral Evensong Tue, Wed, Thu, 1700, Fri 1900, Sun 1530. During GMT 0830-1730, BST 0830-1800, Jul-Aug, 0830-2000. Tel: (01284) 754933.* &

✿ **Saint James's Chapel,** (EH) Lindsey: Small medieval chapel once attached to nearby castle. *All year at any reasonable time.*

✿ **Saint Olaves Priory,** (EH) Herringfleet: Priory remains with early 14th century undercroft with brick vaulted ceiling (see also nearby windmill). *Key to undercroft available from Miss Rutley at the Priory House. At any reasonable time.*

Sutton Hoo Burial Site, Sutton Hoo, Woodbridge: Sutton Hoo is a group of low, grassy burial mounds overlooking the river Deben in south east Suffolk. Excavations in 1939 brought to light the richest burial ever discovered in Britain - an Anglo Saxon ship containing a magnificent treasure. It is thought to have been the grave of Raedwald, one of the earliest English Kings known, who died in 624/5AD. The Sutton Hoo treasure has become one of the principal attractions of the British Museum, but its discovery raised many questions about the site which remain unanswered. *6 Apr-8 Sep, Sat, Sun, public holidays, 1400-1600. £1.50/50p/£1.50.*

✿ **West Stow Country Park and Anglo Saxon Village,** West Stow: Reconstruction on its original site of 6 Anglo Saxon buildings, built using the original tools and techniques available to the Anglo Saxons. Visitor Centre. Taped guides with sound effects and music bring the village to life. *All year, daily, 1000-1700 (last ticket 1615). Closed 24, 25, 26 Dec. £2.50/£1.50/£1.50. Tel: (01284) 728718.*

 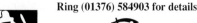

Countryside

LONG WALKS AND DISTANCE PATHS

Bedfordshire

Greensand Ridge Walk: 40 mile footpath from Leighton Buzzard to Gamlingay. Well signposted and waymarked. *Details from Bedfordshire County Council.*

Lea Valley Walk: Walk 9 miles from the source of the River Lea in Leagrave, through Luton Town Centre to East Hyde. Waymarked paths now follow the river 50 miles through Hertfordshire to the River Thames in East London. Guides for the whole walk are available. *Please telephone (01582) 861070 for information. Details from Bedfordshire County Council.*

Stevington Country Walk: This stretch of the former Bedford-Northampton railway between Bromham and Stevington, overlooking the Ouse Valley, links with Stevington Postmill.

Cambridgeshire

Bishops Way: 7-9 miles circular routes on ancient tracks north of Ely. *Details available from Cambridgeshire County Council, Leaflet 40p.*

Clopton Way: 10 mile linear walk from Wimpole to Gamlingay via the prehistoric trackway and deserted medieval village of Clopton. Links in with the Wimpole Way and Greensand Ridge Walk. *Details from Cambridgeshire County Council, leaflet 40p.*

Countryside Cycle Rides: Three sets of route guides for cyclists, with rides from 5 - 25 miles centred around the Fens, the Ouse Valley, and the Cambridge Green Belt. The routes, some of which are waymarked, follow quieter country roads. *Packs of routes covering each area are available from Cambridgeshire County Council, price £1.50.*

Devil's Dyke: This great linear earthwork, which dates from somewhere in the period 350-700 AD, is one of the most spectacular monuments in Britain. Chalk grassland and scrub. *Details from The Wildlife Trust for Cambridgeshire, Enterprise House, Maris Lane, Trumpington, Cambridge CB2 2LE. Telephone (01223) 846363.*

Fen Rivers Way: 17 mile walk between Cambridge and Ely. The path follows well drained floodbank's with stunning views across a fenland landscape rich in wildlife. The route is served by excellent public transport. *A pack containing a Route Guide with helpful local information is available from Cambridgeshire County Council, price £2.00.*

Grafham Water Circular Ride: A circular ride of 13 miles around the reservoir. The route includes ancient woodlands, medieval granges and excellent views across the water. *Details from Cambridgeshire County Council, free leaflet.*

Nene Way: 10 miles, from Peterborough to Wansford along the valley of the River Nene. *Details from Ferry Meadows Country Park, Ham Lane, Peterborough. Telephone (01733) 234443.*

Ouse Valley Way: Long distance river valley walk along the Great Ouse from Eaton Socon to Earith. Total length 26 miles. *Information pack available from Huntingdon Tourist Information Centre, £1.00. Telephone (01480) 388588.*

Three Shires Way: This long distance bridleway runs for 37 miles from the village of Tathall End in Buckinghamshire to Grafham Water in Cambridgeshire. Walkers and cyclists are also welcome to use this fascinating route. *Details available from Cambridgeshire County Council, Telephone (01223) 317445.*

Wimpole Way: 13 miles through woodlands and fields from Cambridge to Wimpole Hall. *Details from Cambridgeshire County Council, leaflet 40p.*

Essex

Epping Forest Centenary Walk: 15 miles through Epping Forest from Manor Park to Epping (links Essex Way to outskirts of London). *Booklet £1 plus 25p p&p from Epping Forest Information Centre, High Beach, Loughton.*

Essex Way: A long distance path stretching across the county of Essex, from Epping in SW to the port of Harwich in NE. A distance of 81 miles, following footpaths and ancient green lanes. *Guidebook £3.00 from Essex County Council Planning Dept, County Hall, Chelmsford. Tel: (01245) 437647.*

Flitch Way: A Country Park passing through 15 miles of countryside along the disused Braintree to Bishop's Stortford Railway in NW Essex. *Other walks and zoned routes for cyclists and horses, telephone (01277) 261343. Rayne Station Visitor Centre, Station House, Rayne, Braintree.*

Forest Way: 25 miles of gentle walking along footpaths and ancient green lanes between the forests of Epping and Hatfield. *Booklet £2.50 from Essex County Council Planning Dept, County Hall, Chelmsford. Telephone (01245) 437647.*

Harcamlow Way: 140 miles in the form of a 'figure-of-eight' footpath walk from Harlow to Cambridge and back. *Booklet £2.50 (inc. postage) from West Essex Ramblers Association, Glenview, London Road, Abridge, Essex. Telephone (01992) 813350.*

St Peters Way: 45 mile walk from Chipping Ongar to ancient chapel of St Peter-on-the-Wall at Bradwell-on-Sea. *Booklet £1.20 (inc. postage) from West Essex Ramblers Association (address above).*

Summer Country Rides: 6 circular off-road rides for horse riders and mountain bikers. The rides vary in length from 6-13 miles. *Guidebook £2.50 from Ways through Essex, Essex County Council Planning Dept., County Hall, Chelmsford. Telephone (01245) 437647.*

Three Forests Way: 60 miles circular walk linking the forests of Epping, Hatfield and Hainault. *Booklet £1.00 from West Essex Ramblers Association (address above).*

Norfolk

Angles Way: Norfolk County Council Recreation Path. 77 miles between Great Yarmouth and Knettishall Heath. A Norfolk Broads to Suffolk Brecks path along the Waverley Valley. *Guide which includes accommodation list £1.50 + 25p p&p, from East Anglia Tourist Board or Peddars Way Association, 150 Armes Street, Norwich, NR2 4EG.*

Around Norfolk Walk: A 220 mile walk following the Peddars Way, Coast Path, Weavers Way and Angles Way, taking in most of Norfolk's varied scenery. *Free leaflet from Norfolk County Council (SAE please).*

Bure Valley Walk: A 9 mile footpath running between Aylsham and Wroxham along the former railway line, along side the narrow gauge track of the Bure Valley Railway, allowing for a relaxing return journey. *Leaflet free from Broadland District Council, Thorpe Lodge, Yarmouth Road, Thorpe St Andrew, Norwich, NR7 0DU. Telephone (01603) 31133.*

Great Eastern Pingo Trail: 8 miles, partly along disused railway line, in Breckland scenery. *Leaflet 65p (inc. p&p) from Norfolk County Council.*

Marriot's Way: 21 mile footpath, bridleway and cycle-route between Norwich and Aylsham along former railway line. *Free leaflet from Norfolk County Council (SAE please).*

Nar Valley Way: A 34 mile footpath from King's Lynn to the Rural Life Museum at Gressenhall. *Free leaflet from Norfolk County Council (SAE please).*

Norfolk Bridle/Cycle Routes: Circular routes (15-25 miles) centred around the villages of Poringland, Reepham, Hockwold, Swaffham and Massingham. *Booklet from Norfolk County Council (SAE please).*

'Off The Beaten Track': Tours of the Broadland District by car or cycle, which as well as taking in much of the beautiful countryside, have a historical content. *Details from Broadland District Council, Thorpe Lodge, Yarmouth Road, Thorpe St Andrew, Norwich NR7 0DU. Free of charge.*

Peddars Way and Norfolk Coast Path with Weavers Way: Official long distance footpath of 93 miles, between Knettishall Heath and Holme, then along the coast to Cromer. Through heath and Breckland woods and varied coastal scenery. Plus Norfolk County Council Recreational Path from Cromer to Great Yarmouth of 56 miles. *Guide which includes accommodation list, £2.10 + 28p p&p from East Anglia Tourist Board or Peddars Way Association, 150 Armes Street, Norwich, NR2 4EG. Official guide available from HMSO £8.99 + p&p.*

Wash Coast Path: A 10 mile route between Sutton Bridge Lighthouse and West Lynn giving spectacular views of the saltmarshes and the Wash. *Free leaflet from Norfolk County Council (SAE please).*

Weavers Way: 57 mile walk from Cromer to Great Yarmouth via Blickling and Stalham. *Free leaflet from Norfolk County Council (SAE please).*

Suffolk

Constable Trail: A 9 mile walk through the landscape and villages associated with the artist's childhood and life. Four shorter walks available. *Booklet £1.25 inc postage from Hugh Turner, Croft End, Bures, Suffolk CO8 5JN. Telephone (01787) 227823.*

Gipping Valley River Path: Located along the 17 mile long former tow path between Ipswich and Stowmarket alongside the River Gipping. *Free leaflet from Suffolk County Council (SAE please).*

Painters Way: 28 mile walk along the valley of River Stour, from Sudbury to Manningtree through countryside which inspired Gainsborough, Constable and Munnings. *Booklet £1.25 inc postage from Hugh Turner, Croft End, Bures, Suffolk, CO8 5JN. Telephone (01787) 227823.*

Stour Valley Path: 60 miles from Newmarket to Cattawade along the valley of the River Stour. *Laminated walk cards from Suffolk County Council, £1.80.*

Suffolk Coast Path: 45 mile path along coast from Bawdsey to Kessingland. *Guidebook available. Details from Suffolk County Council.*

Suffolk Way: A walk of 106 miles crossing distinctive Suffolk countryside from Constable Country at Flatford to Lavenham, continuing to Framlingham and Walberswick, after which it follows the heritage coast to Lowestoft. *Guidebook £2.85 (inc. p&p) from Footpath Guides, Old Hall, East Bergholt, Colchester CO7 6TG.*

Icknfield Way

The Icknfield Way Path follows part of the oldest road in Britain for over 120 miles. It connects the ridgeway at Ivinghoe Beacon, Buckinghamshire, with the Peddars Way at Knettishall Heath, Suffolk. Walker and horse rider routes are available.

SHORTER WALKS

Bedfordshire

Circular Walks: 14 circular walks through the county, which are clearly waymarked and vary in length from 2½ to 11 miles. *Further information from Bedfordshire County Council.*

Guided Walks: Led by the County Council's experienced staff all year round. *Telephone (01234) 228310 for a free copy of the latest walks' programme. £1.00/ 50p/50p each walk.*

Cambridgeshire

Coe Fen and Paradise Trails: Nature trails in Cambridge on common land beside River Cam. *Guide books from The Wildlife Trust for Cambridgeshire, Maris Lane, Trumpington, Cambridge. Tel: (01223) 846363*

Ely Easy Access Trail: A 2 mile trail along the river and nature trail in Ely. Accessible to people of all ages and abilities. Paths are not surfaced so access will deteriorate in winter. *Leaflet from Cambridgeshire County Council, (SAE please).*

'Gentle Strolls' - Booklet featuring nine easy walks near Cambridge, between 1 and 3 miles with information on wildlife and history. Price £1.50 *from The Wildlife Trust for Cambridgeshire, Maris Lane, Trumpington, Cambridge. Telephone (01223) 846363.*

Giants Hill, Rampton: 12th century moat and castle mound, and grassland. Interpretative boards. *Further information from Cambridgeshire County Council, (SAE please).*

Peterborough: Circular walks in rural Peterborough of between 1-11 miles through landscapes including undulating farmland, ancient woodland, riverside scenery and a variety of wildlife. *'Country Walks and Gentle Strolls Volumes I and II'. Available from TIC, 45 Bridge Street, Peterborough. Telephone (01733) 317336.*

Roman Road Walk: (Linton-Hildersham) 6½ mile circular walk, along a Roman trackway and the historic villages of Linton and Hildersham. *Details from Cambridgeshire County Council, leaflet 40p.*

Roman Road Circular Walk: (Stapleford-Wandlebury) 6 mile circular waymarked walk, passing from Stapleford along the River Granta up to Copley Hill, along the Roman Road and back through Wandlebury. *Details from Cambridgeshire County Council, leaflet 40p.*

Shepreth Riverside Walk: Attractive tree-fringed meadows alongside River Cam between Shepreth and Barrington. Walk now available through Malton Lane. Walking, picnics, nature study, small car park. *Further details from Cambridgeshire County Council.*

Wandlebury Country Park Nature Trails: 3 short trails around hilltop crowned by the Wandlebury Ring - an ironage fort. Mainly woodland with some chalk grassland, fine views.

Wicken Walks: Walks through cross section of Fen landscape. *Details from Cambridgeshire County Council, leaflet 40p.*

Woodman's Way: Circular waymarked walk of 6 miles through the once wooded islands of March and Wimblington. *Details from Cambridgeshire County Council, leaflet 40p.*

Essex

Backwarden Nature Reserve Nature Trail, Danbury: 1½ mile trail through heath and woodland. Blackthorn thickets, pools, marsh and bogland. *Leaflet 25p (plus SAE) from Essex Wildlife Trust. Telephone (01206) 729678.*

Basildon Greenway: A series of circular footpaths and connecting linear walks in and around Basildon countryside. *Leaflet 50p from Pitsea Hall Country Park. Telephone (01268) 550088.*

Broaks Wood: Nr Halstead, Essex (A1017 between Gosfield and Sible Hedingham). Waymarked trail with hide. Picnic site. Car parking.

Chalkney Wood: Nr Earls Colne, Essex (A604). Waymarked trail with on site interpretation. Car Parking.

Crays Hill Circular Walk: 5 mile waymarked circular walk centred on the old village of Crays Hill. *Leaflet 20p from Pitsea Hall Country Park. Telephone (01268) 550088.*

Lee Valley Park Circular Walks: Further information from Lee Valley Park Countryside Centre. *Telephone (01992) 713838.*

Maldon Trail: Historic route through Maldon, passing many buildings dating from 15th, 16th, 17th centuries. *Leaflet available from Maldon Tourist Information Centre. Telephone (01621) 856503.*

Norsey Wood Local Nature Reserve: Walk through ancient woodland of archeological and conservation importance which is still managed by traditional methods. There is a waymarked nature trail and easy access trail to follow and staff on site every day (except Christmas). *Further information from Norsey Wood Information Centre. Telephone (01277) 624553.*

North Blackwater Trail: Leaflet describing picturesque route along the riverside, passing marshes and through villages, available from *Maldon Tourist Information Centre. Telephone (01621) 856503.*

Plotland Trail and Museum, Dunton, Basildon: Trail through former plotland area. *Further information from the Warden, Tel: (01268) 419095.*

Ramsden Crays Circular Walk: Approx. 3 mile waymarked walk. *Leaflet 20p from Pitsea Hall Country Park. Telephone (01268) 550088.*

Wildside Walks: 6 walks to help you explore Essex County Parks and their surrounding countryside. *Available from Essex County Council Planning Dept, County Hall, Chelmsford. Telephone (01245) 437647. Price £2.50.*

Countryside

Norfolk

Bacton Wood Forest Walks: 3 forest walks 2km, 3km and 4km through gentle hilly woodland east of North Walsham. 30 species of tree.

'Broadland Country Walks': A series of 15 shorter walks varying from 2-8 miles, covering much of the Broadland District. *Set of leaflets available from Broadland District Council, Thorpe Lodge, Yarmouth Road, Thorpe St Andrew, Norwich NR7 0DO. Free of charge.*

Burlingham Woodland Trails: 3 woodland walks (1, 2 and 3 miles) through the Burlingham estate, 8 miles east of Norwich includes a trail for the less able and pushchairs/ wheelchairs. *Booklet £1.50 (inc. postage) from Norfolk County Council.*

◎ **Felbrigg Woodland & Lakeside Walks & Family Woodland Trail:** (National Trust): These waymarked walks are in the grounds of Felbrigg Hall. Please keep dogs on leads. *All year, daily, dawn to dusk, exc. 25 Dec.*

Kelling Heath Nature Trail: 2½ mile woodland nature trail with conservation lake and other points of interest, magnificent views. Historic sites. Adjacent to North Norfolk Steam Railway. *Leaflet, parking and information from Kelling Heath Holiday Park, Weybourne. Telephone (01263) 588181.*

◎ **Mannington Walks:** Waymarked walks and trails through woodlands, meadows and farmland. *Information Centre, Car Park £1.00.*

Parish Walks: A series of leaflets, describing short circular walks centred on villages throughout Norfolk. Recent additions - Filby, Southrepps, Winterton and Thurning. *Free leaflets from Norfolk County Council (SAE fro further details).*

South Norfolk Footways: Circular walks in the parishes of Diss, Framlingham Earl, Hingham, Long Stratton, Loddon, Mulbarton, Poringland, Pulham, Shotesham and Wymondham. *Free leaflet (send SAE) from TIC, Mere's Mouth, Mere Street, Diss IP22 3AG. Telephone (01379) 650523.*

Walks around Pretty Corner: Approx 250 acres of woodlands for fine and easy walks. Starting from Pretty Corner Main Car Park at the A148 near Sheringham.

◎ **Wolterton Park:** Waymarked paths through historic park with lake and views of Hall. Orienteering Trail, Adventure Playground. *Car Park £2.00.*

Suffolk

Countryside Walks: A series of well signposted circular walks. *Further details of walks/leaflets, 20p each, from Suffolk County Council (SAE please).*

Dunwich Forest: Nr Dunwich Village. Waymarked Forest Trail with *locally available leaflet 20p.* Picnic site. Car parking.

Gipping Valley: 8 circular walks, waymarked, linked to River Path. 3-7 miles. *Details from Suffolk County Council (SAE please).*

Lavenham, Long Melford and Sudbury Walks: 1-4 mile walks along the dismantled railway lines through beautiful countryside. *Leaflet 20p from Suffolk County Council.*

Orford Walks: 4 walks in and around Orford. One suitable for wheelchairs. *Leaflet 20p from Suffolk County Council.*

Rendlesham Forest: Phoenix Trail (E Woodbridge off B1084). Series of waymarked forest walks to suit a range of abilities including wheelchairs. Picnic site and toilets.

Round Walks from Bures St Mary: Seven round walks from under 3 miles to over 7 miles in length using all the footpaths and bridleways through the hills, valleys and woodlands around Bures. *Booklet £1.25 inc. postage from Hugh Turner, Croft End, Bures, Suffolk CO8 5JN. Telephone (01787) 227823. (Published in conjunction with Bures St Mary Parish Council).*

St Cross Farm Walks, South Elmham Hall, St Cross, Harleston: Self guided trails around farm with ruined minster. *£1.00 per adult.*

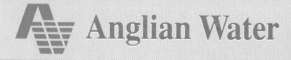

Shotley Peninsula Walks: Walks of about 6 miles include Shotley Gate, Erwarton, Pin Mill, Woolverstone, Holbrook, Freston, Brantham and Bentley. *Further details and free leaflets from Babergh District Council, Planning Dept, Council Offices, Corks Lane, Hadleigh, Suffolk. Telephone (01473) 822801.*

Stour Valley Countryside Walks: Arger Fen Woodland (Nayland) and from Bures (2-4 miles). *Free leaflet from Suffolk County Council (SAE please).*

Thornham Walks (off A140, 3m SW Eye): 12 miles of footpaths on Thornham Estate, the unspoilt country home of the Henniker family. Half mile path suitable for wheelchairs and pushchairs. All terrain wheelchairs. Audio Tours. Picnic Area. Tea Rooms. *Open 0900-1800 daily. May close Oct-Feb. Admission £1.00/free. Telephone (01379) 788153 for events.*

Walberswick Walk: Circular walk starting from the village green, along the seashore, river estuary, through the marshes and across heathland. *Leaflet 20p from Suffolk County Council (SAE please).*

COUNTRY AND LEISURE PARKS

Bedfordshire

Aspley Woods: There are many miles of woods in these 800 acres of attractive woodland, which are covered by an Access Agreement between Bedfordshire County Council, Milton Keynes Borough Council and the Bedford Estate. *Telephone (01525) 237760 for more information.*

Dunstable Downs, Beds County Council: Highest point in the county with superb views over the county and the vale of Aylesbury. Watch the gliders and walk among the chalk downland flora and butterflies at this Site of Special Scientific Interest and Scheduled Ancient Monument. Visitors Centre.

Harrold Odell Country Park, Beds County Council: Landscaped lakes attract many wildfowl varieties. Extensive reedbeds, river meadows, riverbanks. Path around lake suitable for wheelchairs. Award winning Visitors Centre.

Henlow Common: This grassland site, close to the River Ivel, has a variety of wetland habitats. It is excellent for wildlife and peaceful walking.

Priory Country Park, Bakers Lane, Bedford: 228 acres open country, 80 acres of water. Wildlife conservation area, angling, sailing. Visitor Centre.

Stewartby Lake Country Park, Beds County Council: Disused clay pit, now the largest expanse of water in the country. Attracts a rich variety of birds in autumn winter. Water sports. Part of area is a nature sanctuary where dogs must be kept on a lead. *For more information Tel (01525) 237760.*

Stockgrove Country Park, Beds County Council: Renowned for diverse wildlife, from birds of prey to 260 species of moth. Parkland, oak woodland, coniferous plantations, lake and wildlife. Wheelchairs available. Visitors Centre.

Sundon Hills Country Park, (Upper Sundon, Luton) Beds County Council: 250 acres of rolling chalk downland with excellent views of surrounding area. One of the highest points in Beds, this tranquil and unspoilt chalk downland is part of the Chiltern Hills, an Area of Outstanding Natural Beauty. Beech hangers and wooded combes to be found in the park.

Totternhoe Knolls Nature Reserve: Beautiful views, flowers, trees, butterflies and ruined Norman Castle are all features of this chalk grassland area.

Whipsnade Heath: Scrub and contorted trees create an unusual woodland habitat on this 30 acre heath. In spring the glades are a carpet of bluebells.

Cambridgeshire

Ferry Meadows Country Park, Nene Park, Nr Peterborough (off A605 2m W of City centre): Sailing, windsurfing, hire craft available at Water Sports Centre. Fishing, miniature steam railway, boating, picnicking, walking, nature reserve, visitor centre, conservation garden.

Grafham Water (5m SW Huntingdon off B661): This 2½ sq mile man-made reservoir has fishing and sailing facilities and many water birds. 3 nature trails, 2 bird hides (one with facilities for disabled), pleasure boat trips. Picnic sites, restaurant, cafe, free parking, public footpaths, toilets (disabled facilities), cycle hire and visitor exhibition centre.

Hinchingbrooke Country Park: 156 acres of woods, lakes and meadows. Water sports, countryside events and walks. Displays at the Visitors Centre. Facilities for the disabled. Ranger service available. *Telephone (01480) 451568.*

Wandlebury (3m SE Cambridge off A1307): Parkland with Iron Age hill fort, picnics, woodland walks and nature trail. Dogs on leads.

Wimpole, (National Trust) Nr New Wimpole: Walks in park landscaped by Bridgeman, Brown and Repton, surrounding Wimpole Hall.

Essex

Belhus Woods (1m N Aveley), Essex County Council: 158 acres, woodlands, lakes and open areas for walking and picnicking. Fishing from 0800 to dusk. Proposed horse-ride. Visitors Centre. Ranger service. *Telephone (01780) 865628.*

Brentwood Park, Warley Gap: Ski centre, golf range, woodland walk. Health club and leisure facilities. *Tel: (01277) 211994.*

Chalkney Wood, Earls Colne, Essex County Council: Ancient woodland site of 63 acres. *Telephone (01206) 383868.*

Cudmore Grove, East Mersea, Essex County Council: Access to a pleasant beach and grassland for picnics. 35 acres. Information Room. Ranger service. *Telephone (01206) 383868.*

Epping Forest: 6,000+ acres, mostly within Essex, owned by the Corporation of the City of London. Much of it is SSSI and includes ancient woodlands of beech, oak and hornbeam, grasslands and attractive water areas. Two Iron Age earthworks visible. *Official guidebook available from Epping Forest Centre at High Beach, price £1.50 + 29p p&p & The Official Map of Epping Forest, produced by Ordnance Survey, 1:25000 Price £4.50 + 29p p&p.*

Garnetts Wood, Barnston, Nr Dunmow, Essex County Council: Ancient woodland of 62 acres. *Telephone (01376) 340262.*

Grove Woods, Rochford District Council: 40 acres of recent woodland between Eastwood and Raleigh. Walks among old orchards and overgrown ruins of small holdings. Waymarked circular route, surface suitable for wheelchairs. Permissive waymarked horse route.

Hadleigh Castle Country Park, Essex County Council, Southend and Castle Point Borough Councils: 450 acres of downland, woodland and marshes. Wildlife area. Horse ride. Ranger service. *Telephone (01702) 551072.*

Hainault Forest, Romford Road, Chigwell: 600 acres of ancient woodland, a lake and a Rare Breeds Farm. Managed by the London Borough of Redbridge on behalf of Redbridge and Havering London Boroughs & Essex County Council. *Adm. free, parking fee Sun & Bank Hols. Easter-Oct, 1000-1700. Tel: 0181 500 7353. Contact Rory Sidwell/Andrea Green. Refreshments, guided walks & events by arrangement. MG3 (wheelchair toilets).*

Harlow Town Park: Fully landscaped 70ha park with scenic walks and views. Pets Corner. Pitch 'n' Putt. Adventure Playground. Paddling Pool. Cafe. Riverside Walk and Wetland Conservation Area.

Hatfield Forest (4m E Bishop's Stortford): 1,000 acres of wooded medieval landscape and nature reserve with lake. Miles of peaceful woodland walks including 1¼ mile waymarked trail. *£2.50 per car.*

High Woods Country Park, Colchester Borough Council: 330 acres of attractive woodland, grassland, farmland and wetland. Numerous footpaths. Visitors centre, ranger service with programme of activities and guided walks for visitors and schools. Bookshop and toilets.

Hockley Woods, Rochford District Council: 260 acres of ancient coppice woodland, the largest in Essex. Pleasant walks and a horse trail. Picnic and play area. Two waymarked routes. Rustic products, including picnic benches and home grown charcoal can be purchased on the site. Guided walks every Wednesday.

Langdon Hills (1m SW Basildon), Essex County Council: Divided into two parks, Westley Heights and One Tree Hill, overlooking the Thames Estuary with a range of scenery including open grassland, deciduous woodlands, and sandy heaths. Horse ride through park. Information at One Tree Hill plus AA viewpoint. Ranger Service. *Telephone (01268) 542066.*

Countryside

Lee Valley Regional Park: Stretches 23 miles along the Lea Valley from London's East End, through Essex to Ware in Hertfordshire. Parkland, picnic sites, angling, camping, sports centres, marinas, bird watching and a farm. Countryside Centre at Abbey Gardens, Waltham Abbey, Essex EN9 1LQ. *For further information. Tel (01992) 713838.*

Maldon Promenade: 100 acres of formal and informal parkland adjoining River Blackwater. Riverside walks, picnics, children's play area.

Marks Hall Estate, Coggeshall: Country Estate with ornamental grounds, lakes, parkland and fledgling arboretum. Woodland walks, and waymarked trails ideal for wildlife and bird watching. Visitors centre in restored Essex barn. *Easter-31 Oct daily, closed Mon (exc. BH Mon). Car park/ woodland walks open all year. £2.50 per car. Telephone (01376) 563796.*

Marsh Farm County Park, South Woodham Ferrers, Essex County Council: 320 acres of country park operating as a modern livestock farm. Country walks around the sea wall, farm tracks and nature reserve. Visitors centre. Picnic area. See also Animal Collections. *Telephone (01245) 321552.*

Pitsea Hall Country Park, Pitsea: Country park with an emphasis on conservation and natural history. Attractions include a marina, craft workshops, National Motorboat Museum and relocated historic buildings.

Programme of Ranger Guided Activities: Talks can be arranged. *Further details from the Ranger Service, Weald Country Park, South Weald, Brentwood. Telephone (01277) 216297/261343.*

Thorndon (2m S Brentwood), Essex County Council: 540 acres. Thorndon North is almost totally woodland with pleasant walks and a horse ride. Thorndon South has woodland walks, fishing and some extensive views of the Thames Estuary. Ranger service. Park mobility buggy available. Countryside Centre. *Telephone (01277) 211250.*

Weald (1m NW Brentwood), Essex County Council: 428 acres of woodland, lakes and open parkland, open to the public for informal recreation. Fishing & horse riding. Visitors Centre, ranger service. *Tel (01277) 261343.*

Norfolk

Fritton Lake Countryworld (6m SW Gt Yarmouth on A143): 250 acres of wood, grassland and formal gardens. 170 acre lake – fishing, rowing, pedalos, launch trips. 9 hole golf, putting, crazy golf. Large adventure playground. Children's farm. Wildfowl reserve. Heavy horses (daily rides). Falconry Centre (daily flying displays exc. Fri). Craft workshop. Cafe. Shop.

Holt Country Park (1m S Holt on B1149): Conifer wood and heathland with walks, nature trail. Car parking, picnic areas and toilets. 98 acres woodland and 113 acres heathland.

High Lodge Forest Centre, Visitor Centre in the heart of Thetford Forest, (off the Thetford to Brandon Road, B1107): Forest drive, shop, refresh- ments, waymarked trails, cycle hire, orienteering, squirrels maze, play- ground, picnic areas, educational visits, events. *Forest Office, Santon Downham. Telephone (01842) 810271.*

Lynford Arboretum, (1m E Mundford off A1065): Over 200 tree species in attractive parkland. Walks around ornamental lake and into the forest.

Sandringham (7m NE King's Lynn on A149): Wood and heathland. Nature trails. 650 acres. *Visitor Centre open April-Oct and wknds Mar & Dec.*

Sheringham Park (National Trust), Sheringham (car access off A148 Cromer to Holt Road): Rhododendrons, woodland, spectacular views of park and coastlines. *Car park £2.30 ('95).*

Thetford Forest Park: 50,000 acres of pine forest with heathland and broadland areas. Waymarked walks and trails from over a dozen car parks & picnic sites. *Forest Office, Santon Downham. Phone (01842) 810271.*

Wolterton Park: 340 acres of historic parkland with market trails. Orienteering, adventure playground, Hawk and Owl Trust Exhibition. Special events programme. Toilets. *Car Park £2.00*

Suffolk

Alton Water, Holbrook Road, Stutton, nr Ipswich: Water park with walks, nature reserves and picnic areas. Cycle tracks and cycle hire. Watersports centre offering sailing and windsurfing. Coarse angling, day tickets available. Visitor Centre serving snacks.

Brandon (½ m S Brandon): Lake, lawns, tree trail, Victorian walled garden, Visitor Centre, toilets, woodland picnic areas and forest walks. 32 acres. Cycle hire school holidays and weekends. *Visitor Centre open: Apr-Sep 1000-1700 weekdays, 1000-1730 weekends, Oct-Mar 1000-1600 daily.*

Clare Castle, Clare, Nr Sudbury: Ruins of Clare Castle and baileys. A former railway station with visitor centre, waterfowl, nature trail, history trail, walks, picnic areas, toilets. 25 acres.

Ickworth Park, (National Trust) Horringer (3m SW Bury St Edmunds, on A143): Walks through woodland and by canal. Leaflet available from machine at car park £1.00. £1.75/ 50p payable on entrance to park.

Knettishall Heath (5m E Thetford): Attractive Breck landscape, heather, grass heath and mixed woods, 'Peddars Way' long distance footpath starts at W end. 'Angles Way', the Broads to the Brecks path finishes at E end. Toilets and extensive picnic area. 400 acres.

Museum of East Anglian Life, Stowmarket: Enjoy an interesting walk along the Nature Trail within the 70 acre site. Picnic areas provide glorious views of the watermill and windpump and ensure peace and tranquillity.

West Stow Country Park (6m NW Bury St Edmunds, off A1101): Grassland, heathland, lake and river with many walks. Reconstructed Anglo-Saxon village (see Ancient Monuments section). 125 acres. Children's play area. Visitor centre, car parking, picnicking and toilet facilities.

Adjoining Counties

Rockingham Forest Tourism - Can help you discover Northampton-shire's countryside. Stately homes, where to stay, leisure drives, list of guides, walks, what's open. *For further information Oundle TIC, 14 West Street, Oundle PE8 4EF. Telephone (01832) 274333.*

USEFUL ADDRESSES

Department Planning and Transportation, Norfolk County Council, County Hall, Martineau Lane, Norwich. Telephone (01603) 222776.

Environment & Transport Department, Suffolk County Council, County Hall, Ipswich. Telephone (01473) 265131.

Leisure Services, Bedfordshire County Council, County Hall, Bedford. Telephone (01234) 228671.

Rural Group, Department of Corporate Planning, Cambridgeshire County Council, Shire Hall, Castle Hill, Cambridge. Tel: (01223) 317445.

Planning Department, Essex County Council, County Hall, Chelmsford. Tel: (01245) 492211.

Nature Reserves

Ordnance Survey grid references have been provided for some of the reserves which are less easy to locate. For further details please contact the Naturalists' Organisations, addresses and telephone numbers on page 62.

Bedfordshire

Cooper's Hill, nr Ampthill (TL 028376) (Ampthill Town Council/BWT): One of the best examples of Heathland in Bedfordshire, supporting populations of characteristic insects and lizards.

Felmersham Graval Pits, nr Felmersham (SP 991584) (BWT): Disused gravel workings; open water, marsh, grassland, hedges and developing woodland with rich plant life. Excellent site for damselflies and dragonflies.

Flitwick Moor, off Flitwick-Maulden road, turn off by Holly Farm (TL 046354) (BWT): Once valley fen and heath; now contains a variety of habitats including damp birch woodland, open water, unimproved grassland and sphagnum moss.

The Lodge, RSPB Headquarters (1m E Sandy off B1042): Mature woodland, pine plantations, birch and bracken slopes with a remnant of heath and an artificial lake, 4 nature trails. Formal gardens. Many breeding birds, muntjac deer are often seen. *Reserve and gardens, daily 0900-2100 or sunset when earlier. £2.00 (free RSPB members).*

Totternhoe Knolls, nr Dunstable (SP 986216) (BWT): A long, partly wooded chalk ridge, subject to quarrying since Saxon times. Plants include kidney and horseshoe vetch, clustered bellflower and wild thyme.

Cambridgeshire

Brampton Wood, nr Huntingdon (TL 185698) (CWT): Second largest woodland in county, covering 327 acres, supports a remarkable variety of plants and animals, inc. huge numbers of butterflies, birds and insects.

Gamlingay Wood, (TL 143671) (CWT): 120 acres of ancient ash/ample wood, dating back to the 13th century. The wood boosts particularly rich flora including oxlips, bluebell and yellow archangel.

Hayley Wood, nr Gamlingay (TL 294534) (CWT): Ancient woodland of tall oak standards forming a canopy above mixed coppice and smaller trees of field maple, ash hazel and hawthorn. Bluebell, oxlip, other spring flowers.

Fowlmere, E of A10 Cambridge to Royston road, nr Shepreth (RSPB): Reedbeds, pools, watercress beds. Kingfishers, turtle doves, water rails. Access at all times from reserve car park. *Non members £1.00. Warden: Mike Pollard, 19 Whitecroft Road, Meldreth, Royston, Cambridgeshire.*

Ouse Washes, nr Manea reached from A141 Chateris-March road (RSPB/CWT): Extensive wet meadows. Breeding black-tailed godwits. The most important inland site in Britain for wintering ducks and swans. Observation hides, information centre and toilets. *Access free at all times from reserve car park. Warden C Carson, RSPB, Welches Dam, Manea, March.*

Wildfowl & Wetlands Trust, Welney Centre, Welney: Year round reserve with numerous hides and a large observatory overlooking some 900 acres of the Washes. Around 3,500 wild swans and many thousands of wildfowl in winter, in summer notable for waders and other birds and pleasant walks in the unique washland habitat. *All year, daily 1000-1700 (except 25 Dec). Nov-Feb, special evening visits to watch the swans under floodlights, pre-booking essential Tel: (01353) 860711. £3.00/£1.50/£2.20/ family £7.50.*

Essex

Abberton Reservoir, nr Colchester (EBWS): Special protected area for wild duck, swans and other water birds. Visitor centre with panoramic views. Two nature trails and 5 bird hides. Access to perimeter road restricted to EBWS permit holders, although visible from roads. *All year, daily exc. Mon (open Bank Hol Mon), 0900-1700, closed 25 & 26 Dec.*

Chigborough Lakes, 3 m E Maldon, off B1026 (EWT): Former gravel pit with 4 lakes, various ponds, willow swamp, scrub and grassland. Good for scrub and water birds. Entrance (TL 877086) turn left up Chigborough Lane off B1026 3 m E of Maldon. Small car park half mile on your left).

Colne Estuary, (EN) East Mersea; foreshore, beach and marshes.

Cranham Marsh, One of the last remnants of sedge fen in Essex. Spring-fed stream serving marshes and woodlands. Major work underway to raise falling water tables to protect flora such as yellow loose strife and betony. Entrance (TQ 567856). Recommend parking in Park Drive or Argyle Gardens, Upminster, and then footpath to reserve.

Danbury Complex, Mostly SSSI. This superb group of reserves along the Danbury Ridge includes ancient woodland, coppice, pollards, heath, meadows, spring-fed streams and bogs. Woodland birds, mammals and flowers; meadow flowers including orchids, eyebright and harbell; insects including many butterflies and dragonfies. Please keep to the public footpaths where possible. This complex also includes **Backwarden** 30 acres, **Blake's Wood** 107 acres, **Scrubs Wood** 10 acres, **Birch Wood** 15 acres, **Hitchcock's Meadow** 10 acres, **Little Baddow Heath** 50 acres, **Pheasanthouse Wood** 17 acres, **Poors Piece & Smaller Poors Piece** 11 acres, **Woodham Walter Common** 80 acres.

Fingringhoe Wick Nature Reserve 3 m SE Colchester (EWT): 125 acres of woodland and lakes by the Colne estuary. Nature trails, observation tower and 8 hides. Conservation Centre. *All year, daily ex Mon, 0900-1700 (open until 1800 in summer). Closed 25 & 26 Dec.*

Hanningfield Reservoir, At least 30 acres of this 100 acres mixed woodland are ancient in origin. Reservoir itself is SSSI, with large numbers of wildfowl, swifts, swallows and martins. A network of permissive paths cover much of this beautiful reserve, while three bird hides allow the whole reservoir to be scanned (Map ref. TQ 737976).

Hunsdon Mead, Superb flood meadow owned jointly by Essex and Herts & Middlesex Wildlife Trusts. Supports plants like cowslips and yellow rattle and good winter bird numbers. Entrance (TL 42114) park at Roydon station and walk NE along Stort Navigation.

John Weston Reserve, Walton-on-the-Naze (EWT): Small reserve forming part of a much larger complex of cliffs, rough grassland, scrapes and saltings which form the Naze. Nature Trail.

Langdon Nature Reserve, SW Basildon (EWT): 460 acres of woodland, flower meadows, lakes and former plotland gardens, including the ancient woodlands of Marks Hill. Conservation Centre under construction will offer observation room, gift and bookshop, toilets and school facilities. Due to be finished in 1996. *Tel: (01268) 419095.*

Parndon Wood: (SSSI) Local nature reserve set in 21 ha Oak with Hornbeam Coppice Woodland, nature trail, study centre, viewing hides. *Open Suns all year round, 0900-1300 & 1400-1800.*

Phyllis Currie, The great variety of habitats result from the foresight of the late Phyllis Currie and her husband who left the reserve to the Trust. The focus is a large lake with waterfowl, fish and many aquatic insects which can be seen from the bird hide. Secondary woodland, scrub, pine plantation and meadow make for good birdwatching and insect life. Entrance (TL 723182) from A130 in Great Leighs at St Anne's Castle take the minor road west for 2/3 miles, then 200 yards up Dummey Lane is reserve car park.

Pound Wood, One of the larger remaining blocks of ancient woodland in SE Essex. There is a great range of woodland, including sweet chestnut, birch, hornbeam, and hazel (TQ 816888/818886).

Roding Valley Meadows, (TQ 434954) from Oakwood Hill, off Rectory Lane, Loughton (EWT): Largest water meadows left in Essex with flower rich meadows and marsh alongside the River Roding. Variety of birds including kingfisher and good insects. Entrance from Oakwood Hill, off Rectory Lane, Loughton.

Rushy Mead, A short walk along the Stort Navigation towpath S from Bishops Stortford, or entrance from the Bishops Stortford/Hatfield Heath road (TL 497197). The reserve shows how wetland habitats - reed/sedge beds and woodland - are best managed to encourage a variety of animals like riverine birds and dragonflies and plants like marsh marigold and iris.

Shadwell Wood, 18 acres SSSI. Ancient woodland coppice produces a variety of woodland products as well as supporing the rich flora - oxlip, herb paris, ramsons and four orchid species. Entrance (TL 573412) by track on W side of road from Saffron Walden 1½ miles before Ashdon.

Stour Wood and Copperas Bay, off B1352 road from Manningtree to Ramsey (RSPB): Mixed woodland and mudflats on Stour estuary. Ducks, geese and waders numerous in autumn and winter. Nightingales and wood-peckers. Access at all times to hides overlooking estuary from reserve car park. *Donations. Warden: R Leavett, 24 Orchard Close, Gt Oakley, Harwich.*

Thorndon Countryside Centre, 3m S of Brentwood off A128. A joint venture between EWT and Essex County Council, situated in the Thorndon Country Park North, which inc. some fine areas of woodland and nature trails. Centre has activity displays, gift and bookshop, separate education room, toilets and refreshments. It was built mainly of wood blown down in the 1987 storm. *Open daily ex Mon, 1000-1700. Tel: (01277) 232944.*

Two Tree Island (Leigh NNR), One of the Trust's largest reserves comprising of the east half of the island with 130 acres of saltings and over 400 acres of mudflats. Important site for winter wildfowl inc. brent geese, many duck and waders which can be seen from the hide. The island itself, formerly a refuse tip, has been capped and reseeded. Entrance (TQ 824852). Take road round side of Leigh station and over bridge, car park is on left.

Wildside Walks: 6 walks to help you discover the nature reserves of Essex. *Wildside walking pack £2.50 from Essex County Council Planning Department, County Hall, Chelmsford.*

Norfolk

The Norfolk Coast

Blakeney Point (NT): Shingle spit, sand dunes, seals, shop and display in Lifeboat House. Access for disabled. Hides. Access by boat from Morston or Blakeney. *Morston and Blakeney Car park charge.*

Cley Marshes (NWT): Fresh water and salt marshes, large number of rare migrants which appear each year. Visitor Centre with magnificent views; displays on conservation and history of the Cley area. Gift shop. No dogs please. *Vistior Centre Apr-Oct, Tue-Sun, 1000-1700. Closed Mon, open Bank Hols. Marshes all year, access by permit available from Visitor Centre or Watchers's cottage in winter. Admission charge for non-members.*

Holkham (EN): Sand/mud flats, salt marsh, sand dunes with Corsican pines.

Holkham Hall Lake: Freshwater 1 mile in length on which moorhen & coot, grebes, cormorants, swans, geese and ducks can be seen. *Advance notice to Estate Office for large groups please, Tel: (01328) 710227.*

Holme Bird Observatory Reserve (NOA): 6 acres. Permanent warden; 300 species. Hides. Nature Trail. "The only accredited birds observatory in Norfolk" (B.O.C. British Observatories Council). Bird ringing carried out under National Ringing Scheme organised by British Trust for Ornitholgy. *Visitors welcome all year, permits available on the spot.*

Scolt Head Island: (EN) Island reserve with extensive salt marshes and sand dunes. Nature Trail. *Access by ferry from Brancaster Staithe and Burnham Overy Staithe, Apr-Sep.*

Snettisham, signposted from A149 road from King's Lynn to Hunstanton (RSPB): Gravel pits on the Wash. Spectacular flocks of waders at high tides, breeding terns, ducks. Observation hides. Information centre. *Access at all times from public car park at beach. Warden: P Fisher, 13 Beach Rd, Snettisham, King's Lynn.*

Titchwell, off A149, W of Brancaster (RSPB): Reedbeds, lagoons, saltmarsh and sandy beach. Nesting avocets, marsh harriers and bitterns. Good variety of birds all year. Access at all times along the west bank. Observation hides, visitor centre, shop, toilets. *£2.00 car park charge for non members. Warden: N. Sills, Three Horseshoes Cottage, Titchwell, King's Lynn.*

Winterton Dunes (EN): Large sand dune area with coastal plants & birds.

Broadland

Berney Marshes and Breydon Water, nr Great Yarmouth (RSPB): Flooded grazing marsh and estuary mudflats. Waders and wildfowl present throughout the year. No road access. Norwich-Great Yarmouth train stops at Berney Arms halt. Also reached by foot along Weaver's Way or by boat from Breydon Marine or Great Yarmouth, bookable in advance with the warden: *D Barrett, RSPB, Ashtree Farm, Breydon Marina, Butt Lane, Burgh Castle, Great Yarmouth.*

Broadland Conservation Centre, Ranworth (NWT): Floating gallery for moored on Ranworth Broad; displays on conservation and the history of the Broads approached by a 350 metre nature trail through woodland to the waters edge. No dogs. *1 Apr-31 Oct, daily, 1000-1700, gift shop, adm. free.*

Bure Marshes (EN): Extensive fen, broads, fen woodland and Hoveton Great Broad; nature trail can only be reached by boat, upstream from Salhouse Broad. *Early May-mid Sep (exc. weekends).*

Cockshoot Broad (NWT): Boarded walkway (¾ mile) along River Bure and Cockshoot dyke leading to bird hide overlooking the Broad. No dogs.

Hickling Broad, (EN, NWT): Large Broad, open reed and sedge beds, oak woodland. Passage waders in large numbers in spring and autumn; bittern heron and bearded tit in summer. Stronghold of swallowtail butterfly. Boats may pass along public channels. No dogs please. *Visitor Centre, Stubb Rd, Hickling, 1 Apr-30 Sep, daily, 1000-1700. Reserve all year, daily, 1000-1700, £2.00/NWT members free. Water trail daily depart 1030 and 1400 from Pleasure Boat Inn. Advance booking essential. Tel: (01692) 598276.*

A new windsurfing beach at Hickling Broad was opened on 1 September 1995. Wildlife will also benefit because of a zoning agreement by windsurfing club members to keep away from two winter bird refuges in the broad, which is internationally important for overwintering birds. Members of Hickling Windsurfing Club will have free use of the new beach; non-members will pay £7 per day (including car park), collected by a newly-appointed warden employed by partners in the project Norfolk Wildlife Trust, who manage Hickling Broad.

Horsey Mere (NT): Winter wildfowl, with occasional swans; extensive reed beds and proximity to sea give it a special attraction to birds of passage. *Restricted access by boat.*

How Hill, Wildlife Water Trail, Broads Authority: Water trail by small electric launch. Trail covers river and dykes through marshes and fens of the How Hill Nature Reserve. Guide describes area, walk to bird hide. *1 Apr-31 May & 1-31 Oct, Sat, Sun, Bank Hols & half term week, 1100-1500, 1 Jun-30 Sep, daily, 1000-1700. £2.50/£1.50.*

Strumpshaw Fen, signposted from Brundall off A47 Norwich to Great Yarmouth road (RSPB): Broads, reedbeds and woodland with many birds including marsh harriers and kingfishers. Wild flower meadows, dragon-flies and butterflies also notable. Information centre, observation hides and toilets. *All year, 0900-2100 or sunset when earlier. Non members £2.50. Warden: M Blackburn, Staithe Cottage, Low Road, Strumpshaw.*

Surlingham Church Marsh, N of A146 Norwich-Lowestoft road (RSPB): Former grazing marsh with dykes and pools. Nesting little ringed plovers and common terns. Circular walk of 1½ miles starting by Surlingahm Church. Observation hides. Wellingtons or boots advisable. *Access at all times. Warden: Pete Bradley, 2 Chapel Cottages, The Green Surlingham,*

Inland Norfolk

East Wretham Heath (NWT): Grassland heath with some woodland. Typical Breckland country, which in other areas has been much altered by recent afforestation. Sandy soil supports many continental plants unusual in England. *All year (exc. Tue, Christmas and New Year) 1000-1700.*

East Winch Common, off the A47 at East Winch (NWT): One of the few large remnants of heathland in the county. Plants include heather, purple moor grass, sundew and beautiful marsh gentian. Dragonflies, damselflies and a variety of birds. Nature trail. No dogs please.

Foxley Wood, 6m NE East Dereham (NWT): Largest ancient woodland in the county. Wide rides benefit butterflies and the site is rich in wildflowers in the spring and summer. No dogs please.

Honeypot Wood, from the A47 W East Dereham take the road to Wendling (NWT): Honeypot Wood is a remnant of the ancient woodland that once covered Norfolk, there are rare plants and wild flowers in abundance. Concrete rides enable wheelchairs to get about the wood with comparative ease. No dogs please.

Narborough Railway Line, 1m S Narborough Village (NWT): A disused railway embankment compsed of chalk ballast and supporting one of the best examples of chalk grassland in the county. The site is being managed jointly with norfolk Branch of the British Butterfly Society. No dogs please.

Nature Reserves

Roydon Common, 3 miles NE of King;s Lynn off A148 (NWT): One of the few remaining areas of heathland in Norfolk. Car park at start of nature trail at eastern end of nature reserve. No dogs please.

Thompson Common, 4m S Watton via B111 (NWT): A mosaic of grasslands, pingos (shallow ponds formed during the ice age), scrub and woodland. Shetland ponies and roe deer graze the common. Stow Bedon car park links with Great Eastern Pingo Trail and reserve nature trail. Please keep to marked trail. No dogs please.

Wayland Wood, 1m SE Watton, access from A1075 (NWT): Ancient and historic wood, managed in the traditional way as coppice with oak standards. Wayland is mentioned in the Domesday book, its name deriving from the Viking 'Wanelund', meaning sacred grove. No dogs please. *Open at all times.*

Suffolk

Bonny Wood, (TM 076520) Barking Tye, nr Needham Market (SWT): Ancient woodland with marvellous spring flowers. Leaflet available.

Bradfield Woods (TL 935581) 5m SE Bury St Edmunds (SWT): Outstanding ancient woodland coppiced since medieval times. Visitor Centre. Leaflet available. Guided walks for groups by arrangement with the warden. *Tel: (01449) 737996.*

Bromswell Green, (TM 296504) nr Melton (SWT): Variety of woodland, estuary and meadow habitats. Nature trail.

Carlton Marshes, (TM 508918) nr Lowestoft (SWT): Grazing marsh and fen; wetland birds. Visitor Centre. *Guided walks for groups by arrangement with the warden. Suffolk Broads Wildlife Centre on site. Tel: (01502) 564250.*

Cornard Mere, (TL 887388) nr Sudbury (SWT): Wetland important for birds and flowers.

Cavenham Heath, (EN). Area of heathland supporting wide range of birds. Access to area south of Tuddenham-Icklingham track only. Parking at Temple Bridge.

Darsham Marshes (TM 420691) (SWT): Marsh, fen and woodland. Excellent birdlife and flora. Leaflet available.

Dunwich Heath (NT): One mile of sandy beach and gravel cliff with 214 acres of heathland. Exhibition, tea room, shop and holiday flats. *All year. Car park £1.00 (£1.50 Jul & Aug).*

Framlingham Mere (TM 284638) (SWT): Wet meadows and large shallow mere. Near castle. Circular walk. Good water birds.

Groton Wood, (TL 976428) nr Sudbury (SWT): Superb broadleaved wood, with large ancient small leaved lime grove. Bluebells and orchids. Leaflet available.

Havergate Island, Orford (RSPB): Britain's largest colony of avocets also breeding terns. Many wading birds in spring and autumn. Short boat crossing by permit in advance from *The Warden J Partirdge, 30 Munday's Lane, Orford, IP12 2LX (please enclose SAE). Members £3.00, non members £5.00 payable in advance. Visiting times Apr-Aug 1st and 3rd weekends plus every Thursday Sep-Mar, 1st Saturday of each month.*

Hazelwood Marshes, (TM 435575) (SWT): 4m west of Aldeburgh. Grazing marsh with wide range of birds. Stunning views of Alde Estuary up to Iken and Snape.

Lackford (TL 803708) 6m NW Bury St Edmunds (SWT): Award winning large gravel pits restored for wildlife. Much to see in summer & winter. Hides.

Landguard, (TM 285315) nr Felixstowe (SWT): Wonderful coastal flora. Migrant and coastal birds.

Martins Meadows, (TM 227573) nr Monewden (SWT): One of the finest hay meadows in Britain. Keep to edges of meadows.

Minsmere, nr Westleton (RSPB): 2,000 acres of marsh, lagoon, reedbed, heath and woodland. Immense variety of birds including bitterns, marsh harriers and avocets. *All year daily (ex Tue) 0900-2100, or sunset when earlier. Closed 25 & 26 Dec. Non-members £3.00/£1.50/£2.00. Access at all times from Dunwich cliffs to free public hides on beach. Warden: G Welch, Minsmere Reserve, Westleton, Saxmundham, Suffolk.*

Needham Lake & Nature Reserve, Needham Market: Large man-made lake, with nature reserves and wildlife areas. Picnic area. Fishing andnon-motor water sports. *Open all year.*

Newbourne Springs, (TM 271433) (SWT): Woods, fen, heath and reedbed with song-birds in spring, inc. nightingales. Visitor Centre. Leaflet available.

North Warren, off B1122 one mile N Aldeburgh and from Aldeburgh-Thorpeness coast road (RSPB): Heathland, fen and grazing marshes. Breeding waders, heathland birds. *Access at all times. Warden: R Macklin, Race Walk, Priory Road, Snape, Saxmundham.*

Orford Ness, (NT): Shingle spit, important for plants and birds. Formerly Ministry of Defence Site. 4 mile circular walk. *Open Thu, Fri, Sat Apr-Oct. Access by ferry from Orford Quay. For ferry bookings, Tel: (01394) 450637. NT Warden, Tel: (01394) 450900.*

Redgrave & Lopham Fen, (TM 046797) (SWT): Large sedge and reed bed at source of rivers Waveney & Little Ouse. Boardwalk for disabled.

Reydon Wood (TM 476790) (SWT): Ancient woodland and green lane. Nature trail provided. Leaflet available.

Trimley Marshes (TM 263532) (SWT): Marshes good all year, near estuary. Visitor Centre. 1 mile walk to hides.

Walberswick and Westleton Heaths, nr Saxmundham (EN): Heathland and coastal habitats supporting varied flora/fauna. *Access by public footpaths.*

Waveney and Little Ouse. Boardwalk accessible for the disabled. Leaflet available. *Reserve office Tel: (01379) 88618.*

Wicken Fen (NT): Practically the last remaining undrained fen with general access; interesting for plant and insect life, waterfowl in winter and breeding marsh birds in summer. Display. *All year, daily (exc. 25 Dec), dawn-dusk. Parties to book in advance, Tel: (01353) 720274. £2.50/£1.25.*

Wolves Wood, beside A1071 2m E Hadleigh (RSPB): Mixed deciduous wood with nightingales, woodpeckers and hawfinches. Observation hide and informatin centre. Access at all times from car park. Donations welcome. *Warden: c/o Stour Wood Reserve, 24 Orchard Close, Great Oakley, Harwich.*

Naturalists' Organisations

(With abbreviations as used in text.)

Broads Authority, 18 Colegate, Norwich, Norfolk. Tel: (01603) 610734.

BWT: The Wildlife Trust for Bedfordshire, Priory Country Park, Barkers Lane, Bedford, MK41 9SH, Tel: (01234) 364213.

CWT: The Wildlife Trust for Cambridgeshire, Enterprise House, Maris Lane, Trumpington, Cambridge, CB2 2LE, Tel: (01223) 846363.

EBWS: Essex Birdwatching Society, The Saltings, 53 Victoria Drive, Great Wakering, Southend-on-Sea, Essex.

EN: English Nature: (Norfolk Team), 60 Brancondale, Norwich, Norfolk, NR1 2BE. Tel: (01603) 620558.

EWT: Essex Wildlife Trust, Fingringhoe Wick Nature Reserve, nr Colchester, Tel: (01206) 729678.

NT: The National Trust, Blickling, Norwich, Norfolk, Tel: (01263) 733471.

NOA: Norfolk Ornithologists' Association, Aslack Way, Holme-next-the-Sea, nr Hunstanton, Tel: (01485) 25226.

NWT: Norfolk Wildlife Trust, formerly known as the Norfolk Naturalists Trust, 72 Cathedral Close, Norwich, Tel: (0603) 625540. For a guide to all 37 NWT reserves, contact the above, £2.99 (free to new members).

RSPB: Royal Society for the Protection of Birds, HQ: The Lodge, Sandy, Beds, Tel: (01767) 680551. East Anglia Office, Stalham House, 65 Thorpe Road, Norwich, Tel: (01603) 661662.

SWT: Suffolk Wildlife Trust, Brooke House, The Green, Ashbocking, Ipswich. Tel: (01473) 890089.

AMPTHILL

Ampthill, one of Bedfordshire's finest historic towns lies 8 miles south of Bedford. Radiating out from its crossroads are picturesque narrow streets lined mainly with Georgian houses, many of which were restored in the early 1950's by the former president of the Royal Academy, the architect and writer, Sir Albert Richardson. There are also many interesting Tudor buildings, and a cross now marks the spot where the 15th century castle stood, where Catherine of Aragon was sent while Henry VIII arranged the annulment of their marriage. Market day Thursday. Early closing Tuesday. *Further information from Sandy TIC.*

BECCLES

The imposing tower of St Michael's church here dominates the Waveney valley and marks Beccles as a town of ancient distinction. Conservation has helped preserve the picturesque old town with its many beautiful buildings exhibiting a rich variety of architectural styles. Curiosities include the impressive tower built separately from St Michael's church and the existence of two market places, one of which is mentioned in the Domesday Book, along with the fact that Beccles was a noted herring fishery! The river Waveney is integral to the history and development of Beccles, the common and fen being claimed from the extensive tidal marshes. Today, Beccles is the southern gateway to the Broads system and local boat-hire gives access to the beautiful reed-fringed waterways abundant with wildlife. Special trails around Beccles Marsh also give walkers a rewarding view of Broadland landscape. Beccles is a lovely blend of old and new, a thriving town with a range of shops, pubs and eating places (early closing Weds.) plus market and auction on Fridays. *Further information from TIC.*

BEDFORD

The ancient county town of Bedford dates back to before Saxon times. The River Great Ouse flows through the town on its journey to the Wash. Since Victorian times the river has been cherished and attractive gardens, water meadows and riverside walks line the banks. The Embankment is one of the country's finest river settings with its graceful suspension bridge and bandstand, which today still plays host to concerts throughout the summer. The Bedford River Festival is held in May, in even numbered years. Held annually in May is the town's

regatta which attracts oarsmen from all over the country. Bedford is internationally famous as the home of John Bunyan, author of The Pilgrim's Progress. His life story is portrayed in the Bunyan Museum, and the 16th century Moot Hall at Elstow. The town is dominated by fine buildings, which include the Bedford Museum and award winning Cecil Higgins Art Gallery and Museum. Market days Wednesday and Saturday. Early closing Thursday. *Further information from TIC.*

BISHOP'S STORTFORD

Superbly situated in rural Hertfordshire right on the border with Essex, is the ancient market town of Bishop's Stortford. The town grew up around the ford over the river now known as the Stort. Good communications have always played an important part in the history of Bishop's Stortford. It lay on the Roman road between St Albans and Colchester and during medieval times, was a staging post on the mail coach routes between London and both Cambridge and

Newmarket. A number of 16th and 17th century Inns still exist as well as the remains of a Norman Castle. Bishop's Stortford has not lost its identity as a traditional market town with markets still being held on Thursday and Saturday and is a favoured commuter area for the city of London, which can be reached in just 35 minutes by rail. Cecil Rhodes, the founder of Rhodesia, now Zimbabwe, was born in the town and his childhood home, Nettleswell House, now houses his Memorial Museum. Early closing Wednesday. *Further information from TIC.*

BUNGAY

An unspoilt market town standing on Suffolk's border with Norfolk, on the banks of the River Waveney. The Domesday Book noted 5 churches in Bungay and of these 2 remain. Bungay Castle, rebuilt in about 1300, stands as a reminder of the town's turbulent past. Largely rebuilt after the Great Fire in 1688, the town has many fine Georgian buildings. The Market Place contains the Butter Cross, on top of which is the figure of Justice. There is wide variety of shops, all within easy walking distance of the Market Place. The town is encompassed by a well-signed footpath walk, the Bigod Way, providing a range of country walks 2 to 10 miles in length. *For free Holiday Guide, Tel: (01502) 565989 (24hr answerphone).*

BURNHAM-ON-CROUCH

The largest town in the area known as the Dengie Hundred, a peninsula bounded northward by the River Blackwater and southward by the River Crouch. Throughout its history, Burnham has maintained a strong maritime flavour culminating today in its title "Pearl of the East Coast" and is today a major yachting centre. There are various attractions including the large yacht harbour, a riverside country park, a museum, a sports centre, pleasant shopping area and a good selection of pubs and restaurants. Early closing Wednesday. *Further information from Maldon TIC.*

BURY ST EDMUNDS

An ancient market town, full of history and Suffolk charm, and ideally situated for touring East Anglia. Cambridge, Ely and the Suffolk coast are within easy reach, as are Ickworth House, Clare Priory and Euston Hall. The country park at West Stow features a unique reconstructed Anglo-Saxon village and there are country parks at Clare and Nowton on the outskirts of the town. Bury St Edmunds has a wealth of historic buildings. The boards are still trodden at the Theatre Royal, a Regency theatre designed by William Wilkins, and the Market Cross Art Gallery was designed by Robert Adam. Moyse's Hall Museum in the Market Place is a Norman building which houses local history collections and the Manor House is a new museum of fine arts and time keeping. There is a leisure centre with indoor swimming pools, a cinema and open air markets on Weds. and Saturday. The Bury festival takes place each May. Early closing Thursday. *Tourist Information Packs (£2 inc postage) from TIC.*

CAMBRIDGE

The river, and the Roman road, made Cambridge an important settlement and market from early times. The Saxon tower of St Benet's Church, the mound built by William the Conqueror for his castle, and several medieval churches all survive. The Folk Museum (Castle Street) and the University Museum of Archaeology and Anthropology (Downing Street) have interesting items from the city's past. The University was established in the 13th century, and the first college, Peterhouse, founded in 1284. the later medieval colleges, including King's and Trinity, were all built in or beside the existing town. The more modern colleges are scattered over west Cambridge, with the new faculty buildings. (Individual visitors may generally walk through the college grounds, but party organisers must contact the Tourist Office preferably well before their visit.) The Fitzwilliam Museum is one of the principal museums of fine and applied arts in Britain. Market days Mon-Sat. *Leaflet and Guide from TIC.*

COGGESHALL

Coggeshall, is different - with two National Trust properties, Marks Hall nature reserve, and its own professionally trained guides, it is well worth a visit. Sitting peacefully on the river Blackwater, Coggeshall exudes a sense of timelessness with meandering streets and Medieval houses - many having woodcarving or colourful pargeting. Stories of ley lines, ghosts and "Coggeshall Jobs", (a ludicrous way of getting something done) are legion, and known throughout East Anglia. Coggeshallians laugh at their reputation, but are proud of their history, the history of ordinary people, their struggles through religious and political persecution, of Martyrs, marauding gangs, and recessions which in turn brought the cloth, embroidery and lacemaking industries to an end. Coggeshall boasts unusual specialist shops, antiques, good pubs, traditional teas/homemade cakes, a five star hotel, B&B's and restaurants to suit all pockets. Free parking, coaches welcome. *To book a guide Tel: (01376) 563242/562885 or Fax: (01376) 563885.*

COLCHESTER

As Britain's oldest recorded town, Colchester has over 2000 years of history to discover. It's a history involving the Romans, the Saxons and the Normans, which has been interpreted and displayed in the towns five museums. A 'must' on any visit is Colchester Castle Museum, which is now one of the most exciting hands-on historical attractions in the country. Only here you can touch real Roman pottery, feel what it is like to wear Medieval clothes, and experience Colchester's murkier past by visiting the Castle prisons. Here witches were interrogated by the infamous Witchfinder General, Matthew Hopkins, in the 17thC, but Colchester does not just rely on the richness of its history to keep its visitors enthralled. Colchester today is a flourishing, modern town offering the widest choice in family leisure and the very best in shopping variety, to tempt all tastes and age groups. Most of the big-name stores are here as well as specialist shops you can browse in. Market days are Friday and Saturday, early closing day is Thursday. After shopping, take a break in the town's award-winning Castle Park, just a few yards from the High Street. *Further information about Colchester, daily walking tours and open-top bus tours from the Visitor Information Centre, Tel: (01206) 282920.*

DEDHAM

Dedham Vale is described as 'Constable Country', and it was this countryside which inspired John Constable's paintings. A footpath leads along the edge of the River Stour to Flatford Mill and Willy Lott's cottage, the scene of his famous 'Hay Wain'. The village has a charm fitting with the mellow countryside. The grammar school which the young painter attended still exists although it now stands as 2 private houses. St Mary's Church commands the central position in the village, the building of which was financed by the wool merchant Thomas Webbe. South of the village the road

passes Castle House, the home of the painter Sir Alfred Munnings. Early closing Wednesday. *Further information from TIP, Duchy Barn.*

DISS

Diss is a thriving market town set in the Waveney valley. It still retains much of its picturesque old world charm despite seeing a certain amount of modern development. The

older part of the town is found around its market place and the site of the six acre mere – a lake which is a haven for ducks. St Mary's church is a fine imposing building which dominates the market place and has watched history pass it by for seven centuries. The streets leading from the church, the market place and mere feature a wealth of interesting architecture, and a variety of specialist shops and restaurants. Market and auction day Friday. Early closing Tuesday. *Further details from TIC.*

DUNSTABLE

At the junction of the 4000 year old Icknield Way and Roman Watling Street lies Dunstable, created early in the 12th century by Henry I. An Augustinian priory was founded here in 1131, and was later chosen by Henry VIII for the trial of his first wife, Catherine of Aragon. Very fine Norman work remains from the priory, including the nave arcade and the west front. The town is on the edge of the highest point in Bedfordshire, the Dunstable Downs, which offer stunning views over the county and are rich in wildlife. Market days Wednesday, Friday and Saturday. Early closing Thursday. *Further information from TIC.*

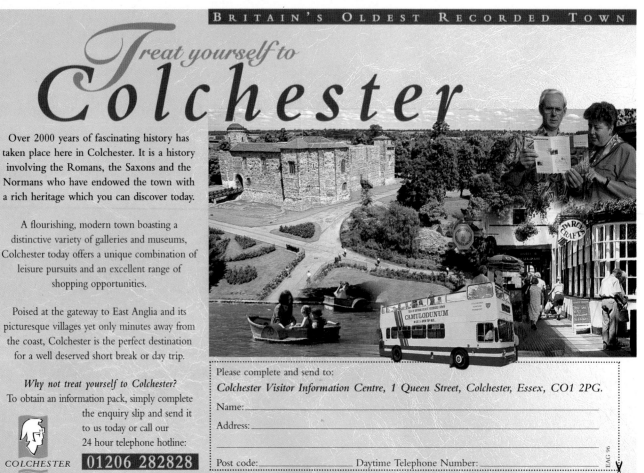

Heritage Towns

ELY

Ely Cathedral is a superb architectural achievement of the Middle Ages and is a dominating feature of the Fenland skyline. The Octagon is an engineering masterpiece and the Lantern above it is one of the finest examples of 14th-century carpentry. The great Lady Chapel (1321) retains the beauty of its carvings and tracery. It has a fine long Nave and the choir has 14th century stalls. Stained glass museum in North Triprium. Nearby is Oliver Cromwell's House which houses a themed tourist information and visitor centre. The Ely museum occupies one of the many old monastic buildings which surround the Cathedral. Along and near the Riverside Walk are interesting old houses and the attractive Maltings public hall. Antique and craft market Saturday, general market Thursday. Early closing Tuesday. *Mini-guide available from TIC.*

EYE

Retains the peaceful atmosphere and character of a small 18th century market town resting in the heart of the Suffolk countryside. The first definite evidence of a settlement dates from Roman times. The castle mound, which dates back to 1156, affords panoramic views of Eye and its surrounding countryside. The Church of St. Peter and St. Paul, founded in the 12th century with its magnificent tower and rood screen is particularly worth a visit. Town trail available. Early closing Tuesday. *Further information from Stowmarket TIC.*

FAKENHAM

A thriving market town with a weekly auction. The town is home to Fakenham Race Course, one of the finest rural national hunt courses in the country, ten pin bowling, a good selection of shops and restaurants which are complemented by a whole range of interesting places to visit including Fakenham Museum of Gas, Pensthorpe Waterfowl Trust, Mill Farm Rare

Breeds and the Thursford Collection. Market day Thursday. Early closing Wednesday. *TIC. For a free guide write to: Coast & Countryside Dept EG96, P.O. Box 666, Norfolk, NR13 6LH. Tel: (01603) 721717 (24 hours).*

FRAMLINGHAM

A quiet market town with many attractive buildings. The striking 12th century castle, built by Roger Bigod, is mainly intact and marvellous views may be seen from its battlements. The Lanman Museum in the castle grounds provides a valuable insight to the lives of the town's people. The Church of St. Michael contains historic tombs and effigies. It has close links with the Mowbrays and Howards, two important medieval families. The town has an interesting shopping centre and good sports centre. Market day Saturday. Early closing Wednesday. *Further information from Aldeburgh TIC.*

HADLEIGH

This busy market town in the valley of the River Brett is of special historical and architectural importance. At one time a Viking Royal Town, it later rose to become one of the more prosperous towns in the country through its wool trade during the 14th century and 15th century. The medieval heart of Hadleigh, St Mary's Church, the Deanery Tower and the Guildhall bears witness to its historical importance. Today the long High Street has a wide variety of shops offering personal and friendly service. Hadleigh offers free parking. Market days Friday and Saturday. Early closing Wednesday. *Accommodation list from TIC.*

HARLESTON

Harleston is in the heart of the beautiful Waveney Valley, a favourite spot for artists. The town has an abundance of fine historical buildings such as Candlers which was built during the reign of Queen Anne. The Swan Hotel, another fine building, was built by the notorious Robert Cook, accused of treason and

later pardoned by Henry VIII during 1550. The parish church of St. Mary's at Redenhall, built in 1260, is considered to be one of the finest in South Norfolk. The town has an exceptional range of shops for its size, catering for all needs. the Wednesday market is a must for visitors, with many colourful stalls selling an array of goods. Early closing Thursday. *Further information from Diss TIC.*

HARWICH & DOVERCOURT

Harwich still has a strong flavour of the medieval sea-faring township it once was. Christopher Jones, master of the Mayflower was married here, and Charles II took the first pleasure cruise from Harwich. During the time Samuel Pepys was MP for the town Harwich was the headquarters of the King's navy. Now, lightships, buoys and miles of strong chain are stored along the front and passengers arriving on the North Sea ferries at Parkeston Quay see the nine-sided High Lighthouse as the first landmark. Southwards along the coast is Dovercourt, with its indoor swimming pool, the residential and holiday suburb of Harwich. Market day Friday. Early closing Wednesday. Holiday guide to the Essex Sunshine Coast from *Council Offices (EDU), Thorpe Road, Weeley, Clacton on Sea, Essex, CO16 9AJ. Tel: (01255) 830566. Information also from Harwich TIC. Tel: (01255) 506139.*

Heritage Towns

HERTFORD

With over 1,000 years of history, the County Town of Hertford still has many historic buildings and street names which have changed little since 1610. The 15C Gatehouse on the site of the original moated castle beside the placid River Lee, has beautiful grounds encircled by a massive flint and stone curtain wall built by Henry II. among other buildings of note are the Georgian Shire Hall, the Quaker Meeting House - oldest in the world still in use today - and the Verger's House - now one of the towns' many antique shops. Hertford's interesting local museum is itself housed in a listed 17th century building and has a recently added knot garden in that century's style. There are two fine parish churches and nestling in the hillside overlooking the ancient meads stands the 12C Church of St Leonard with its Norman font, Anchorite's cell and 13C wall paintings. *Further information from Hertford TIC. Tel: (01992) 534322.*

HOLT

A small, attractive country town just inland from the coast and nestling in undulating North Norfolk countryside. The main street is lined by Georgian buildings mainly built after the fire of 1708. The town has many picture galleries and bookshops. Holt is well known for the public school Greshams, founded in 1555. The North Norfolk Steam Railway has its terminus on the outskirts of the town, connecting Holt with the seaside resort of Sheringham. Market day Friday. Early closing Thursday. *For a free guide write to: Coast and Countryside, Dept EG96, Brochure Despatch Centre, Unit 28, Mackintosh Road, Rackheath Industrial Estate, Norwich, Norfolk NR13 6LH. Tel: (01603) 721717 (24 hours).*

HUNTINGDON

Historically significant as the birthplace of Oliver Cromwell, popular as a National Hunt Racing venue, and now famous as the busy market town at the heart of John Major's Parliamentary constituency, Huntingdon was originally the old county town of one of England's smallest rural shires. The town grew up around a river crossing on the Great Ouse and by Norman times it was a provincial town with no less than 16 churches. The Black Death put an end to the town's early prosperity and it did not really return until the 18th century when improved roads saw the town gain importance as a staging post for coaches travelling on the Great North Road. Huntingdon's most famous son is Oliver Cromwell (born 1599). The Cromwell Museum now houses an interesting collection of personal items and portraits which once belonged to Cromwell and his family. Hinchingbrooke House on the outskirts of Huntingdon is the ancestral home of the Cromwell family. It opens to the public on Sunday afternoons. Market days Weds and Saturday. Early closing Wednesday. *Further information from TIC. Tel: (01480) 388588.*

IPSWICH

Ipswich is possibly England's oldest Anglo-Saxon town. It is well worth a visit for its heritage, leisure and shopping facilities. Christchurch Mansion (1548), set in beatiful parkland and furnished as a country house, contains the finest collection of Constable and Gainsborough paintings outside London. Ipswich Museum contains replicas of the Sutton Hoo and Mildenhall Treasures and a Roman Villa display. The Ancient House has the country's finest example of pargeting. Ipswich has twelve medieval churches, one of which, St Stephens' houses the new TIC. The Tolly Cobbold brewery offers fascinating guided tours. Sport and leisure facilities are excellent including the awarrd winning Crown Pools. Most indoor and outdoor sports are available. Ipswich Town Football Club provides professional football, with speedway and stock car racing just outside the town. First class live entertainment is provided by The Corn Exchange, the Wolsey Theatre and the Regent Theatre. There are seven cinema screens, two night clubs and a wide variety of restaurants. Market days Tuesday, Friday and Saturday. *Regular guided tours and a series of walks from the TIC. A tourist and accommodation guide is available.*

KING'S LYNN

King's Lynn entertained King John before his last journey to Newark Castle, where he died. His baggage-train, following after him, badly miscalculated the tide and was lost crossing the Wash. People still look for the treasure and Lynn makes visitors believe in treasure trove. Medieval streets run down to the quays, merchant's houses with their private warehouses still present an aspect of considerable wealth and two guildhalls still function. One is the Town Hall, now housing Tales of the Old Gaol House, a crime and punishment attraction as well as the splendid civic treasures, including a magnificent set of Charters dating right back to the days of King John (access through TIC) and the other is the King's Lynn Arts Centre, home of the King's Lynn Festival (held the last two weeks of July). There are three museums including the Town House Museum of social history and True's Yard, a museum of King's Lynn's fishing quarter, two market places (with markets on Tuesday, Friday and Saturday), many fine buildings to visit, plus Lynnsport and Leisure Park, East Anglia's newest and largest sports and leisure complex, and a cinema. The surrounding countryside is attractive, and contains several historic houses open to the public, including Sandringham, as well as a variety of other attractions. Early closing Wednesday. *Brochure from TIC.*

LAVENHAM

A magnificent example of a Suffolk wool town with many superb ancient buildings. The preparation of wool and yarn and the manufacture of various kinds of cloth were the source of Lavenham's wealth for at least 500 years and once made it one of the richest towns in England. The church of St Peter & St Paul with its fine 141ft tower stands proud to the southwest and like the 16th century Guildhall and Little Hall (both in the Market Place) is evidence of this wealth. Little Hall, dating from the late 14th century, has been a family home for most of its 600 years. The Guildhall, one of the finest Tudor half-timbered buildings in the country, now contains an exhibition of local history and of the woollen cloth industry. *Further information from Lavenham TIC*

LEIGHTON BUZZARD

Situated on the Grand Union Canal, Leighton Buzzard has in modern times become famous for sand. It is essentially a market town and has a wide Georgian High Street with mews shops, an ancient street market and a fine parish church, which dates from 1277. It has a 190 foot spire, medieval graffiti and 13th century ironwork. The 15th century pentagonal market-cross at the centre of the town, has played host to witch trials, horse auctions and the calling of marriage banns. The Leighton Buzzard Narrow Gauge Railway was built in 1919 to carry sand from the quarries, but now offers passenger trips around the town. Market days Tuesday and Saturday. Early closing Wednesday. *Further information from TIC, District Library, Vernon Place, Dunstable, Bedfordshire, LU5 4HA. Tel: (01582) 471012.*

LITTLE WALSINGHAM

A busy pilgrimage centre since the middle ages. The high street opens out into a square in the centre of which is a 16th century octagonal pump-house. Many of the religious buildings can still be seen including the Abbey and hostels used by the pilgrims over the centuries. There is an Anglican shrine built in 1931 which may be visited and a few miles away at Houghton St Giles is the Slipper Chapel. *Further information available from TIC. For a free guide write to: Coast and Countryside, Dept EG96, Brochure Despatch Centre, Unit 28, Mackintosh Road, Rackheath Industrial Estate, Norwich, Norfolk NR13 6LH. Tel: (01603) 721717 (24 hours).*

LONG MELFORD

This lovely village set in the heart of South Suffolk, boasts one of the most spectacular churches in the county plus two magnificent Tudor mansions, both of which are open to the public. The heart of Long Melford is set along a broad street over a mile in length which is well known for antiques and other specialist shops. Above all, it is a place for walking around and exploring. There are plenty of high quality restaurants and pubs and a picnic site just outside the village. *More information and an accommodation booklet are available from Lavenham/Sudbury TIC.*

LUTON

The fortunes of Luton were largely founded on the straw hat industry, which grew in the 17th century throughout the south of the county. Luton is proud of this tradition and tells the history of the industry in its museum. In recent years it has become a centre for modern industry, including car manufacturing. The Mossman Collection is a unique and nationally important collection of horse-drawn vehicles. The collection is located in Stockwood Park, together with the Stockwood Craft Museum and the Hamilton Finlay Sculpture Garden. Market days Monday to Saturday. Early closing Wednesday. *Further information from TIC.*

MALDON

The attractive town of Maldon lies on the Rivers Chelmer and Blackwater and is home to the Thames sailing barges which can be seen by the Hythe quay. The town, granted a Royal Charter in 1171, has many interesting old buildings, including the 15th century Moot Hall and 17th century Plume Library. The large Promenade Park, with avenues of mature trees and grass areas running down to the banks of the River Blackwater, is a haven for visitors of all ages. Market days Thursday and Saturday. Early closing Wednesday. *Explore the town or the surrounding district by obtaining various free publications, including the Mini-Guide, from the TIC.*

Heritage Towns

MANNINGTREE

The Charm of Manningtree is that it lies on the River Stour in the beautiful rolling countryside so elegantly depicted by artists through the years. It has been a market town since 1238, and is still a busy shopping centre. It is the smallest town in Britain, and a stroll through the streets reveal the variety of its past. There are still traditional shops, as well as handcraft and specialist outlets. Being ten miles from Colchester, Harwich and Ipswich, it is a popular and ideal place for relaxed shopping. The views over the river are well known to birdspotters, sailors and ramblers. The town has an intriguing past - as a river crossing, a market, a smuggler's haven and the home of the Witchfinder General.

MARCH

Occupying an island in the fens, March has a known history of 1,400 years. The old course of the River Nene winds its way through the centre past a beautiful park and picturesque riverside walks. The town is an oasis in the flatlands and has a good shopping centre, ideal for river tourists. The medieval church of St Wendreda treasures a stunning 15th century double hammerbeam angel roof which displays 118 oak angels in full flight. A medieval stone base of a calvary cross stands by the wayside leading to the church. Market days Wednesday and Saturday. Early closing Tuesday. *Further information from Wisbech TIC. Tel: (01945) 583263.*

NEEDHAM MARKET

A small town in the Gipping Valley with many pleasant country and riverside walks. It boasts Mid Suffolk's most popular recreation site, Needham Lake, with its fishing and picnic facilities. There are many attractive buildings in the town and of particular interest is the church interior with its dramatic hammerbeam roof. Craft and antique shops add further interest. Town Trail available. Early closing Tuesday. *Further information from Stowmarket TIC.*

NEWMARKET

James I was the first King to visit Newmarket, primarily because the hunting was so good, but it was his Scottish nobles who introduced racing to England and found the heath at Newmarket so ideal for the matches which were then run usually between two horses at a time. Charles II was single-minded in his devotion to racing from the first, and Newmarket became during the racing season, in fact if not in name, the alternative court to Whitehall. The Rowley Mile racecourse takes its name from his hack Old Rowley. Nell Gwynn's cottage can still be seen, having escaped the fire of 1683 which consumed

most of old Newmarket. The town became firmly established as the centre of horse racing and breeding a position which it still maintains, embodied in the handsome buildings of the Jockey Club in the High Street. The National Horse Racing Museum and the National Stud are well worth a visit. Market days Tuesday and Saturday. Early closing Wednesday. *Further information from TIC.*

NORTH WALSHAM

A small market town just nine miles from the coast and as many from the Norfolk Broads. A distinctive market cross in the sixteenth century is the focal point of the town. A wide variety of shops and restaurants and attractions to visit including the Norfolk Motor Cycle Museum, the Cat Pottery and Worstead Festival held in August each year. Market day Thursday. Early closing Wednesday. *Further information from TIC. For a free guide write to: Coast & Country-side, Dept EG96, P.O. Box 666, Norwich,, NR13 6LH. Tel: (01603) 721717 (24 hrs).*

NORWICH

'Norwich has everything' said Pevsner, the eminent architectural historian and looking at the City's heritage it's easy to see why. One of England's finest Norman Cathedrals, as well as the striking Catholic Cathedral: more pre reformation churches than any other City in Europe; the Norman Castle - described as 'the most ambitious secular building of its generation anywhere in Europe'; the most complete Medieval street pattern in England with 1500 historic buildings within its walled centre - incidentally the largest of its kind in the country; the 'grandest market place in all England'; the finest regalia collection and finest Guildhall outside London and so the list goes on. Happily the catalogue of assets does not stop with its historic treasures. The 'City in an orchard' offers miles of riverside walks, a unique collection of 1930's parks, 150 acres of Mousehold Heath within the built up area and, most recently, the remarkable Castle Green Park. No ordinary park, this 4 acre oasis of grass, trees, waterfeatures and promenades, nestling in the shadow of the Castle keep, is located on top of the discretely designed Castle Mall shopping centre. The centre is naturally lit by an elegant glass and iron roof light reminiscent of the Palm House at Kew Gardens while each level of the scheme links directly into the City's extensive pedestrianised shopping network. The Mall's stores, including Disney and Virgin, complement the City's traditional shopping centre, which is the largest in the region. In addition to one of the largest Marks and

Spencers outside London, the centre boasts a major branch of the John Lewis Partnership, Jarrolds department store and, as well as a full representation of the usual high street multiples, an extensive array of independent speciality shops and restaurants in a network of intimate paved lanes and alleyways. For further diversion the City offers such diversities as one of Britain's outstanding regional theatres, the award winning Sainsbury Centre for the Visual Arts, the works of the Norwich School of Painters and Endsleigh League football - 'a fine City, truly, view it from whatever side you will.' *Information pack available from TIC.*

ORFORD

A thriving port when Henry II had a castle built there in 1165. At that time the shingle spit seperating the river from the sea ended near the quay. Since then the spit has extended 5 miles to the south west resulting in the port's decline, but not affecting the village's beauty. The National Trust has now opened up Orford Ness to visitors limited to 96 a day. Ferry must be booked in advance with the Warden. The 90ft keep, all that remains of the castle, provides excellent views of the brick and timber cottages below and across to the marshes beyond. Good restaurants and walks. Car park by harbour. Early closing Wednesday. *Further information from Aldeburgh TIC.*

PETERBOROUGH

Steeped in history. Peterborough has developed into a modern city that tastefully combines the old with the new to offer an attractive and enchanting place to visit. The richness of Peterborough's history is encapsulated in its Norman Cathedral of St Peter which stands at the very heart of the city. Further evidence of Peterborough's past can be found at Flag Fen Bronze Age Excavations and the Museum and Art Gallery. Rail enthusiasts can visit Railworld or travel back in time on the Nene Valley Railway through Ferry Meadows Country Park to central Peterborough. Peterborough's prosperity has allowed its leisure industry to thrive and a full range of sporting facilities are on offer. Watersports, boating, horse-riding, golf, fishing, nature walks and cycling are some of the leisure pursuits to be found at Nene Park. Combine these elements with excellent shopping, easy access and a wide range of accommodation - it makes Peterborough the ideal city. *Various leaflets and guides are available from the TIC.*

ROYSTON

Royston lies at the crossing of the ancient Icknield Way and Ermine Street, and is said to have been named after the Lady Roysia who placed a cross set in stone to mark this crossing. The town has several interesting houses and inns, and an unusual bell shaped cave, thought to be pre Roman. There is a small local history museum. Market days Wednesday and Saturday. *Further information from Royston Town Hall, Royston, Herts SG8 7DA. Tel: (01763) 245484.*

SAFFRON WALDEN

The ancient town of Saffron Walden has revolved around its market for many generations. The medieval market rows are well preserved and timber-framed buildings abound, many decorated by pargeting. The church, reputed to be the largest in Essex, dominates the town and nearby are the remains of the Norman Castle. On the Common is a rare earth maze, also a restored hedge maze at Bridge End Gardens. The Museum is known for its ethnographic department and also houses a large collection of local interest including many Saxon finds. The Saffron Crocus can be seen flowering outside the Museum in the autumn. It has never been proved that Cromwell's headquarters were in the Sun Inn but Henry Winstanley was certainly born in the town. Nearby is the Jacobean mansion of Audley End. Market days Tuesday and Saturday. Early closing Thursday. *Town Trail leaflet from TIC.*

ST ALBANS

St Albans has been welcoming visitors for centuries, from medieval pilgrims to the shrine of St Alban to modern-day tourists. They too come to see the shrine amid the inspiring setting of the Cathedral, and to explore the site of Roman Verulamium, home to the award winning Verulamium Museum and its fabulous mosaics, and the unique Roman theatre. St Albans is a city easily explored on foot. Visitors can walk from Verulamium through the charming village of St Michaels, with its 16th century water-mill and up Fishpool Street, past centuries of delightful houses. Or they can stroll through Verulamium Park up to the Abbey and the town. The 100 acre park covers the site of the Roman town and boasts the remains of the Roman walls and Hypocaust as well as attractive lakeside walks. Once in the town the visitor can enjoy the plesures of a modern, thriving city, and the contrasts of the old and the new. Attractive shopping centres are only a short walk away from the 15th century Clock Tower, a rare example of a town belfry. The post Roman history of the town can be discovered at the Museum of St Albans on Hatfield Road. St

Albans is also home to the Organ Museum, a magnificent collection of working mechanical instruments, and the Mosquito Museum, which displays the prototype of this famous aircraft. St Albans maintains an enviable blend of beautiful buildings, busy streets, attractive shops and inviting pubs. It hosts over two hundred independent shops and over one hundred eating places. This mixture of past and present provides a unique atmosphere in which to linger, gaze and enjoy, while the twice weekly street market, with its hustle, bustle and colour is as popular now as when first established in 948AD. Held every Wednesday and Saturday, the market stretches the length of St Peters Street and offers goods of every kind from fruit and vegetables to books, records and bric-a-brac. Steeped in history and ideally situated just outside London, St Albans has two railway stations, is close to the M1 and M25 and has ample car parking. It offers a real day out, a unique heritage, original shops, and, should you get tired, plenty of places to eat and drink! *Further info. from TIC. Tel: (01727) 864511.*

ST IVES

An attractive riverside market town, St Ives grew up on the site of a busy Easter Fair at a river crossing on the Great Ouse near the old Saxon village of Slepe. In its heyday in the 13th century, the fair was one of the 4 biggest in the country, and merchants from all over Western Europe came to buy cloth on Huntingdonshire looms. The most notable landmark in St Ives today is the 15th century stone bridge and bridge chapel in the town centre. At that time in England there were many such chapels but now only 3 others remain. These chapels provided a retreat for travellers, and it is believed they also served as toll houses. Oliver Cromwell is St Ives most famous resident. His short residence is marked by the impressive statue in the market place, which was erected in 1901 to mark the 300th anniversary of his birth. Market days Monday and Friday. Early closing Thursday. *Further information from Huntingdon TIC. Tel: (01480) 388588.*

Heritage Towns

ST NEOTS

Standing proudly on The River Great Ouse, St Neots grew up around a 12th century Benedictine Priory. A market charter was granted in 1130 and the town flourished. The old Priory was finally closed and demolished during the Dissolution of the Monasteries (1536-1539). In the 17th and 18th centuries there was much rebuilding in the town. The river was dredged, and sluices were built enabling goods to be brought in by water. Today the importance of the town's position on the Great North Road can be seen in the handsome rectangular market place and the town's surviving coaching inns and hostelries. On fine summer days visitors and residents alike make their way to the Riverside and Priory Parks to boat or fish, enjoy a picnic, listen to a band concert or simply take in the natural beauty. Walking enthusiasts can join the Ouse Valley Way in Riverside Park or set off on the Town Trail from the Market Square. The 15th century parish church of St Mary is a well known local landmark with its 130ft church tower and splendid perpendicular architecture. Market day Thursday. Early closing Thursday. *Further information from Huntingdon TIC. Tel: (01480) 388588.*

SAXMUNDHAM

A quiet market town with some interesting buildings, hotels and restaurants. The church of St John the Baptist has a hammerbeam roof, and a piscina in the south wall of the Sanctuary dates from the 13th Century, and is well worth a visit. At nearby Leiston there are the romantic ruins of

Leiston Abbey, part of which is now a music school. The Long Shop Museum in the centre of the town houses a good collection of traction engines and steam rollers and a history of the Garrett products, from 1852.

STOWMARKET

Stowmarket is a busy market town and an important shopping centre for the surrounding countryside. During the 17th and 18th centuries, the town was a noted centre of the woollen trade and the River Gipping was canalised between Stowmarket and Ipswich to carry the town's trade. A walk can be taken along the former towpath through the woods and meadows by the river. Stowmarket's Museum of East Anglian Life is worth a visit. Market days Thursday and Saturday. Early closing Tuesday. *Stowmarket Guide and Further information available from TIC.*

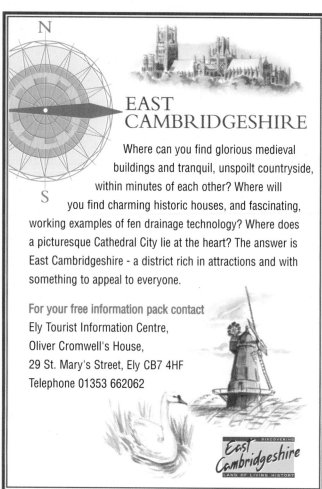

SUDBURY

Sudbury is a thriving market town, very much the centre of the smaller villages and communities which surround it. Mentioned in the Domesday Survey of 1086, Sudbury stands on the River Stour which winds round three sides of the town. River meadows surrounding the town provide excellent walking. Sudbury still retains many ancient and interesting buildings. The weaving industry here dates back to the 13thC, even today the finest silk, including that used in the Princess Royal's wedding dress, is woven in Sudbury. The present centre is Market Hill, dominated by St Peter's church, no longer used for regular worship, but now home for concerts and exhibitions. Before the door stands the bronze statue of Thomas Gainsborough, the town's most famous son. Gainsborough's House, where the famous painter was born, is now preserved as a delightful museum with an exhibition gallery. Market days Thurs and Sat. Early closing Wed. *Leaflet and accommodation list from TIC.*

SWAFFHAM

First-time visitors to Swaffham are always impressed at the extent of the triangular- shaped market place which gives the town an air of expansive tranquillity, transformed every Saturday by the famous open-air market and lively public auction. Around the market place are many fine Georgian buildings. Close by stands the majestic church of St Peter and St Paul, one of the finest of the medieval churches in East Anglia. It has a magnificent hammer-beam roof, with carved angels. Swaffham is an ideal base for touring the beautiful Norfolk countryside and visiting the many attractions. Craft market Wednesday. Early closing Thursday. *Further information and free brochure from Swaffham TIP. Tel: (01760) 722255.*

THAXTED

Thaxted has been a community since Saxon times, with its greatest days in the 14th and 15th centuries when it prospered because of its cutlery industry. It was at this time that the Guildhall was built and that the present shape of the town grew up, with little houses, some white, some colour-washed or half timbered, winding

down the hill past the church into Town Street. The tall spire of the church is one of the landmarks of Thaxted, soaring 181 feet above the town. The other well-known sight is the windmill built in 1804 by John Webb. From the top floor the view of the town and surrounding countryside is quite outstanding. Market day Friday. Early closing Wednesday. *Further information from Saffron Walden TIC.*

THETFORD

Thetford has been a thriving market town since before the Norman Conquest, and many traces of its fascinating past remain, from the Iron Age ramparts surrounding the Norman castle mound, to the stately priory ruins and the fine buildings of the town centre's Conservation area. 1000 years ago Thetford was one of the largest towns in the country, archaeological digs have revealed important Roman, Saxon and Iron Age finds. Thetford is a wonderful centre for river and forest walks. It has an excellent little museum in

the picturesque 15th century Ancient House, just a few yards from the birthplace of Thomas Paine, "Father of the American Revolution". The Charles Burrell Museum tells the story of this once world famous manufacturer of steam traction engines. There are excellent recreation and cultural facilities with the long awaited regional centre for swimming, including family leisure pool, opening in August 1996. Thetford offers the best of both worlds a lively town in lovely countryside. Market days Tuesday and Saturday. Early closing Wednesday. *Further information available from Ancient House Museum, White Hart Street, Thetford. Tel: (01842) 752599.*

WARE

Ware is an historic old town which still retains the character of its Medieval High Street, Tudor waggon-ways and riverside. Situated on the old North Road, Ware became an important stopping place in the middle ages with numerous inns. The great bed of Ware was built for one of these, The White Hart. Later the town became an important malting centre and some of the malting buildings still survive. There are charming riverside gazebos on the River Lea. The many attractive buildings include St Marys Church, founded in 1380 and Place House, built in 1290. *Further info. available from Ware Priory, (01920) 460316. It is possible to arrange tour guides. See also Scotts Grotto, Ware Priory and Ware Museum.*

WISBECH

The present day character of Wisbech is mainly that of a prosperous Georgian market town. The North Brink, the Crescent and Museum Square must be among the finest examples of Georgian street architecture in the country. The town grew up around its port, trading from medieval times but flourishing commercially with the draining of the Fens in the 17th century. The years 1700-1850 witnessed tremendous growth, which established the fine buildings seen today. Whilst the port has declined in importance, Wisbech remains the market centre for a large agricultural and horticultural area. Of particular note in the town are buildings including Elgood's historic brewery, Peckover House and Gardens, the Old Market, the Market Place and the Crescent area (including the Wisbech and Fenland Museum). Octavia Hill, one of the founders of the National Trust, was born in Wisbech. A museum commemorating her life and work in housing reform has recently been opened on the South Brink. The Angles Centre presents theatre and exhibitions all year. A modern shopping centre complements the traditional retail areas. Auctions of plants and produce Mon to Fri, 1600 at Cattle Market Chase and household effects and bygones on Wed and Sat, 1000. Market days Thurs and Sat. Early closing Wednesday. *Free Mini Guide and Visitor Guide from TIC.*

Heritage Towns

WOBURN

A small and beautifully preserved Georgian town, acknowledged as one of the most important historic towns in Britain. Woburn Abbey, home of the Dukes of Bedford for over 300 years is set in a magnificent 3000 acre deer park. The house was rebuilt in the mid 18th century and contains an extensive art collection. Britain's largest drive-through safari park, Woburn Safari Park is home to a variety of species. The Heritage Centre is housed in old St Mary's church, combining a museum of Woburn's history with Tourist Information. *Further info. from Woburn Heritage Centre.*

WOODBRIDGE

Built on the banks of the Deben, it is not hard to believe this quiet, mainly Georgian town has a history of shipbuilding and sail-making. The name 'Woodbridge' derives from the Saxon language meaning Woden's town, and in later years people have been searching for centuries to find the wooden bridge after which the town was supposedly named! Its famous Elizabethan Statesman, Thomas Seckford has left his mark on the town. His endowment of almshouses in Woodbridge and investment in properties in London means the Seckford Foundation is still in being today. The Shire Hall on Market Hill was built by him and now houses the Suffolk Horse Museum. The Seckford family home is now a hotel outside Woodbridge. The famous Tide Mill has been restored to full working order and is open to the public. From the quay enjoy a walk along the river wall path. St Mary's church has a large 15th century West tower with strange buttresses that change shape as they ascend. *Tourist Information from: Council Offices, Melton Hill (01394) 383789.*

WYMONDHAM

Wymondham (pronounced "Win-dum") retains all the character of a historic market town. The recently restored ancient octagonal timber framed Market Cross dominates the Market Place. The Green Dragon public house is the oldest inn. It has a fine half timbered facade with a gabled dormer window and a carved head of a bearded man supporting the jetty. Wymondham Abbey, founded in 1107 is dominated by its two tall towers which appear against the skyline from whatever side one approaches. The interior is very impressive with its ranks of arches and windows soaring up to the beautiful hammerbeam roof. The local museum tells the story of the town, which was once an important weaving centre. Opened in 1845 the railway station once served an important junction. It has been beautifully restored and now houses a museum of railway memorabilia. Market day Friday. Early closing Wednesday. *Further details from TIP.*

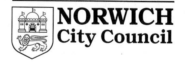

Beside the Seaside

Aldeburgh

The wide High Street, with its cottages and shops, runs north-south a stone's throw from the shingle beach where the lifeboat is always ready. Fishermen draw their boats up on to the beach and sell their fish. The Moot Hall, the Tudor centre of the town (now a museum) stands exposed only yards from the sea, which over the centuries has whittled away the shoreline. Benjamin Britten and Peter Pears began the Aldeburgh Festival in 1948 and it has developed into a year-round programme of music and arts, shared between Aldeburgh and Snape Maltings concert hall. The Aldeburgh Festival is in June, the Maltings Proms in August. Thorpeness village, a seaside village created in 1910 is just two miles up the coast. Winner of the Tidy Britain Group Seaside Award for cleanliness of beach and water. TIC. Dog ban in season.

Brightlingsea

Once an important fishing town, Brightlingsea is now a yachting centre with one of the best stretches of sailing on the East Coast. Superb walks along the banks of Brightlingsea Creek and the River Colne offer the naturalist a chance to study birdlife on the saltings. *Holiday guide to the Essex Sunshine Coast from Council Offices (EDU), Thorpe Road, Weeley, Clacton-on-Sea, Essex, CO16 9AJ. Tel: (01255) 830566.*

Clacton-on-Sea

Clacton-on-Sea's south facing long sandy beach is part of the sunshine holiday coast of Essex. Clacton is a strikingly clean town with lovely seafront gardens and walks. The town offers a wide variety of shops. There is good choice of accommodation competitively priced ranging from hotels and guest houses to self catering flats, and holiday parks. It is an ideal place to stay or as a base from which to

visit other parts of East Anglia. The town and surrounding area has been the venue for several television programmes including Travelog, the BBC1 holiday programme, and an episode of Eastenders. There is a varied programme of entertainment and events taking place throughout the year in and around the town. There are various amusement centres, including the arcades, Pavillion and the Pier. The two theatres Princes Theatre and West Cliff are open all year with many well known 'stars' performing at both venues. TIC. *Guide to the Essex sunshine Coast from Council Offices (EDU), Weeley, Clacton-on-Sea, CO16 9AJ. Tel: (01255) 830566.*

Cromer

Dominated by its parish church the town of Cromer stands in a cliff top setting, with wide sandy beaches running down to the sea. It is famous for its fishing boats that still work off the beach and offer freshly caught crabs. The town boasts a fine pier theatre, museums and lifeboat station along with the usual seaside attractions. A week not to be missed is carnival week held in August. TIC. *For a free guide write to Coast and Countryside, Dept EG96, Brochure Despatch Centre, Mackintosh Road, Rackheath Industrial Estate, Norwich, Norfolk, NR13 6LH. Tel: (01603) 721717 (24 hrs).*

Felixstowe

A popular resort town between the estuaries of the rivers Deben and Orwell on the Suffolk coast. It is popular as a family resort with a playground, boating lake, pier, model yacht pond, miniature railway, amusement park and the beach itself which is safe at all states of the tide and is a mixture of sand and shingle. The Spa Pavilion Theatre presents a lively and wide-ranging programme of entertainment throughout the year and the Leisure Centre has three swimming pools and a sauna, fitness area and lounge bars. Felixstowe is justly proud of its gardens which provide a floral welcome all year. The resort is an ideal centre from which to tour the lovely and historic Suffolk countryside. Sea and river trips. Events: May Folk Festival, Historic Vehicle Rally, Drama Festival; July Raft Race, East of England Lawn Tennis Championships; Aug/Sep Felixstowe Carnival; Oct Half Marathon; Nov Fishing Festivals. TIC.

Frinton-on-Sea & Walton-on-the-Naze

Frinton, sited on a long stretch of sandy beach, is quiet, secluded and unspoilt. Its main shopping street has been dubbed the 'Bond Street' of East Anglia. Summer theatre and other open-air events take place throughout the season. A variety of attractive hotels and guest houses face the magnificent greensward. There are excellent tennis and golf clubs. Frinton recently hosted the BBC1 'Clothes Show', and has featured in the BBC1 'Holiday' programme and Channel 4 'Travelog'. Walton is more fun of the fair. It is a jolly, quaint resort which focuses on the pier with all its attractions, including a ten pin bowling alley. The seafront gardens are colourful and the beach has good sand. To the rear of Walton are the Backwaters, a series of saltings and little harbours leading into Harwich harbour adjacent to the modern indoor swimming pool is the Columbine Centre, a multi purpose centre.TIP. *Holiday Guide to the Essex Sunshine Coast from Council Offices (EDU), Weeley, Clacton-on-Sea, Essex, CO16 9AJ. Tel: (01255) 830566.*

Great Yarmouth

Is one of Britain's most popular seaside resorts with wide sandy beaches and the impressive Marine Parade which has colourful gardens and almost every imaginable holiday attraction and amenity. The award-winning Marina Leisure and Fitness Centre, offers a huge variety of all-weather sports and entertainment facilities, including a swimming pool with waves! Gorleston-on-Sea has a wide promenade lined with gardens and old streets dating from the days when it was an important sea port. The sandy beaches outside the town are unspoilt. Great Yarmouth is also an interesting historical centre, sections of the old town wall remains and there are numerous museums and other places of historic interest to be explored. Boating: Yacht Station and Port of Yarmouth Marina; day cruises to the Broads, Broads sailing and day boats for hire. Entertainment: Huge variety, including star-name live shows at various theatres and venues - Britannia Theatre Tel: (01493) 842209 Jul-mid Sep. Gorleston Pavilion Tel: (01493) 662832 early Jun-end Sep. Hippodrome Tel: (01493) 844172, early July-Sep. Wellington Pier Theatre Tel: (01493) 842244 or 843635, early Jul-mid Sep. Winter Garden Tel: (01493) 857425, Jun-Sep, variety family entertainment. Royalty Theatre Tel:

(01493) 842043, early Jul-mid Sep, summer show and latest film presentations. St Georges Theatre Tel: (01493) 858387 Jun-Sep, summer show; remainder of year, concerts, recitals, plays etc. Marina Centre Piazza Tel: (01493) 851521 entertainment nightly, Jul-Sep. Also horse racing and numerous other holiday attractions incl. The Sealife Centre, Ripley's 'Believe it or Not' exhibition, 'Treasure World' underseas exhibition, and a huge Pleasure Beach with all the latest rides. *Full details of all facilities and accommodation incl. in Holiday Guide available from TIC, Tel: (01493) 332200.*

Hunstanton

Hunstanton possesses two quite distinct physical features: it is famous for its striped cliffs, made of successive layers of carr stone, red chalk and white chalk; and unlike any other resort in East Anglia, the town faces west. In 1996 it celebrates its 150th birthday as a seaside resort (purpose-built in 1846) with many special events and a birthday party on 18 August. Winner of several Seaside Awards for cleanliness of beach and water. Hunstanton's wide sandy beaches are excellent for bathing, and it is also popular with boating, windsurfing and water-skiing enthusiasts. Hotels and guest houses are bounded to the south by well laid out caravan sites and holiday centres and to the north, cliffs slope away to the dunes and quiet sandy beaches. The focal point of the town is the large, open greensward known as 'The Green', and there are the lovely Esplanade Gardens sloping gently down to the sea. The Oasis all weather leisure centre, Princess Theatre, Jungle Wonderland and the Sea Life Centre are favourite attractions for visitors. *Free brochure from TIC.*

Lowestoft and Oulton Broad

Lowestoft, Britain's most easterly town, successfully combines its role as a leading holiday resort with that of a modern fishing and commercial port. Lowestoft South Beach is winner of the European Blue Flag and Tidy Britain Group Seaside Award for cleanliness of beach and water. Oulton Broad, one of the finest stretches of inland water in England, offers the chance to get afloat in a range of craft from modern cruiser or day boat to sailing

dinghy or rowing boat. Add to the natural amenities such facilities as theatre, the East Point Pavilion visitor centre, indoor and outdoor swimming pools, attractive parks, putting and bowling greens, tennis courts, boating lakes, sports centre, family theme park, exciting events and festivals, museums, high speed motor boat racing, and concerts, naturist beach, and you have the making of an ideal family holiday. The staff of the tourist information centre in the East Point Pavilion will do all they can to make your stay a happy one. They will offer help in finding accommodation, and suggest things to do and places to visit, and arrange a tour of the fishing industry or book a theatre seat. Lowestoft and Oulton Broad is a fine holiday centre where a warm welcome is assured. TIC. *Free holiday guide available from Waveney Tourism, Room EA1, Mariners Street, Lowestoft NR32 1JT. Tel: (01502) 565989 (answerphone).*

Sheringham

Sheringham is a mixture of Victorian and Edwardian houses which has grown up around its fishing traditions. The original village is still the haunt of seafarers who carry on the brave tradition of manning the lifeboat. Sandy beaches and a range of amusements and activities are to be found in and around Sheringham. Attractions include the North Norfolk Steam Railway, museums, theatre and the Splash Fun Pool. TIC. *For a free guide write to Coast and Countryside, Dept EG96, Brochure Despatch Centre, Unit 28, Mackintosh Road, Rackheath Industrial Estate, Norwich, Norfolk, NR12 6LH. Tel: (01603) 721717 (24 hours).*

Southend-on-Sea

Southend is one of the best loved and most friendly resorts in Britain, featuring the very best ingredients for a break at the seaside. Attractions include the longest pleasure pier in the world, Seaside Award winning beaches, Sea Life Centre, Peter Pan's Playground, Never Never Land, Clifftop Bandstand, Shuttle Train, cliffs Pavilion, Art Gallery, Museums and the fishing village of Old Leigh to name but a few, and with a full calendar of exciting special eventse throughout the year, entertainment is provided for everyone. Join one of the Marketing Depart's organised Floral

Trail Guided Tours around the parks and gardens, and discover why Southend has won awards in 'Britain In Bloom' for three years running and a gold medal in the 1995 Chelsea Flower Show. New for 1996 - Peter Pan's Adventure Island, a water theme park which will include a Log Flume Ride, Lazy River Boat Ride, Sea Serpent Slides and Flying Shark Roller coaster, making it on of the finest theme park attractions in the south of the country. *For free guide and money saving voucher book please write or telephone: Marketing Department, P.O. Box 6, Civic Centre, Southend-on-Sea, Essex, SS2 6ER; Tel: (01702) 215119. TIC (01702) 215120.*

Southwold

Southwold is an elegant and attractive town standing on the cliff top facing the sea, with its mixture of sand and shingle beach. Winner of the European Blue Flag and Tidy Britain Group Seaside Award for cleanliness of beach and water. Fishermen's cottages, pleasant old streets and green open spaces give it much character. Discreetly fashionable as a Victorian bathing place, there is still an atmosphere of old-fashioned charm. Trade with northern Europe has left its mark on many buildings in Southwold, which show a marked Dutch influence, although the battle of Sole Bay between the Dutch and English fleets was just off the coast here (and commemorated in the local brewery's Broadside Ale). TIC. *Free holiday guides available from Waveney Tourism, Room EA1, Mariners Street, Lowestoft, Tel: (01502) 565989 (answerphone).*

Wells-next-the-Sea

A small but busy port for coasters and the local whelk and shrimp boats. Wells is a town of narrow streets and flint cottages with interesting shops. There are two steam railways, a small line runs from the quay to the Pinewoods Caravan Park which offers pitch and putt, a canoeing lake and the beach beyond; or you can enjoy a ride on the narrow gauge railway to Walsingham. Sandy beaches, nature reserves and miles of footpaths make Wells-next-the-Sea an ideal holiday town. Winner of the Tidy Britain Group Seaside Award for cleanliness of beach and water. TIC. *For a free guide write to Coast and Countryside, Dept EG96, Brochure Despatch Centre, Mackintosh Road, Rackheath Industrial Estate, Norwich, Norfolk, NR13 6LH. Tel: (01603) 721717 (24 hours).*

Good Beach Guide

On the north Norfolk coast there are wonderfully big beaches where the sea goes out for miles and where it is possible to get away from everything. On the East Coast beaches tend to be narrower, and shelve steeply. Suffolk beaches are always safer and more attractive at low tide when there is normally a strip of clean sand and the beaches shelve less steeply. (Tide tables can always be found in the East Anglian Daily Times.) At Hunstanton the high tide comes right up to the promenade as it does at Clacton, ensuring a clean beach but restricted space as high water approaches. Beware undercurrents particularly where beaches shelve steeply, and remember that the current flows south on the flood and north on the ebb and can run quite strongly, especially when the wind is in the same direction. Although East Anglia has more sunshine than most parts of the country there can be onshore easterly winds so a windbreak can be useful. Groynes constructed to stop erosion also make useful shade and shelter for picnics. Beware of strong offshore winds; these take effect 50 to 100 metres from the beach, air beds and small inflatables are very vulnerable.

Norfolk

1 Hunstanton

Winner of Seaside Awards for the last five years. Sandy beaches make an ideal playground for children, whilst windsurfers find the Wash an excellent location for their sport. To the north there are red and white cliffs and then sand dunes and a quieter beach at Old Hunstanton. The beach is very gently shelving and when the tide goes out it makes a pleasant walk for a swim. Deck-chairs. Pony rides. Pitch and putt, putting, bowls and crazy golf courses. Specially designed route for wheelchairs along the seafront. Car parking. Toilets. Dog Ban. TIC.

2 Holme-next-Sea

A long unspoilt sandy beach with a wild area of dunes and marshes at Gore Point. Nearby 400-acre nature reserve. Approached via Holme village (approx 2 miles). Car parking. Toilets.

3 Brancaster

Very quiet broad sandy beach with dunes. Approached by lane leading north from the village. The tide retreats for more than a mile to the east, but not so far to the west. Car parking. Toilets.

4 Holkham

A huge private sheltered sandy beach with dunes backed by pine trees. A favourite spot for picnics and swimming. The tide goes out for miles. Car parking along Lady Anne's Drive on payment of fee in summer, but free in winter.

5 Wells-next-the-Sea

The wide spacious beach is a mile from the town, and is reached across dunes, or by the narrow gauge railway. Consisting of sand and shingle, the beach has a large boating lake known as Abraham's Bosom and pine trees on one side with the harbour channel on the other side. Winner of the Tidy Britain Group Seaside Award (Resort Beach category). Car parking. Toilets. Wells is famous for its cockles, whelks and shrimps. Dog Ban. TIC.

6 Sheringham

A beach of sloping pebbles and shingle above sand. Rocks and groynes with shallow pools at low tide. Low cliffs. Fishing boats are hauled up on the beach. Amusements and refreshments. Deck-chairs. Car parking. Toilets. Dog Ban. TIC.

7 East Runton & West Runton

Gently shelving sand and shingle beaches backed by low crumbling cliffs. Groynes. Rocky at low tide. Car park. Dog ban at West Runton. Toilets.

8 Cromer

Gently shelving sandy beach with shingle and pebbles, the west beach is more shingly than the east one. Shallow pools at low tide. Cliffs. Pier with entertainment. Famous lifeboat. Crab fishing. Deck-chairs. Car parking. Toilets. Dog Ban. TIC.

9 Overstrand

Gently shelving sandy beach with pedestrian access. Groynes, pleasant cliff-top walks. Small car park. Toilets. Dog Ban.

10 Mundesley

Winner of the Tidy Britain Group Seaside Award (Resort Beach Category). Quiet holiday resort built in a dip in the coast line. Cliff path access to a smooth sandy beach between groynes. Deck-chairs. Car parking. Toilets. Dog Ban.TIC.

11 Winterton-on-Sea

Very wide sandy beach backed by extensive sand dunes. Pools at low tide. Nature reserve. Car park. Toilets. TIP.

12 Hemsby

Wide sandy beach scattered with stones and backed by grassy dunes. Amusements and deck-chairs. Boat trips. Car parking. Toilets. TIP.

13 Scratby/California

Low cliffs and wide sandy beach. Shallow pools at low tide. Amusements on cliff top at California. Car park at Scratby. Toilets. TIP.

14 Caister-on-Sea

Wide sandy beach which shelves steeply in some places. At the north end, towards California, there are low sandy cliffs. Low sea wall with dunes behind. Boat trips. Volunteer Lifeboat Station. Deckchairs. Car parking on Beach Road (central beach). Toilets. Picnic area. TIP.

15 Great Yarmouth

Very long sandy beach lined by the Marine Parade with its colourful gardens and countless attractions and amenities. Two piers with entertainment. Dunes at North beach. Boat trips, trampolines, and numerous refreshment stalls. Marina Centre. Deckchairs. Beach huts and tents. Car parking. Toilets. Dog Ban. TICs.

16 Gorleston-on-Sea

Wide sandy beach. Dog ban on northern section from ravine to harbour. Pier, forming part of harbour entrance. Amusements. Low cliffs between sea wall and promenade. Beach chalets. Deck-chairs. Car parking. Toilets. Dog Ban. TIP.

17 Hopton

Flat sandy beach with some shingle beneath low cliffs. TIP.

Suffolk

18 Corton

Sand and shingle beach, with southern area available to naturists. Car parking in official car park. Dog Ban.

19 Lowestoft

South Beach is the sandy pleasure beach with two piers. Winner of the European Blue Flag and Tidy Britain Group Seaside Award (Resort Beach category). Punch and Judy. Deck-chairs. Amusements. The East Point Pavilion is an indoor visitor centre. Lowestoft Ness Point is Britain's most Easterly Point. Car parking. Toilets. Dog Ban. TIC. The North Beach, is somewhat quieter and sandy with cliffs and sand dunes.

20 Pakefield

Sandy beach scattered with shingle below low grassy cliffs. Car parking. Toilets. Dog Ban.

21 Kessingland

Easy access to pebble and shingle beach with some sand. Low cliffs. River. Suffolk Wildlife Park nearby. Winner of the Tidy Britain Group Seaside Award (Rural Beach category). Dog Ban.

22 Southwold

Part sand, part shingle beach depending upon tides, with some dunes for sheltered picnics. Uncommercialised, but pots of tea are available on the beach. Short pier with amusements and refreshments. Deck-chairs and beach huts. Parking. Toilets. TIC. Winner of the European Blue Flag and Tidy Britain Group Seaside Award (Resort Beach category). Dog Ban.

23 Walberswick

Approached over The Flats, the beach is sand and shingle with sand dunes. It becomes steeper and more shingly to the south with some pebbles. Popular with painters and birdwatchers. Stall selling fish on beach. Limited car parking. Toilets.

24 Dunwich

Short walk to shelving sand and shingle beach above sand. High eroding cliffs should be avoided. There is marsh, dunes and more sand to the north. Winner of the Tidy Britain Group Seaside Award (Rural Beach category). Nature reserve at nearby Dunwich Heath. Occasional underwater exploration of old submerged town destroyed by storms – they say you can hear the church bells from beneath the waves! Car parking. Toilets.

25 Thorpeness

Steeply shelving shingle beach with some sand at low tide. Dunes and low cliffs starting to the north. Curious holiday resort developed in early 1900s with varied architectural styles. Winner of the Tidy Britain Seaside Award (Rural Beach Category). Car parking (limited). Toilets.

26 Aldeburgh

Quiet unspoilt resort. Long steeply shelving shingle beach with groynes. Winner of the Tidy Britain Group Seaside Award (Rural Beach category). Lifeboat. Fishing boats hauled up, with stalls selling fresh fish daily. Car parking. Toilets. Dog Ban. TIC.

27 Shingle Street

As its name suggests, a steep shingle beach particularly good for bracing walks and beachcombing (sometimes you can find amber). Popular for offshore fishing. Very limited roadside parking.

28 Felixstowe

Popular south-east facing holiday resort with Leisure Centre (three swimming pools), seafront gardens, pier, museum, amusements and entertainment. Shelving sand and shingle beach with little tidal movement. Some groynes down to pebbles and sand. Low cliffs to the north. Deck-chairs and beach huts for hire. Car parking. Two-mile long promenade with public seating. Toilets. Dog Ban. TIC.

Essex

29 Walton-on-Naze

Traditional resort with a gently shelving sandy beach. Groynes, cliffs and dunes at The Naze a grassy area on low cliffs giving excellent views of the busy shipping lanes around Harwich and Felixstowe. Nature trail. Pier and groynes. Pony rides, deck-chairs. Putting and tennis. Refreshment kiosks at regular intervals along the seafront. Car parking. Toilets. TIC.

30 Frinton-on-Sea

Wide expanse of greensward on top of low cliffs above a wide gently shelving sandy beach. A first-class golf course plus excellent cricket, tennis and squash facilities. A resort of peace and tranquility. Deck-chairs. Toilets. Car parking. Dog Ban.

31 Holland-on-Sea

Good sandy beaches which are usually quieter and less crowded than nearby Clacton. Groynes. Deck-chairs. Adjoining is the Holland Haven Country Park. Picnicking facility. Car parking. Toilets. Dog Ban.

32 Clacton-on-Sea

Gently sloping long sandy beach. Amusements and entertainments. Pier featuring spectacular rides, roller skating rink, SeaQaurium and night spot. Magic City the latest childrens fun filled attraction. Leisure centre and children's adventure world. Pavilion Entertainment Centre. Deck-chairs. Car parking. Toilets. Dog Ban. TICs.

33 Southend-on-Sea

Seven miles of sea and foreshore with sand and shingle beach. Expanse of seaside provides walks, traditional seaside entertainment, boat trips, water sports. Longest pleasure pier in the world with pier trains, Sea Life Centre, Peter Pan's Pleasure Park, Never Never Land Fantasy Park, colour illuminations. Popular beaches include East beach at Shoeburyness which is a winner of the Tidy Britain Group Seaside Award (Rural Beach category). This stretch of the coast has a wide expanse of grass, as well as a shingle beach ideal for young children to play. Additional beaches include Three Shells Beach, winner of the Tidy Britain Group Seaside Award (Resort Beach category), Thorpe Bay and Chalkwell. Leigh Old Town, Bell Wharf Beach. Restaurants, refreshment kiosks, archway cafes, deckchairs, boat trips, car parking, toilets. Dog Ban. TIC.

TIC: Tourist Information Centre

TIP: Tourist Information Point

Dog Ban: 1 May-30 Sep, dogs banned from the main beach areas. Further details from the nearest TIC.

Premier Seaside Award logo

European Blue Flag logo

Seaside Awards/Blue Flag Awards

The Tidy Britain Group Seaside Award covers both the beach and the bathing water. The beach must be free of litter, pollution and large amounts of rotting seaweed. The water quality must meet the mandatory standard of the EC Bathing Water Directive, and a Seaside Award flag confirms this. In addition there area number of separate qualifications which rural and resort beaches must meet, individually.

The European Blue Flag, also administered by the Tidy Britain Group, is a European award for resort beaches only and allows comparison of standards between and within the countries of the European community.

For details of the Seaside Awards/ European Blue Flag Awards and a list of 1995 award beaches (available June), contact The Tidy Britain Group: Tel: (01603) 762888.

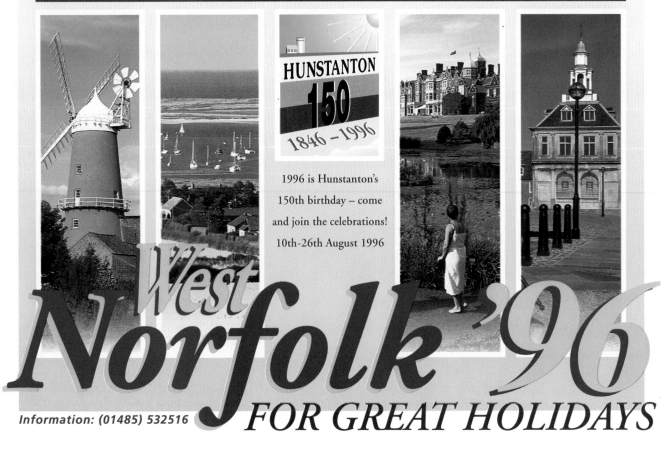

Boat Hire

Cruiser Hire

Blakes Holidays Ltd, Wroxham, Norfolk: Cruisers, yachts and houseboats on the Norfolk Broads. Narrow boats on the Cambridgeshire waterways. Choose from a wide selection from 2-12 berth. Tel: (01603) 782911 (instant bookings/general enquiries). Blakes Country Cottages. Tel: (01282) 445225. Free colour brochure (01603) 782141/783226 (recorded message).

Broads Tours Ltd, Wroxham, Norfolk. Tel: (01603) 782207. Broads cruiser line and self drive day boats. *Apr-Nov.*

Broom Boats Ltd, Riverside, Brundall, Norfolk. Tel: (01603) 712334: 2-9 berth boats, weekly hire.

Compass Craft, Ferry View Estate, Horning. Tel: (01692) 630401: 2-10 berth boats, weekly hire, and or midweek and weekends.

Freshwater Cruisers, Riverside Estate, Brundall, Norfolk, Tel: (01603) 713507: 2-6 berth cruisers. Weekly hire.

Grebe Canal Cruises, Pitstone Wharf, Leighton Buzzard, Beds. Tel: (01296) 661920: 4 and 6 berth boats for weekly and short break hire.

Greenway Marine Ltd, Riverside, Loddon, Norfolk. Tel: (01508) 520397: 2-8 berth boats, weekly hire.

Highcraft, Griffin Lane, Thorpe St Andrew, Norwich. Tel: (01603) 701701: Motor cabin cruisers. Day, picnic boats and rowing boats from Norwich Yacht Station, Riverside Road.

King Line Cruisers, Horning, Norfolk. Tel: (01692) 630297: 2-6 berth cruisers. Weekly, day boats by hour-day-week. Riverside cottages with facilities for wheelchairs.

Maffett Cruisers, Chedgrave, Norfolk, Tel: (01508) 520344: 2-6 berth cruisers. 1 dual position steerer, traditional broads cruiser. Weekly hire.

Moore & Co. Tel: (01603) 783311: 2-8 berth cruisers. Self drive day launches. Self-catering riverside properties, moorings and indoor pool. Boat repairs.

River Craft From, Stalham Yacht Services, Stalham, Norfolk. Tel: (01692) 580288: 2-10 berth Broads Cruisers, house boats, day launches. Weekly, daily and hourly hire available.

VIP Harvey Eastwood, Riverside, Brundall, Norfolk. Tel: (01603) 713345: 2-8 berth cruisers.

Narrowboat Hire

Blackwater Boats, on the Chelmer and Blackwater Navigation: 4 berth luxury narrow boats. Day hire, short breaks, long holidays. Tel: (01206) 853282.

Fox Boats, 10 Marina Dr. March, Cambs. Tel: (01354) 52770: 9 narrow boats, short break/weekly hire. 28½ miles of Fenland Waterway, stretching from the River Nene, to the River Ouse, which offers possible cruises to nearby Ely, Bedford, Cambridge, Peterborough, Oundle and Northampton.

Day Boat Hire

BEDFORDSHIRE

Leighton Buzzard
Grebe Canal Cruises, Pitstone Wharf, Leighton Buzzard, Beds. Tel: (01296) 661920): Small Narrow boats for full day hire. Galley and toilet.

CAMBRIDGESHIRE

Cambridge
Scudamores Boatyards, Mill Lane, Granta Place. Tel: (01223) 359750: Punts and rowing boats fro hire on 'the backs' and River Granta.

Huntingdon
Huntingdon Marine & Leisure Ltd, Bridge Boatyard. Tel: (01480) 413517: Day boat hire. Boat engine, chandlery & inflatable sales.

Purvis Marine Boatyard, Hartford Rd. Tel: (01480) 453628. Canoes, rowboats, motor launches and day boats. From £9.00 per hour, £55.00 per day.

ESSEX

Dedham
C.D. & M Maestrani, The Boatyard, Mill Lane. Tel: (01206) 323153/ 322045: Rowing boats and canoes. Evening bookings for parties. Teas, ices and snacks.

Mersea Island
Eastcoaster Sailing, 5 Prince Albert Road. Tel: (01206) 382545: Specialises in sailing holidays, sail training, charter and can also offer a unique day's sailing for business entertaining.

Walton Backwaters
Secret Charters, 'Pippins', Abberton Road, Layer-de-la-Haye, Colchester. Tel: (01206) 734727: Skippered Catamaran Day Cruises from Walton Backwaters. Children welcome.

NORFOLK

Acle
Anchor Craft, Acle Bridge. Tel: (01493) 750500: Day launches, cruisers.

Hickling
Whispering Reeds Boatyard. Tel: (01692) 598314: Rowing boats, sailing boats, motor launches, cruisers, houseboats for hire. Slipway and gantry facilities available.

Horning
Ferry Boatyard Ltd, Ferry Road. Tel: (01692) 630392: Cruisers, day launches and picnic launches. Modern workshop facilities with electric hoist, boat sales and marina moorings.

Potter Heigham
Herbert Woods, Broads Haven. Tel: (01692) 670711: All weather cabin type day launches, either electric or diesel. Passenger boats make regular trips to Hickling Broad.

Wroxham
Broadland Passenger Craft, Hoveton/Wroxham. Tel: (01603) 782527. Local excursions, telephone for details.

Faircraft Loynes, The Bridge. Tel: (01603) 782207: All-weather cabin-type day launches. Hire cruisers available fro weekly cruises. Passenger boats make regular trips to visit various Broads. Facilities on certain boats to accommodate wheelchairs.

Moore & Co, Hotel Wroxham, Car park. Tel: (01603) 783311: All weather diesel self-drive day launches and luxury motor cruisers.

SUFFOLK

Brandon
Bridge House Hotel. Tel: (01842) 813137: Rowing boats and canoes. Licensed riverside restaurant.

Bungay
Outney Meadow Caravan Park. Tel: (01986) 892338: Rowing boats, skiffs and canoes. Hourly or daily hire.

Lowestoft
Day Launch Hire, Yacht Station, Oulton Broad. Tel: (01502) 513087/ 589556: All weather inboard motor launches.

Sudbury
The Boathouse Hotel. Tel: (01787) 379090. Rowing boats for hire by the hour on the Stour. Afternoon cream teas.

Regular Excursions

BEDFORDSHIRE

◎ **Grebe Canal Cruises,** Pitstone Wharf, Leighton Buzzard, Beds. Tel: (01296) 661920: 1½ hour and 5½ hour cruises into the Chiltern Hills.

ESSEX

Harwich

Harwich Ferry and Services, The Quay. Tel: (01255) 502004. Pleasure steamer offering daily 1 hour harbour cruises along the River Orwell, afternoons and evenings. Private hire, special occasions - phone for details.

Southend-On-Sea

Special paddle steamer trips on PS Waverley to various destinations, including London. For details and bookings contact TIC.

HERTFORDSHIRE

Broxbourne

◎ **Lee Valley Boat Centre.** Tel: (01992) 462085. Rowing boats and motor boats for hire by the hour; electrically powered day boats to seat 8 people for hire by the day/ half-day. Traditional narrow boats for hire by the week or 3 day mini break. *Telephone for further details.*

Watford

◎ **'Arcturus' Day Cruises,** Cassio Wharf. Tel: (01438) 714528: Famous Star Class, wooden boat built 1934. Public trips from Ironbridge Lock in Cassiobury Park. *Easter-Oct, Sun & Bank Hol 1430 and 1600; also Tue & Thu in Aug 1400 and 1530.*

NORFOLK

Blakeney

Colin Bishop Ferry Service. Tel: (01263) 740753: Trips to Blakeney Point and the seals.

Broads

Wherry Sailing Tours, Broads Authority. Tel: (01603) 610734: Sailing trips on wherries (traditional Broads sailing craft). Up to 12 passengers, plus crew. During Summer. *For dates/other details contact Broads Authority.*

Horning

Mississippi River Boat, Double Decker, Paddle Steamer, based at the Swan Hotel, Horning. Tel: (01692) 630262. 1½ hour public trips throughout the season. Private hire for up to 100 people. *Ring for details.*

Hunstanton

◎ **Searle's Hire Boats,** South Beach Road. Tel: (01485) 534211: Jul-Sep: Motor launch carrying up to 60. Cruises to Seal Island viewing the seals of the Wash. Also ½ hour coastal cruises. Fishing trips. Speedboat rides. 20 min trips in WWII ex-army DUKWS, to view Hunstanton from the shoreline.

Norwich

Southern River Steamers, Elm Hill & Thorpe Station. Tel: (01603) 624051: two river boats seating 84 & 92 for 1½ and 3 hour Broadland river cruises and city cruises. Also available for private hire to groups.

Stalham

Stalham Water Tours, 28 St Nicholas Way, Tel: (01692) 670530 answerphone: All weather luxury cruiser for 1-2½ hour Broads cruises. Light refreshments. Departs Richardson's Boatyard, Stalham. Visit to How Hill Gardens, *Mon-Fri & Sun afternoons.*

Wroxham

Broadland Passenger Craft, Hoveton/ Wroxham. Tel (01603) 782527: 45 Seater passenger craft with facilities for people with special needs. 2½ or 3½ hour trips down the river from Wroxham.

◎ **Broads Tours Ltd.** Tel: (01603) 782207: 1¼. 1½, 2 and 3½ hour Broadland tours in all-weather. Passenger boats (traditional style and double decker boats). Largest boat takes 170. *May-Sep*

SUFFOLK

Lowestoft

Day Trips along the Suffolk Coast, The Yacht Station, Oulton Broad, Lowestoft. Tel: (01520) 513087/ 589556: 2/ 3 hour Sea Trips along the coast. Day trips to Southwold, and Gt Yarmouth returning via The Broads.

Orford

Lady Florence. Tel: (0831) 698298: Four hour lunch cruises on the rivers Alde and Ore. Dinner cruises in the summer. Coal fire in winter. Bar. Informative commentary. *All year round (including Christmas Day).*

Oulton Broad

Waveney River Tours Ltd, Mutford Lock, Bridge Road. Tel: (01502) 574903. 'Waveney Princess', with licensed bar, up to 125 passengers. 'Enchantress', up to 92 passengers. Light refreshments. Broads trips. *Easter, end May-end Oct.*

Snape

◎ **Snape Maltings.** Tel: (01728) 688303: One hour trip on the River Alde aboard Edward Alan John, a covered boat carrying up to 70 passengers. Departure times dependent on tides. Reduction for pre-booked groups. *Details and times on request.*

Waldringfield

◎ **Waldringfield Boat Yard.** Tel: (01473) 736260: Cruises on the River Deben, morning, afternoon and evenings. Reservations must be made.

Woodbridge

Frank Knights Shipwrights Ltd, Ferry Quay. Tel: (01394) 382318/ (01473) 624524: Trips in the launch 'Duchess 11' operate from Woodbridge Quay throughout the summer months, commencing Easter. View the River Deben at its best.

Boat Hire For Groups

BEDFORDSHIRE

Leighton Buzzard

◎ **Grebe Canal Cruises,** Pitstone Wharf, Leighton Buzzard, Beds. Tel: (01296) 661920: 60 seater wide beam vessels. Meals including Cream Tea served while cruising.

◎ **Leighton Lady Cruises,** Brantoms Wharf. Tel: (01525) 384563: 70 foot narrow boat. Heated passenger saloon with cushioned seats, seating up to 54. Cream teas and buffet available on request. *Phone for public trips list.*

ESSEX

Chelmsford

Chelmer & Blackwater Navigation Ltd, Paper Mill Lock, Little Baddow. Tel (01245) 225520: Modern pleasure barge, with bar and refreshments. Charter for groups of up to 48. Individual trips Sun and Mon of Ban Hol weekends. *Apr-Oct.*

NORFOLK

Norwich

Norfolk Wherry Trust, 14 Mount Pleasant, Norwich. Tel: (01603) 505815: Owns 'Albion' the last trading wherry. Charters available for up to 12 people. Membership includes special cruises and two journals each year.

Wherry Yacht Charter, Barton House, Hartwell Road, The Avenue. Tel: (01603) 782470: Broadland cruising on historic wherry yachts 'Olive' and 'Norada', and pleasure wherry 'Hathor'. For groups of up to 12 on each.

Sailing Boats (see section on Sailing Schools on page 94)

NORFOLK

Wroxham

◎ **Camelot Craft,** The Rhond, Hoveton. Tel: (01603) 783096: Yacht hire on the Norfolk Broads, weekly, weekends and daily hire. Tuition available.

SUFFOLK

Snape

◎ **Snape Maltings,** Ethel Ada Thames Sailing Barge. Tel: (01728) 688303/ (01473) 822054: Cruise the beautiful unspoilt East Anglian rivers aboard a comfortably converted Thames Sailing Barge. Sailing weekends, barge matches, sea shanty or birdwatching cruises and day trips. Advance bookings, scheduled trips or special charters.

Events

East Anglia offers a range of exciting and varied events to suit all tastes, from airshows to arts festivals, from historical re-enactments and cheese rolling contests to craft fairs and agricultural shows. Or for the more unusual, try the world snail racing, conker & peashooting championships, all held in the region during the year. On this page we have brought together just a small selection of events taking place during 1996. Dates which were provisional at the time of going to press are indicated by an * , and we suggest you call to confirm the details. For further information on the events listed or on other events taking place during 1996, contact the East Anglia Tourist Board on (01473) 822922.

Norwich Cathedral & Diocese Anniversary Celebrations 1096-1996
From January to December
(see also 11-14 July, 13 July, 6-11 Aug and 21 Sept)
Various venues, Norwich, Norfolk

January

12th-14th	**Whittlesey Straw Bear Festival** Various venues, Whittlesey

February

14th-25th	**King's Lynn Mart** Tuesday Market Place, King's Lynn

March

16th-17th	**National Shire Horse Show** East of England Showground, Peterborough
28th Mar- 1 Apr	**Aldeburgh Early Music Festival** Snape Maltings Concert Hall, Snape
30th-31st	**Thriplow Daffodil Weekend** Various venues, Thriplow

April

5th-8th	**Great Easter Egg Hunt, Quiz & Re-creation of Tudor Life** Kentwell Hall, Long Melford
6th-8th	**Southern Skirmish - American Civil War Re-enactment** Knebworth House, Knebworth,

May

4th-6th	**Tudor May Day Celebrations** Kentwell Hall, Long Melford
5th-6th	**The Knebworth Country Show** Knebworth House, Knebworth
6th	**Stilton Cheese Rolling Contest** Stilton, Peterborough
6th	**Ickwell May Festival** Ickwell Green, Biggleswade
9th-12th	**Living Crafts at Hatfield House** Hatfield House, Hatfield
9th-25th	**Bury St. Edmunds Festival** Various venues, Bury St. Edmunds
11th-12th	**Bedford Regatta** Various venues, Bedford
11th-12th	**Fighter Meet 1996** North Weald Airfield, North Weald
18th-25th	**Chelmsford Cathedral Festival** Chelmsford Cathedral,
19th	**BMF Rally** East of England Showground, Peterborough
25th-26th	**Air Fete '96** RAF Mildenhall, Mildenhall

25th-26th	**Bedford River Festival** Various venues, Bedford
25th-27th	**Re-creation of Tudor Life at Whitsuntide** Kentwell Hall, Long Melford
26th-27th	**Braintree Country Fair & Festival** Towerlands Centre, Panfield Road, Braintree
26th-27th	**LTS Southend Air Show** Western Esplanade, Southend-on-Sea
27th	**Luton Carnival** Various venues, Luton
29th-30th	**Suffolk Show** Suffolk Showground, Ipswich

June

7th-23rd	**Aldeburgh Festival of Music and the Arts (49th)** Snape Maltings, Snape, Suffolk
14th-16th	**Essex County Show** Essex Showground, Great Leighs
15th-30th	**Hunstanton & District Festival of Arts** Various venues, Hunstanton
16th Jun- 7th Jul	**Historical Re-creation of Tudor Life** Kentwell Hall, Long Melford (Sat/Suns only) & Fri 5th July
22nd-23rd	**Festival of Gardening at Hatfield House** Hatfield House, Hatfield
22nd Jun- 3rd Jul	**Peterborough Cathedral Festival** Peterborough Cathedral
26th-27th	**Royal Norfolk Show** Norfolk Showground, Norwich
29th Jun- 7 Jul	**Harwich Festival** Various venues, Harwich

July

During July *	**World Snail Racing Championships** Congham, nr. King's Lynn, Norfolk
11th-14th	**Flower Festival in Norwich Cathedral** Norwich Cathedral, Norwich, Norfolk
13th	**Tendring Hundred Show** Lawford House Park, Lawford
13th	**Lord Mayor's Street Procession** Various venues, Norwich
13th	**World Pea Shooting Championships** Village Green, Witcham, Cambridgeshire
13th-14th	**Wings & Wheels Model Spectacular** North Weald Airfield, Epping
16th-18th	**East of England Show 1996** East of England Showground, Peterborough
19th-28th	**Festival of St. Albans** Various venues, St. Albans
20th Jul- 3rd Aug	**King's Lynn Festival 1996** Various venues, King's Lynn
26th-28th	**32nd Charles Wells Cambridge Folk Festival** Cherry Hinton Hall Grounds, Cherry Hinton
28th	**Fireworks & Laser Symphony Concert** Knebworth House, Knebworth

| 28th Jul-
3rd Aug | **Great Yarmouth & Gorleston Carnival 1996**
(procession on 28th)
Various venues in Gorleston & Great Yarmouth |
| 31st | **Sandringham Flower Show**
Sandringham Park, Sandringham |

August

1st-31st	**Snape Proms** Snape Maltings Concert Hall, Snape
2nd-4th	**Southend Jazz Festival** Various venues, Southend-on-Sea
3rd-6th	**NSRA Hot Rod Championships** Knebworth House, Knebworth
6th-11th	**'Fire from Heaven'- Drama of Norwich Cathedral's History** Norwich Cathedral, Norwich
17th	**Illuminations Switch On & Firework Spectacular** Various venues, Southend-on-Sea
17th-18th	**Hertfordshire Craft Fair** Knebworth House, Knebworth
18th	**Hunstanton's 150th Birthday Party** Various venues, Hunstanton
21st*	**Cromer Carnival** Various venues, Cromer
24th	**Thames Sailing Barge Race** Seafront, Southend-on-Sea, Essex
25th	**Festival of Bowls (50th Anniversary)** Various venues, Great Yarmouth
Bank Holiday*	**The Chelmsford Spectacular 1996** Hylands Park, Chelmsford, Essex
26tth	**St. Albans Carnival** Various venues, St. Albans

September

1st	**Herring Festival** Hemsby Beach, nr. Great Yarmouth
5th-8th	**Burghley Horse Trials 1996** Burghley House & Park, nr. Stamford
7th	**Anniversary Finale Concert - Musical Extravaganza with Fireworks** Norwich Cathedral Close, Norwich
13th-17th	**Glenn Miller Festival** Various venues, Bedford
30th Sep- 6th Oct	**Cathedral & Abbey Church of St. Alban Flower Festival** Cathedral & Abbey Church of St. Alban

October

10th-20th	**Norfolk & Norwich Festival 1996** Various venues, Norwich
13th	**World Conker Championships 1996** The Village Green, Ashton, Cambridgeshire
17th-20th	**Aldeburgh October Britten Festival** Snape Maltings Concert Hall, Snape
28th Oct- 2nd Nov	**19th CAMRA Beer Festival** St. Andrews & Blackfriars Hall, Norwich

November

| Nov -Dec | **Christmas Carol Concerts**
The Thursford Collection, Thursford |

Events

December

Dec   **Christmas Concerts**
           The Village, Fleggburgh, nr. Great Yarmouth

18th-19th* **Victorian Christmas Fair**
           Various venues, Bedford

Horseracing

Racing at Fakenham - Tel: (01328) 862388

Racing at Great Yarmouth - Tel: (01493) 842527

Racing at Huntingdon - Tel: (01480) 453373

Racing at Newmarket - Tel: (01638) 663482

The National Trust

The National Trust organises a wide and varied range of special events at their properties in East Anglia, during the year. For a free programme contact The National Trust on (01263) 733471.

Local Theatres

Bedfordshire

Luton, St. Georges Theatre (01582) 21628

Cambridgeshire

Peterborough, Key Theatre (01733) 52437
Wisbech, Angles Theatre (01945) 474447

Essex

Basildon, Towngate Theatre (01268) 531343
Chelmsford, Civic Theatre (01245) 495028

Colchester, Mercury Theatre (01206) 573948
Colchester, Lakeside Theatre (01206) 873261
Colchester, Arts Centre (01206) 577301
Grays, Thameside Theatre (01375) 383961
Harlow, The Playhouse (01279) 424391
Southend-on-Sea, Cliffs Pavilion (01702) 351135
Southend-on-Sea, Palace Theatre (01702) 342564

Norfolk

King's Lynn, Arts Centre (01553) 773578
Norwich, Theatre Royal (01603) 630000
Norwich, Arts Centre (01603) 660352
Norwich, Maddermarket Theatre (01603) 626560
Norwich, Puppet Theatre Administration (01603) 615564
    Box Office (01603) 629921

Suffolk

Bury St Edmunds, Theatre Royal (01284) 755469
    Box Office (01284) 769505
Eye, Theatre (01379) 870519
Felixstowe, Spa Pavilion Theatre (01394) 283303
    Box Office (01394) 282126
Ipswich, Wolsey Theatre (01473) 253725
Ipswich, Regent Theatre (01473) 281480
Ipswich, Eastern Angles Theatre Co (01473) 218202
    Box Office (01473) 211498
Lowestoft, Marina Theatre (01502) 573318
Sudbury, Quay Theatre (01787) 374745
Snape Concert Hall (01728) 452935
    Box Office (01728) 453543
Woodbridge, Riverside Theatre (01394) 382174

Cambridgeshire

◎ **Big Sky Adventure Play,** 24 Wainman Road, Shrewsbury Avenue, Woodston: A full range of soft play activities for 0-12 years old including slides, climbs, inflatables and ball pools - all in a completely safe environment. Electric mini go-karts suitable for 3-8 year olds. Full catering facilities for children and parents. *All year, daily, 0930-1830; closed 25, 26 Dec, 1 Jan. Children £2.99. Tel: (01733) 390810.*

◎ **Wildtracks,** Chippenham Road, Kennett: Off-road activity park embracing all kinds of activities for children and adults, inc. karting, quad bikes, moto cross, 4 wheel driving and instruction. In addition the largest collection of drivable tanks and military vehicles in the UK. *All year, daily, 0900-1800; closed 25 26 Dec unless by arrangement. Tel: (01638) 751918.* ♿

Essex

◎ **E&M Harrison (Clacton) Ltd Clacton Pier,** 1 North Sea, Clacton-on-Sea: Largest fun pier in Europe. 12 fairground rides, arcades, shops, cafes, restaurants, side shows, pub with children's play area, disco and sea aquarium. Disco and pub open all year. Rides and attractions open Easter to 31st October. *Easter-31 Oct, daily, 1000-1700 onwards, depending on time of year. Tel: (01255) 421115.* ♿

Never Never Land, Western Esplanade, Southend-on-Sea: Never Never Land is a unique and original children's adventure park where fantasy becomes living, animated reality with many fairytale features and special effects, including the familiar stories of Jack and the Beanstalk, Merlin the Magician, fairy castles and futuristic themes such as Masters of the Universe, Badger's house from Wind in the Willows, Snow White's Cottage and the Old Women who lived in a Shoe. *7 Apr-31 Oct, Sat, Sun, 1100-2130. All local school holidays 7 days a week, 1100-2130. £1.80/ £1.20/£1.20. Tel: (01702) 460618.* ♿

Peter Pan's Playground, Sunken Gardens West, Western Esplanade, Southend-on-Sea: Rides and attractions include roller coaster, big wheel fantasy dome, Sky Lab, giant Pirate Ship. Fast food kiosks. New for 1993, the Looping Barracuda. *Open daily, Easter-30 Sep, 1 Oct-Easter, weekends only, closed 25 Dec. Tel: (01702) 468023.* ♿

◎ **Southend-on-Sea Pier,** Western Esplanade, Southend-on-Sea: Train ride along the pier approx. 1.3 miles. Pier Museum at North Station, amusements novelty shop, restaurant, licensed public house. Guided tours at Lifeboat House. Music and entertainment at pier Head in June, July and August. Punch and Judy also. *Phone for details. Tel: (01702) 215622.* ♿

Peter Pan's Playground, Essex

Peter Pan's Playground (illuminated), Essex

Walton-on-the-Naze Pier, Pier Approach, Walton-on-the-Naze: Pier with arcade, prize bingo, diner, ten pin bowling centre, fishing, adult and junior rides, Pirate Pete's indoor soft play area, arcade bingo, soft play area. *All year, daily. Rides 13 Mar-22 May, Sat, Sun, 1000-dusk; 22 May-18 Sep, daily, 1000-2130; 18 Sep-31 Oct, Sat, Sun, 1000-dusk; open, 30 Mar-14 Apr and Bank Holidays, 1000-dusk. Tel: (01255) 672288.* ♿

Hertfordshire

Activity World, Longmead, Birchwood, Hatfield: Large childrens indoor adventure play centre with 6,000 sq ft of giant slides, ball pools and mazes. Birthday parties catered for and special schemes for playgroups and schools. *Daily, 0930-1930. Closed 25, 26 Dec. £2.40. Tel: (01707) 270789.* ♿

Adventure Island Playbarn, Parsonage Lane, Sawbridgeworth: A 200,000 high quality barn conversion into an indoor children's play centre, incorporating toddler area for the under 5's, soft play, slides, aerial runway, ball ponds, plus other exciting children's play modules. A picnic area also includes a bouncy castle, and outdoor child- rens activity garden. There is an indoor refresh- ments area, adequate car parking and birthday parties & school groups are catered for. A major extension during June 95 has doubled the size of playspace & seating available. A permanent marquee now holds the bouncy castle & hot food. *Every day, 1000-1800. Closed Christmas 24, 25, 26 Dec. £2.00. Tel: (01279) 600907.* ♿

Norfolk

◎ **Dinosaur Natural History Park,** Weston Estate, Weston Longville: The park is in 300 acres of unspoilt woodland with life size models of dinosaur around the walk. On the trail you will find our Bygone Museum, The Teddy Bear's Picnic and our tribe of Neanderthall Man. New this year is our life size Mammoth, Norfolk's largest. On to our information Centre then back to the play area, refreshments and gifts. First aid and baby room. Crazy golf is £1.00 per person extra. *1 Apr-31 Oct, 1000- 1800; please ring for further information.. £3.75/£2.75. Tel: (01603) 870245.* ♿

Funstop, Exchange House, Louden Road, Cromer: Children's indoor adventure centre with giant slide, ball bond, tubes, scrabling nets, special under 4's area, super snack bar and lots more. *Jan-Mar, Fri, Sat, Sun and school holidays, 1000-1800; Apr-Oct, daily, 1000-1800; Nov-Dec, Fri, Sat, Sun and school holidays, 1000-1800. Tel: (01263) 514976.*

Jungle Wonderland CHS Amusements, 1st Floor Pier Entertainment Centre, The Green, Hunstanton: Adventure playground catering for children 2-12 years. Soft play area for toddlers, ball pool, Kenny the Croc slide, and many more play with the jungle theme. 80 seater diner that can cater for birthday and Christmas parties (we do sell a selection of bottled alcoholic beverages) also a gift shop. Height limit of approx. 5ft. *31 Mar-31 Oct, daily, 1000-1800; school summer holidays, daily, 1000-1900; Nov-Mar, Fri-Sun, 1000-1800; autumn, winter, spring school holidays, daily, 1000-1800; closed 25, 26 Dec. £1.95. Tel: (01485) 535505.*

Family Fun

Louis Tussauds House of Wax, 18 Regent Road, Great Yarmouth: Waxworks exhibition, torture chambers, chamber of horrors. Hall of funny mirrors. Family amusement arcade. *Easter-31 Oct, daily, times variable. £2.50/£1.50/£1.50. Tel: (01493) 844851.*

◎ **Pettitt's Animal Adventure Park**, Camphill, Reedham: Children's theme park. Rides, shows, animals and craft demos. New for 1996 - Junior Roller Coaster, The Black Mamba. *5 Apr-31 Oct, Sun-Fri; Sat only on Bank Hols and school holidays. £5.25/£4.95/£3.95. Tel: (01493) 700094.* &

◎ **Pleasure Beach,** South Beach Parade, Great Yarmouth: Situated on the sea front the Pleasure Beach is a 6 acre leisure park featuring over 70 rides and attractions. Entry is completely free. Visitors can come and go as they please. Rides are paid for by tokens purchased from pay boxes and machines inside the park. The Pleasure Beach is currently rated in the top ten of all leisure parks in the country with in excess of 2 million visitors a year. Ample car parking adjacent to the park. *24 Mar, 1300-1800; 31 Mar-11 Apr, weekends & Bank Hols in April and May; 25 May-15 Sep, daily. Tel: (01493) 844585.* &

◎ **The Village,** Burgh St Margaret, Fleggburgh: Set in over 35 acres of parkland. Traction eng- ines, Victorian Gallopers, narrow gauge railway, working crafts, concerts on the Mighty Compton Cinema Organ, farm animals, working steam exhibits, vintage vehicles, live shows and children's adventure playground, traditional fair- ground Picnic areas, New Regent restaurant, BBQ food, pub, tearooms, fish & chips. *Feb half term; 5 Apr-31 Oct, Nov, Dec, daily, 1000-1730, closed last 2 weeks Dec. Tel: (01493) 369770.* &

World of Wax, 68 Marine Parade, Great Yarmouth: Waxworks include, fairyland, horrors, crown jewels, pop stars and royalty. *Open, daily, Apr, May, Oct, 0930-1800; Jun-Sep, 0930-2130; Nov-Mar, Sat, Sun; Open all school holidays; closed 25 Dec. £2.00/£1.50/£1.50. Tel: (01493) 842203.*

Felixstowe, Suffolk

Suffolk

◎ **Charles Manning's Amusement Park**, Sea Road, Felixstowe: Large thrilling rides and attractions; traditional amusement park. Night- club and lazer shooting - new in 1994 Paintball shooting - new in 1995 The Big Red Fun Bus and the Labyrinth Ghost Train. *4 Apr-29 Sep, Sat, Sun and school holidays; Sun and Bank Holidays, please phone for exact opening times. Tel: (01394) 282370.*

◎ **Cragg Climbing Wall**, Mid Suffolk Leisure Centre, Gainsborough Rd, Stowmarket: East Anglia's leading wall. Group bookings, instruction courses, individual climbing and competi- tions. Suitable for novice and advanced climbers. Installed by Entre-Prises, the world's market leader in climbing walls. The new wall offers an advanced modular panelled section together with 5 other individual sections. With its 7m high lead wall 2m overhang and its realistic rock relief it allows the nearest thing possible to an ideal cragg. *All year, daily, 0800- 2300; closed 25 Dec. Tel: (01449) 674980.* &

◎ **Pleasurewood Hills Family Theme Park**, Corton, Lowestoft: One of Britain's major Theme Parks. Offering up to 8 hours of family magic every day in summer; you pay only once and then everything's free. Everything you climb and ride on, all the hairy scary rides and all the shows, as many times as you like, and there are over 50 to choose from. *Telephone for opening times. £9.50/£8.50/£5.50. Tel: (01502) 508200.* &

Sport for All

East Anglia offers a full and varied range of opportunities for those who wish to take part in sport and physical recreation. The listing that follows provides some of the basic information for visitors to the region. Additional advice and information can be obtained from the Sports Help-Line, Tel: (01234) 345222.

An annual publication entitled **Directory of Sport in the Eastern Region** is available from the Sports Council (Eastern Region), at Crescent House, 19 The Crescent, Bedford, MK40 2QP.

Artificial Ski Slopes

Bassingbourn
Bassingbourn Ski Club, Bassingbourn Barracks, Tel: (01462) 434107

Brentwood
⊛ **The Ski Centre at Brentwood Park**, Warley Gap, Tel: (01277) 211994

Harlow
Harlow Ski School, Harlow Sports Centre, Tel: (01279) 21792

Ipswich
Suffolk Ski Centre & Golf Driving Range, Bourne Terrace, Wherstead, Tel: (01473) 602347

Norwich
Norfolk Ski Club Ltd, Whitlingham Lane, Trowse, Tel: (01603) 662781 for details and practice times.

Cycling

An Information Sheet on cycle hire and routes is available from the East Anglia Tourist Board.

Golf Courses

⊛ **Stoke By Nayland Golf Club**, Keepers Lane, Leavenheath: Two 18 hole courses laid out over natural meadowland. Restrictions on visitors at weekends and Bank Holidays.

A comprehensive list of Golf Courses in East Anglia is available from the East Anglia Tourist Board.

Ice Skating

Chelmsford
Riverside Ice and Leisure Centre, Victoria Road, Tel: (01245) 269417: Ice rink, 3 pools, 6 court sports hall, gymnasium, squash courts, snooker hall and health suite.

Leisure Pools

BEDFORDSHIRE

Oasis Leisure Pool, Cardington Road, Bedford, Tel: (01234) 272100: Waterslides, fountains, bubble burst, outside river ride, quiet pool, spa baths. Conditioning gym, sauna and sunbeds.

ESSEX

Blackwater Leisure Centre, Maldon, Tel: (01621) 851898: Leisure pool with flumes, baby/toddlers pool, health and fitness area, solarium, cafeteria.

Colchester Leisure World, Cowdray Avenue, Tel: (01206) 766500: Extensive leisure complex offering a wide range of facilities including leisure pool , bubble lounge, children's fountain, 25m competition pool and teaching pool. Also badminton courts, sauna, jacuzzi, bar and restaurant and concert hall.

NORFOLK

⊛ **Great Yarmouth's Marina Leisure and Fitness Centre**, Marine Parade, Gt Yarmouth, Tel: (01493) 851521: Tropical leisure pool with wave machine and Aquaglide, sports hall, multi-gym. Table tennis, snooker, pool, squash courts, sauna/solarium, restaurants, bars, children's play area, entertainment, indoor bowls, roller skating, conference facilities.

⊛ **Hunstanton Oasis** (Promenade), Tel: (01485) 534227: Exciting family leisure centre on seafront. Indoor and outdoor leisure pools, aquaslide, toddler pools, whirlpool spa, soft play area with toddler slides, swings and see-saw, indoor bowls, squash courts, cafeteria, bar, sun lounge.

⊛ **Norwich Sport Village & Broadland Aquapark**, Drayton High Road, Hellesdon, Tel: (01603) 788912: Indoor and outdoor tennis, squash, multi sports hall, health & fitness centre including gymnasium, sauna/steam rooms, plunge & spa pool, bars, restaurants and hotel. The Aquapark is a 6 lane, 25m competition pool and has 2 giant water flumes.

⊛ **The Splash Leisure Pool**, Weybourne Road, Sheringham, Tel: (01263) 825675: Giant waterslide and splash pool, wave pool, children's paddling pool and walrus slide. Health and fitness club. Ice-cream parlour, poolside bar and fast-food. Shop.

East Anglia has a good selection of golf courses.

SUFFOLK

⊛ **Bury St Edmunds Leisure Centre**, Beetons Way, Tel: (01284) 753496/7: 33m pool, 20m learner pool, leisure pool with flumes. Sports hall, 2 ancillary halls, 3 squash courts, climbing wall, weight and fitness training, sporturf all weather pitches, saunaworld. Cafe and bar.

⊛ **Felixstowe Leisure Centre**, Undercliff Road West, Tel: (01394) 670411: Features include

leisure swimming pool, learner pool, sauna, sunbeds, bowls hall, fully licensed lounges and bars, multi-purpose entertainment and conference hall, amusement area, cafe and refreshment facilities, tourist information centre.

⊛ **Crown Pools**, Crown Street, Ipswich. Tel: (01473) 219231: Award winning 3 pool complex, 8-lane 25m competition pool, beach entry free-form leisure pool with wave making machine, waterfall fountains, inflatable slide and teaching pool, surrounded by an oasis of tropical plants. Full theatrical lighting system. Bar, restaurant and cafeteria.

⊛ **Kingfisher Leisure Pool**, Friars Meadow, Sudbury, Tel: (01787) 375656: Leisure pool including 25m pool, 55m flume ride, wave machine, water cannon, health suite and gymnasium.

Roller Skating

Bury St Edmunds
⊛ **Rollerbury**, Station Hill, Tel: (01284) 701216: Roller-skating, skating lessons, cafe and bar.

Colchester
⊛ **Rollerworld**, Eastgates, Tel: (01206) 868868: Great Britain's largest roller-skating rink, 25m x 50m maple floor. Roller hire, roller cafe, roller bar. Sound and lightshow, Quasar at Rollerworld: serious fun with a laser gun.

Ipswich
Roller King Skating Centre, Gloster Rd, Martlesham Heath, Tel: (01473) 611333: Maple floor, skate hire, skating lessons, snack bar, licensed bar.

Southend-on-Sea
Roller City, Aviation Way, Tel: (01702) 546344: Roller rink, skate hire, shop, snacks available.

Swimming Pools

The swimming pools list gives information about **extra facilities** that can be found at each pool site, the following abbreviations are used:

🏃 Athletic track
🧗 Climbing wall
♿ Provision for those with a disability
🤿 Diving pool
⛳ Golf course
𝖸 Health and fitness suite
L Learner pool
≋ Outdoor pool
✳ Outdoor sports pitch
⌂ Sports hall
🎾 Squash courts

BEDFORDSHIRE

Bedford
Robinson Pool, Bedford Park. Tel: (01234) 354901. 𝖸 *L* ♿

Dunstable
Dunstable Park Recreation Centre, Court Drive. Tel: (01582) 608107. ⌂ ✳ 𝖸

Houghton Regis Sports Centre,
Parkside Drive. Tel: (01582) 866141.
⌂ ♿

Flitwick
Flitwick Leisure Centre, Steppingley Road. ⌂

Leighton Buzzard
Tiddenfoot Leisure Centre, Mentmore Road.
Tel: (01525) 37565. ⵏ ♿

Luton
Lea Manor Leisure Centre, Northwell Drive.
Tel: (01582) 599888. ⌂ ♿

Lewsey Park Pool, Pastures Way.
Tel: (01582) 604244. ⵏ ♿

Putteridge Recreation Centre, Stopsley.
Tel: (01582) 31664. ⌂ ♿

Wardown Swimming & Leisure Centre,
Bath Road. Tel: (01582) 20621. *L* ⌂ ♿

Kempston
Kempston Pool, Hillgrounds Road.
Tel: (01234) 843777. ⵏ ♿

CAMBRIDGESHIRE

Bottisham
Bottisham Village College, Lode Road.
Tel: (01223) 812148.

Cambridge
Abbey Pool, Whitehill Road.
Tel: (01223) 213352. ⵏ *L* ❋

Kings Hedges Pool, Kings Hedges Road.
Tel: (01223) 353248.

Parkside Pool, Parkside. Tel: (01223) 350008.
ⵏ *L* ♿

Ely
Paradise Pool, Newnham Street.
Tel: (01353) 665481. ♿

Eynesbury
St Neots Indoor Pool, Barford Road.
Tel: (01480) 74748. *L*

Huntingdon
Huntingdon Recreation Centre,
St Peters Road. Tel: (01480) 454130. 🏹 ♿

March
George Campbell Pool, City Road.
Tel: (01354) 53511. ♿

Melbourn
M C Splash. Tel: (01763) 261508. ⵏ ⌂

Peterborough
Jack Hunt Swimming Pool, Ledbury Road.
Tel: (01733) 264644. 🚴 ⵜ ♿

Orton Longueville Pool, Orton Longueville
School. Tel: (01733) 231971. ⌂

Regional Swimming Pool, Lancashire Gate.
Tel: (01733) 51474. ⵏ *L* ♿

Ramsey
Ramsey Sports Centre, Abbey Road.
Tel: (01487) 710275. ♿

St Ives
St Ivo Recreation Centre, Westwood Road.
Tel: (01480) 64601. 🚴 🏹 ⵏ ⌂ ♿

Swavesey
Swavesey Village College, Swavesey.
Tel: (01954) 30366/30373. 🏹

Whittlesey
Manor Leisure Centre, Station Road.
Tel: (01733) 202298. ♿

Wisbech
Hudson Pool, Harecroft Road.
Tel: (01945) 584230.

Crown Pools, Ipswich

ESSEX

Basildon
Gloucester Park Swimming Pool,
Town Centre. Tel: (01268) 523588. ⵏ ♿

Billericay
Billericay Swimming Pool, Lake Meadow,
Recreation Ground. Tel: (01277) 657111.

Braintree
Riverside Pool, St John Avenue.
Tel: (01376) 23240. ⵏ 🏹

Brentwood
Brentwood Centre, Doddinghurst Road.
Tel: (01277) 229621. 🏹 ♿

Canvey Island
Waterside Farm Sports Centre,
Somnes Avenue. Tel: (01268) 694343. ⵏ ⌂ 🏹

Chelmsford
Riverside Pool, Victoria Road.
Tel: (01245) 269417. ⵏ 🏹 ♿

Clacton on Sea
Clacton Leisure Centre, Vista Recreation
Ground. Tel: (01255) 429647. ⵏ ♿

Corringham
Corringham Swim & Squash Centre,
Springhouse Road. Tel: (01375) 678070. 🏹 ♿

Dovercourt
Dovercourt Swimming Pool, Wick Lane.
Tel: (01255) 508266. ♿

Dunmow
Dunmow Sports Centre, Helena Romanes
School. Tel: (01371) 873782. ⵏ ❋ 🏹 ♿

Grays
Blackshots Swim & Leisure Centre,
Blackshots Lane. Tel: (01375) 372695. 🚴 ⵏ ❋

Halstead
Halstead Swimming Pool, Parsonage Street.
Tel: (01787) 473706. ⵏ

Harlow
Harlow Swimming Pool, First Avenue.
Tel: (01279) 446430. ⵏ ♿

Stewards School Pool, Stapletye.
Tel: (01279) 444503. ⵏ ♿

Hawkwell
Clements Hall Leisure Centre, Clements Hall
Way. Tel: (01702) 207777. 🚴 ⵏ ⌂ 🏹 ♿

Leigh on Sea
Belfairs Swimming Pool, Fairview Gardens.
Tel: (01702) 712155.

Loughton
Loughton Pool, Traps Hill.
Tel: (0181) 508 1477. ⵏ ♿

Ongar
Ongar Sports Centre, Fyfield Road.
Tel: (01277) 363969. ⵏ ❋ ♿

Pitsea
Pitsea Swimming Pool, Rectory Drive.
Tel: (01268) 556734. ♿

Saffron Walden
Lord Butler Leisure Centre, Peasland Road.
Tel: (01799) 26600. ⵏ 🏹 ♿

Shenfield
Shenfield Sports Hall, Oliver Road.
Tel: (01277) 226220. *L*

Shoeburyness
Shoeburyness Swimming Pool,
Delaware Road. Tel: (01702) 293558.

South Ockendon
Belhus Park Leisure Complex, Belhus Park.
Tel: (01708) 852248/856297. ✓ ⵏ 🏹 ♿

Southend on Sea
Southend Swimming Pool, Warrior Square.
Tel: (01702) 464445. ⵜ ⵏ ♿

Tendring
Walton Pool, Bachhouse Meadow,
Walton on the Naze. Tel: (01255) 676608.

Thundersley
Runnymede Sports Hall, Runnymede Chase.
Tel: (01268) 756514.

Waltham Abbey
Waltham Abbey Pool, Roundhills Estate.
Tel: (01992) 716733. ⛹ ♿

Wickford
Wickford Swimming Pool, Market Avenue.
Tel: (01268) 765460. ♿

Witham
Bramston Sports Centre, Bridge Street.
Tel: (01376) 519200. 禾 ♿ ⛹

HERTFORDSHIRE

Bishops Stortford
Grange Paddocks Pool, Rye Street.
Tel: (01279) 652332. ⛹

Buntingford
Ward Freeman Pool, Bowling Green Lane.
Tel: (01763) 72566.

Sawbridgeworth
Leventhorpe Pool, Cambridge Road.
Tel: (01279) 722490.

Ware
Fanshawe Pool, Park Road.
Tel: (01920) 466967. ⛹

NORFOLK

Bradwell
Phoenix Pool, Mallard Way.
Tel: (01493) 64575. ♿

Diss
Diss Swimming Pool, Victoria Road.
Tel: (01379) 652754. ⛹ ♿

Dereham
Breckland Pool, Quebec Road.
Tel: (01362) 693419. ⛹ ♿

Downham Market
Downham Market Swimming Pool, War
Memorial Playing Fields. Tel: (01366) 383822.
❋ 禾 ♿

King's Lynn
St James Swimming Pool, Blackfriars Street.
Tel: (01553) 764888.

Norwich
St Augustines Swimming Centre,
St Augustines Gate. Tel: (01603) 620164. ⛹ 禾 ♿

Sprowston
Sprowston Swimming Pool, Sprowston High
School, Cannerby Lane. Tel: (01603) 31133.

SUFFOLK

Bungay
Waveney Valley Pool, St Johns Hill. ♿

Hadleigh
Hadleigh Swimming Pool, Stonehouse Road.
Tel: (01473) 823470. ♿

Haverhill
Haverhill Sports Centre, Ehringshausen Way.
Tel: (01440) 702548. 肀 ⛹ ⌂ ♿

Ipswich
Fore Street Baths, Fore Street.
Tel: (01473) 253089.

Leiston
Leiston Sports Centre, Red House Lane.
Tel: (01728) 830364. ⌂

Lowestoft
Waveney Sports & Leisure Centre,
Water Lane. Tel: (01502) 69116. ⛹ 禾 ♿

Mildenhall
Mildenhall & District Swimming Pool,
Recreation Way. Tel: (01638) 712515. ♿

Newmarket
Newmarket Swimming Pool, High Street.
Tel: (01638) 661736.

Stowmarket
Mid Suffolk Leisure Centre, Gainsborough
Road. Tel: (01449) 674980. ♿ 肀 ⌂ ❋ *L* 禾 ⛹

Stradbroke
Stradbroke Pool, Wilby Road.
Tel: (01379) 384376. ♿

Woodbridge
Deben Swimming Pool, Station Road.
Tel: (01394) 380370. ♿

Watersports & Outdoor Sports

BEDFORDSHIRE

Cardington Canoe Slalom Course, Bedford.
Tel: (01582) 503851 (bookings).

The Outdoor Centre, Hillgrounds Road,
Kempston. Tel: (01234) 854959. Archery,
climbing wall, canoeing, caving, training courses.

Priory Water Sports Assoc, Bedford. Tel: (01234)
212584: Canoeing, sailing, wind- surfing.

CAMBRIDGESHIRE

Grafham Water, Huntingdon, Tel: (01480)
810521: Windsurfing, canoeing, dinghy
sailing, cycle trail, trout fishing.

Mepal Outdoor Centre, Ely, Tel: (01354)
692251: Sailing courses, climbing, archery,
canoeing, artificial caving system, residential
accommodation, fast-food restaurant.

Tallington Lakes Watersports Centre,
Tallington Lakes Leisure Park, Tallington, nr
Stamford, Lincs: Main Office (01778) 346342.
Waterski and jetski (01778) 347000. Dry ski
slope, (01778) 344990. Windsurf, canoe and
dinghy hire (01788) 380002.

Wyboston Lakes Watersports Centre,
Huntingdon, Tel: (01480) 213100: Personal
watercraft, waterskiing.

ESSEX

Bradwell Field Studies and Sailing Centre,
Bradwell Waterside, nr Southminster, Tel: (01621)
776256: Offshore cruising, dinghy sailing,
canoeing, windsurfing. RYA Approved Centre.

**Channels Windsurfing, Mountain Bike and
Canoe Centre,** Belstead Farm Lane, Little
Waltham, Chelmsford, Tel: (01245) 441000.

Channels Watersports Centre, Alexandra
Lake, Lakeside, Thurrock, Tel: (01708) 865745:
Dingy sailing, windsurfing, mountain biking,
canoeing and diving.

Chalkwell Windsurfing Club, Chalkwell
Beach, Leigh-on-Sea, Tel: (01702) 79896: Car
park, toilets. Tuition arranged. Regular racing.

🌀 **Gosfield Lake & Leisure Park,** Church
Road, Gosfield, Halstead, Tel: (01787) 475043:
Water skiing, pitch 'n' putt, fishing, restaurant.

Harlow Outdoor Pursuits Centre, Burntmill
Lane, Harlow, Tel: (01279) 432031: Sailing,
windsurfing, power boats, narrow boats, canoeing, rock climbing. Outside catering facilities.

Mill Dam Lake, St Osyth, Tel: (01255) 820535:
Waterskiing, sailing, personal watercraft.

Southend Marine Activities Centre, Eastern
Esplanade, Southend, Tel: (01702) 612770:
Tuition in sailing, canoeing, windsurfing and
power boat driving during evenings, weekends
and school holidays.

NORFOLK

Roanoke Day Centre, Neatishead, Norwich,
Tel: (01692) 630572. Sailing, canoeing. For
people with disabilities.

Surf 55, 55 St James's Street, King's Lynn, Tel:
(01553) 764356. Waterbase: Pentney Leisure
Lakes, King's Lynn. Windsurf, mountain bike
and kite centre.

Taverham Mills, Taverham Mills Fishery Lodge, Norwich, Tel: (01603) 861014. Top quality coarse fishing for lake and river. Self-catering Holiday Lodge has 10 twin-bedded rooms, and a fully fitted communal kitchen, and is within casting distance of the water.

SUFFOLK

Windsurfing Seasports, The Beach, Sea Road, Felixstowe. For information telephone Niconeys Gym: (01394) 273264: Car park, club, changing facilities, toilets, comprehensive rescue facilities. Shop, hire, tuition.

Alton Water Sports Centre, Alton Water, Stutton, Ipswich, Tel: (01473) 328408: Windsurfing, sailing, canoeing and cycle trail. Tuition and equipment hire. Cafeteria, chandlery, changing facilities, toilets. R.Y.A Approved Centre.

Suffolk Water Park, Bramford, Ipswich, Tel: (01473) 830191: Windsurfing tuition, sales, changing rooms, snack bar.

Sailing Schools

There are many opportunities in East Anglia for sailing, both inshore and offshore. In fact the region is well known for its sailing centres, such as Burnham-on-Crouch and the Norfolk Broads, to name just two. Listed here are Royal Yachting Association recognised sea schools. Further information on the RYA and sailing courses can be obtained from: Royal Yachting Association, Romsey Road, Eastling, Hants SO50 9YA. Tel: (01703) 627400.

CAMBRIDGESHIRE

East Coast Offshore Yachting, 1 Moory Croft Close, Great Staughton. Tel: (01480) 861381. Courses: Competent Crew, Day Skipper, Coastal Skipper - Sail. Based at Suffolk Yacht Harbour, River Orwell. Friendly, quality tuition in varied and interesting cruising grounds, courses tailored to individual requirements. Own boat tuition, deliveries and shore based courses available all year.

ESSEX

Bradwell Outdoor Education Centre, Bradwell Waterside, Southminster. Tel: (01621) 776256. Courses: Competent Crew, Day Skipper, Coastal Skipper - Sail. Based at Bradwell Creek, River Blackwater. Yacht equipped to current RYA/DoT requirements. The majority of cruises sail the East Coast between Dover and Great Yarmouth, offering challenging passage making, interesting pilotage and picturesque scenery. One day Taster courses for beginners and special feature courses also available.

The Cirdan Trust Sailing School, Fullbridge Wharf, Maldon. Tel: (01621) 851433. Courses: Competent Crew, Day Skipper, Coastal Skipper - Sail. Based at Brightlingsea. Practical RYA courses all levels, all year round. Coastal Skipper/Yachtmaster assessment courses including RYA examinations. Special courses to suit groups at discount price. Vessel is centrally heated for winter sailing with most modern navigation equipment.

Crouch Sailing School, 15 Granville Terrace, Burnham-on-Crouch. Tel: (01621) 784140. Courses: Competent Crew, Day Skipper, Coastal Skipper - Sail. Based at Burnham-on-Crouch. 3 and 5 day courses, designed to gain the full RYA certificates from Competent Crew to Yachtmaster. Our aim is to give as much one-to-one tuition as possible. Our courses are friendly, adventurous and good fun.

Essex Sailing School, 35 Bramley Way, Mayland, Chelmsford. Tel: (01621) 741818. Courses: Competent Crew/Helmsman, Day and Coastal Skipper - Sail/Power. Based at Maylandsea, River Blackwater. We offer the complete range of RYA courses, from beginner to Yachtmaster direct assessment. 'See how you like it' weekends are available for your very first time afloat. Good road and rail links to our marina base with ample parking. Individual nautical training ashore and afloat in both sail and power craft.

The Multihull Sailing School, 20 Ashleigh Drive, Leigh-on-Sea. Tel: (01702) 79156. Courses: Competent Crew, Day Skipper, Coastal Skipper - Sail. Based at Portsmouth and Burnham-on-Crouch. Offering a full range of RYA and tailored cruising courses, operating from Solent and East Coast bases is the school at which to learn multihull sailing. Modern, extensively equipped cruising multihulls, specialising in tuition on Prout catamarans. Be it long distance cruises, fun multihull experience weekends or RYA practical courses we guarantee you high quality tuition, fun and lots of time on the water.

Sailtrain, 18b Southend Road, Hockley. Tel: (01702) 206289. Courses: Competent Crew, Day Skipper, Coastal Skipper - Sail. Based at Shotley Point Marina, River Orwell. Sailtrain offers an all year round programme from the 'see how you like it' and 'just plain cruising' up to 'Yachtmaster'.

HERTFORDSHIRE

Foreign Exchange Marine Enterprises, 28 Dickinson Avenue, Croxley Green. Tel: (01923) 710164. Courses: Competent Crew, Day Skipper, Coastal Skipper - Sail. Based at Portsmouth Harbour. Our sailing is varied and adventurous including racing, adventure holidays, corporate events, women's groups, RYA practical courses and own boat tuition.

NORFOLK

Norfolk Broads School of Sailing, The Rhond, Hoveton. Tel: (01603) 783096. Sailing courses in cruising yachts to RYA standards. Also sailing yacht hire on the Norfolk Broads, weekly, weekend or daily. Tuition available (Camelot Craft).

Tama Sailing, 55 Eastern Road, Thorpe St Andrew, Norwich. Tel/Fax: (01603) 35431. Courses: Competent Crew/Helmsman, Day Skipper, Coastal Skipper - Sail/Power. Based at Pin Mill, River Orwell. The East Coast of Suffolk, Essex and Kent is a delightful cruising ground with interesting navigation around many offshore sand-banks. Also, cruising to foreign waters of France, Belgium and Holland offers and additional challenge. Send for brochure.

SUFFOLK

East Anglian Sea School, Studio One, Fox's Marina, The Strand, Ipswich. Tel: (01473) 684884. Courses: Competent Crew/Helmsman, Day Skipper, Coastal Skipper, Sail/Power. Based at Fox's Marina. Take your RYA course in uncrowded waters, practice navigation and boat handling with professional instructors aboard a well maintained fleet of 32' yachts.

North Sea Yachting & Motor Cruising, 2 Wherry Lane, Ipswich. Tel: (01473) 232221. Courses: Competent Crew/Helmsman, Day Skipper, Coastal Skipper - Sail/Power. Based at Ipswich and Titchmarsh. Practical YHA courses all year round. Special Coastal Skipper/Yachtmaster assessment courses including RYA exam. 'Come Sailing' holidays on the East coast and to continental ports and Channel Islands. Beginners very welcome.

Seatrain Sailing, Bridge House, Mill Road, Friston, Saxmundham. Tel: (01728) 688875. Courses: Competent Crew, Day Skipper, Coastal Skipper - Sail. Based at Orford. Exceptionally comfortable boats in some of Europe's finest and most enjoyable waters. The unspoilt coasts of Suffolk and Essex, the busy ports of Harwich and Felixstowe, and the proximity of the Dutch and Belgian ports offer a unique training experience.

Shotley Marina Sea School (Sail & Motor Cruising) Ltd, Shotley Gate, Ipswich. Tel: (01473) 788982. Courses: Competent Crew/ Helmsman, Day Skipper, Coastal Skipper - Sail/Power. Based at Shotley Marina. Excellent operating base with training rooms. Sheltered sailing in bad weather, from absolute beginner to Yachtmaster Ocean.

Sailing on Cockshoot Broad, Norfolk

People to Help You Explore the Area

Guided Tours by Registered Blue Badge Guides

Each registered Guide has attended a training course sponsored by the East Anglia Tourist Board and can be identified when wearing the 'Blue Badge'. Regional Blue Badge Guides are further qualified to take individuals or groups around the region for half day, full day or longer tours if required. For a list of these Guides and an information sheet on Guiding Activities, please contact the East Anglia Tourist Board. The 11 towns/cities listed below support registered Guides. *Please contact the Tourist Information Centre (see pages 64 to 74) in the town/city for further information unless otherwise indicated.*

BURY ST EDMUNDS

Regular Town Tours: Tours lasting 1½ hours leave from the Tourist Information Centre, Tickets can be purchased in advance, or on the day. Tel: (01284) 764667.

Tours for Groups: Guides can also be arranged for groups at any time, if enough notice is given.

CAMBRIDGE

Regular Walking Tours: Individual visitors may join tours which leave the Tourist Information Centre daily and up to 4 times a day in summer. Colleges are included as available, generally not those which charge admission.

City Centre Tours: These tours do not go into the colleges, but explore the street scenes and the historic past of the city. Evening drama tours take place during mid summer.

Group Tours: Guides are available at any time for private groups. Each tour lasts about 2 hours. One guide can escort up to 20 people. Guides to accompany groups throughout East Anglia also available. Tel: (01223) 463290/322640.

College Tours for Groups: All parties of 10 or more who intend to tour the colleges must be accompanied by a Cambridge registered Blue Badge Guide. Colleges which charge admission are only included on request (cost added to tour price). Most colleges are closed to the public during examination time, mid Apr-end Jun.

Fitzwilliam Museum, Trumpington Street. Regular tours take place during the summer and last about 1¼ hours. Groups may also book tours during museum opening times. Tel: (01223) 332904.

COLCHESTER

Regular Town Tours: Tours leaving the Tourist Info. Centre daily during summer, Mon-Sat 1400, Sun 1100. Duration about 1¾ hours.

Group Tours: May be booked at any time of year. Please give at least four days notice.

ELY

Cathedral & City Tours: Guides available for pre-booked groups all year Tours may inc. the Cathedral and city, or Oliver Cromwell's House.

Cathedral Only Tours: Groups may book a special guided tour of Ely's magnificent Cathedral. Contact The Chapter Office, Tel: (01353) 667735 Mon-Fri, 0900-1600.

Regular Tours: Individuals may join these tours in Jul & Aug. Tours include the city or Oliver Cromwell's House.

Oliver Cromwell's House Tours: available for pre-booked groups all year round. The tour may be combined with a city tour.

Theme Tours: Tours arranged as required. E.G., local pubs, ghosts, haunted places, the fens drainage story, photographic spots. By appt only.

IPSWICH

Regular Town Tours: Individuals may join the tours which leave the Tourist Info. Centre, May-Sep, Tue 1415. Tours take about 1 hour.

Group Tours: Tours can be arranged for groups all year. Please give at least one week's notice.

KING'S LYNN

Regular Town Tours: Individuals may join the tours which leave the Tourist Info Centre May-Oct, Wed & Sat; Sun, Mon, Fri in Aug and Sep each afternoon during Festival Week at 1400. Tour takes about 1 hr. For details Tel: (01553) 763044.

Group Tours: Guided tours can be arranged for groups by contacting the King's Lynn Town Guides on (01553) 765714, 1800-2100 weekdays.

NORWICH

Regular City Tours: Historic Norwich walking tours leave the Tourist Info. Centre, lasting 1½ hours. Sat, Apr-Oct at 1430. Mon-Sat from 22 May-30 Sep at 1430. Aug only 1030 & 1430. Sun only Jun-end Sep at 1030. Easter Sun and Mon, Spring and August Bank Holiday Mons.

Group Tours: Guides are available at any time for private groups, on a variety of themes. Each tour lasts about 1½ hours, one guide can escort up to 20 people. Guides for City Coach tours are also arranged, lasting approx 75 mins.

Day or Half Day Group Coach Tours: Guides are available for tours of East Anglia. Assistance with itineraries. Tel: (01603) 666071.

PETERBOROUGH

Group Tours: Guides are available for city and cathedral tours at any time for private groups, each tour lasts approx 1½ hours. Regular tours during July and August every Wednesday and Saturday leaving from the Tourist Information Centre. Tel: (01733) 317336 for details.

SAFFRON WALDEN, THAXTED & UTTLESFORD

Guided walking tours of Saffron Walden and/or Thaxted on Suns by arrangement. For specialist group tours contact Mrs Kirkpatrick, Tours Organiser. Tel: (01799) 526109 or 510445.

ST ALBANS

For information on guided tours, contact the Tourist Info. Centre, Town Hall, Market Place, St Albans, Herts AL3 5DJ. Tel: (01727) 864511.

WALSINGHAM

Walking guided tours round the historic village of Walsingham. Apr-30 Sep, Wed and Thu, 1100; Jul and Aug, Thu, 1430.

Other Tours

Bedford - For walking tours of Bedford, contact the TIC, 10 St Paul's Square, Bedford MK40 1SL. Tel: (01234) 215226.

Cambridge & East Anglia Guided Tours - Half, full day or short break tour itineraries. Specialist tours arranged. All tours accompanied by Blue Badge Guides. Contact Tours Organiser, TIC, Wheeler Street, Cambridge CB2 3QB. Tel: (01223) 463290/322640, Fax (01223) 463385.

Cycle Hire Centre. Byways Bicycles has a choice of cycles for hire, to suit all ages. Follow a planned route showing you local places of interest, pubs, tea rooms or picnic places, or choose your own. Cycling holidays also arranged. Byways Bicycles, Darsham, Nr Saxmundham, Suffolk IP17 3QD, Tel: (01728) 668764. Open Easter and May-Oct, 1000-1800 (at other times by appointment). Closed Tue.

Guide Friday Limited. Guided City tours leave every 15 minutes in summer and include a visit to the American Memorial Cemetry at Madingley. Tickets valid all day and the tour can be joined at Cambridge Railway Station or official stops in the City. Open all year round except for Christmas. Tel: (01223) 362444.

Just Pedalling. Well known for their cycling holidays. Also day or weekly hire of 3 speed and mountain bikes. Conveniently situated in the Broads area where cycling is easy and interesting. Open all year. Contact: Alan Groves, Just Pedalling, 9 Church Street, Coltishall, Norfolk NR12 7DW. Tel: (01603) 737201.

The National Stud, Newmarket. 75 minute conducted tours. The 8 horse stallion unit and up to 100 mares and foals are included in the visit. The guides give a full insight in to the workings of a modern thoroughbred stud. Open early Mar-end Aug, plus Sept & Oct Race Days. Booking essential Tel: (01638) 663464.

Rockingham Forest Tourism - Can help you discover Northamptonshire's countryside. Stately homes, where to stay, leisure drives, list of guides, walks, what's open. Contact them at: c/o Civic Centre, George Street, Corby, Northants NN17 1QB.Tel: (01536) 407507.

Windmill Ways Walking and Cycling Holidays in Norfolk. Leisurely breaks to suit individual tastes. Start and finish when you choose; travel at the pace you wish; complete personal service. Accommodation booked in quality guesthouses and hotels; maps, routes and local information provided; baggage transported; excellent touring, mountain or tandem bikes with back-up service. Colour brochure available. Windmill Ways, 50 Bircham Road, Reepham, Norfolk NR10 4NQ. Tel: (01603) 871111.

Bedfordshire

⊛ Bromham Mill & Art Gallery

A restored 17th century watermill, now run as a working museum. In addition to the supporting interpretative exhibitions on milling, agriculture and waterways history, the mill houses an art gallery and craft work outlet. The Gallery's rolling programme of exhibitions offers high quality professional work from artists within Bedfordshire and nationally. During 1996, visitors can see solo, group and themed exhibitions, including photography and contempory design projects. Craft work is also exhibited, through links with the Crafts Council recognised Fenny Lodge Gallery. Most of the art and craft work is for sale. Bromham Mill, picnic area and nature reserve, set amongst river meadow, adjoining the River Great Ouse and 26 arch, 13th century Bromham Bridge, offers a delightful setting for a relaxed outing. Fresh coffee and speciality teas served during opening hours: Mar-Oct, Wed-Fri, 1030-1630, Sat, Sun and Bank Holidays, 1130-1800 (1995 times). Small admission fee to Mill. Party groups and guided tours welcome, special rates available. Bromham Mill Gallery, West End of Bromham Bridge, Bromham, Bedfordshire. Tel: (01234) 824330 or 228671. Please phone for a programme.

Taste & Try Days

A tour that's different - and entertaining! Sample the delights of food and wine from around the world. Mediterranean, Caribbean, Mexican, Stir-Fry, Traditional British - these are just a few of the themes chosen for you to taste and try! Each recipe presented in a simple light-hearted style in a relaxed atmosphere. If you like what you taste, then recipes and take-home packs are available from our fine food shop. Forthcoming programme and booking form from Harpers Taste and Try Events, Bell Farm, Studham, Dunstable, Beds, LU6 2QG. Tel: (01582) 872001.

Cambridgeshire

⊛ Unusual gifts of good taste in craft gallery beside the cathedral. Tea room. We sell treen, woodwork, leatherware, ceramics, jewellery and toys. Open all year, daily except Sunday, 0900-1730. 16-18 High Street, Ely, Cambs. Tel: (01353) 664731.

⊛ **Sacrewell Farm & Country Centre** is interesting and educational - superb for parties and school visits - but above all it is **friendly** and **fun**. Meet our farmyard animals or enjoy the many 'hands on' bygones, quizzes and games. Play on trampolines, roundabouts and swings. Travel any of the numerous farm, nature and general interest trails, bury yourself in the history of the place and relish the immense power and ingenuity of our ancient watermill reopened in 1993 after extensive renovation. We are open every day, 0900-1800. 'The Miller's Kitchen' provides refreshments and a souvenir/gift shop is open daily 0930-1730. Admission to the Centre £3.00/£2.00/£1.00 with party rates and conducted tours available. Ample parking; caravans and campers welcome; provision for picnics. Situated off the A47, 8 miles west of Peterborough. Telephone (01780) 782254.

Essex

⊛ One of East Anglia's leading Art and Craft Centres, this thriving complex is set in the famous village of Dedham, in the heart of Constable Country. The imaginatively converted church now has three extensive floors: The GROUND FLOOR shows a huge array of British, and other, crafts including silkpainting, studio pottery, silk waistcoats, dried flower displays and superb craft jewellery. Also a candle workshop. The restaurant serves an excellent range of wholefood/vegetarian fayre all day. The FIRST FLOOR houses hand crafted furniture, ties (with a difference!), hats,

wedding dresses, our ceramic sculptor and resident artists can often be seen at work. TOY MUSEUM - see entry in Museums section. The Skylight Gallery on the SECOND FLOOR provides an excellent venue for a more paintings and studio/workshops. Open Mon-Sun, 1000-1700 all year (but closed Mon during Jan-Mar). Admission 50p/30p (family £1.00) High Street, Dedham, Nr Colchester, Essex. 1 mile off main A12 between Colchester and Ipswich. Tel: (01206) 322666. Restaurant (01206) 322677.

Norfolk

⊛ Situated at Neatishead near Wroxham, in the heart of the Norfolk Broads. A small farm specialising in growing and selling quality Dried Flowers direct to the public. The Flower Arranging Workshop and Showrooms are open throughout the year with advice and help readily available. A huge selection of flowers are on sale - dried by the bunch; silk flowers, baskets of all sizes, brassware, sundries and books. Dozens of Dried Flower Arrangements, large and small are always in stock or made to special order. Details of winter day classes available on request. Evening group demonstrations and tours by appointment. A selection of flowers can be seen growing during the summer. The farm is well signposted off the A1151 Wroxham to Stalham road. Free entry and ample free parking. Light refreshments. Open throughout the year Tue-Sat 1000-1600; Sun 1100-1600. Mon during July and Aug, Bank Holidays 1000-1600 (closed Dec 24-mid Jan). Tel: Wroxham (01603) 783588.

⊛ Situated 9 miles from Great Yarmouth on the banks of the River Bure, boasts England's largest variety of handcrafted candles, with many that are unique. The Centre also has a good selection of modelling kits. The candle shop and workshop is open daily (except Sat) from Easter to the end of Oct from 0900-1730 and during Nov and Dec from Thu to Sat 1000-1600 with free admission. Free parking and river moorings in village. Telephone Great Yarmouth (01493) 750242.

The Textile Centre

Set in traditional Norfolk barns the designs of Sheila Rowse are screen printed on to textiles and then made up into aprons, teatowels and many other items. Processes can be viewed on weekdays and a large shop stocks other textiles, books, clothes and original gifts. Cafe - serving Ploughman's lunches, coffee, tea and homemade baking. Open Mid Mar-mid Nov, Mon-Fri, 0930-1730, Sat, Sun and Bank Holidays 1000-1700. Facilities for people with special needs. Free entry and car park. Tel (01328) 820009. Hindringham Road (B1388) Great Walsingham.

Great Walsingham Gallery

The gallery is set in a beautiful courtyard in converted barns in the village of Great Walsingham. Regular exhibitions are held of paintings, also displays of sculpture, pottery, patchwork and handmade furniture. On sale, fine art prints, photo frames, mirrors and greetings. A comprehensive picture framing service is available. Members of Fine Art Trade Guild. Open Mar-Dec, Mon-Fri, 0900-1730, Sat, Sun, 1000-1700; Jan-mid Mar, Tue-Fri, 0900-1730, Sat, 1000-1700. Tel: (01328) 820900.

Taverham Craft and Country Shopping Centre
is a purpose-built centre for the finest in traditional crafts, hand made on the premises by local crafts people in a glorious countryside setting in the heart of the Wensum Valley to the west of Norwich. The workshops have been built to the highest standards in traditional style, and are grouped around a charming paved quadrangle. Inside you'll find many different crafts, from embroidery and lacemaking to sugar craft, painting and framing. Watch the crafts people at work, talk to them about their skills, and come away with a pretty and practical keepsake. Plus garden centre, coffee bar, pet food and corn stores. Facilities for the disabled: coach parties welcome. Car parking for 1000 cars. Open Mon-Sat, 1000-1700, Sun 1100-1700. Taverham Craft Centre, Fir Covert Road, Taverham, Norwich (situated 7 miles from Norwich on the A1067 Norwich /Fakenham road). Tel: (01603) 860522. Please phone before calling for specific crafts and/or purchases.

Norfolk Children's Book Centre

Surrounded by fields, the Centre displays what we are told is the best collection of children's and teachers' books in East Anglia. Here you will find a warm welcome, expert advice and an abundance of the best, the latest and the classics in children's fiction and non-fiction. Open during school holidays, Mon-Sat, 1000-1600, term time Wed, 1000-1200 and Sat 1000-1600. Teachers welcome any time, please phone. Find us between Aylsham and Cromer just off the A140. Look out for the signposted left turn 600 yards north of Alby Crafts. Tel: (01263) 761402.

VISIT

VISIT

A BLACK SHEEP SHOP

BLACK SHEEP

JERSEYS, ACCESSORIES AND GIFTS

A WARM INVITATION

to two nearby places of unusual interest en route to Blickling. Black Sheep is known for its special range of superb quality Country Clothes made from natural undyed wools totally grown and made in Great Britain.

VISIT AYLSHAM open Mon-Sat, 0900-1730 - all Sundays in Aug-Sep and 6 Sundays prior to Christmas. See the Workshop - garments in creation - Showroom and Shop with design stock range in addition to bargains galore surplus to export orders, etc.

VISIT INGWORTH - 1½ miles down the road - glimpse the Black Sheep at home - the foundation and inspiration for the business. Barn selection of design stock range promoted off the beaten track in glorious rural surroundings. Open Easter-mid Nov, 1030-1700, Tue-Sun - also Bank Holidays.

A WARM AND COURTEOUS WELCOME AWAITS YOU ALWAYS. If you cannot visit us - THEN SEND FOR A FREE COLOUR CATALOGUE to BLACK SHEEP LTD, 9 PENFOLD STREET, AYLSHAM, NORFOLK, NR11 6ET or telephone (01263) 733142/732006.

Black Horse Bookshop

Latest books on a wide range of subjects, including almost everything in print about East Anglia. Other departments include maps, art books, architecture and reference books. Books posted to all parts of the world. Open 6 days a week. Official agent for HMSO. 8 & 10 Wensum St, Norwich. Tel: (01603) 626871 and 613828

Sutton
Pottery

Sutton is a small Broadland village 17 miles north-east of Norwich via the A1151, and 16 miles north of Great Yarmouth just off the A149. Malcolm Flatman makes and designs a large range of microwave and dishwasher safe stoneware pottery and tableware items in a selection of glazes. Many lamps and decorative pieces are 'one-offs', and Malcolm will produce items to customers' own designs. Visitors are welcome in the workshop to see work in progress and to purchase from a selection of finished pottery. Please telephone at weekends, and before a long journey. A price list is available on request, and telephone and postal enquiries are welcome. Pottery can be posted to customers if required. Sutton (Windmill) Pottery, Church Road, Sutton, Norwich, NR12 9SG. Tel: (01692) 580595.

The Gallery contains the skills of many British craftsmen, shown to perfection in this beautifully restored set of Norfolk farm buildings. Also Studio-workshops, Furniture Showroom, Lace Museum, Bottle Museum and Gift Shop. The Tea Room serves a varied menu of home made food. Extensive and interesting Gardens. Free car park. Coaches by appointment. Open 16 Mar-22 Dec. Tue-Sun, 1000-1700; weekends only 13 Jan-16 Mar, 1000-1700; Open Bank Holidays. On A140 between Cromer and Aylsham. Tel: (01263) 761590.

⊚ The Picturecraft Art Gallery
North Norfolk's Art Centre

Discover one of the largest, privately owned art galleries in the country when visiting the historic Georgian town of Holt. Gold Award Winners of the coveted NatWest Business Award Scheme 1991. Difficult to find, so look for the brown & white 'Art Gallery' Tourist Information signs in the town centre. No admission charges and large free car park. Extensive artists' material shop and specialist picture framing service. Video presentations on painting techniques. Demonstrations and one-man-shows. Easy access to all departments makes wheelchair visitors especially welcome. Members of the Fine Art Trade Guild and Guild of Master Craftsmen. Open Mon-Sat, 0900-1700. (Thu 0900-1300). Tel: (01263) 711040 Gallery; 713259 Frame Desk; 712256 Art Shop. 23 Lees Courtyard, Off Bull Street, Holt. NR25 6HP

See Glassmaking at Caithness Crystal King's Lynn

⊚ Watch the highly skilled glassmaker, at NO CHARGE, creating items before your eyes, in the manner it has been made for centuries. You will be able to view the operation at close quarters and feel the heat from the furnace. Well stocked factory shop, open 7 days a week Easter to Christmas, 6 days during the rest of the year, selling a wide selection of giftware, tableware, paperweights and glass animals. Glassmaking throughout the year, Mon-Fri and weekends mid June-mid Sep. Well worth a visit. Caithness Crystal, 10-12 Paxman Road, Hardwick Industrial Estate, King's Lynn. Tel: (01553) 765111.

Wroxham Barns
The craft centre in East Anglia

⊚ Wroxham Barns Ltd

Collection of beautifully restored 18th century barns, situated 1½ miles north of Wroxham set in 10 acres of Norfolk parkland, providing the setting for one of the finest rural craft centres in East Anglia. Visit thirteen craftsmens workshops with crafts as diverse as decorative glass making, wooden toys, stitchcraft and wood turning. The Gallery Craft and Gift Shop is

home to a wonderfully varied collection of gifts and interesting crafts. Upstairs in the Gallery Collection choose from a selection of classic, county clothing. At the Old Barn Tearooms enjoy delicious homemade cakes, traditional cream teas and light lunches. Also Williamson's Traditional Fair and Junior Farm for the children. Open daily throughout the year, 1000-1700 except 25, 26 Dec. (Williamson's Fair open 31st March - 15th September 1996, 1100-1700. Tel. (01603) 783762).

LANGHAM
FINE HANDMADE CRYSTAL

⊚ Langham Glass - Norfolk

In a large beautiful Norfolk barn complex, teams of glassmakers can be seen working with molten glass using blowing irons and hand tools that have been traditional for hundreds of years. There is an enclosed children's adventure playground, factory gift shops, museum, restaurant, video and walled garden, also a newly converted Antiques and Collectable shop. Open 7 days a week all year 1000-1700. Glassmaking Easter-31 Oct (Sun-Fri); 1 Nov-Easter (Mon-Fri). Group visits welcome. The Long Barn, North Street, Langham, Holt, Norfolk, NR25 7DG. Tel: (01328) 830511.

⊚ Langham Glass - Cambridge

Set besdie the river Cam, opposite Magdalene College in a resdtored listed building previously used as a bonded warehouse, Langham Glass has a large factory shop, glassmaking demonstrations and Cambridge experience video. Open all year, group visits welcome. Thompson's Lane, Quayside, Cambridge, CB5 8AQ. Tel: (01223) 3299144

⊚ The Particular Pottery

MICHELLE and DAVID WALTERS work in an old Baptist Chapel (1807) which has been sympathetically restored, resulting in a stunning studio and showroom. Visitors can watch David potting away, and buy from his wide range of distinctive thrown and decorated Porcelain. A comprehensive range of contemporary Crafts and top quality makers of the Suffolk Craft Society and other Craftspeople, is available from on-going exhibitions in the Gallery area. Kenninghall is on the B1113, not far from Banham Zoo. Visitors are very welcome, Tue-Sat, 0900-1700. Closed Sun and Mon unless by prior appointment. Tel: (01953) 888476.

⊚ Sainsbury Centre for Visual Arts

The Sainsbury Centre has been described as 'the jewel in the crown' of East Anglia's rich visual arts scene. Paintings, sculpture and drawings by Bacon, Degas, Epstein, Giacometti, Moore and Picasso are displayed alongside one of the finest collections of non-western art outside London. Housed in one of Britain's most distinctive post-war buildings, designed by world-famous architect Sir Norman Foster. The Centre also has a programme of world-class special exhibitions, events and educational work. There is a Gallery Cafe and Shop, and facilities for special functions, banquets, meetings and conferences. Open all year, Tue-Sun, 1100-1700. Admission Adults £1.80/Children 50p/Concessions 50p ('95). Sainsbury Centre for Visual Arts, University of East Anglia, Norwich, NR4 7TJ. Tel: Galleries (01603) 456060, Groups (01603) 592467, Administration (01603) 592467.

Suffolk

CRAFT SHOP - TEA ROOM

◎ At Monks Eleigh, in the heart of the Suffolk countryside between Hadleigh and Lavenham, Corn Craft specialise in growing and supplying corn dollies and dried flowers for the gift trade. A wide range of their own products, along with an extensive selection of other British crafts is available from the craft shop and new flower shop, beautifully set amongst the farm buildings. Coffee, cream teas, home made cakes and other light refreshments are served in the converted granary adjoining the shop. Ample space and easy parking. Evening demonstrations of corn dolly making are given by arrangement. Contact Mrs Win Gage. Open every day throughout the year from 1000-1700, Sunday 1100-1700. Bridge Farm, Monks Eleigh, Suffolk. Tel: (01449) 740456.

◎ **Snape Maltings Riverside Centre**

This remarkable collection of old maltings buildings is set on the banks of the River Alde on the Suffolk Heritage Coast. Shops and galleries include House and Garden (furniture, rugs, quilts, kitchenware and fine foods plus pots and plants in the garden); Snape Craft Shop; Gallery; Countrywear; Maltings Music, Books and Toys and a special Christmas Shop (open Sep-Dec). Fresh home-cooked food in the Granary Tea Shop, River Bar and the Plough and Sail pub. Open all year, daily 1000-1800 (1000-1700 in winter). Snape Maltings, near Saxmundham, Suffolk IP17 1SR. Tel: (01728) 688303/5.

For all who love Flowers

◎ **Swan Craft Gallery**

Gallery owner, author and designer Mary Lawrence creates her original Real Flower Jewellery, each a stunning miniature flower composition using flowers grown and pressed here in Ashfield-cum-Thorpe to make the elegant colour co-ordinated designs for which Mary is internationally renowned. You will be welcome in our Gallery in the restored stable of this former 17th century Inn, where in addition to this Flower jewellery, you will also enjoy browsing amongst the many carefully chosen Crafts and a fine mix of new and traditional hand decorated gifts, ceramicss, Suffolk keyboxes, lampshades, accessories and designer fashions. We are situated on the main A1120 at Ashfield between Stowmarket and Yoxford. Open from Apr to Christmas on Tue to Sat and Bank Holidays 0930-1700. On Sun from 1400-1700. Tel: (01728) 685703.

SUFFOLK *craft* SOCIETY

The Suffolk Craft Society represents 170 professional designer craftspeople. Their 25th annual summer exhibition will be held at the Peter Pears Gallery, Aldeburgh, from 20 Jul-26 Aug and offers an ideal opportunity to view - and purchase - crafts of outstanding design and workmanship. Details of members - including Basketmakers, Book binders, Calligraphers, Furniture-makers, Glass engravers, Jewellers, Musical Instrument makers, Potters, Print makers, Sculptors, Textile artists, wood carvers and turners - can be found in **The Crafts in Suffolk,** £5.50, available from selected East Anglian bookshops or by contacting The Exhibition Organiser, Bridge Green Farm, Gissing Road, Diss, Norfolk IP22 3UD. Tel: (01379) 740711.

Watson's Potteries

Earliest record of Wattisfield potters is 1646. The Watson family have perpetuated the craft for nearly 200 years. Original Suffolk Collection of printed terracotta ware includes kitchen and gift items, unique terracotta wine coolers, herb, spice and storage jars, lasagne dishes, bread bakers, etc. See original kiln, tour factory by appointment, visit shop selling our own quality seconds. Wattisfield (A143 between Bury and Diss). Tel: (01359) 251239.

Horseracing is part of British history. Explore this fascinating story at the National Horseracing Museum. A beautiful collection of racing art, personalities, objects and history, to interest both racing enthusiasts and casual visitor alike. Fine gift shop, gardens, licensed cafeteria. Open, Tue 2 Apr-Sun 8 Dec, Tue-Sat 1000-1700, Sun, 1200-1600, Bank Hols and Mon in Jul and Aug Mon-Sat 1000-1700, Sun, 1200-1600. Adults £3.30, over 60 £2.00, Child £1.00. 10% Reduction for adults and over 60's in groups of 20 or more. Equine tours available, charges on request (booking essential). The National Horseracing Museum, 99 High Street, Newmarket, CB8 8JL. Tel: (01638) 667333.

NURSEY & SON LTD

Established 1790. Mens and ladies flying jackets, leather and suede jackets, sheepskin coats, slippers, gloves, hats, rugs etc. The factory shop has a good selection especially for Gifts, also a wide variety of sub-standard Products and Oddments. Mon-Fri 1000-1300, 1400-1700. Closed 27 July. Re-open 12 August. Access, Visa. 12 Upper Olland St, Bungay. Tel: (01986) 892821.

Tolly Cobbold & The Brewery Tap

First built in the 18th century on the banks of the River Orwell at Ipswich, and rebuilt in 1896, Tolly Cobbold is one of the finest Victorian breweries in the country. Taste the malt and smell the hops as we guide you through the brewing process, and then relax in the traditional Brewery Tap pub with a complimentary drink. Fully guided tours all year Fri at 12 noon, May-Sep, **daily** at 12 noon. Groups (10+) all year 1000-2000 by arrangement - £3.75 (Min age 14 years). Brochure & details: Cliff Road, Ipswich, Suffolk IP3 0AZ. Tel: (01473) 231723, Fax: (01473) 280045.

Bury St Edmunds Art Gallery

Robert Adam's only public building in the East of England. The magnificent cruciform upper floor is used for a programme of changing exhibitions across the visual arts with a special emphasis on contemporary craftwork. Craft shop with a selection of prints, ceramics, wood, glass, textiles and jewellery, books, cards and children's gifts. Open all year, Tue-Fri, 1030-1700, Sat, 1030-1630; closed 25 Dec-8 Jan. Disabled access. Entrance 50p concessions 30p. Tel: (01284) 762081

MILESTONE·HOUSE·POTTERY
HIGH STREET·YOXFORD·SUFFOLK

Milestone House Pottery

Turn off the A12 into Yoxford High Street to find this pottery with its attractive Trafalgar balcony. We make our stoneware domestic pottery and import a selected few from Africa. Also available are automata (toys for big people!), greeting cards, kites and many other things to make a visit worthwhile and interesting. Open Easter-Christmas, 1000-1700. Closed Wed 1300 and Sun. Winter opening Thu-Sat, 1000-1700. Milestone House Pottery, High Street, Yoxford, nr Saxmundham, Suffolk, IP17 3EP. Tel: (01728) 668465.

BRUISYARD
VINEYARD & WINERY
HERB & WATER
GARDENS

A 10-acre vineyard and winery producing the estate-bottled Bruisyard St Peter wine, situated west of Saxmundham. Wines, vines, herbs, souvenirs, etc for sale. Open 15 Jan-24 Dec, daily, 1030-1700. Conducted tours. Parties of 20 or more by appointment. Large herb and water gardens, shop, restaurant, children's play area and picnic area. Free wine tasting for vineyard and winery visitors. Bruisyard Wines, Church Rd, Bruisyard, Saxmundham, Suffolk, IP17 2EF. Tel: (01728) 638281.

The PARISH LANTERN — Original Crafts, Gifts, Pictures, and Teas on the Village Green at Walberswick

I am sure you will agree that there is something for everyone at the Parish Lantern including delicious light refreshments and a warm and friendly welcome. Before the advent of street lamps the only light in the village was provided by the moon which was called The Parish Lantern. Walberswick is one of the few villages still using the moon in this way. Open daily, 1000-1700. Sat & Sun only during Jan, Feb and Mar. Tel: (01502) 723173.

⊚ Carters Teapot Pottery

It doesn't have to be tea time to visit this Pottery making highly collectable teapots, in the beautiful village of Debenham. Visitors can see from the viewing area how these world renowned teapots are made and painted by hand. Pottery shop selling teapots, mugs, quality seconds and individual house plaques made to order. Situated just off the High Street, follow the teapot signs. Parking available. Tea and coffee served in the courtyard at weekends - weather permitting. Open Mon-Fri, 0900-1730, Sat & Bank Hols 1030-1630, Sun, Easter & Christmas, 1400-1700. Low Road, Debenham, (Stowmarket) Suffolk, IP14 6QU. Tel: (01728) 860475.

⊚ Gainsborough's House is the birthplace of Thomas Gainsborough, one of England's greatest painters. It is now an art gallery and museum with more of his work on show than anywhere else in the world. The House also supports contemporary art vigorously by mounting a programme of exhibitions in two galleries and in the garden. 1995 exhibitions include: **Richard Bawden: retrospective,** 9 Mar-21 Apr; **Drawings for All '96: open drawing competition,** 27 Apr-16 Jun; **Nicola Hicks: Sculpture in the gardens,** 22 Jun-11 Aug. Open all year, Tue-Sat, 1000-1700, Sun and Bank Holidays, 1400-1700, 1 Nov-Easter, closes at 1600. Admission, adults £2.50, children £1.50, senior citizens £2.00. Gainsborough's House, 46 Gainsborough Street, Sudbury, Suffolk, CO10 6EU. Tel: (01787) 372958.

ALDRINGHAM CRAFT MARKET

Family business, established 1958. Three relaxed and friendly galleries offering wide and extensive ranges of British craft products, original paintings, etchings and prints, studio, domestic and garden pottery, wood, leather, glass, jewellery, toys, kites, games, books, maps and many other good things, including ladies' clothes, knitwear and toiletries.

We only stock sensibly-priced, high quality products

Easy and ample car parking; childrens' play area; frequent exhibitions; coffee shop in season.
OPEN Mon to Sat 10.00~5.30.
Sun 2.00~5.30(all year), 10.00~12.00
(Spring & Summer)

Aldringham, Near Leiston,

 Suffolk IP16 4PY
Tel: 01728 830397

Afternoon Teas

What can be more tempting than a traditional English cream tea? You can be sure of a delicious selection of home made goodies at any of the following tea rooms, so forget about your waist line, and treat yourself!

To help you find the tearooms nearest to you we have marked the locations with a teacup symbol on the maps on pages 119-124. Establishments which are members of the Tourist Board have ◎ after the text.

Cambridgeshire

ELY
Steeplegate
16/18 High Street
Tel: (01353) 664731
Proprietor: Mr J S Ambrose
Seats: 40
Open: Daily except Sun.
Home-made cakes, scones and fresh cream teas served in historic building backing onto cathedral. Medieval vault on view. Craft goods also sold. Small groups welcome. ◎

Hertfordshire

HARE STREET VILLAGE
The Old Swan Tea Shop
Nr Buntingford (on B1368)
Proprietors: Lynda & Bill Sullivan
Tel: (01763) 289265
Seats: 40 inside, 50 in garden
Open: Apr-Oct, Thu-Sun, 1000-1900, Nov-Mar, Thu-Sun, 1000-1800 and all Bank Holidays except Christmas and by arrangement.
A picturesque 15th century Hall House within two acres of gardens and orchard, situated in beautiful East Hertfordshire. Specialising in traditional home baking. Licensed and open for morning coffee, lunches, afternoon teas, early evening meals. Also Sunday roasts, but please boo. Non-smoking inside. Parties welcome by arrangement. ◎

Norfolk

BRESSINGHAM
Pavilion Tea Room
Bressingham Plant Centre, nr Diss (on A1066, 3 miles west of Diss).
Tel: (01379) 687464/688133
Open: daily including Sundays, 1000-1730 except Christmas Day and Boxing Day.
Enjoy delicious gateaux and patisserie, a light meal or Special Cream Tea in the bright and airy surroundings of our new Pavilion Tea Room, in the peaceful setting of our famous 2 acre Plant Centre, where you'll find over 5,000 varieties of colourful garden plants.

GREAT BIRCHAM
Great Bircham Windmill
Nr King's Lynn
Tel: (01485) 578393
Proprietors: Mr and Mrs Wagg
Seats: 45
Open: 31 Mar-30 Sep, daily (ex. Sat), 1000-1800.
Tea rooms adjacent to the windmill. Bread, tea-cakes and rolls made in our own bakery. Cream teas, home-made cakes, free car park. ◎

HEACHAM
Norfolk Lavender Ltd
Caley Mill, Heacham
Tel: Heacham (01485) 571965/570384
Seats: 38 all year, 88 in summer
Open: Apr-Sep, 1000-1700, Oct-Mar, 1030-1630. Closed for Christmas holiday.
Average price: £2.20
Cakes and scones home-made, cream teas a speciality. Booked cooked meals/Sunday lunches October-March. Tea room in old millers cottage in the middle of lavender/herb gardens. ◎

HETHERSETT
Park Farm Country Hotel
Tel: (01603) 810264
Set amidst beautiful landscaped gardens, this Georgian Country House hotel is an ideal peaceful setting to relax, and enjoy our morning coffee and afternoon teas. Our homemade biscuits and homemade cakes are our speciality. ◎

HORSHAM ST FAITHS
Elm Farm Chalet Hotel
(Off A140 Cromer road)
Nr Norwich
Tel: (01603) 898366
Proprietor: W R Parker
Open: All year, Mon-Sat, 1000-1700
Situated in centre of picturesque village. Home-made cakes, scones, cream teas, fruit and cream served in garden or lounge. Light lunches. Parties welcome by prior arrangement. ◎

KING'S LYNN
Caithness Crystal
10-12 Paxman Road, Hardwick Industrial Estate
Tel: (01553) 765111
Seats: 84
Open: Mon-Sat, 0930-1630, Sun Easter-Dec, 1100-1600
A pleaant welcome awaits you in our restaurant serving a wide selection. Morning coffee, light snacks and home made cooked lunches. Afternoon teas with home made fruit pie and cakes. Coach parties and groups most welcome. Special menu available for parties to pre-book meals. ◎

NORWICH
Norwich Cathedral Visitor Centre and Buffet
62 The Close, Norwich NR1 1EH
Tel: (01603) 766756
Seats: 68
Open: Mon-Sat, 1030-1630
Refreshments served in an ancient room above the Cloisters, on of the earliest parts of the former monastery. Locally-baked cakes and scones; delicious light lunches, sandwiches etc. Tea, coffee, soft drinks. Open air terrace in summer months.

THURSFORD
The Thursford Collection
Thursford, Fakenham
Tel: (01328) 878477
Proprietor: Mr J Cushing
Seats: 92 inside, 150 outside
Admission: £4.40/£2.00/£4.00
Afternoon cream teas on the lawn served from our Garden Conservatory. Teas and light refreshments also served in our 'Barn'. ◎

WALSINGHAM
Sue Ryder Coffee Room and Retreat House
The Martyrs House, High Street
Tel: (01328) 820622
Seats: 60
Open: All year, 0930-1730
Light meals and snacks: cakes and pastries home-made. Coach parties welcome by appointment. Bed & Breakfast accommodation available with evening meal if required.

WROXHAM
The Old Barn Tearooms, Wroxham Barns
Tunstead Road, Hoveton
Tearooms: Tel: (01603) 784571
Seats: 85
Open: All year, 1000-1700
Pleasant tea room set in a craft centre just 1.5 miles from Wroxham. Morning coffees, light lunches prepared on the premises, cream teas and home-made cakes are all available. Pre-booked coach parties are welcome. ◎

Suffolk

ALDRINGHAM
Aldringham Craft Market
Aldringham, nr Aldeburgh
Tel: Leiston (01728) 830397
Contact: Margaret Huddle
Seats: Inside 6, Outside 30
Open: Spring-late Autumn, Mon-Sat, 1000-1730, Sun 1000-1200, 1400-1730
Home-made cakes, scones, fresh coffee, etc, offered in our Coffee Shop. Adjacent lawn, climbing frame, etc, provides ideal venue for family break when visitign our extensive arts, crafts and gifts Galleries. Easy car parking.

BRUISYARD
Vineyard and Herb Centre Restaurant
West of Saxmundham
Tel: (01728) 638281
Seats: Inside 25, Outside 24
Open: 15 Jan-24 Dec, daily, 1030-1630
Morning coffees, light lunches, afternoon teas. Home-made cakes and scones, herbal and speciality teas. Winery tours and tastings, herb and water gardens. Vineyard shop with wines, vines, herbs, crafts and gifts.

BUTLEY
Butley Pottery and Tea Room
Mill Lane, Butley, Woodbridge
Tel: (01394) 450785
Seats: 30 plus outside
Open: Apr-Sep, daily; Oct-Mar, Wed-Sun, 1030-1700.
A selection of tasty lunches with salad; home made cakes and scones; tea and coffee. Served in the relaxed atmosphere of the renovated thatched barn in peaceful rural surroundings. Live music most Sunday lunch times. Turn off the B1084 in Butley down Mill Lane. Evening parties can be catered for by appointment. Bring your own wine.

CAVENDISH
The Sue Ryder Coffee Room and Museum
High Street
Tel: (01787) 280252
Seats: 110
Admission to museum: 80p/40p
Open: Daily, 1000-1730; Closed 25 Dec.
Lunches and light refreshments: cakes and pastries home-made. Gift shop.

FELIXSTOWE
Ferry Cafe
Felixstowe Ferry
Tel: (01394) 276305
Proprietor: Laura Balsom
Seats: 53
Open: All year, 7 days a week
Teas with home made scones, cakes and pies, served in unique setting alongside mouth of River Deben with extensive fishing and boating activities. Also golf coarse nearby. Early breakfasts, superb fish and chips, and light meals all day. Parties catered for with free parking. Bed and breakfast also available.

HARTEST
Giffords Hall
Hartest, on B1066, south of Bury St Edmunds
Tel: (01284) 830464
Proprietors: The Kemp family
Seats: Indoors 40, Outside 50
Open: Easter-31 October
Cream teas and delicious home made cakes are served in the delightful converted stable block which adjoins the farm shop of this 33 acre small country living. Visitors can also explore the smallholding, vineyard and winery. Coaches welcome by appointment.

HELMINGHAM
Helmingham Hall
between Ipswich and Debenham on B1077
Tel: (01473) 890363
Owner: Lord Tollemache
Open: 28 Apr-8 Sep, Sun, 1400-1800; Wed, 1400-1800 by appointment.
Admission: £3.00/£1.50/£2.50
Home made cakes and scones served in the old Coach House or outside in the courtyard, make a welcome end to a visit to the gardens at Helmingham Hall.

IPSWICH
The Sue Ryder Coffee Room
Sue Ryder Home, The Chantry, Hadleigh Road
Tel: (01473) 287999
Seats: 75
Open: Tue-Sun, 1000-1730
Light refreshments, cakes and pastries homemade. Coach parties welcome by appointment. Please write to: Miss C Milton.

LAVENHAM
The Vestry Tea Rooms
The Centre, High Street, Lavenham
Tel: (01787) 247548
Proprietor: Mr K Morgan
Seats: 40
Open: All year, daily, 1030-1730
This cosy tea room is set in a converted Victorian chapel which is now a shopping centre. Morning coffee, snacks, afternoon teas, home made cakes. Hot meals available all day. Sunday roast, including sweet and coffee, £5.50. Easy parking and wheelchair access. Coach parties and groups welcome, by appointment if possible.

MONKS ELEIGH
Corn-Craft Tearoom & Coffee Shop
Monks Eleigh, Nr Lavenham
Tel: (01449) 740456
Seats: 40 inside, 30 outside
Open: All year, daily, 1000-1700, Sun, 1100-1700.
Corn-Craft serves morning coffee, cream teas, delicious home-made cakes and other light refreshments in a converted granary, beautifully set amongst farm buildings adjoining the craft shop. Ample parking. Coach parties welcome by appointment. For details of the craft shop refer to entry in Crafts section.

NEWMARKET
The National Horseracing Museum
99 High Street
Tel: (01638) 667331
Contact: Sharon Darler
Seats: 70; marquee in garden seats further 70
Open: 52 weeks of the year, Tue-Sat, 1000-1630; Sun, 1200-1600.
Our licensed coffee shop is open for morning coffee, light refreshments, home cooked lunches and afternoon teas throughout the year, even when the museum is closed for the winter. Pre-booked coach parties are welcome.

STOWMARKET
Museum of East Anglian Life, 'Brambles'
Tel: (01449) 675964
Open: Easter to end October; Apr, May, Oct, Tue-Sun and Bank Holidays, June-Sep, daily.
Enjoy morning coffee, home made scones and cakes and light lunches in the rural calm of the Museum in the heart of Stowmarket. Afternoon teas and parties catered for. (For details of Museum refer to entry in Museums section).

THORPENESS
Gallery Coffee Shop
Barn Hall
Tel: Aldeburgh (01728) 453105
Fax: (01728) 453946
Proprietors: Mr & Mrs J Strowger
Seats: 60 inside, 100 outside
Open: All year, 0930 to dusk
A licensed restaurant situated next to beach with pleasant garden overlooking boating lake. Specialising in cream teas, gateaux and ice cream desserts, with extensive craft and gift shop. Coach parties welcome by appointment.

WALBERSWICK
Mary's
The Street
Tel: (01502) 723243
Proprietors: Rob & Felicity Jelliff
Seats: 45
Open: Apr-Oct, daily (ex for Mon, other than Bank Holidays, Open Mon in Aug); Nov-Mar, Fri, Sat and Sun.
Morning coffee, lunch, afternoon and high teas, dinner Friday and Saturday. Home-made cakes and cream teas a speciality, served in the garden in fine weather. Parties welcome by appointment and lunch/dinner reservations advisable.

THE PARISH LANTERN
on the Village Green
Tel: (01502) 723173
Open: Jan-Mar, Sat and Sun only. Apr-Dec, daily.
Visit our tea room and garden where you can enjoy morning coffee, light refreshments, cream teas and home baked cakes. Also original crafts, gifts and pictures. We serve all day. You will be very welcome.

Local Produce

Cambridge's Independent Family Brewery

North Brink Brewery was established in 1795, when it was converted from an 'Oyl' Mill and Granary into today's classic Georgian Brewery. All Elgood's beers are brewed using the finest natural ingredients - Malt, Hops, Sugar, Yeast and 'roasted' Barley, to give our beers that distinctive Elgood's flavour and character. We currently brew:- **GREYHOUND STRONG BITTER:** A premium cask conditioned ale, ABV 5.2%. Plus a new addition to our portfolio to celebrate 200 years of brewing **BICENTENARY PAGEANT ALE,** 4.3% ABV. **CAMBRIDGE BITTER:** Cask conditioned, malty and fruity with a delicate hop aroma, ABV 3.8%. **FENMAN SPECIAL:** A fine Keg beer with a strong Regional following, ABV 3.8%. **MELLOW MILD:** Our Gold Medal winning Keg Mild, ABV 3.6%. **BOTTLED FENMAN PALE ALE:** Traditionally brewed with all the sparkle of a freshly pulled pint, ABV 3.6%. Seasonal Brews - **BLACK DOG MILD:** a cask conditioned traditional dark mild, ABV 3.6%. **BARLEYMEAD:** Brewed each Autumn with the fresh harvest of hops and

THE SIGN OF REAL ALE

THE SIGN OF QUALITY

ELGOOD'S

barley, ABV 4.8%. **NORTH BRINK PORTER:** Available on draught for the winter months, and throughout the year in bottles, ABV 5%. **WENCESLAS WINTER WARMER:** The King of Winter Ales, ABV 7.5% - a very strong beer for the real ale enthusiasts, brewed late November. These fine ales, plus Elgood's estate of Public houses and a growing Free Trade, have hiven Elgood's a well founded reputation and enabled Elgood's to stay fiercely independent. For group brewery tours contact, Jennifer Elgood. Tel: (01945) 583160.

'A SMALL COUNTRY LIVING'
HARTEST • SUFFOLK

Gifford's Hall
Hartest, on B1066 south Bury St Edmunds

A small country living with 12 acres of vines and a winery producing delicious white and rosé wines, as well as fruit liqueurs to traditional recipes. Vegetables are also produced in the organic vegetable gardens, free range eggs, honey, jams and cut flowers. Home made cream teas and cakes are available in the converted stable adjoining the farm shop. Visitors are welcome between 11 and 6, seven days a week from Easter-31 October and can explore the 33 acre smallholding, visit the winery and enjoy a free wine tasting. Groups welcome by appointment either daytime or evenings. Tel: (01284) 830464.

Congham Hall Herb Gardens
Grimston, King's Lynn

At Congham Hall, one of East Anglia's highest rated Country House Hotels, the proprietors have created a unique Potager and Herb Garden which features around five hundred different herbs. The Potager is a vegetable garden based on XVII Century design and this supplies specialist vegetables and salads to the hotel kitchen who also make great use of the abundant supply of fresh herbs. Tours of the Gardens including a lunch based on the use of herbs and a talk by Mrs Forecast the proprietor and the Hotel Chef can be arranged. Gardens are open to the public Apr-Oct 1400-1600 daily except Sat. No facilities for coaches. Please telephone Mrs C Forecast on Hillington (01485) 600250.

The Flower Shop
2A Cumberland St, Woodbridge, Suffolk IP12 4AB Tel/Fax: (01394) 384109
Well established Interflora shop offering high quality personal floral services on a wide basis, through designer and diploma florists. Fresh, dried and silk - weddings, functions, funerals, gifts and arrangements, indoor landscaping and maintenance service. Telephoned orders welcome. Medal winner of the 1994 Chelsea Show.

Starston Fayre Dairy Ice Cream at Cranes Watering Farm Shop

Starston, Norfolk

Fresh Dairy Ice Cream made here on the farm from the milk of our own Jersey and Guernsey cows. Creams - including clotted cream are also made here, and we stock our own dairy fed pork and lots of other local produce. Customers are welcome to picnic on the farmhouse lawn and stroll around the farm - maps are available free from the shop. Open Tuesday, Wednesday, Friday, Saturday only, 0900-1700. On the road between Dickleburgh and Harleston. Tel/Fax: (01379) 852387.

Bruisyard Vineyard & Herb Centre

10-acre vineyard and winery producing the estate-bottled Burisyard St Peter wine, situated west of Saxmundham. Wines, vines, herbs, souvenirs etc for sale. Open 15 January-24 December, daily, 1030-1700. Conducted tours, Parties of 20 or more by appointment. Large herb and water gardens, shop, restaurant, children's play area and picnic area. Free wine tasting for vineyard and winery visitors. Bruisyard Wines, Church Road, Bruisyard, Saxmundham, Suffolk IP17 2EF. Tel: Badingham (01728) 638281.

Restaurants

Bedfordshire

OLD WARDEN, (5 minutes from the A1 and 15 minutes from Bedford)

⚜ **The Hare and Hounds**
Tel: (01767) 627225

Large platefuls of excellent home cooked food are served every day and evening at the Hare and Hounds, Old Warden. The village designed in the 19th century by the Ongley family to reflect a Victorian model village, was later continued by the Shuttleworth family in the 1870s. Approaching Old Warden you will pass the Swiss Garden and the Shuttleworth Collection of Historic Aircraft and Vehicles, both of which are recommended for a memorable visit. Across the lake is the Shuttleworth Mansion, built to a Jacobean design in the late 19th/20th centuries. The Hare and Hounds, also built in the 1870s, is still in its original form with old oak beams, fire places and inglenook corners. For people wishing to stay overnight, accommodation is available next door at the family run Old Warden Guest House. Food is served in all four bars and the extensive garden and patio. The menu ranges from snacks to full meals, with a delightful choice of starters and puds. Daily special cater for all tastes - traditional, seasonal, international and vegetarian. Real ales compliment any meal as does the extensive wine list. *Open: daily. Prices from: £.25 for snacks, £5.95 for full meals.*

Cambridgeshire

KEYSTON (off A14 between Huntingdon & Thrapston)

⚜ **The Pheasant Inn**
Tel: (01832) 710241

A delightful thatched village pub, its 17th century interior decorated with farming bygones beneath the old beams. Chef Patron Martin Lee produces a sophisticated menu which is acclaimed in every major national guide. In both the restaurant and the bar area you can enjoy imaginative and interesting dishes, competitively priced and finely presented, with several real ales and over 15 wines by the glass. Should the sun shine, enjoy eating outside overlooking the village green. *Open: daily. Average prices: lunch or dinner à la carte £17.00, bar food from £3.25.*

MADINGLEY (2m NW Cambridge)

⚜ **Three Horseshoes**
Tel: (01954) 210221

Just outside Cambridge, this enchanting thatched village inn is one of the busiest quality restaurants in East Anglia. Richard Stokes' creative cooking has a clear Mediterranean bias, but concentrates on maximising the flavour of the best possible ingredients, whatever they may be. The pretty conservatory and the informal bar area both provide a relaxed atmosphere. Also on offer are superb wines (national winner of 1994 Italian wine list of the year award) and three real ales in perfect condition. *Open: daily. Average prices: lunch & dinner à la carte £19.00, bar food from £3.95.*

CAMBRIDGE

⚜ **Midsummer House**
Midsummer Common
Tel: (01223) 369299 Fax: (01223) 302672

Idyllically situated on Midsummer Common in the heart of Cambridge and on the banks of the River Cam, this Award Winning Victorian House Restaurant offers stylish, contemporary European cuisine using traditional techniques and regional ingredients by Chef Anton Escalera. With an outstanding wine list - the perfect setting for a memorable lunch or dinner. *Closed Mondays. Open for Lunch and Dinner. Prices from: Lunch £17.00, Dinner £26.00.*

HUNTINGDON

⚜ **The Old Bridge Hotel**
Tel: (01480) 52681

The ultimate 'country hotel in a town'. The lounges extend into a really splendid conservatory with attractive and comfortable cane chairs and tables amidst lush green plants in great tubs. Here one can enjoy exceptional brasserie style food, with a lavish buffet. Also a top-class, panelled restaurant with a wine list regularly named as one

of the finest in the UK. Enjoy tea, coffee and drinks any time of day in the comfortable lounge and bar or outside on the patio. *Open: daily. Average prices: 3 course restaurant meal £17.50. Brasserie meals from £3.95.*

CAMBRIDGE

⚜ **Panos**
Hills Road
Tel: (01223) 212958

This popular Cambridge restaurant cooks stylish French/Greek style dishes and even offers a traditional 'Mezze' as a first course amongst a special 3 course set dinner. The service here is extremely welcoming and the food is delicious. There is a good variety on the menu including classic Greek dishes like Fillet Suvlaki to more French style dishes like Crevette Provençales with rice and Greek Salad. The lunch menu is imaginative and varied and is very competitively priced at £14.50 for 3 courses and there is always a daily 'special' available. Desserts are all home-made and are quite delicious, they include Crépe Suzette and Baklava. Turkish coffee is offered in addition to regular house coffee. A wide selection of wines are available at reasonable cost. *Open: Mon-Fri, lunch & dinner, Sat dinner, Sun, closed. Lunch £14.50. Dinner £18.95.*

CAMBRIDGE

⚜ **Park Terrace**
Tel: (01223) 367480

Tucked away behind the University Arms Hotel and bordering the cricket square of Parker's Piece is Hobbs Pavilion. A selection of savoury and sweet pancakes are filled with fascinating combinations from Bumper Vegetarian (Cheese, Spinach, Basil, Tomatoes), to Hobbs Special Restaurants Steak with mashed potatoes. A full range of first courses is available from the blackboard, we had Gazpacho which was one of the most flavoursome I had ever tasted even to Spanish standards. To follow I had the Super Pizza Pancake filled with Cheese, Tomatoes, Basil and Garlic Mushrooms which was also delicious (£4.60). Also on the blackboard is a selection of wines served by the bottle or glass, and there is a good selection of soft drinks available including 'Citron Presse' (lemon juice, water and sugar on the side). I also found the list of 'Digestifs' interesting and enterprising which included Marc de Bourgogne, Marc de Gigondas and some single estate Cognac all at £5.00 per large measure. This is a good place to take children of all ages. Seats 60. *Open: 1200-1415 lunch, 1900-2145 dinner. Closed Sun, Mon, Bank Holidays, mid Aug-mid Sep. Average price: £14.50 dinner with coffee, per head. WE ARE 100% NON-SMOKING.*

MELBOURN

◎ **The Pink Geranium**
Tel: (01763) 260215

For over 35 years The Pink Geranium has operated as a high quality restaurant with great emphasis on a homely but professional atmosphere within this 15th century idyllic thatched cottage. Chef/proprietor Steven Saunders is well known for his TV. appearances, in particular BBC TV's 'Ready, Steady Cook' which gives The Pink Geranium its high profile attracting clientele from all over the the country. Lobster with tarragon velouté, Wild Venison with juniper berries, King Scallops, Sea Bass with tapenade are just a few examples of the quality of ingredients used. The À la carte menu costs approximately £45.00 per person but the daily menus are only £24.95 & £29.95 in the evening and £15.95 & £18.95 at lunch times. Sunday lunch is a popular occasion for families (£19.95 inc VAT) and Steven Saunders operates a first class outside catering company (up to 300 guests) as well as his famous Cookery School from the restaurant. The Pink Geranium was voted National Restaurant of the year in 1995 and holds a stack of food awards in all major guides. It is one of the prettiest and most highly acclaimed restaurants in the country today. Open: Tue-Fri, lunch & dinner, Sat dinner, Sun lunch.

FENSTANTON

◎ **King William IV**
High Street
Tel: (01480) 462467

A charming 17th century Inn in a pretty village off the A604 near St Ives. There is a pleasant relaxing atmosphere in this low beamed pub run by the very hospitable landlord, Jeremy Schonfeldt and his staff. All food is fresh, well varied and reasonably priced. The menu is comprised of things like Seafood Pancake, Steak and Kidney

Pudding (in a suet case), or Lamb and Apricot pie with Ginger. There are always 2 or 3 vegetarian dishes available and a wide selection of wines and beers. Every Wednesday evening they have a Blues or Jazz band playing and they frequently have speciality evenings. During the summer you can relax outside and there is ample parking around the attractive village. Seats 50 in the restaurant, half of which is non-smoking. Egon Ronay pub and Good Food Guide recommended.

Essex

ARDLEIGH, nr COLCHESTER

◎ **The Wooden Fender**
Harwich Road
Tel: (01206) 230466

The Wooden Fender is easily recognised by its brightly coloured fairy lights, on the Colchester to Harwich road. It is renowned for its history as the meeting place of Matthew Hopkins, the "Witchfinder General" and his henchmen who decided the fate of 29 local witches over a pint or two of local ale. The ale is still excellent, with Adnams and Greene King as well as guest beers to be sampled. The Egon Ronay recommended establishment offers not only 50 different bar meals (which includes dishes from China, Indonesia, Italy, Thailand and India) but also a 12 choice vegetarian and a childrens menu. Eat either a la carte in the restaurant, or in the bar where snacks are good value and the choice extensive. With 84 covers, coach parties, banquets and wedding receptions are welcomely catered for. *Open: lunch & bar meals daily, restaurant nightly except Tues evening. Average prices: bar meals £2.60-£5.50, A la Carte £15.00-£20.00 - children half price. Access, Visa & Amex accepted.*

HALSTEAD

◎ **The White Hart**
Great Yeldham
Tel: (01787) 237250

The White Hart was built in 1505 and has been one of England's most beautiful inns for centuries. The timbered exterior is matched by the heavily beamed interior, complete with no less than four fireplaces. The huge gardens run along both sides of a stream. Refurbished in 1995 to its former beauty, the White Hart is now part of

'Huntsbridge', a partnership of Chefs who each serve the highest quality food within the relaxed, informal atmosphere of an inn of character and historic charm. Chef Patron is Roger Jones, previously of The Pheasant at Keyston in Cambridgeshire, where he received acclaim from all the guide books. Real ales and Huntsbridge's renowned selection of wines complete the picture.

ROXWELL, Nr CHELMSFORD

◎ **Farmhouse Feast**
The Street
Tel: (01245) 248583

The name of this restaurant conjures up an image of kitchen tables laden with nourishing and delicious country products, and indeed the feeling of plenty comes across as soon as you enter and are confronted by a table groaning under the weight of assorted hors d'oeuvres. Make your choice, but I advise restraint: save space for the rest of the meal! A tureen of home-made soup is to follow and then a choice of four main courses including vegetarian dishes. For dessert there is no problem with indecision for you help yourself from the buffet and can sample a little of two or even three extravaganzas. Coffee and petits fours complete the feast. Three course menus are also offered for lunch and dinner, with price reductions for Senior Citizens and early diners. *Open for lunch Tue-Fri, average price £12.00, dinner. Tue-Sat. Farmhouse Feast £23.50, 3 courses (exc. Sat) £14.00.*

Hertfordshire

HATFIELD

◎ **The Old Palace**
Hatfield Park
Tel: (01707) 262055/272738

If you are in the mood for something completely different, The Old Palace is the place for you! Every Tuesday, Thursday, Friday and Saturday evening a magnificent banquet is held in The Great Hall of Hatfield Park and comprises a five course meal of royal proportions including red or white wine or mead. You will be served by buxom serving wenches in constant attendance and your glass is frequently replenished. On Tuesdays and Fridays, in addition to the fun and games of the Elizabethan era, you can enjoy the jests and songs of an earlier era, that of Henry VIII who joins you in his full splendour. The Great Hall is laid with long banqueting tables joining all folks together and merriment from a troupe of costumed minstrels and players singing songs and performing ceremonies will keep you more than entertained. Warming soup is poured from huge earthenware jugs and a traditional English Fare is served. The staff are amazingly helpful and friendly and an endless supply of food and wine is served. Prices are very reasonable and inclusive. Please call for details. See Historic Houses entry for Hatfield House.

WARE

⊚ **Byrche's at The Priory**
High Street, SG12 9AL
Tel: (01920) 486500 Fax: (01920) 486110

This delightful restaurant is named after Thomas Byrche, a scrivener and yeoman of Ware, and the first occupier of the Priory (Friary) following King Henry VIII's dissolution of the monasteries in 1538. Byrche's is situated in the Priory's beautifully rebuilt Victorian greenhouse conservatory overlooking the river and gardens. Just outside, the colourful community waterfowl live out, before you, the busy life of the waterfront as you drink, eat and chat inside. The stunning and novel design of the restaurant coupled with the excellent quality of the fare will make your visit a memorable one which you will want to repeat again and again. *Open for Sunday lunches and from 1100-1500 Tue-Fri (Sat until 1700) for coffees, lunches, snacks and teas and then 1900 until late for dinners. Closed Mon.*

Norfolk

CAWSTON (10m N of Norwich)

⊚ **Grey Gables Country House Hotel and Restaurant**
Tel: (01603) 871259

A beautiful former rectory set in wooded grounds. In the winter there is an inviting log fire which, together with the elegant candlelit dining room, make Grey Gables the ideal setting for a relaxing, romantic meal. The

cooking is traditionally prepared and cooked by Chef/Proprietor, Rosalind Snaith using fresh, local produce. There is a fine wine cellar with many French & German classics, as well as ports and wines from Italy, Spain, Australia, New Zealand, California, Washington, Chile, England and The Lebanon. The sweets are gorgeous and each customer is served with three sweets to sample-an excellent idea! 8 Hotel Rooms from £20.00-£30.00 per person. *Open: daily. Average prices: lunch bookings by arrangement, dinner £17.00 per person. Light supper also available Sun-Thu, £10.00 per person.*

KING'S LYNN

⊚ **Farmers Arms and Garden Restaurant, at Knights Hill Hotel**
South Wootton
Tel: (01553) 675566

Dinner at the **Garden Restaurant** is a civilised and leisurely affair in stylish, elegant surroundings. The menu is light and caters for a variety of tastes. Oak smoked salmon and prawns makes a delicious starter. Main courses include Supreme of Duck Victoria. The **Farmers Arms** is part of the same operation. Originally a barn, this delightful alternative restaurant has been tastefully and skilfully restored and converted. The menu is reasonably priced and comprised of dishes like the Norfolk Kebab of Pitta Bread with slices of roasted turkey with salad. A smooth glass of draught Bass is the perfect accompaniment to this popular but more rustic restaurant. *Garden Restaurant, open evenings and Sunday lunch £15.50-£20.00; Farmers Arms, open all day lunch or dinner £11.00, bar snacks £4.00.*

NORWICH

⊚ **The Trafalgar Restaurant**
Hotel Nelson, Prince of Wales Road
Tel: (01603) 760260

We highly recommend the newly refurbished Trafalgar Restaurant. They present a choice of simple but interesting main courses as well as desserts and traditional puddings from the display. The restaurant is fully air-conditioned with pleasant views of the River Wensum.

Light meals, snacks and informal dining is available in the Quarter-deck conservatory and bar (open every day). *Trafalgar Restaurant - Open: daily (except Sat lunch). Average prices: lunch £9.75, table d'hote £13.50, à la carte dinner from £15.50.*

GRIMSTON (nr King's Lynn)

AT CONGHAM HALL

⊚ **Congham Hall Country House Hotel**
Tel: (01485) 600250

For excellent food, go to Congham Hall. Chef Jonathan Nicolson interprets "modern English cooking" intelligently and with a fine balance of taste and decoration. The restaurant and "orangery" is delightfully decorated in the Georgian manner. On hot summer days we particularly recommend Congham's outdoor lunches-ask about the luncheon club; but eating in the dining room or on the lawn one has the feeling of being part of an English Country Home, which is what Trevor and Christine Forecast set out to achieve when they established Congham as a country house hotel and now appropriately a member of the "Pride of Britain" group and Johansens Hotel of the Year 1993. *Open: daily. Average prices: lunch table d'hote £15.00, Sunday lunch £15.00, dinner from £25.00.*

LONG STRATTON
(10 minutes south of Norwich on the A140)

'Doodlebugs' 1940's Wine Bar, Restaurant, Café

Open 1030-last orders 2145. Open **365** days, all day and evening - no booking necessary. 'An explosion of great tasting food, wine and beer that won't cost you a bomb!' From Blitz to Victory - come and see what kept up the spirits of the nation as Britain makes ready for battle on the home front. Everything from good teas and coffees to tasty snacks and meals. All good home prepared food. **For *your* ration book phone (01508) 530842 or just turn up and chalk up a victory!**

'Snickerdoodles Restaurant'

For those who like classic bistro cooking, this restaurant (adjacent to Doodlebugs) is a must. Guests walk off the pavement into a delightful little room crammed with Victoriana and pine. The Gibbs, (Ray cooks, Penny hosts) offer a five course set menu for £22.95 with about ten or so main courses and sumptuous sauces. Everything, including puddings and bread, are fresh and home made, portions are generous. Portfolio of excellent yet reasonably priced wines. **Phone: (01508) 531845 to reserve your table.**

NORWICH

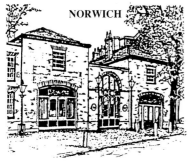

NORWICH

◎ Pizza One Pancakes Too!
24 Tombland
Tel: (01603) 621583

Norwich's own Pizzas, Pastas and French Crêpes. A favourite haunt, where food still has that homemade taste. It's usually crowded with families, businessmen, students and tourists alike. Situated along the Cathedral wall in Tombland, the historic heart of the city, it is the perfect place to stop for lunch, afternoon pancakes or dinner. *Open daily, 1200-2300, Sun, 1200-2200 (closed 25 Dec and 1 Jan). Average price £5.85 – children's portions available. Students discounts on all main courses.*

NORWICH

◎

MUSIC ● CAFE ● BAR
24 Tombland
Tel: (01603) 626099

Take time out to enjoy the truly continental feeling of Boswells. Situated along the Cathedral wall in Tombland in the historic heart of the city, it is in an ideal spot to stop for lunch or afternoon tea next time you are shopping or sightseeing. The Brasserie style menu is varied and delicious, ranging from spectacular sandwiches to three course meals. The unique decor and atmosphere are further enhanced by its 'all day every day' opening hours, live Jazz and old movies. You can now enjoy all this in the open air on the fully licensed forecourt terrace. *Open: Sun 1100-1800; Mon-Sat 1200-0200. Average price under £6.00 (specials for children are available).*

HETHERSETT (Nr Norwich)

◎ Park Farm Country Hotel & Restaurant
Tel: (01603) 810264 Fax: (01603) 812104

Park Farm Hotel has earned a well deserved reputation for good food, a warm welcome and excellent service in this family-run hotel and restaurant. Set in beautiful surroundings, Park Farm provides both French and English cooking prepared with the best local produce. A good selection of menus, both à la carte and table d'hote, whilst the chef's speciality menus have more skilfully prepared dishes. Bar meals and afternoon teas are also available. *Open: daily. Average*

prices: lunch £10.75 (table d'hote), dinner £15.75 (table d'hote), £18.00-£25.00 (à la carte).

WEST RUNTON (Nr SHERINGHAM)

the Pepperpot

◎ The Pepperpot
Tel: (01263) 837578

Tucked away down a narrow lane leading to the beach, it is only the illuminated sign that distinguishes this restaurant from the other private houses. A warm welcome is offered by hostess Barbara (who with husband Ron has run the Pepperpot since March 1992) that complements the immediate feeling of hospitality, comfort and intimacy that suggests itself upon arrival. The A la Carte menu offering three courses, is understated and modest, for the emphasis is on quality through dishes such as delicious breast fillets of duck in peach sauce and incredibly lean steak in a brandy and cream sauce, without forgetting quantity. Desserts are lavish and the wine list is small but thoughtful. *Price per head without wine:3 course set supper menu £16.95. À la Carte £15.00-£24.00.*

NORWICH

◎ Adlard's
79, Upper St Giles Street
Tel: (01603) 633522

In an emerald green jewel of a restaurant a few hundred yards above the market place, chef-proprietor David Adlard and his lovely American wife Mary are responsible for some of the most serious food in East Anglia, served in a genial and unstuffy manner. Awarded 'County Restaurant of the Year' in 'The Good Food Guide 1994', and Regional Winner of Decanter/Sandeman Wine List competition 1995. David's perfectly judged and meticulously prepared dishes utilise much seasonal and local produce Sauces which accompany noisettes of English lamb, breast of Limesdale duck or fillets of brill are always based on excellent stocks, carefully reduced. Pastry for a delicious apple

tart surrounded by caramel sabayon is buttery and feather-light, and ice cream silky and smooth. *Open: Tue-Sat, lunch 1230-1345, dinner 1930-2230, also **dinner on Mondays**. Average price per head, without wine, lunch £16.00, dinner £332.00.*

WELLS-NEXT-THE-SEA

ARK ROYAL

◎ Freeman Street
Tel: (01328) 710478
Proprietors: Roger & Shirley Thake

Situated near the beautiful Wells harbour. This busy pub offers food throughout the day. Children are well catered for with their own room and separate menu (prices starting at £1.95). An excellent variety of food is on offer from home-made Steak and Kidney Pie and Cod and Chips to steaks and fresh lobster. A separate restaurant area, seating up to 70 people, is available should you wish to eat in more comfort. There is an interesting selection of seven traditional ales and many continental lagers. *Open: Mon-Sat all day; Sun 1200-1700, 1900-2200. Average price: Bar snacks £3.95 approx, 3 course lunch or evening meal £7.50-£18.00 approx, (excluding wine).*

NORWICH

◎ Walnut Tree Shades
Old Post Office Court
Tel: (01603) 620166

Situated just off the busy pedestrian shopping area of Norwich. The Castle Mall is only 5 minutes walk away. The restaurant has comfortable bench/sofa seats and walls are packed with American style posters and prints. An original Wurlitzer juke box sits prominently by the bar and rock and blues music plays in the background. It has a nostalgic atmosphere of the 60's and attracts families with children because of the special menu for kids which has puzzles and games for their amusement. The adult menu has a variety of American style starters like Buffalo Wings and Chilli Potato Skins to a more conservative Prawn Cocktail and Paté and Toast. Main courses are also varied from Chicagostyle Hot Dogs to Peppered Steak and Teriyaki Chicken. There is also a good selection of good quality burgers. A stunning cocktail list ranges from Margarita's to Sangria and there is always a special reduced cocktail on offer each night. The wine list offers some interesting wines from California and South Africa. The staff are very welcoming and helpful and all in all it is a well run successful operation. Established since 1984. *Open: Mon-Sat, 1145-1415 and 1830-late. Average price: £12.00 (excluding wine) for 3 courses.*

Restaurants

NORWICH

⊚ Jarrold's Store Restaurant
London Street
Tel: (01603) 660661

There are three restaurants in this large department store. 'Below Decks' in the basement sells sandwiches, coffee, teas, cakes and scones. It is self service - seating approximately 50 and open from 0915-1715. The middle restaurant is called 'Benjamins', has waitress service and offers dishes like homemade soup, hot specials from the blackboard and some imaginative vegetarian dishes. They also have slimmers dishes comprising salads with cottage cheese, prawns, etc., and actually list the calories per dish. No alcoholic drinks are available but a wide range of Benjamin's soft drinks, including hot chocolate and iced coffee are available. A minimum charge of £1.25 is levied between 1145 and 1415 - and food is served up to 1700. The staff are very pleasant and attentive and walk about with hot coffee offering second cups. The third restaurant on the top floor seats 200 people and is open between 0900 and 1715. It offers a wide choice of salads, hot meals and open sandwiches. Wine and low alcohol lager plus a selection of soft drinks are available. This bustling attentive restaurant has good views of the city if you get a table by the window.

WOLTERTON (Nr Erpingham)

⊚ The Saracens Head 'With Rooms'
Tel: (01263) 768909

Only 20 minutes from Norwich, The Saracen's Head is a civilised free house without the intrusion of piped music and fruit machines. It was built in the early 19th century by Lord Walpole as a coaching Inn for his estate. There are log fires, terra-cotta walls, leather bound settles, wicker fireside chairs and fresh flowers on the mantlepieces. It is a well kept, well run house, more a restaurant than a pub. The staff are both welcoming and helpful and the food is fresh and delicious. The Paté Maison was full of flavour and not too rich and the steaks were cooked to perfection. Other dishes include braised local rabbit, grilled fillets of Smoked Mackerel, Venison, Duck and Steaks. Puddings are fairly traditional, e.g., Bread and Butter Pudding, Sticky Toffee Pudding. The wine list is an impressive selection of 30 interesting wines. It made a pleasant change to see a choice of New Zealand, Australian, Spanish and South African wines as well as many of

the more classic French. House wines are also available at £8.25 per bottle. Chef/proprietor Robert Dawson-Smith and his staff run The Saracens Head extremely well and they deserve their popularity. *Open: 7 days a week, 1100-1500, 1800-2300.*

Suffolk

FELIXSTOWE

⊚ Waverley Hotel and Wolsey Restaurant
Wolsey Gardens
Tel: (01394) 282811

At the Waverley Hotel you have the choice of dining in the Wolsey Restaurant or the Gladstone Bar. You will be assured of a delicious choice of meals made with fresh local produce by our award winning chefs. Dramatic views of the North Sea make this a very special place to eat. Conferences, receptions and parties can be catered for. *Open: daily. Average prices: lunch £9.50, dinner £10.00-£14.00. Fax: (01394) 670185.*

IPSWICH

⊚ The Marlborough Hotel, Henley Road
Tel: (01473) 257677

Tucked away in a quiet residential quarter, this solid, red-brick Victorian hotel exudes a strong feeling of comfortable dependability. A beguiling and unexpected inner garden soothes the spirit, as do adventurous dishes such as Oriental Duck Samosa and other exciting combinations from the well-priced set menu. Head Chef, Simon Baxter works hard to retain his 2 rosettes for food and service awarded by the AA Guide. An efficient young staff, led by the owners Robert and Karen Gough, treat parties, businessmen and private diners alike with skill and courtesy. *Average price per head, without wine, £15.00-£25.00.*

WOODBRIDGE

⊚ The Riverside Restaurant
Quayside
Tel: (01394) 382587 Fax: (01394) 382656

The Riverside restaurant is unique as it has its very own theatre/cinema which recently celebrated 80 years unbroken service. The Restaurant offers a special 3 course Dinner and Film package for only £18.00, plus the exciting à la carte menu which is revised seasonally. Choices include, Honey Roasted Boneless Quail with

buttered cabbage, smoked bacon and port wine sauce or our popular Special Platter of hot and cold hors d'oeuvres for 2 or more to share. Main course examples: Char griddled Tuna Nicoise with balsamic dressing. Enjoy a pre-film/theatre drink in the atmospheric bar while you choose from the special menu, eating before or after the film of your choice. True to his word, proprietor Stuart Saunders offers you "The best which is not always the most expensive." *Lunch 1200-1500, dinner 1800-2230, daily. A la carte £15.00-£20.00. Dinner and Film package £18.00. Light lunch from £3.95.*

BURY ST EDMUNDS

⊚ The Angel Hotel, Angel Hill
Tel: (01284) 753926

A trip to Bury St Edmunds would be incomplete without, at least a visit to the Angel Hotel. If most of the houses in Bury St Edmunds look as edible as angel cake, the creeper-clad Angel Hotel must be a plum pudding. In an imposing position overlooking the Abbey Gardens, this fine hotel with its Dickensian connections is owned and run with pleasing professionalism by the Gough family. With two dining areas to choose from, the cosy Pickwick bar or handsome Regency restaurant, the food ranges from sandwiches made from local bread through homely dishes such as venison sausages and mashed potatoes to an upmarket, classic Chateaubriand with Bearnaise sauce. Adnams supplies the beers and the wine list is thoughtful and modestly priced. *Special weekend rates are offered from £34.00 per person including full English breakfast. Conference, banquets and weddings can be catered for, ranging from an intimate dinner for 6 to a wedding extravaganza for 120.*

HOLBROOK

⊚ The Compasses
Tel: (01473) 328332

Holbrook is at the head of Alton Water, an ideal spot for wind surfing, walking and bird watching. The restaurant at the Compasses is recently refurbished, with a varied menu including old favourites as well as some unusual dishes. A fascinating collection of keyrings decorates the walls. The menu complimented by daily specials and roast has a wide variety of English and Continental dishes which together with daily deliveries of fresh fish gives a choice suitable for all tastes. *Average prices, £8.00-£10.00, for two courses. Large car park, childrens play area, garden (booking advised). Table service throughout.*

LAVENHAM

◎ The Angel
Market Place
Tel: (01787) 247388

In one of the best-loved and best-known of Suffolk's medieval villages, the Angel is so resolutely settled into its corner site overlooking the market square that one almost feels that its strong timbers have grown straight from the soil. Two dining rooms, one informally strewn with pine tables, the other rich with mahogany tables and bric-a-brac, offer home-made fresh food: garlic mushrooms, pates, home-made soups and pies, casseroles of pork and apple or steaks and lamb chops, as well as delicious treacle tart or Suffolk apple flan, with a menu that changes daily. The atmosphere is easy, the staff delightful. *Average price per head, without wine, £10.00 lunchtimes £15.00 evenings.*

WOODBRIDGE

◎ Captain's Table
Quay Street
Tel: (01394) 383145

This delightful restaurant is to be found in one of Woodbridge's quaint, narrow streets between the town centre and the yacht haven. The atmosphere is warm and cosy and you will receive the personal and friendly attention of the proprietor's family and helpers. There is a pleasant patio where you can eat during the warmer months, a licensed bar and small car park. As you may have guessed, seafood is the speciality–lobster, oyster, crawfish and fresh salmon when available and there is a comprehensive wine list. *Open: Tues-Sat. Average prices: lunch £6.00, dinner £16.50, 3 course fixed price menu £12.95.*

YOXFORD

◎ JaCey's Charcoal Pit
High Street
Tel: Yoxford (01728) 668298

A friendly informal village restaurant which specialises in Maderian Kebabs, generous skewers of marinated lamb, King Prawns, Tarragon Chicken or the house special of Tender Beef, Cajun sausage, mushrooms and onions, all the Kebabs are presented on long iron stands that are fixed to the tables. Dining this way adds a bit of fun to 'Eating Out'. They also serve many delicious dishes such as Hungarian Lamb, Chicken Piri Piri Rib of beef steak with onion rings, Sword fish steaks. The home-made breads are terrific as are the sweets, which are all home-made, some of the favourites are Banoffi pie, Pavlova and Chocolate Roulade. The very modestly priced wine list is small but interesting. *Open Mon-Sat for dinner. Main course prices range from £5.00-£11.00 with lots of choice in the £5.00/8.00 range. Main courses all include salad, rice, chips or potatoes.*

HINTLESHAM

◎ Hintlesham Hall
Tel: (01473) 652334/268

Set in 170 acres of parkland, Hintlesham Hall with 33 bedrooms and suites, is renowned for its excellent cuisine and luxurious accommodation. There are 5 reception rooms, including the splendid Salon, the intimate book-lined Library, and the mellow pine-panelled Parlour. Throughout the hotel, individuality is displayed in the eclectic selection of modern and traditional works of art, and the fine antiques. The style of cooking is modern British, using local and home-grown produce for the seasonal menus. Above all, the service from the young team is unfailingly pleasant and helpful. Leisure facilities include the Halls own 18 hole championship length golf course and leisure club. *Open: daily, except Sat - lunch time. Average prices: House lunch (A la carte) including coffee and petits fours £21.00. Table d'hote menu Sun to Thu £24.00. Full à la carte every day. £18.50 table d'hote lunch.*

BILDESTON

◎ The Bow Window
116 High Street
Tel: (01449) 740748

Situated in one of the nicest village squares in Suffolk, this pretty pink washed restaurant has an abundance of oak beams, a large inglenook with log fires in season and a walled flower garden for the summer. The restaurant offers simple, high quality food all prepared on the premises using herbs from the kitchen garden. Honest dedication combined with the skilful use of fresh ingredients and attention to detail enables the restaurant to offer a selection of authentic dishes with excellent flavour. Service is relaxed and informal whilst still providing civilised levels of attention and comfort. A range of modestly priced wines from around the world are available to accompany your meal. "Imaginative menus, always prepared with care" **Delia Smith**. *Open: Wed-Sat evenings. 3 course Prix Fixe £11.95, 3 course Carte £16.00. Sun lunch - 3 courses plus coffee £11.95. Perfect for those special celebratory occasions and dinner parties with your own personally chosen menu.*

YOXFORD

◎ Satis House
Tel: (01728) 668418

Satis House will surprise you. You will find nothing more English than this typical country house near to the Suffolk Coast. But step inside and you begin to realise that all is not as it seems. Although English and French dishes are available, Chris and Chiu Blackmore specialise in authentic Malaysian food which is influenced by Malay, Chinese and Indian cooking. The menu is long and exotic and if you find the choice bewildering, I can recommend the House speciality - the "Kenduri". This is a selected range of dishes to suit your individual preference, whether it be for mild, medium, hot or combination of all three. I enjoyed every dish, and lost count of the variety of tasty combinations presented. If I was forced to pick a favourite, I think I would choose the Istana Lamb, cooked in a yoghurt based sauce with herbs and spices, and smothered in fresh coriander. But the joy of this style of eating is that you do not have to choose one dish - it is a feast of many different flavours. May I wish you Selemat Makan - good eating! *Open: Mon-Sat from 1900; lunch by arrangement only. Average price, £20.00-£25.00.*

Accommodation

The Angel
♔♔♔ HIGHLY COMMENDED

Market Place, Lavenham, Suffolk CO10 9QZ
Tel: 01787 247388

This family-run inn overlooks the market place and offers relaxation in a calm and quiet environment. Dating from 1420, it retains a wealth of period features and is ideal for exploring the area. The 8 en suite bedrooms all have telephone, colour TV and tea/coffee making facilities. The restaurant menu changes daily and features fresh local ingredients. Amenities include classical music, attractive gardens and free parking. Logis of Great Britain. AA.

Special Breaks: 3 nights for the price of 2.

Crosskeys Riverside Hotel
♔♔♔ COMMENDED

Hilgay, Downham Market, Norfolk PE38 0LN
Tel: (01366) 387777

A small country hotel beside the River Wissey in converted 17th century buildings. All bedrooms have en suite bath- rooms, colour TV; tea/coffee making facilities (3 four-posters). Restaurant and bar.

Rooms: 3 Double, 2 Twin, 1 Family

B&B Single: £35.00   B&B Double/Twin: £56.00

Bunwell Manor
♔♔♔ COMMENDED

Bunwell, Norfolk NR16 1QU
Tel: (01953) 788304

Just 12 miles south of Norwich, off the B1113. Our country house hotel dates originally from the 16th century. 2 acres of lovely grounds and 10 bedrooms all en suite. Carefully prepared à la carte and table d'hote menus. Ideally peaceful base for touring Norfolk, Suffolk and Cambridgeshire. Full central heating and welcoming log fire in winter. Children and dogs welcome. Special breaks available all year. Fully licensed. AA 2 Star. RAC 2 Star.

Eastcourt
⌂⌂⌂⌂ HIGHLY COMMENDED

2 Abbey Road, Sheringham, Norfolk

Contact: Mrs P Cornish, The Old Chapel,
Edgefield Street, Melton Constable, Norfolk NR24 2AU
FREEPHONE: 0500 400490

The site must be one of the best on the North Norfolk coast. Magnificent views across the rooftops of Sheringham, to the sea and golf course.

2 flats, sleeps 2-4
Open all year.   Weekly rate: from £155.00 to £335.00

Congham Hall
♔♔♔ HIGHLY COMMENDED

Congham Hall Country House Hotel & Restaurant
Grimston, King's Lynn, Norfolk
Tel: (01485) 600250

Luxurious Georgian manor in 40 acres, 6 miles from King's Lynn, 5 miles from Sandringham. Acclaimed by many leading guides. Offering peaceful relaxation and high quality accom- modation and cuisine. Under personal supervision of the owners. RAC Blue Ribbon, AA 3 Red Star and 2 Rosettes. Egon Ronay. Johansens Hotel of the Year 1993. A Pride of Britain Hotel.

Elm Farm Chalet Hotel
♔♔♔ COMMENDED

St Faith, Norwich,
Norfolk NR10 3HH

Tel: (01603) 898366
Fax: (01603) 897129

Hotel in quiet attractive village. Norwich 4 miles. Ideal for touring Norfolk & Suffolk. En suite rooms. Ample parking.

Hopton Holiday Village ✓✓✓✓

Hopton-on-Sea, Great Yarmouth, Norfolk
Tel: 01502 730214

Hopton Holiday Village is situated between Great Yarmouth and Lowestoft, set close by the Norfolk Broads. Facilities include indoor/outdoor swimming pool, kids and teens clubs, evening entertainment.

350 caravans, sleeps 2-8
Open from March to December
Weekly rate: from £99.00 to £484.00

The Marlborough Hotel 👑👑👑👑 COMMENDED

Henley Road, Ipswich, Suffolk   Tel: (01473) 257677

This family owned and run hotel is set in the leafy suburbs of Ipswich opposite the beautiful Christchurch Park. Personal service and superb food has made The Marlborough one of the most recommended hotels in the area. Each bedroom is decorated with care and imagination and a delightful Victorian restaurant overlooks a secluded floodlit garden. Ideal base for touring Constable Country, Suffolk Coastal and striking inland to discover hidden villages and Newmarket.

Rooms: Double £78.00   Single £68.00
(Prices include breakfast and VAT)

Miami Hotel 👑👑👑 APPROVED

Princes Road, Chelmsford, Essex
Tel: (01245) 264848 & 269603
Fax: (01245) 259860

55 bedrooms, all twin/double with colour TV (Sky available) in all rooms, teasmade, shower, WC, direct dial telephone, hair-dryers. Restaurant open 7 days for lunch/dinner. Table d'Hote. A la carte. Bar. Meeting & conference facilities.

Weekend rates, group rates on request.

The Orchards Holiday Village ✓✓✓

At Point Clear, St Osyth, Clacton-on-Sea, Essex
Tel: 01255 820651

Situated in its own grassy parkland yet convenient for Clacton-on-Sea. Facilities include pool, bars, kids and teen clubs and evening entertainment.

150 caravans, sleeps 2-8
Open from March to October.
Weekly rate: from £99.00 to £364.00

Sycamore Farm 🏠🏠🏠 - 🏠🏠🏠🏠 HIGHLY COMMENDED

Edgefield Street, Nr Holt, Norfolk

Contact: Mrs P Cornish, The Old Chapel, Edgefield Street, Melton Constable, Norfolk NR24 2AU
FREEPHONE: 0500 400490

Converted barns and farmhouse 8 miles from coast. For the holidaymaker requiring quality and tranquility. Three nights winter breaks brochure on request.

6 barns, sleeps 2-6. Open all year. Weekly rate: £150.00 to £470.00

Waverley Hotel 👑

2 Wolsey Gardens, Felixstowe, Suffolk IP11 7DF
Tel: 01394 282811 Fax: 01394 670185

All bedrooms have en suite bathrooms, trouser presses, colour television, tea and coffee making facilities, and direct dial telephones. Our Wolsey Restaurant features a high standard of à la carte cuisine featuring fresh local produce. Please contact us for details of weekend breaks and colour brochure. Live jazz every Sunday lunch.
Rooms: Single 5, Double 8, Twin 6, Family 1, Ensuite 20
B&B Single: £40.00   B&B Double: £59.95

ASSISI GUEST HOUSE
CAMBRIDGE

Warm, welcoming, family-run guesthouse, ideally situated for the city, colleges and Addenbrookes Hospital. All modern facilities. Large car park.
Bedrooms:
4 single, 5 double, 6 twin, 1 triple.
Bathrooms: 17 private

Parking for 15
Cards accepted: Access, Visa, Amex

Bed & breakfast per night	£ min	£ max
Single	25.00	29.00
Double	35.00	39.00

ASSISI GUEST HOUSE
👑👑 APPROVED
193 Cherry Hinton Road, Cambridge CB1 4BX
☎ **(01233) 246648 & 211466   Fax: (01233) 412900**

Roslin Hotel
Thorpe Esplanade, Thorpe Bay, Essex
Telephone: 01702 586375

👑👑👑👑 COMMENDED

Overlooking the sea in residential Thorpe Bay.
Offering good food and friendly informal service.
All bedrooms with private facilities, Sky TV, hairdryer, tea/coffee making facilities
Mulberry Restaurant open to non-residents
Large car park

The Wentworth Hotel stands on the edge of the Suffolk coast at the old fishing town of Aldeburgh and has the comfort and style of a country house with open fires and antique furniture. All individually decorated bedrooms have colour television, radio, telephone, hairdryers and tea facilities. The restaurant serves a wide range of dishes using fresh produce and the lunch time bar menu can be enjoyed in the sunken terrace garden.

Aldburgh has quality shops, two excellent golf courses and nearby are long walks, Minsmere bird reserve, Snape Maltings concert hall and of course, miles of beach to sit upon to watch the sea.
Selection of breaks available throughout the year.
WENTWORTH HOTEL,   👑👑👑 HIGHLY COMMENDED
Wentworth Road, Aldeburgh, Aldeburgh, Suffolk IP15 5BD   Telephone (01728) 452312

The House in the Clouds 🏠🏠🏠🏠🏠 COMMENDED

Thorpeness, Nr Leiston, Suffolk
Tel: (0171) 252 0743

A fantasy unmatched in England

Sleeps 10 in 2 double rooms, 3 twin rooms. For extra guests an additional double sofa bed. 3 bathrooms, drawing room, kitchen, dining room and 'The Room at the Top' with the finest views in Suffolk. Situated in 1 acre grounds overlooking Thorpeness Golf Course, Thorpeness Mere and the sea. Close to Snape Maltings, home of Aldeburgh Festival and to Minsmere and other bird and nature reserves.

Available for holidays and short breaks.

Rail

Bedford	Huntingdon
Bury St Edmunds	Ipswich
Cambridge	King's Lynn
Chelmsford	Lowestoft
Clacton-on-Sea	Luton
Colchester	Norwich
Great Yarmouth	Peterborough
Harwich/Dovercourt	Southend-on-Sea
Hertford	Stevenage
Hitchin	Watford

Train information (times and fares) for the whole of East Anglia can be obtained from British Rail, 24 hours, 7 days a week by telephoning (0171) 928 5100.

Car Hire

Avis
Head Office	(0181) 848 8765
Bedford	(01908) 281334
Cambridge	(01223) 212551
Chelmsford	(01245) 496655
Colchester	(01206) 41133
Great Yarmouth	(01493) 851050
Harlow	(01279) 414040
Hemel Hempstead	(01442) 230092
Ipswich	(01473) 273366
Luton	(01582) 454040
Luton Airport	(01582) 36537
Norwich	(01603) 416719
Peterborough	(01733) 349489
Stansted	(01279) 663030

Budget Rent-A-Car
Bury St Edmunds	(01284) 701345
Cambridge	(01223) 323838
Clacton	(01255) 222444
Hitchin	(01462) 431151
Luton	(01582) 503101

Candor Motors Ltd
Braintree	(01376) 321202
Colchester	(01206) 791171

Europcar
Head Office	(01923) 811000
Cambridge	(01223) 233644
Great Yarmouth	(01493) 857818
Ipswich	(01473) 211067
Lowestoft	(01502) 516982
Luton	(01582) 413438
Norwich	(01603) 400280
Welwyn Garden City	(01483) 715179

Hertz Rent-A-Car
Cambridge	(01223) 416634
Colchester	(01206) 231801
Great Yarmouth	(01493) 857086
Ipswich	(01473) 218506
Luton	(01582) 450333

Mildenhall	(01638) 717354
Norwich Airport	(01603) 404010
Peterborough	(01733) 893083
Peterborough Station	(01703) 65252
Welwyn Garden City	(01707) 331433

◎ Willhire Ltd
Brentwood	(01277) 228666
Bury St Edmunds	(01284) 762888
Cambridge	(01223) 414600
Chelmsford	(01245) 265853
Colchester	(01206) 867888
Dereham	(01362) 698158
Ely	(01353) 662118
Great Yarmouth	(01493) 857130
Ipswich	(01473) 213344
King's Lynn	(01553) 764400
Mildenhall	(01638) 717452
Newmarket	(01638) 669209
Norwich	(01603) 416411
Norwich Airport	(01603) 404010
Peterborough	(01733) 340493
Southend	(01702) 546666
Thetford	(01842) 761578

Ferry Companies

◎ Scandinavian Seaways
Harwich (01255) 240808
Harwich-Esbjerg: 3 times a week (Tue, Thu, Sat), every other day in summer
Harwich-Hamburg: Tue & Thu, every other day in summer.
Harwich-Gothenburg: Fri & Sun, (4 June-20 Aug, Tue & Sun).

◎ Stena Line
Harwich (01255) 243333
Head office, Kent (01233) 647047
Hook of Holland-Harwich: twice daily.

Airports

Cambridge Airport,
(Magnet Air Services)
Teversham (01223) 293621/ 292651
Luton Airport (01582) 405100
Norwich Airport (01603) 411923
Southend Airport (01702) 340201
◎ Stansted Airport,
Bishop's Stortford (01279) 680500

Airlines

Air UK (01603) 424288
Destinations from Norwich:
Aberdeen, Amsterdam, Bergen, Edinburgh, Humberside, Jersey, Guernsey, Stavanger, Tees-side.

Air UK (01279) 680146
Destinations from Stansted:
Aberdeen, Amsterdam, Brussels, Dusseldorf, Edinburgh, Florence, Frankfurt, Glasgow, Jersey, Guernsey, Madrid, Newcastle, Nice, Paris, Copenhagen, Munich, Milan, Zurich, Hamburg. (Innsbruck - Sat & Sun in summer).

Britannia Airways (01582) 424155

Premier Holidays,
Cambridge (01223) 516000

Suckling Airways,
Reservations (01223) 293393
Destinations from Cambridge:
Amsterdam and Manchester. Free car park at Cambridge Airport.
Destinations from Luton:
Ireland, Amsterdam, Paris.

Bus & Coach Services

National Express Ltd (0990) 808080

There are many bus service operators throughout the region and each county council has an enquiry number as follows:

Bedfordshire	(01234) 228337
Cambridgeshire	(01223) 317740
Essex	(0345) 000333
Hertfordshire Traveline	(0345) 244344
Norfolk	(0500) 626116
Suffolk	(01473) 265676

Cycle Hire

An information sheet is available from the East Anglia Tourist Board (01473) 822922.

Tourist Information Centres

Pay a visit to your nearest Tourist Information Centre and you may be surprised by the range of services they offer both for visitors and for local people. Things to do, places to eat, how to get there, what to do if it's raining, places suitable for young children, or for the elderly or disabled ... the Tourist Information Centres are expert in answering these kinds of questions. Information covering the whole country can be found at most offices. TICs will book accommodation for you, in their own area, or further afield using the 'Book A Bed Ahead Scheme'. Many TICs specialise in locally produced crafts or goods as well as a wide range of local interest or British travel books.

Bedfordshire

* Not open all year

Bedford, 10 St Pauls Square, Tel: (01234) 215226.
All year, Mon-Sat, 0930-1700, Sun, 1100-1500.

Dunstable,The Library, Vernon Place Tel: (01582) 471012.
All year, Mon-Fri, 1000-1700, Sat, 0930-1600.

Luton, 65-67 Bute Street, Tel: (01582) 401579.
All year, Mon-Fri, 0930-1630, Sat, 0930-1600.

Sandy, Holiday Inn, Garden Court, Girtford Bridge, London Road, Sandy, (Junction A1 & A603).Tel: (01767) 682728
2 Jan-31 Mar, Mon-Thu 0930-1600, Fri, 1000-1600, Sat-Sun 1000-1500
1 Apr-7 Oct, Mon-Thur 1000-1500, Fri, 1000-1600, Sat-Sun 0900-1700
8 Oct-31 Dec, Mon-Thur 0930-1600, Fri, 1000-1600, Sat-Sun 1000-1500

Cambridgeshire

Cambridge, Wheeler Street, Tel: (01223) 322640
2 Jan-31 Mar, Mon-Fri, 0900-1730; 1 Apr-30 Jun, Mon-Fri, 0900-1800; 1 Jul-31 Aug, Mon-Fri, 0900-1900; 1 Sep-31 Oct, Mon-Fri, 0900-1800; 1 Nov-31 Dec, Mon-Fri, 0900-1730; 1 Apr-30 Sep, Sun and Bank Hols 1030-1530; All year Sat, 0900-1700.

Ely, Oliver Cromwells House, 29 St Mary's Street Tel: (01353) 662062.
2 Jan-31 Mar, Mon-Sat, 1000-1715; 1 Apr-29 Sep, Mon-Sun, 1000-1800; 30 Sep-31 Dec, Mon-Sat, 1000-1715.

Huntingdon, The Library, Princes Street Tel: (01480) 388588.
All year, Mon-Fri, 0930-1730, Sat, 0900-1630. Closed Bank Holidays.

Peterborough, 45 Bridge Street, Tel: (01733) 317336.
All year, Mon-Fri, 0900-1730, Sat and Bank Hols 1000-1600.

Wisbech, District Library, Ely Place Tel:(01945) 583263.
All year, Tue-Fri, 1000-1800, Sat, 0930-1700.

Essex

Braintree, Town Hall Centre, Market Square Tel: (01376) 550066.
All year, Mon-Fri, 0900-1700, Sat, 0900-1600.

Brentwood, 14 Ongar Road,Tel: (01277) 200300.
All year, Mon-Sat, 0900-1700

Chelmsford, County Hall, Market Road Tel: (01245) 283400.
All year, Mon-Fri, 0930-1700, Sat 0930-1600. Closed 1 Jan.

Clacton-on-Sea, 23 Pier Avenue, Tel: (01255) 423400.
All year, Mon-Sat, 0900-1700, 20 May-8 Sep, Sun, 0900-1700.

Colchester, 1 Queen Street, Tel: (01206) 282920.
2 Jan-30 Mar, Mon-Sat, 1000-1700,31 Mar-9 Nov, Mon-Tue, 0930-1800, Wed, 1000-1800, Thu-Sat, 0930-1800, Sun, 1000-1700. 11 Nov-31 Dec, Mon-Sat, 1000-1700.

Harwich, Parkeston Quay, Tel: (01255) 506139.
2 Jan-31 Mar and 1 Oct-31 Dec, Mon-Fri, 1000-1730, Sat, 1000-1600; 1 Apr-30 Sep, Mon-Sun, 0645-1900.

Maldon, Coach Lane, Tel: (01621) 856503.
2 Jan-31 Dec, Mon-Fri, 1000-1600 6 Jan-25 Mar and 7 Oct-30 Dec, Sat, 1000-1330; 1 Apr-30 Sep, Sat, 1000-1600.

Saffron Walden, 1 Market Place, Market Square Tel: (01799) 510444.
2 Jan-31 Mar and 1 Nov-31 Dec, Mon-Sat, 1000-1700; 1 Apr-31 Oct, Mon-Sat, 0930-1730.

Southend-on-Sea, 19 High Street, Tel: (01702) 215120.
2 Jan-31 Dec, Mon-Sat, 0930-1700, 21 Jul-1 Sep, 1000-1600.

Thurrock, Granada Motorway Service Area, M25, Grays Tel: (01708) 863733.
1 Jan-31 Mar, Mon-Fri, 0900-1630, Sat, 0930-1630, Sun, 1000-1630.
1 Apr-31 Oct, Mon-Sun 0900-1700. 1 Nov-31 Dec, Mon-Fri, 0900-1630, Sat, 0930-1630, Sun 1000-1630.

Waltham Abbey, 54 Sun Street, Tel: (01992) 652295.
1 Jan-30 Apr and 1 Oct-31 Dec, Tue-Sat, 0930-1630, 1 May-30 Sep, Tue-Sun, 0930-1630.

Hertfordshire

Bishop's Stortford, The Old Monastery, Windhill, Tel: (01279) 655831.
All year, Mon, 0845-1630, Tue-Thu, 0845-1700, Fri, 0845-1645, Sat, 0900-1300.

Hemel Hempstead, Dacorum Info. Centre, Marlowes Tel: (01442) 234222.
2 Jan-31 Dec, Mon-Fri, 0930-1700. 6 Jan-28 Dec, Sat, 1000-1600.

Hertford, The Castle, Tel: (01992) 584322.
2 Jan-31 Dec, Mon-Fri, 0900-1730; 6 Jan-13 Apr and 2 Nov-28 Dec, Sat, 1100-1500; 20 Apr-26 Oct, Sat 1000-1600.

South Mimms, Welcome Break, M25 Motorway Services Tel: (01707) 643233.
All year, 2 Jan- 31 Dec, Mon-Sat, 0930-1730, Sun, 0930-1630.

St Albans, Town Hall, Market Place Tel: (01727) 864511.
2 Jan-6 Apr and 4 Nov-30 Dec, Mon-Sat,1000-1600, 7 Apr-20 Jul, 22 Jul-7 Sep and 9 Sep-2 Nov, Mon-Sat, 0930-1730; 22 Jul-7 Sep, Sun, 1030-1630.

Norfolk

Cromer, Bus Station, Prince of Wales Road Tel: (01263) 512497.
1 Jan-24 Mar and 4 Nov-31 Dec, Mon-Sun, 1000-1600, 25 Mar-21 Jul and 9 Sep-3 Nov, Mon-Sat, 1000-1700 Sun, 1000-1600; 22 Jul-8 Sep, Mon-Sat, 0930-1900, Sun, 0930-1800.

Diss, Meres Mouth, Mere Street Tel: (01379) 650523.
2 Jan-31 Mar and 1 Nov-31 Dec, Mon-Thu, 1100-1500, Fri-Sat, 1000-1600; 1 Apr-31 Oct, Mon-Sat, 1000-1600.

* Fakenham, Red Lion House, Market Place, Tel: (01328) 851981.
25 Mar-21 Apr, Mon-Sat, 1000-1300, 1330-1700, 22 Apr-26 May, Mon-Sat, 1000-1400; 27 May-8 Sep, Mon-Sat, 1000-1300, 1330-1700, 9 Sep-3 Nov, Mon-Sat, 1000-1400.

* Great Yarmouth, Marine Parade, Tel: (01493) 842195/846345.
5-8 Apr, Fri, Sat & Mon 0930-1730; Sun, 1000-1700; 9 Apr-25 May, Mon-Sat, 0930-1700, Sun 1000-1700, 26 May-29 Sep, Mon-Sat, 0930-1730, Sun, 1000-1700. Information between Oct-Apr on (01493) 846345.

* Hoveton,Station Road, Tel: (01603) 782281.
5 Apr-31 Oct, Mon-Sun, 0900-1700.

Hunstanton, Town Hall, The Green, Tel: (01485) 532610.
2 Jan-31 Mar, Mon-Sun, 1030-1600, 1 Apr-30 Sep, Mon-Sun, 0915-1700, 1 Oct-31 Dec, Mon-Sun, 1030-1600.

King's Lynn, The Old Gaol House, Saturday Market Place Tel: (01553) 763044. *2 Jan-31 Dec, Mon-Thu, 0915-1700, Sat, 0915-1700, Sun, 1000-1700. 2 Jan-7 Apr, Fri, 0915-1700, 8 Apr-1 Oct, Fri, 0915-1730, 2 Oct-31 Dec, Fri, 0915-1700.*

* Mundesley, 2a Station Road, Tel: (01263) 721070.
25 Mar-21 Apr, Mon-Sat, 1000-1300, 1330-1700, Sun, 1000-1300, 1330-1600; 22 Apr-26 May, Mon-Sun, 1000-1400; 27 May-8 Sep, Mon-Sat, 1000-1300, 1330-1700, Sun, 1000-1300, 1330-1600; 9 Sep-3 Nov, Mon-Sun, 1000-1600.

Norwich, The Guildhall, Gaol Hill Tel: (01603) 666071.
2 Jan-31 May and 1 Oct-31 Dec, Mon-Fri, 1000-1600, Sat, 1000-1400, 1 Jun-30 Sep, Mon-Sat, 1000-1700.

* Sheringham, Station Approach, Tel: (01263) 824329.
25 Mar-21 Jul, Mon-Sat, 1000-1700, Sun, 1000-1600; 22 Jul-8 Sep, Mon-Sat, 0930-1900, Sun, 0930-1800; 9 Sep-3 Nov, Mon-Sat, 1000-1700, Sun, 1000-1600.

* Walsingham, Shirehall Museum, Common Place Tel: (01328) 820510.
4 Apr-30 Sep, Mon-Sat, 1000-1700, Sun, 1400-1700, 1-31 Oct, Sat,1000-1700, Sun, 1400-1700.

* Wells-next-the-Sea, Staithe Street, Tel: (01328) 710885.
25 Mar-21 Jul, Mon-Sat, 1000-1700, Sun, 1000-1600; 22 Jul-8 Sep, Mon-Sat, 0930-1800, Sun, 0930-1700; 9 Sep-3 Nov, Mon-Sat, 1000-1700, Sun, 1000-1600.

Suffolk

* Aldeburgh, The Cinema, High Street Tel: (01728) 453637.
25 Mar-27 Oct, Mon-Fri, 0900-1715, Sat, Sun, 1000-1715.

* Beccles, The Quay, Fen Lane, Tel: (01502) 713196.
5 Apr-31 Oct, Mon-Sun, 0900-1700.

Bury St Edmunds, 6 Angel Hill, Tel: (01284) 764667.
1 Jan-5 Apr and 1 Oct-31 Dec, Mon-Fri, 1000-1600, Sat, 1000-1300; 6 Apr-30 Sep, Mon-Fri, 0930-1730, Sat, 1000-1600, Sun, 1000-1600.

Felixstowe, Leisure Centre, Undercliff Road West, Tel: (01394) 276770.
1 Jan-31 Mar and 1 Oct-31 Dec, Mon-Fri, 0845-1715, Sat, 1000-1700, Sun, 1000-1300; 1 Apr-30 Sep, Mon-Fri, 0900-1730, Sat, Sun, 0930-1700.

Hadleigh, Toppesfield Hall, Tel: (01473) 823824.
All year, Mon-Fri, 0900-1715. Closed Bank Holidays.

Ipswich, St Stephens Church, St Stephens Lane Tel: (01473) 258070.
All year, Mon-Sat, 0900-1700.

* Lavenham, Lady Street, Tel: (01787) 248207.
1 Apr-28 Sep, Mon-Sun, 1000-1645.

Lowestoft, East Point Pavilion, Royal Plain Tel: (01502) 523000/523057.
2 Jan-3 Jan, Tue-Wed, 1000-1700, 4 Jan-18 Feb, 24 Feb-29 Mar, 30 Sep-27 Oct & 2 Nov-21 Dec, Mon-Fri 1100-1700, Sat-Sun 1000-1700; 19 Feb-23 Feb and 28 Oct-1 Nov, Mon-Fri, 1000-1700. 30 Mar-29 Sep, Mon-Sun, 1000-1800.

Newmarket, 63 The Rookery, Tel: (01638) 667200.
All year, 2 Jan-31 Dec, Mon-Fri, 0900-1700, Sat, 1000-1300.

*Southwold, Town Hall, Market Place Tel: (01502) 724729/523000.
1 Apr-30 Sep, Mon-Fri, 1100-1700, Sat, 1000-1730, Sun, 1100-1600.

Stowmarket, Wilkes Way, Tel: (01449) 676800.
2 Jan-30 Jun, Mon-Fri, 0900-1700, 2 Jan-9 Apr, Sat, 0930-1330; 10 Apr-30 Jun, Sat, 0930-1630;1 Jul-31 Aug, Mon-Fri, 0900-1730, Sat, 0930-1630; 1 Sep-31 Dec, Mon-Fri, 0900-1700, Sat, 0930-1630.

*Sudbury, Town Hall, Market Hill, Tel:(01787) 881320.
1 Apr-28 Sep, Mon-Sat 1000-1645.

Tourist Information Points   *** Not open all year**
Limited information available, no bed booking service.

Bedfordshire

Ampthill, 12 Dunstable Street, Tel: (01525) 402051
All year, Mon-Thurs, 0845-1700, Fri, 0845-1600.

* Woburn Heritage Centre, Old St Mary's Church, Tel: (01525)290631.
1 Apr-Oct, Mon-Fri, 1400-1630, Sat, Sun, 1130-1630.

Essex

* Dedham, Duchy Barn, Tel: (01206) 323447.
Easter-Mid Oct, Mon-Sat, 1000-1300, 1400-1700, Sun, 1400-1700.

* Halstead, Lodge Gate, Townsford Mill, Tel: (01787) 477411.
1 Apr-end Sep, Tue-Fri, 1000-1600, Sat, 1030-1500.

Manningtree, Townsends, 33 High Street, Tel: (01206) 392766.
Feb-Dec, Mon-Sat, 0900-1300, 1400-1630, Wed 0900-1300.

* Walton on the Naze, Princess Esplanade, Tel: (01255) 675542.
14-18 Apr, 27 May-16 Sep, daily, 1000-1700.

* Witham, 61 Newland Street, Tel: (01376) 502674.
Apr-Sep, Mon-Fri, 1000-1530, Sat, 0930-1330. Closed Bank Holidays.

Hertfordshire

Berkhamsted,The Library, Kings Road, Tel: (01442) 877638.
All year, Mon-Fri, 0930-1730, Tue, Thu, 0930-2000, Sat, 0930-1600. Closed Wed & Bank Hols.

Borehamwood, Civic Offices, Elstree Way, Tel: (0181) 207 7496.
All year, Mon-Thu, 0900-1715, Fri, 0900-1700.

Hitchin, The Library, Paynes Park, Tel: (01462) 434738/450133.
All year, Mon, Tue, Thu, Fri, 0930-2000, Sat, 0930-1600.

Rickmansworth, Three Rivers Hs, Northway, Tel: (01923) 776611 ext 1381.
All year, Mon-Fri, 0900-1630.

Stevenage, The Library, Southgate, Tel: (01438) 369441.
All year, Mon-Thu, 0930-2000, Fri, 0930-1700, Sat 0930-1600.

Norfolk

Attleborough, Victoria Gallery, Cyprus House, Queens Square Tel: (01953) 452404.   *All year, Mon-Sat, 0900-1730.*

* Aylsham, Bure Valley Railway Station, Norwich Road, Tel: (01263) 733903.   *Mar-Sep, 0900-1700.*

* Dereham, The Bell Tower, Tel: (01362) 698992.
Easter-Sep, Mon-Sat, 1300-1600.

Downham Market, Town Hall, Bridge Street, Tel: (01366) 387440.
1 Jan-30 Mar & 1 Nov-31 Dec, Mon-Sat, 1000-1630;1 Apr-31 Oct, Mon-Sat, 0945-1700.

* Great Yarmouth, North West Tower, North Quay, Tel: (01493) 332095.
Tel: (01493) 332095, or Broads Authority (01603) 610734 for opening times.

Holt, Sanders Coaches, Market Place, Tel: (01263) 713100.
Mon-Fri, 0900-1600 (1700 summer). Sat 0900-1300 (1600 in summer).

* Loddon, Bridge Stores, 41 Bridge Street, Tel: (01508) 520690.
All year, Sun 0630-1700, Mon-Sat 0630-1800 (1900 summer).

* Ranworth, The Staithe, Tel: (01603) 270453.
5 Apr-31 Oct, daily, 0900-1700.

* Swaffham, Market Place, Tel: (01760) 722255.
Apr-Oct, Mon-Sat, 1000-1630.

Thetford, Ancient House Museum, 21 White Hart St, Tel: (01842) 752599.
All year, Mon, 1000-1300, 1400-1700, Tue-Sat, 1000-1700, end May-29 Sep, Sun 1400-1700. Closed 1 Jan, 5 Apr, 25, 26 Dec.

Felixstowe: regional winner of England for Excellence

* Watton, The Clock Tower, High Street, Tel: (01953) 882058/884224.
May-Sep, Mon, Sat, 0930-1200 and on request.

* Wymondham, Market Cross, Market Place, Tel: (01953) 604721.
5 Apr-30 Sep, Mon-Sat, 1000-1600, July, Aug 1000-1700, B Hols 1000-1300.

Suffolk

Beccles, Public Library, Blyburgate, Tel: (01502) 714073.
All year, Mon-Sat, 0930-1700.

* Santon Downham, High Lodge Visitor Centre, Tel: (01842) 815434.
Easter-end Sep, daily, 1000-1700. Winter weekends.

Woodbridge Public Library, New Street, Tel: (01394) 382896.
All Year, Mon, Sat, 0930-1700, Tue-Fri, 0930-1730. Closed Bank Hols.

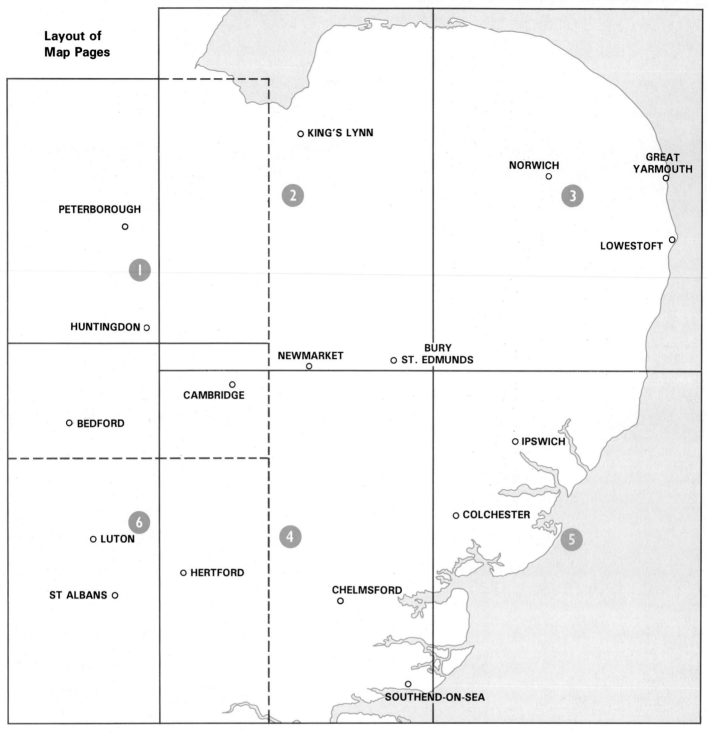

Layout of Map Pages

PETERBOROUGH ○

1

HUNTINGDON ○

○ KING'S LYNN

2

NORWICH ○

3

GREAT YARMOUTH ○

LOWESTOFT ○

NEWMARKET ○

BURY ST. EDMUNDS ○

CAMBRIDGE ○

BEDFORD ○

IPSWICH ○

6

LUTON ○

○ HERTFORD

4

COLCHESTER ○

5

ST ALBANS ○

CHELMSFORD ○

SOUTHEND-ON-SEA ○

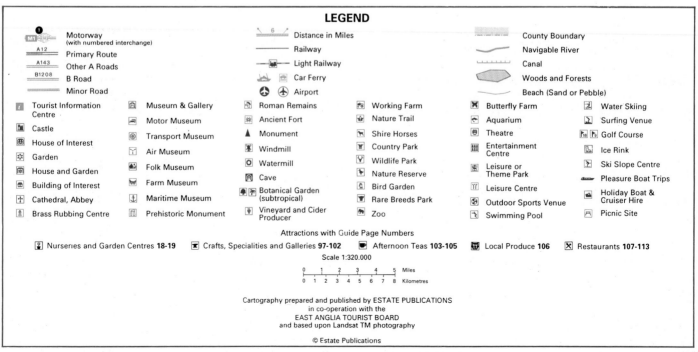

LEGEND

M1	Motorway (with numbered interchange)
A12	Primary Route
A143	Other A Roads
B1208	B Road
	Minor Road

- Tourist Information Centre
- Castle
- House of Interest
- Garden
- House and Garden
- Building of Interest
- Cathedral, Abbey
- Brass Rubbing Centre
- Museum & Gallery
- Motor Museum
- Transport Museum
- Air Museum
- Folk Museum
- Farm Museum
- Maritime Museum
- Prehistoric Monument
- Roman Remains
- Ancient Fort
- Monument
- Windmill
- Watermill
- Cave
- Botanical Garden (subtropical)
- Vineyard and Cider Producer
- Working Farm
- Nature Trail
- Shire Horses
- Country Park
- Wildlife Park
- Nature Reserve
- Bird Garden
- Rare Breeds Park
- Zoo
- Butterfly Farm
- Aquarium
- Theatre
- Entertainment Centre
- Leisure or Theme Park
- Leisure Centre
- Outdoor Sports Venue
- Swimming Pool
- Water Skiing
- Surfing Venue
- Golf Course
- Ice Rink
- Ski Slope Centre
- Pleasure Boat Trips
- Holiday Boat & Cruiser Hire
- Picnic Site

- Distance in Miles
- Railway
- Light Railway
- Car Ferry
- Airport

- County Boundary
- Navigable River
- Canal
- Woods and Forests
- Beach (Sand or Pebble)

Attractions with Guide Page Numbers

- Nurseries and Garden Centres **18-19**
- Crafts, Specialities and Galleries **97-102**
- Afternoon Teas **103-105**
- Local Produce **106**
- Restaurants **107-113**

Scale 1:320.000

0 1 2 3 4 5 Miles
0 1 2 3 4 5 6 7 8 Kilometres

Cartography prepared and published by ESTATE PUBLICATIONS
in co-operation with the
EAST ANGLIA TOURIST BOARD
and based upon Landsat TM photography

© Estate Publications

Index